DIVIDED AGAINST ZION

CASS SERIES: ISRAELI HISTORY, POLITICS AND SOCIETY
Series Editor: Efraim Karsh

ISSN: 1368–4795

This series provides a multidisciplinary examination of all aspects of Israeli history, politics and society, and serves as a means of communication between the various communities interested in Israel: academics, policy-makers, practitioners, journalists and the informed public.

1. *Peace in the Middle East: The Challenge for Israel*, edited by Efraim Karsh.
2. *The Shaping of Israeli Identity: Myth, Memory and Trauma*, edited by Robert Wistrich.
3. *Between War and Peace: Dilemmas of Israeli Security*, edited by Efraim Karsh.
4. *U.S.–Israeli Relations at the Crossroads*, edited by Gabriel Sheffer.
5. *Revisiting the Yom Kippur War*, edited by P. R. Kumaraswamy.
6. *Israel: The Dynamics of Change and Continuity*, edited by David Levi-Faur.
7. *In Search of Identity: Jewish Aspects in Israeli Culture*, edited by Dan Urian.
8. *Israel at the Polls, 1996*, edited by Daniel J. Elazar and Shmuel Sandler.
9. *From Rabin to Netanyahu: Israel's Troubled Agenda*, edited by Efraim Karsh.
10. *Fabricating Israeli History: The 'New Historians'*, second revised edition, by Efraim Karsh.
11. *Divided Against Zion: Anti-Zionist Opposition in Britain to a Jewish State in Palestine, 1945–1948*, by Rory Miller.
12. *Peacemaking in Israel after Rabin*, edited by Sasson Sofer.

Divided Against Zion

Anti-Zionist Opposition in Britain
to a Jewish State in Palestine
1945–1948

Rory Miller

*Lecturer in Mediterranean Studies
King's College, London*

FRANK CASS
LONDON • PORTLAND, OR

First published in 2000 in Great Britain by
FRANK CASS & CO. LTD.
Newbury House, 900 Eastern Avenue
London, IG2 7HH

and in the United States of America by
FRANK CASS
c/o ISBS, 5804 N. E. Hassalo Street
Portland, Oregon, 97213-3644

Copyright © 2000 Rory Miller.

British Library Cataloguing in Publication Data
Miller, Rory
  Divided against Zion: anti -Zionist opposition in Britain
to a Jewish state in Palestine, 1945–1948.–(Cass studies
in Israeli history, politics and society)
  1.Jews – Politics and government – 20th century 2. Zionism –
History – 20th century 3. Israel – Foreign public opinion,
British 4. Israel – Foreign relations – Great Britain
5. Great Britain – Foreign relations – Israel – 1936–1945
6. Palestine – Foreign relations – Great Britain 7. Great
Britain – Foreign relations – Palestine – 1936–1945
I. Title
320. 5'4'095694'09044

ISBN 0-7146-5051-X (cloth)
ISBN 0-7146-8102-4 (paperback)
ISSN 1368-4795

Library of Congress Cataloging-in-Publication Data
Miller, Rory, 1971–
  Divided against Zion: anti-Zionist opposition in Britain
to a Jewish state in Palestine, 1945–1948 / Rory Miller.
    p. cm. – (Cass series – Israeli history, politics, and society; 1)
  Includes bibliographical references and index.
  ISBN 0-7146-5051-X (cloth: alk. paper) – ISBN 0-7146-8102-4
(pbk.: alk. paper)
    1. Zionism – Great Britain – History. 2. Arab Office (London,
England) 3. Committee for Arab Affairs (London, England)
4. Jewish Fellowship (London, England) 5. Great Britain –
Foreign relations – Middle East. 6. Middle East – Foreign
relations – Great Britain. 7. Jewish–Arab relations –
History – 1917–1948. I. Title. II. Series.
DS149.5.G4 M55 2000
327.4105694'09'044–dc21   00-035899

All rights reserved. No part of this publication may be reproduced, stored in or introduced into a retrieval system or transmitted in any form or by any means, electronic, mechanical, photocopying, recording or otherwise, without the prior written permission of the publisher of this book.

Printed in Great Britain by
MPG Books Ltd, Bodmin, Cornwall

*For My Parents
Marion and Alan*

Contents

Acknowledgements	ix
Abbreviations	xi
Introduction	1
1. Antecedents and Outlook: The Post-War anti-Zionist Effort in Context	5
2. The Committee for Arab Affairs and the Arab Cause	23
3. Zionist Responses to the English Anti-Zionist Constituency	55
4. The Jewish Fellowship and the Battle over Zionism in Anglo-Jewry	82
5. Common Arguments, Common Goal: Anti-Zionist Arguments against the Creation of a Jewish State	121
6. The Failure to Co-operate: Sir Edward Spears, the CAA and the Jewish Fellowship	156
7. An Example of Anti-Zionist Co-operation: The CAA and the Arab Office	193
8. Fundamental Issues, Fundamental Divisions	215
Conclusion	246
Bibliography	253
Index	267

Acknowledgements

I would like to thank Clare Brown, archivist at the Middle East Centre, St Antony's College, Oxford University, for her assistance on my many visits to use the Spears papers and sundry other collections. Moreover, I would like to acknowledge the permission from Dr Eugene Rogan, Director of the Middle East Centre, St Antony's College, for allowing me to quote from and refer to collections of private papers held at the Centre, specifically the papers of Nevill Barbour, Estelle Blyth, Humphrey Bowman, Richard Crossman, Jerusalem and the East Mission, Elizabeth Monroe, Harry Philby and Hubert Young.

I would also like to thank Colonel J.A. Aylmer, literary executor of Sir Edward Spears's private papers collection at the Middle East Centre, St Antony's College, for allowing me access to the Spears papers when they were closed to public viewing, and then for his prompt permission to allow me to cite from them in the course of this book.

I would also like to acknowledge and thank Pembroke College, Cambridge University, for allowing me access to and permission to cite from the Ronald Storrs papers; Mr Pinfold, Librarian, Rhodes House Library, Oxford University, for allowing me to refer to and quote from the Fabian Colonial Bureau archives; Dr C.M. Woolgar, Archivist and Head of Special Collections, at the Hartley Library, University of Southampton, for allowing me permission to cite from the collections of private papers of the following individuals held in the Hartley Library archives: Selig Brodetsky, Ivan Greenberg, Basil Henriques and Harold Reinhart.

On a personal note, I would like to thank Gus Nichols, Andy McConnell, Alan Shaw, Dermot Brosnan, Nick Williams and Stephen Douglas for the interest they have shown in my work and the encouragement that they have given me the last few years. I would especially like to thank Simon Meldrum and Petros Panayiotou for their support while I was completing this project in

1998. I would also like to give special thanks to Professor Efraim Karsh, who has guided me in my studies and given me many opportunities for which I am grateful.

I would like to thank all my family, especially John and Enid Silverstone in London and, in Dublin, my grandparents, Sybil and Leslie Silverstone, Lisa and Ken Milofsky, Daniel and Amanda Miller, and Emma and Colin Sheena. All have shown me great support over the years.

Finally, I would like to dedicate this book to my parents, Marion and Alan, whose support has made this and so much more possible. Recognising this fact here is hardly enough of an appreciation, but it is a start.

Abbreviations

AACIP	Anglo-American Committee of Inquiry on Palestine
ACJ	American Council for Judaism
AHC	Arab Higher Committee
AJA	Anglo-Jewish Association
AO	Arab Office
CAA	Committee for Arab Affairs
CO	Colonial Office
DP	displaced person
FO	Foreign Office
HMG	His Majesty's Government
JA	Jewish Agency for Palestine
JF	Jewish Fellowship
MEPC	Middle East Parliamentary Committee
MESC	Middle East Supply Centre
MOI	Ministry of Information
NZO	New Zionist Organisation
PIC	Palestine Information Centre
PLO	Palestine Liberation Organisation
RCAS	Royal Central Asian Society
RIIA	Royal Institute of International Affairs
UNSCOP	United Nations Special Committee on Palestine
WJC	World Jewish Congress
WZO	World Zionist Organisation
ZF	Zionist Federation of Great Britain and Ireland

SOURCES

ABD	Archives of the Board of Deputies of British Jews
AJAP	Anglo-Jewish Association Papers
ANB	*Arab News Bulletin*
BARB	N. Barbour papers

BBCWAR	BBC written archives
BLYTH	E. Blyth papers
BOW	H. Bowman papers
BROD	S. Brodetsky papers
CAB	Cabinet papers
CROSS	R. Crossman papers
FCBA	Fabian Colonial Bureau Archives
FO	Foreign Office
GREEN	I. Greenberg papers
HENP	B. Henriques papers
JC	*Jewish Chronicle*
JEMP	Jerusalem and East Mission papers
JO	*The Jewish Outlook*
JRCAS	*Journal of Royal Central Asian Society*
MONPA	E. Monroe papers
PHIL	H. Philby papers
PPP	M. Philips Price papers
REIN	H. Reinhart papers
SPSP	E. Spears papers
STOP	R. Storrs papers
TBJSBH	Typescript biographical journal of Sir Basil Henriques
WEINP	Weiner Library, press cuttings
YOUNG	H. Young papers
ZR	*Zionist Review*

Introduction

Between November 1944 and August 1945 three bodies, one Jewish and two Gentile (one Arab and one English), were formed in London with the aim of providing organised and effective opposition to Zionist aspirations in Palestine, which after the Biltmore Declaration of May 1942 primarily centred on the gaining of a Jewish state.[1] By 1949, in the wake of the creation of the State of Israel, all three bodies had disbanded.

This book examines the relationship between these three bodies: (1) the Jewish Fellowship, (2) the Arab Office, and (3) the Committee for Arab Affairs. In doing so it has the objective of examining active anti-Zionism. This is one of the least documented and understood, yet important and interesting aspects of British involvement in Palestine. Indeed, while there has been much analysis of Britain's official Palestine policy and the dynamics of the Anglo-American relationship over Palestine in the final years of the British Mandate, and while in recent times the Arab and Jewish sides of the conflict have been subject to an extensive (and often intensely critical and revisionist) historical illumination, there has been little written on either the subject of anti-Zionism in general or the anti-Zionist effort in Britain in particular.[2]

Rather, anti-Zionism, as an issue in and of itself, has been viewed as a minor adjunct in the history of the Palestine question and the Zionist movement. This is somewhat understandable, given the fact that anti-Zionism (both Jewish and Gentile), from the earliest Herzlian era, through the Balfour Declaration of 1917 and up to the end of the Mandate in 1948, was to a large extent a reaction and response to Zionism and what were perceived to be the various successes and excesses of the Zionist endeavour. Anti-Zionism had no programme of its own, no clear goals and as it has been said of the Popular Front's opposition to fascism in France during the 1930s, the anti-Zionist effort throughout these years was primarily against something, most notably any apparent Zionist advances towards autonomous statehood in Palestine, rather than for anything. Above and beyond this is the fact that the Zionists' ultimate success in gaining a state in Palestine in 1948 further reduced the belief in the importance of anti-Zionism during the Mandatory era as a subject worthy of anything more than cursory historical study.

Yet this is a pity. For regardless of the changing distribution of international power which saw a rise in the role of the United States in international affairs and an increase in the United Nations' involvement in deciding Palestine's fate, Britain, as the Mandatory power for Palestine, was, in the post-war era, still considered of vital importance in any decision affecting the final status of the country.

As shall be seen, this was certainly the view of the Arab leadership within the Arab League, an organisation that both sponsored the Arab Office and was at the forefront of the diplomatic battle against Zionism in the western world. Those English Jews and Christian Gentiles most committed in their opposition to Zionism were British citizens and as such felt a unique responsibility, as much a right as a duty, to take a stand on the Palestine question even if this meant that at times their staunch opposition to Zionism put them in potential conflict with the Mandatory power, their own government.

In these terms the efforts of the London-based anti-Zionists under study have a centrality and relevance in any discussion of the dynamics of the debate over Palestine in Britain in the years between 1945 and 1948. Indeed the nature and identity of these anti-Zionist men and women, their motivations and arguments, the intellectual and political resources on which they drew, are all questions of interest in any historical study of the final years of the British Mandate.

This book hopes to illuminate these various and varied aspects of the anti-Zionist effort in Britain at this time. It hopes to show how in the post-war era Jewish and Gentile anti-Zionists shared a determined opposition to a Jewish state in all or any part of Palestine at, what all agreed, would be a critical time in deciding whether a Jewish state, so abhorred, would be achieved. It hopes to show how these groups shared a tendency to view Zionism primarily as a propaganda phenomenon that had to be fought by propaganda means, and in doing so how they used common arguments against Zionism: that Jews were a religious community, rather than a national entity, and therefore had no right to a state;

that Zionism resulted in a dual loyalty among Jews; that Zionism was an illegitimate creed, no less than the successor to Nazism in the post-war world.

In these terms the Committee for Arab Affairs (CAA) and the Arab Office provided forums through which the Arab case over Palestine could be presented, just as the Jewish Fellowship provided a forum where the Jewish anti-Zionist case could be set out. Indeed the existence of a virulent Gentile anti-Zionist constituency, arguing in similar terms to Jews against Zionism, in itself came to be perceived by the Zionists as proof that the Jewish Fellowship was at best giving credibility to Gentiles and at worst deliberately co-operating with them to harm Jewish aspirations in regard to gaining a Jewish state.

Yet the varying relationships between the CAA, the Arab Office and the Jewish Fellowship contradict this Zionist belief. For while the Arabs did have influential support in their opposition to Zionism, the Jewish Fellowship found itself isolated both within Jewry and from non-Jewish anti-Zionists. Despite efforts at co-operation between Jewish and Gentile anti-Zionists in the pre-war era and up to the months immediately preceding the creation of the CAA, and despite the use of common arguments against Zionism, the constituency of Jewish anti-Zionists, as represented by the Fellowship, and the Gentile anti-Zionists, of the CAA, did not co-operate in any effective way, especially when compared to the close relationship that developed between the CAA and the Arab Office at the same time.

In December 1943 the author and Arabian adventurer Freya Stark, a propagandist for the Ministry of Information during the war and herself a devoted anti-Zionist, was of the opinion that 'it is obviously very difficult for a moderate Jew to steer between Scylla and Charybdis'.[3] The 'moderate' Jews Stark referred to were those whom political Zionists in the post-Biltmore era would have had no compunction about calling anti-Zionist: that is, they were Jews opposed to the policy of creating an autonomous Jewish state in all or any part of Palestine.

Charybdis, the dangerous whirlpool of Greek epic that lay opposite the lair of the monster Scylla, is an interesting metaphor to use in describing the situation facing those Jews who opposed Zionism. But the meaning is clear. For to be between Scylla and Charybdis was to be caught between the whirlpool and the monster. In other words, in the view of Stark, those Jews opposed to Zionism would face isolation from a Jewry largely sympathetic to Zionist aspirations and from the Gentile world. For they would be

4   *Divided Against Zion*

acceptable to neither.

It is the central intention of this work to examine, to analyse and finally to show that in the context of the three-way relationship between the Jewish Fellowship, the Arab Office and the Committee for Arab Affairs, during the post-war battle over Zionism, and despite common arguments and a common objective – the prevention of a Jewish state – Stark's 1943 Scylla and Charybdis metaphor, made at the height of the war before the return to peace made Palestine an issue of priority once more, was not only prescient but prophetic.

NOTES

1. The Biltmore Declaration, which saw the official adoption of a Jewish state policy by the mainstream Zionist movement, was adopted at a meeting at the Biltmore Hotel, New York, 9–11 May 1942. Six hundred American Zionists and 60 Zionist leaders from around the world, including Chaim Weizmann and David Ben-Gurion, attended this meeting. For an examination of the causes and reactions to the Biltmore Declaration see J.C. Hurewitz, *The Struggle for Palestine* (New York: W.W. Norton, 1950), chapter 12 'The Statists and their Opponents', pp. 156–66, and chapter 15 'The Biltmore Controversy', pp. 195–211.
2. For a classic study of high politics in the early years of the British Mandate see Elie Kedourie's *In the Anglo-Arab Labyrinth: The McMahon–Husayn Correspondence and Interpretation, 1914–1939* (Cambridge: Cambridge University Press, 1976). Also see Bernard Wasserstein, *The British in Palestine: The Mandatory Government and the Arab-Jewish Conflict, 1917–1929* (Oxford: Basil Blackwell, 1990) and Isaiah Friedman, *The Question of Palestine: British, Jewish and Arab Relations, 1914–1918* (New Brunswick: Transactions, 1992). For studies of the later years of the British Mandatory era, see Michael Cohen, *Palestine, Retreat from Mandate: The Making of British Policy, 1936–1945* (London: Elek, 1978) and *Palestine and the Great Powers, 1945–1948* (Princeton, NJ: Princeton University Press, 1982); Martin Jones, *Failure in Palestine: British and United States Policy after the Second World War* (London: Mansell, 1985); Ronald Zweig, *Britain and Palestine During the Second World War* (London: Royal Historical Society, 1986); Neil Caplan, *Futile Diplomacy: Vol. II, Arab–Zionist Negotiations and the End of the Palestine Mandate* (London: Frank Cass, 1986). Also see William Roger Louis and Robert W. Stooky (eds), *The End of the Palestine Mandate* (London: Tauris, 1985), which includes a detailed bibliographical essay by Stooky on writings on Palestine during the Mandate, pp. 149–65. There has also been a revisionist reappraisal of the Palestine question. See, for example, Avi Shlaim's *Collusion Across the Border: King Abdullah, the Zionist Movement and the Partition of Palestine* (Oxford: Oxford University Press, 1988) and Ilan Pappe's *The Making of the Arab–Israeli Conflict, 1947–1951* (London: Tauris, 1992).
3. Freya Stark to Elizabeth Monroe, 20 December 1945, MONPA.

1 Antecedents and Outlook: The Post-War Anti-Zionist Effort in Context

ANTI-ZIONISM AND NON-ZIONISM IN ANGLO-JEWRY

As has already been stated in the Introduction, compared with the vast literature on the Zionist movement and the diplomatic battle over Palestine, the literature on active opposition to Zionism on a non-official or non-institutionalised basis among the members of the British elite both inside and outside Jewry is sparse.[1] As such, it is important at this point to set out the antecedents of the Jewish Fellowship, the Arab Office and the Committee for Arab Affairs, and to highlight the most prominent personalities and ideas within the post-war anti-Zionist movement.

The Jewish Fellowship (hereafter, the Fellowship), had been founded in 1942, but was only officially organised and presented as a functioning body in September 1944. Its founder and chairman, Basil Henriques, was a member of one of the leading families in Anglo-Jewry who, as warden of the Bernard Baron St George's Jewish Settlement and a magistrate in juvenile cases, had devoted his life to working with underprivileged Jewish youth in the East End of London.[2]

Former MP Sir Jack Brunel Cohen (Conservative MP for Fairfield, in Liverpool, 1918–31) was the president of the Jewish Fellowship and the body included some of the most eminent names in Anglo-Jewry and many of those members of the community held in the highest regard in the non-Jewish world including: Sir Robert Waley Cohen, president of the United Synagogue, the leading Orthodox Jewish body in the community, who was heralded in some quarters as the 'uncrowned king of Anglo-Jewry';[3] Sir Leonard Lionel Cohen, who in 1946 became the first Jewish Lord Justice; D.L. Lipson (Independent Conservative MP for the constituency of Cheltenham,

1937–50); Colonel Louis Gluckstein (Conservative MP for Nottingham East, 1931–45); Rabbi Dr Israel Mattuck, Rabbi of the Liberal Synagogue; Viscount Bearsted; and Lord Swaythling, to name but a few.

It is important to note that the Fellowship was not alone within Jewry in opposing the creation of a Jewish state in Palestine at this time. Other groups, such as the Anglo-Jewish Association (hereafter, the AJA) and Agudath Yisra'el also opposed such an eventuality in these years. As such it could be argued that these other Jewish groups could be included in what is after all a work concerning the relationship between Jewish and Gentile opponents of a Jewish state in Palestine. However, these bodies have been excluded from this discussion except when their position highlights the isolation of the Fellowship within Jewry.

Despite an increasingly acrimonious relationship with the Zionist movement in the post-war era, the AJA was perceived by the Zionists as a non-Zionist body – prepared to work with the Zionists for the practical benefit of the Yishuv (the Jewish settlement in Palestine) – rather than an avowedly anti-Zionist body. Unlike the Fellowship it had not been founded in the turmoil surrounding the Biltmore Declaration of 1942, but had existed since 1871 as a charitable and cultural body. Likewise, though the AJA, under the presidency of the highly regarded Leonard Stein,[4] was in the years under examination officially opposed to a Jewish state, it differed from the Fellowship, whose total membership was anti-Zionist, because many of its members supported Zionism and opposed the official position of the AJA leadership.[5]

Thus the difference between the AJA and the Fellowship was profound. For while the latter was against a Jewish state on principle, even if Jewry made up the vast majority of Palestine's population and the Arab minority supported the creation of a Jewish state, the AJA was opposed to a state on the basis that at the present time such an entity provided neither an answer to the Jewish problem nor security for those Jews already in Palestine. Hence, as shall be seen in the course of this work, the Fellowship gained no official sympathy or support from the AJA or its president Leonard Stein.

The religious anti-Zionists of Agudath Yisra'el[6] shared with the Fellowship members a philosophical and immutable opposition to the creation of a Jewish state. Religious anti-Zionists viewed Zionism as a catastrophic, pseudo-messianic ideology that would forestall redemption by human action. Yet Agudists viewed Liberal Judaism, with which the Fellowship came to be intimately associated (see Chapter 4), as almost as great anathema as a secular Jewish state in Palestine. Added to this was the fact that Orthodox religious anti-Zionism, motivated as it was by the tenets of traditional Judaism and Jewish insularity, could in no way be perceived, or presented (as the Fellowship was within Jewry), as a betrayal of Judaism through allying with Gentiles.

Thus neither Agudath Yisra'el nor the AJA saw the Fellowship as an ally or a friend in their opposition to a Jewish state. Nor were either of them perceived by Zionists in the way that the Fellowship was – as a purely extra communal assimilationist body attempting to destroy Jewish hopes for Palestine in the non-Jewish world at a time of both great emotional and political sensitivity (given the recent Holocaust in Europe and the sense that a final decision over Palestine was forthcoming).

The fundamental goal of the Fellowship, a body which Gideon Shimoni has appropriately called 'the last stand of anti-Zionism' in Anglo-Jewry,[7] was to provide a Jewish forum where political Zionism, with its objective of a Jewish state in Palestine, could be publicly and vigorously opposed on the grounds that Jewry was a religion not a nation and hence had no right to gain a state.

As such the religious rejuvenation of Jewry became a central plank of the Fellowship platform, embodied in its constitution, adopted at its first annual meeting and central to all Fellowship literature. The Fellowship's earliest pamphlet, *What the Fellowship Stands For*, informed the reader that 'the bond that unites all Jews throughout the world is Judaism' and stressed that the Fellowship's objective was to

> Uphold the principle that Jews are a religious community ... stimulate Jewish life in this country ... to seek to revive the Jewish religious spirit among Jews and to place the Torah, the Synagogue and the ethics of Judaism at the heart of Jewish life.[8]

But the Fellowship had a second and directly related objective. As Sir Jack Brunel Cohen informed the Fellowship council, the body also had the duty 'to remove the impression ... that although Jews British by birth ... [they are] Jewish by nationality'.[9] For the Fellowship the concept of a Jewish state was untenable because Jewry was a religion, not a political entity. Political Zionism totally contradicted the post-emancipatory belief that Jews were Jews only in religion and British citizens in every other aspect of life.

Thus the Fellowship was the ultimate expression, within the assimilated sector of British Jewry, of the long-time opposition to the Zionist movement and particularly its doctrine that the Jews were an ethnic minority and the Jewish problem was a national problem. Such opposition to the implications of Zionism, from Jews who viewed the issues facing Jewry from a post-emancipatory perspective, had existed in the Jewish world from the earliest Herzlian times. For example, the attack on the first Zionist Congress in 1897 by the 'protest Rabbis', though emanating from a group of Orthodox Jewish ministers was partly argued in emancipatory terms.[10]

Likewise from the earliest years of the Zionist movement it was secular Jewish opposition to Zionism that predominated within Anglo-Jewry. Most notable amongst this group was the highly influential journalist and Jewish diplomat Lucien Wolf[11] and the patrician theologian and father of Liberal Judaism in Britain, Claude G. Montefiore.[12] Arguing against Zionism on the basis that the emancipation of the Jews into Gentile society, rather than a Zionist separatist and nationalist approach, provided the best opportunity for the future of Jewry, this ideological group gained its first public and organised expression with the birth of the League of British Jews in November 1917, in the wake of the Balfour Declaration.

The League described itself as an association of British subjects professing the Jewish religion, and claimed as its objective the upholding of the status of British subjects professing the Jewish religion and the resistance of allegations that Jews constituted a separate political nationality.[13] It had been founded by those members of the Anglo-Jewish elite who had been most vocal in promoting the emancipatory ideology within Jewry in the years before the Balfour Declaration.

As Shimoni has stated, the League's fundamental ideological argument was that emancipation was a 'universally valid panacea for the contemporary Jewish condition'.[14] Through its journal *Jewish Opinion* (later *The Jewish Guardian*), and with a membership fluctuating between 400 and 1,300 members, the League of British Jews continued to present its position until 1930.

By this time however, as Ben Halpern has shown in his masterly work *The Idea of the Jewish State*,[15] assimilationist anti-Zionism, as embodied in the League, lost much of its influence as Zionists looked to co-operate with their ideological opponents. This had the result of turning many Jews who were ideologically anti-Zionist, and still philosophically opposed to a Jewish state and the idea of Jewry as a nation, into non-Zionists.

This shift in attitudes gained its most concrete expression in the expansion of the Jewish Agency into a partnership between Zionists and non-Zionists in 1929. And though there was a resurgence of active assimilationist opposition to Zionism in the wake of the extremely important report of the 1937 Royal Commission on Palestine,[16] which called for the partition of Palestine, and then, after the Zionist Biltmore Declaration of 1942, which made an autonomous Jewish state in Palestine the declared objective of the Zionist movement, the atmosphere of non-Zionism fostered in the 1920s (and embodied by the AJA in later decades) meant that the ideology that the League stood for lost much of its momentum and credibility.

Zionist polemics in the late 1940s would constantly condemn the Fellowship as nothing but a 'revival of the League of British Jews'.[17] In response, the Fellowship, aware of the danger of being labelled a continuation of this elitist, and ultimately unsuccessful, body and determined to present itself as a group with the goal of rejuvenating the religious life of Jewry, denied that it was a reconstitution of the defunct League. Yet there is little doubt that one can trace back many of the ideas and motivations of the Jewish Fellowship (not to mention some of its leading supporters) to the League. Indeed the Fellowship shared the League's assimilationist, secularised, negative attitude toward Zionism, so concisely summed up by historian Walter Laqueur. For the Fellowship, like the League before it, Zionism

> as a secular movement ... was incompatible with the religious character of Judaism; as a political movement ... was inconsistent with the spiritual emphasis in Judaism; as a nationalist movement it was out of keeping with the universalist character of Judaism; and it was a threat to the welfare of Jews as it confused Gentiles in their thinking about Jews and thus imperilled their status.[18]

THE ARAB CAUSE IN LONDON

If the antecedents of the Fellowship can be found in the polemical arguments of men like Lucien Wolf and Claude Montefiore and in the existence of the League of British Jews, it is possible to find the historical roots of the Arab Office and the Committee for Arab Affairs in such earlier manifestations of organised Gentile anti-Zionism as the Palestine Information Centre and the Arab Centre, both founded in London in the 1930s.

Recent leading opponents of Zionism and the State of Israel, such as Christopher Mayhew, have argued that the efforts of Englishmen to explain the Arab point of view before 1967 consisted simply of 'the spontaneous initiatives of a few courageous men'.[19] But in reality, the exertions of Arab and Gentile English anti-Zionists during the Mandatory period can be viewed as the building blocks on which later, more contemporary anti-Israel and pro-Arab bodies, such as the Council for the Advancement of Arab British Understanding (CAABU) have been built.[20]

The first Arab effort to present their case over Palestine in London can be traced back to 1921 with the arrival of a delegation of Christian and Muslim Palestinian Arab leaders.[21] More delegations followed over the next decade and the idea for a permanent Arab propaganda office in London was first proposed in a serious way in 1934 among the Palestinian Arab leadership linked to the Husseini family and its patriarch the Mufti of Jerusalem, Al-Hajj Muhammad Amin al-Husseini.[22]

However, it was not until the arrival of a Palestinian delegation in London in 1936 that the objective of establishing a permanent Arab propaganda office came to fruition. As delegation member Dr Izzat Tannous, a Nablus-born physician, educated in Beirut and London, has recalled, during the four-month visit the delegation was motivated by 'the need of the British public for Arab information' and as such established a permanent office in London in order 'to continue the good work we [the Arab delegation] had begun'.[23]

Thus was born the Palestine Information Centre (hereafter, the PIC). Interestingly it had been planned to call the body the Pro-Arab League, but Freya Stark suggested the name PIC as a less aggressive alternative.[24] The objectives of this body were threefold:

1. To supply reliable information for those who wish to have a clearer understanding of the Palestine problem, and in particular,

to defend the rights of the Arab population in accordance with the undertakings given and the declarations made from time to time by the British government.
2. To provide a meeting place in a central locality where Arabs from Palestine visiting this country may meet their English friends for social purposes and for the exchange of information.
3. To collect and supply information to the press and interested persons on Arab political, economic and religious matters.[25]

The establishment of the PIC and the setting out of a clear set of objectives were a turning point in the Gentile propaganda effort in London. As the *Arab News Bulletin* (the paper of the post Second World War Arab propaganda body in London, the Arab Office) would state in 1948, the PIC was 'the first office to put the Arab view before the British public'.[26] Moreover, the PIC attempted to do this through a partnership between Arabs and English supporters of the Arab cause. This was extremely significant, both for the everyday workings of the body and for the precedent it set for the close relationship between Arabs and their British supporters for the remaining years of the Mandatory era.

As Tannous recalls, the official decision to form the PIC was taken with 'ten of our British friends'.[27] Miss Frances Newton, Dame Justice of the Order of Jerusalem, a long-time resident of Haifa and Jerusalem, a leading advocate of the Palestinian cause and honorary secretary of the new committee, was more specific in her recollection that it had been the English supporters of the Arabs, who 'for some years had felt very strongly that English voices should be raised in defence of the Arab cause', who had approached the Arab delegation in July 1936 and who had initiated the plan for the PIC.[28]

Apart from Emile Ghoury, a close adviser of the Mufti and later a member of the Jordanian parliament, who acted as the Arab delegate to the PIC, the body was dominated by English Arabists. The MP Sir Ernest Bennett was chairman. Other leading members included Mrs Steuart Erskine, the author and publicist, whose 1935 book *Palestine of the Arabs* was heralded as an important contemporary contribution to the Arab propaganda cause; Colonel Stewart Newcombe, Lawrence's colleague in Arabia during the First World War, and a man who would later join the CAA; Miss Estelle Blyth, daughter of the Anglican Bishop of Jerusalem; and journalist J.M.N. Jeffries.[29]

The PIC worked primarily under British auspices into 1937,

producing and distributing pamphlets on Palestine and challenging the Zionist position at, for example, the 1937 hearings of the Royal Commission on Palestine.[30] However, it was also during this year that the composition of the PIC began to change, when in January 1937, in the wake of the Royal Commission hearings in Jerusalem, Izzat Tannous, who had been instrumental on the Arab side in establishing the PIC, returned to London to take charge of this body and, as he phrased it, 'thus fill a vacancy in the field of Arab information and propaganda'.[31]

The return of Tannous to London in an official capacity as a professional propagandist marked the beginning of a process that saw the propaganda efforts in London move from predominantly English to Arab control – a shift that occurred with the full support and active encouragement of the PIC's English members. For example, it was the PIC's honorary secretary, Miss Frances Newton, who visited Palestine in 1937 specifically to discuss the future of the PIC with the Mufti of Jerusalem. At this meeting she proposed that the time had come for Arab propaganda work in London to be taken over by the Arabs themselves, who would be directly responsible to the Mufti and the Jerusalem-based Arab Higher Committee. As Newton recalls in her autobiography the Mufti approved this proposal and Tannous and Emile Ghoury, the PIC's Arab delegate, were appointed to head what was henceforth to be known as the Arab Centre.[32]

These veteran Arab propagandists were joined by other London-based Arabs in their effort to present the Arab position. Musa al-Husseini, a cousin of the Mufti who was studying at the University of London and who had been involved in the negotiations between the 1936 Arab delegation and their 'British friends' which had led to the founding of the PIC, became a senior member of the Arab Centre. Other Arabs who increased their involvement included the lawyer George Mansour, at the time vice-president of the Arab Labour Union of Jaffa, Nicola Ziadeh, later Professor of Arab History at the American University of Beirut, Awni Daoudi, one-time adviser to King Sinusi of Libya, Esa Nachley, later chairman of the Palestine Information Centre in New York, and representatives seconded from the Iraqi legation in London, Abdul Ghani Dallyi and Abdur-Rahman Bazzaz.[33]

This change from the PIC to the Arab Centre was a determined effort by the Arabs to present their own case over Palestine. Under the agreement reached between Newton and the Mufti, the English members of the PIC would continue to support the Arab Centre only in an advisory capacity.[34] Yet in reality this reorganisation did not see a reduction in the central role that English supporters of the Arabs played in presenting the Arab case. In fact if anything their involvement only deepened. Frances Newton 'came almost every day', Mrs Steuart Erskine became 'the soul of the centre', and others such as Colonel Stewart Newcombe, the former Palestine Administration officials Ernest Richmond and C.R. Ashbee and the BBC journalist Nevill Barbour, who like Newcombe would later join the CAA, also played an important part in organising the Arab Centre and setting out its propaganda.[35]

An especially close relationship developed between Tannous and the journalist J.M.N. Jeffries. Jeffries had acquired his life-long rabidly anti-Zionist stance during his time as the *Daily Mail*'s Near East correspondent during the First World War. He had been a founding member of the PIC and was the author of two of the central pieces of English anti-Zionist propaganda before the Second World War: *The Palestine Deception: A Daily Mail Enquiry on the Spot* (1923) and *Palestine, the Reality* (1939).[36]

In June 1938 the Arab Centre moved its premises from Victoria Street to a more spacious home in Grand Building, Trafalgar Square, where it was better able to host visitors (who included the Emir Feisal and other 'important personages from the Arab and Muslim world'),[37] and to carry out what was deemed to be its most important work: the efficient distribution of literature and the provision of statements on behalf of the Arab case to both the press and public.

As such, a weekly *Arab Centre Bulletin*, devoted to the Arab case over Palestine, the defence of the Arab Revolt and the renunciation of the partition as a possible solution to the Palestine crisis, was published and distributed. With an original mailing list of 5,000, this bulletin was circulated to members of both Houses of Parliament, as well as to the media and political associations. The Centre also carried out its propaganda effort in other forums. For example, in August 1938 it published in the press, *The Arab Charter for Palestine*, an open letter to MPs, written by Tannous. This set out the Arab Centre's plan for a solution to the Palestine problem on the basis of the suspension of Jewish immigration, the end of the British Mandate and the creation of a unitary and independent Palestinian state.[38]

Efforts such as the *Arab Centre Bulletin* and *The Arab Charter for Palestine* suggest a certain sophistication and seriousness in the Arab propaganda effort at this time of debate over Palestine that is conventionally and conveniently ignored.[39] And in retrospect Izzat Tannous, the head of the Arab Centre, who would also become a member of the Arab Office in the post-war era, was of the opinion that the Arab Centre in short time 'came to be known as the official organ which represented the people of Palestine' and, moreover, that the Centre came to symbolise 'the revived Arab hope in Palestine and raised Arab morale'.[40]

By 1939 the Arabs planned to intensify their propaganda efforts in London.[41] The war halted this aspiration but it also made such efforts increasingly unnecessary. For with the commencement of hostilities the British government not only postponed any decision on the fate of Palestine but based its Palestine policy on the implementation of the May 1939 Palestine White Paper. This document limited Jewish immigration levels into Palestine and combined with the accompanying Land Transfer Regulations that restricted the sale of land to Jews in Palestine on the basis of their religion. As such, for all practical purposes, it put a freeze on the development of the Yishuv.[42]

Indeed, Arab propaganda during the war years, particularly the defence of the White Paper, became the responsibility not of the Arabs but of the British government that had introduced it. The most obvious and notable example of this was the visit by Freya Stark to the United States in 1943–44. This visit arranged by the Ministry of Information, for whom Stark worked in the Middle East during the war, had the objective of presenting the British–Arab position over Palestine, in an effort to reduce American anti-British feeling that had been rising since the introduction of the Palestine White Paper in 1939.

Regardless of the fact that both Stark and the Ministry of Information vigorously denied that she was on a pro-Arab propaganda tour of the United States, there is no doubting (especially on the evidence of her private correspondence from that visit) the validity of the Zionist claims of the time that her tour was British-sponsored pro-Arab anti-Zionist propaganda.[43]

Once the Allied victory was ensured and discussion on a post-war settlement began to be considered, the issue of Palestine again came to the forefront, and with this the Arab belief in the need to return to the propaganda arena was reborn. At the seventh meeting of the Pan

Arab Conference in Alexandria in October 1944 (a conference that resulted in the formation of the Arab League), the possibility of forming Arab publicity bureaux to explain the Arab position on crucial issues, such as Palestine, throughout the western world was addressed.[44] As such, in the spring of 1945, and after much debate between the member countries of the Arab League, Arab Offices under the sponsorship of the Arab League were set up in Washington, Jerusalem and London.

The last of these, being the capital city of the Mandate government, was considered by far the most important of the three. Indeed the Arabs made no secret of the importance that they attached to London. The *Manchester Guardian*, in a long and detailed article on the Arab Office in 1945, was of the view that 'the London office is clearly intended to be the most important'.[45] Nor was this belief in the importance of London to fade as the battle continued. In his autobiography, Cecil Hourani, a leading member of the Washington Arab Office, stated that even after the partition vote at the United Nations in November 1947, London was considered to be more important than Washington: 'nearer to the centre of decision-making … as such the efforts of the Arab Office were concentrated there'.[46]

Musa al-Alami, a former government advocate in Palestine and the unofficial Palestinian representative to the Arab League, became overall director of the new bureaux. The London Arab Office was under the direction of Edward Atiyah, formerly public relations officer in the Sudan government. Other members of the Arab Offices included Ahmed Shukairi, the first leader of the Palestine Liberation Organisation (PLO), Jamal Nasir, a future Jordanian minister of justice, Wasfi Tal, a future Jordanian prime minister, Bedia Afnan, whose husband was Iraq's long-standing representative at the United Nations, Khulusi Khairi, the foreign minister in the short-lived Iraqi–Jordanian Union of 1958 and scholars such as Cecil Hourani, Walid Khalidi, Burhan Dajani, Najla Izzedin, Charles Issawi and most notably, for his centrality to the Arab Office effort, Albert Hourani, a future leading academic on the Arab world.

The Arab Office was deemed essential because it was believed that there did not exist the necessary propaganda capabilities for fighting Zionism in England at the end of the war. Indeed the Iraqi delegation attending discussions on the setting up of Arab propaganda offices at a conference on Arab union in Alexandria, argued in favour of the creation of Arab Offices precisely because the existing Arab legations in England were diplomatic institutions and as such could not undertake 'the free and organised propaganda which circumstances demand'.[47] And as colonial official John Bennet, a member of the Minister of State's Office in Cairo who had served in the Sudan with Atiyah and was in close contact with Arab Office leaders in the run up to the body's founding, admitted in a memorandum submitted to the Foreign Office in March 1945: 'fundamentally what they [Arabs] want the London office for is to build up for the Arabs a position in influential British circles ... access to departments, MPs, press and so on'.[48]

In these terms, and in as much as its formation was motivated by the same belief in the need to tackle 'the huge network of intrigue which Zionism has built up in London',[49] the Zionists and influential and seasoned Arabists such as Lord Killearn (formerly Sir Miles Lampson, ambassador to Egypt and high commissioner to the Sudan during 1936–46) were correct in their view that the Arab Office was but a 'reopening' and a 'a re-establishment' of the pre-war Arab propaganda effort that had been epitomised by the PIC and the Arab Centre.[50]

SIR EDWARD SPEARS AND THE ARAB CAUSE

The same can be said of the Committee for Arab Affairs under the chairmanship of Sir Edward Spears. Spears is one of the least-known public figures of British twentieth-century life. Nonetheless, he qualifies for the title of leading Gentile opponent of Zionism in the last years of the Mandate. Indeed his importance to the post-war anti-Zionist effort means that it is necessary to investigate his background in some detail.[51] Born in France in 1886 into an Anglo-French–Irish family he began his public career in the British army. With the aid of fluent French he served in Anglo-French liaison in the First World War and rose to the rank of brigadier-general at the tender age of 31 in 1917. He was elected to parliament in 1921, but only established himself as a parliamentarian of standing when he won the Carlisle seat as a Conservative in 1931 – a seat he was to hold until 1945.

With the start of the Second World War, Churchill, who had become a close friend of Spears during their shared time on the

Western Front in 1915 (he was godfather to Spears' only son, and Spears had strongly supported Churchill's opposition to appeasement in the House in the 1930s), sent Spears as his personal representative to the French prime minister, Paul Reynaud, with the rank of major-general.

After the French surrender to Germany, Churchill appointed Spears, whose military and political experience had been entirely centred on the Anglo-French relationship, as the British minister plenipotentiary in the Levant states (Syria and Lebanon) with ambassadorial status. The local Arab leaders in Beirut and Damascus quickly came to view Spears, a friend of Churchill and a critic of de Gaulle, as a perfect foil to French colonial aspirations in the region. He was treated with almost regal deference by the locals and in turn he became a champion of Arab independence.[52]

On his return to England in December 1944 his newly found devotion to the Arab cause was translated into the advocacy of Arab opposition to Zionism in England. Retaking his seat in parliament he founded the Middle East Parliamentary Committee, to promote Arab rights from within the House of Commons. After his defeat in the 1945 parliamentary election, he founded the Committee for Arab Affairs (hereafter, the CAA).

Spears was the chairman and most devoted member of this body, and was instrumental in motivating a group of leading English Arabists and anti-Zionists to work tirelessly to prevent the creation of a Jewish state in Palestine. This group included Sir Ronald Storrs, the first Governor of Jerusalem after the British conquest of Palestine in 1917; the civil servant and refugee expert Sir John Hope-Simpson; Colonel Stewart Newcombe; the missionary and preacher Dr (Agnes) Maude Royden-Shaw, who had been a leading suffragette before the First World War and who commentated on economic, ethical and religious aspects of the women's movement; Professor G.R. Driver, the Oxford Hebraist; the Revd Dr Alfred Guillaume, Professor of Old Testament at the University of London; the journalists and broadcasters Nevill Barbour and Kenneth Williams; and present and former MPs, including Ralph Beaumont, Henry Longhurst, M. Philips Price, Kenneth Pickthorn, Richard Rapier Stokes and E.H. Keeling.

Indeed, it is impossible to view the practical Gentile anti-Zionist effort in these years outside the context of this group under the direction of Spears. Other attempts to promote the Arab cause over Palestine in England at this time failed to achieve any level of consistency or legitimacy. Most notably this is true of the Anglo-Arab Friendship Society, founded in London in 1946 by the anti-Zionist stalwart Frances Newton. This body had its roots in the PIC and Arab Centre and was under Newton's direct control. As she informed the Arabist Harry Philby, Newton saw this new committee as an opportunity to enable the 'Arab cause to have their opinion voiced through a corporate body'.[53] Yet regardless of its attempt to court publicity (holding a press conference to announce its formation), and the track record of its founders in promoting the Arab case,[54] it failed to make any impression in the post-war era.

Newton's society had little appeal to the CAA membership which spearheaded the Gentile English anti-Zionist co-operation with the Arab Office, and which viewed her effort as an anachronistic attempt at promoting the Arab cause. Specifically, the CAA was appalled by her committee's outdated and unpopular close support and association with the Mufti of Jerusalem, who in the post-war era was *persona non grata* within the British establishment for his co-operation with the Nazis during the war.[55]

As such Newton came under intense pressure from Spears and the CAA to close down the society. What particularly troubled this dominant group of English Arabists was the closeness of names of Newton's Anglo-Arab Friendship Society and the Anglo-Arab Association, a body founded in 1946 by the CAA with the aim of providing a forum for supporters of the Arab cause by bringing all pro-Arab groups in Britain under one umbrella group (see chapter 2 for an account of this body).

In an attempt to dissuade Newton from continuing her efforts she was offered the position of vice-president of the Anglo-Arab Association if she wound up her own group. Her obstinate refusal resulted in the commencement of legal proceedings by Spears' solicitors so that Newton would be forced publicly to state that her organisation and Spears' were in no way related. Ultimately Newton, who refused all overtures to work with the Anglo-Arab Association, agreed to distance her society from the Anglo-Arab Association.[56] With this the Anglo-Arab Friendship Society faded out, amid bitter recriminations.

But even more important than the dominance of Spears and the CAA of the Gentile anti-Zionist effort was the fact that in the context of the relationship between Jewish, Gentile and Arab anti-Zionists, and the Zionist perception of that relationship, Spears came to be viewed by all parties as the central figure in the anti-Zionist movement in this era, and the pivot around which all anti-Zionist efforts revolved. Thus it is with Spears and the CAA that we shall begin.

NOTES

1. This is truer for the Gentile anti-Zionist effort than the Jewish one. There has been an important, if limited, amount of scholarship on the subject of Jewish assimilationist anti-Zionism during the Mandate era. See especially, chapter 5 of Ben Halpern's *The Idea of the Jewish State* (Cambridge, MA: Harvard University Press, 1961). See also Gideon Shimoni's articles 'From Anti-Zionism to Non-Zionism in Anglo-Jewry, 1917–1937', *Jewish Journal of Sociology*, XXVIII: 1 (June 1986), pp. 19–47 and 'The Non-Zionists in Anglo-Jewry, 1937–1948', *Jewish Journal of Sociology*, XXVIII: 2 (December 1986), pp. 89–115; Walter Laqueur, 'Zionism and its Liberal Critics, 1896–1948', *Journal of Contemporary History*, 6 (1971), pp. 161–82; Robert S. Wistrich, 'Zionism and Its Jewish "Assimilationist" Critics (1897–1948)', *Jewish Social Studies*, 4: 2 (winter 1998), pp. 59–112.
2. On Henriques see Leonard Montefiore's homage, 'B.L.Q.H.', *Jewish Monthly*, 1: 8 (November 1947), pp. 9–11. Also see Henriques' memoirs, *The Indiscretions of a Warden* (London: Methuen, 1937) and L.L. Loewe's *Basil Henriques: A Portrait* (London: Routledge & Kegan Paul, 1976).
3. See Elazar (pseud.), writing on the occasion of Waley Cohen's 70th birthday, 'Sir Robert at Seventy', *Jewish Monthly*, 1: 7 (October 1947), p. 38.
4. Leonard Stein was a highly respected barrister, scholar and member of the Anglo-Jewish community. He had served as political secretary of the World Zionist Organisation from 1929–39, and legal adviser to the Jewish Agency from 1930–39. As president of the AJA, 1939–49, he was one of the most eminent non-Zionists in the community. Stein was also a member of the board of directors of the *Jewish Chronicle* and the author of *The Balfour Declaration* (London: Vallentine Mitchell, 1961).
5. Leading AJA members who opposed the group's official position on Palestine and supported the Zionist stance included Rabbi I.J. Unterman, William Goldstein (member of the AJA council), Dr L. Kirsch, Herbert Michaelis, Louis Nathan, Shabtai Rowson, Lionel Jacobson (chairman of the Newcastle Jewish Representative Council), Mark Labovitch (president of the Leeds Jewish Representative Council) and Dr Philip Wigoder, a leading member of the Manchester Jewish community.
6. Agudath Yisra'el was founded in 1912 in Kattowitz, primarily by German, Polish and Hungarian Jews. See *The Purpose and Programme of the World Agudist Organisation* (London: Agudath Yisra'el, 1937), p. 8. See also the practical attack on Zionism by an adherent of Agudath, Rabbi Dr Ignaz Maybaum, 'Zion and Galuth', *Jewish Monthly*, 1: 2 (May 1947), pp. 34–5.
7. Shimoni, 'The Non-Zionists in Anglo-Jewry, 1937–1948', *Jewish Journal of Sociology*, p. 102.
8. *What the Jewish Fellowship Stands For* (London: JF, October 1944), p. 2; *Constitution of the Jewish Fellowship*, as adopted at general meeting, 14 October 1945, point 1, p. 1.
9. Brunel Cohen, *Address to the Jewish Fellowship Council*, 20 June 1945, p. 4.
10. On the emancipatory aspect of this statement see Ben Halpern, *The Idea of the Jewish State*, pp. 144–5.
11. For Wolf's anti-Zionist arguments see 'The Zionist Peril', *Jewish Quarterly Review*, XVII: 3 (October 1904), pp. 1–25. For an academic analysis of Wolf's position within Anglo-Jewry and towards Zionism see Mark Levene's 'Lucien Wolf: Crypto-Zionist, Anti-Zionist or Opportunist *Par Excellence*?', *Studies in Zionism*, 12: 2 (autumn 1991), pp. 133–48 and his *War, Jews and the New Europe: The Diplomacy of Lucien Wolf, 1914–1919* (Oxford: The Littman Library of Jewish Civilisations, 1992).
12. Claude G. Montefiore was one of the most influential members of Anglo-Jewry in the twentieth century. Among his many achievements he was the founder and co-editor (with Israel Abrahams) of the *Jewish Quarterly Review* in 1886. He was the founder of the Jewish Religious Union in England in 1901, which in turn led to the establishment of the Liberal Synagogue in 1911. He was president of the Anglo-Jewish Association,

1895–1921. His many publications include *Liberal Judaism and Authority* (London: 1919); *Liberal Judaism and Convenience* (London: 1924) and *The Place of Judaism Among the Religions of the World*.
13. On the League of British Jews see Laurie Magnus, *Old Lamps for New: An Apologia for the League of British Jews* (London: 1918) and *The Need for the League* (London: 1917). One can find the reports of the League's annual meetings at the Mocatta Library, University College, London. Also see Stuart Cohen, *English Zionists and British Jews: The Communal Politics of Anglo-Jewry, 1895–1920* (Princeton, NJ: Princeton University Press, 1982) and 'Ideological Components in Anglo-Jewish Opposition to Zionism Before and During the First World War: A Restatement', *Jewish Historical Studies*, Transactions of the Jewish Historical Society of England, XXX (1987–88), pp. 149–62 and 'The Conquest of the Community? The Zionists and the Board of Deputies in 1917', *Jewish Journal of Sociology*, XIX: 2 (December 1977), pp. 157–84. Also see Eugene Black's *The Social Politics of Anglo-Jewry, 1880–1920* (Oxford: Basil Blackwell, 1988).
14. Shimoni, 'From Anti-Zionism to Non-Zionism in Anglo-Jewry, 1917–1937', p. 23.
15. Ben Halpern, *The Idea of the Jewish State*, especially chapters 2 and 5.
16. See Cmd. 5479, Report of the Palestine Royal Commission, July 1937.
17. See Israel Cohen, *Zionist Review*, 12 March 1948, p. 8.
18. Walter Laqueur, 'Zionism and its Liberal Critics, 1896–1948', p. 180.
19. Christopher Mayhew (with Christopher Adams), *Publish it Not: The Middle East Cover-up* (Harlow: Longman, 1975), p. 43. Mayhew had been an Under-Secretary of State at the Foreign Office in the Attlee government that handed over the Palestine Mandate to the United Nations in 1947.
20. For other English Gentile anti-Zionist arguments in the contemporary era see Michael Palumbo, *Imperial Israel: The History of the Occupation of the West Bank and Gaza* (London: Bloomsbury, 1996); Claud Morris, *The Last Inch: A Middle East Odyssey* (London, New York: Kegan Paul International, 1996).
21. See the Palestine Arab Delegation's *The Holy Land: The Moslem–Christian Case Against Zionist Aggression* (London: 1921). Also see Doreen Ingrams, *Palestine Papers, 1917–1922, Seeds of Conflict* (London: John Murray, 1972), pp. 137–51 and David Cesarani 'Anti-Zionist Politics and Political Antisemitism in Britain, 1920–1924', *Patterns of Prejudice*, 23: 1 (1989), pp. 28–45.
22. Mrs Steuart (Beatrice Caroline) Erskine, *Palestine of the Arabs* (London: George Harrap, 1935), p. 168. Al-Hajj Muhammad Amin al-Husseini was a Palestinian Arab nationalist leader. Born into an influential Jerusalem family, he played a leading role in the anti-Jewish riots of 1920. In 1921 he was appointed Grand Mufti (expounder of Muslim law) by Herbert Samuel in an attempt to appease the Arab nationalists. He used his religious role to consolidate his position as the most powerful Arab leader in Palestine, adopting an extremist anti-Jewish and anti-British attitude in the process. He headed the Arab Higher Committee, played a central role in the Arab Revolt in Palestine, from where he was expelled in the late 1930s. He collaborated with Nazi Germany during the Second World War. In 1946 he escaped from French detention and continued to direct Arab affairs from his exile in Cairo.
23. Izzat Tannous, *The Palestinians: A Detailed Documented Eye-witness History of Palestine under the Mandate* (New York: IGT, 1988), pp. 186–7.
24. See Freya Stark to Venetia Buddicom, 20 July 1936, reprinted in Lucy Moorehead (ed.), *Freya Stark, Letters: Vol. 3, The Growth of Danger, 1935–1939* (London: Compton Russell, 1986), p. 42.
25. Frances Newton, *Fifty Years in Palestine* (Wrotham: Cold Harbour Press, 1948), p. 282.
26. *Arab News Bulletin*, 69 (14 August 1948), p. 4.
27. Tannous, *The Palestinians*, p. 187.
28. Newton, *Fifty Years in Palestine*, p. 281.
29. Other members of the PIC executive were Mr Archer Crust, Mr Ruthven Guest, Mrs L. Swinburne and Mrs Cecil Brooke.
30. For the PIC's arguments in relation to the 1937 Royal Commission on Palestine see *Crisis in Palestine: The Task of the Royal Commission: Has There Been a Breach of Faith?* (London, 1937). For other examples of PIC propaganda and for correspondence concerning the PIC see file 4, Box LXV, JEMP.
31. Tannous, *The Palestinians*, p. 189.

Antecedents and Outlook 21

32. Newton, *Fifty Years in Palestine*, p. 282.
33. Tannous, *The Palestinians*, p. 214.
34. Newton, *Fifty Years in Palestine*, p. 282.
35. See, for example, Newcombe's *The Future of Palestine* (London: 1938) and Barbour's *A Plan for a Lasting Peace in Palestine* (London: 1938). Both published by the Arab Centre.
36. See J.M.N. Jeffries, *The Palestine Deception: A Daily Mail Enquiry on the Spot* (London: Daily Mail, 1923) and *Palestine, the Reality* (London: Longmans, Green, 1939).
37. Newton, *Fifty Years in Palestine*, p. 283.
38. See Tannous, *The Arab Charter for Palestine* (London: Arab Centre, 1938).
39. Other Arab Centre propaganda works included *The Causes of the Arab Revolt* (1938); Tannous and Newton's *Palestine: The Way to Peace* (1938) and two pamphlets by Newton, *Punitive Measures in Palestine* and the subsequent *Searchlight on Palestine: Fair Play or Terrorist Methods?*. Both were published in 1938 and their claims of British brutality against Arabs in Palestine caused much controversy.
40. Tannous, *The Palestinians*, pp. 201–3.
41. See report of meeting between Colonial Office official H.L. Baggallay and George Antonius, 30 March 1939, PRO/FO 371/23232.
42. *Palestine: A Statement of Policy*, Cmd. 6019 (London, 1939). The most important aspects of the White Paper for the Arab cause were the immigration clauses of the document which limited Jewish immigration into the country to 75,000 over the following five years after which the Arabs of Palestine would have the final say on future levels of Jewish immigration. See chapter 8 for a detailed examination of the White Paper.
43. For Stark's candid private correspondence on her tour see her letters to Elizabeth Monroe, in the Monroe Collection, MEC, St Antony's College, Oxford. Also see *Freya Stark, Letters: Vol. 5, New Worlds for Old, 1943–1946*, ed. Lucy Moorehead (London: Compton Russell, 1986). For the Zionist view of Stark's tour see 'Miss Freya Stark's Tour', *Zionist Review*, 19 May 1944, and *New Judea* (April 1944), p. 115. For a general description of her tour and the controversy surrounding it, including questions raised about the trip in the House of Commons, see Molly Izzard, *Freya Stark: A Biography* (London: Hodder & Stoughton, 1993) and Caroline Moorehead, *Freya Stark* (London: Viking, 1985).
44. Minutes of the seventh meeting of the Pan Arab Union Conference, Alexandria, Egypt, 5 October 1944, PRO/FO 371/45235.
45. *Manchester Guardian*, 20 August 1945.
46. Cecil Hourani, *An Unfinished Odyssey: Lebanon and Beyond* (London: Weidenfeld & Nicolson, 1984), p. 71.
47. 'Memorandum of the Government of Iraq on the Founding of the Arab Offices', 17 August 1944, PRO/FO 371/45235. On the objectives that the Council of the Arab League set out for the Arab Offices see 'Material for a History of the Arab Union, 1939–1945', by Colonel de Gaury, research department, FO, 28 March 1947, PRO/FO 371/45241, p. 11.
48. Bennet to Robin Hankey, 29 March 1945, PRO/FO 371/45238.
49. Al-Sayed Hamdi al Bajahji, seventh meeting of the Pan Arab Union Conference, 5 October 1944, PRO/FO 371/45235.
50. See 'Arab Propaganda Offices', *Zionist Review*, 1 June 1945, p. 1 and Killearn to FO, 18 January 1945, PRO/FO 371/45235.
51. There has only been one attempt to address the life of Spears (1886–1974) in biographical form. See Max Egremont's *Under Two Flags: The Life of Major-General Sir Edward Spears* (London: Weidenfeld & Nicolson, 1997). However Egremont concentrates his study on Spears' life-long relationship with France and in doing so pays scant attention to the issues of Zionism and Palestine, neither of which even gains a reference in the index.
52. For a contemporary summary of the French situation in the Levant see Charles-Andre Julien, 'French Difficulties in the Middle East', *Foreign Affairs*, 24: 2 (January 1946), pp. 327–36. For Spears' own autobiographical account of his time in the Levant see *Fulfilment of a Mission: The Spears Mission to Syria and Lebanon, 1941–1944* (London: Leo Cooper, 1977). See also Philip Khoury's *Syria and the French Mandate: The Politics of Arab Nationalism, 1920–1945* (London: Tauris, 1987) and Aviel Roshwald, *Estranged Bedfellows: Britain and France in the Middle East during the Second World War* (New York and Oxford: Oxford University Press, 1990).

53. Newton to Philby, 20 July 1946, Box 10/4, PHIL.
54. Other founding members of the Anglo-Arab Friendship Society included Douglas Reed, Captain Alan Graham, the Earl of Norbury and Lady Makins.
55. For this body's support of the highly unpopular Mufti see *The Truth about the Mufti* (London: Anglo-Arab Friendship Society, 1946). Also see Newton's defence of the Mufti in her autobiography, *Fifty Years in Palestine*, p. 293.
56. On this incident see Newton to Spears, 6 and 9 August 1946, Box 11/1 and N. Maurice to R. Bertrand (Spears' solicitor), 25 September, 1946; Bertrand to Maurice, 26 September 1946, Box 11/1. Also see W.G. Baillie to Newton, 18 October 1946; Newton to Baillie, 21 October 1946, Box 11/2. Finally see Sir John Hope-Simpson to Spears, 27 July 1947; Spears to Hope-Simpson, 30 July 1947, Box 11/1 (all SPSP).

2 The Committee for Arab Affairs and the Arab Cause

Sir Edward Spears was not a veteran member of the English Arabist community, but only became interested in Middle Eastern politics during his time as minister plenipotentiary in the Levant states in the years between 1941 and 1944. Like many a convert to a particular cause he was a fervent one, especially vocal in his condemnation of French actions in the Levant and in his belief that Arab friendship was more important to Britain than that of the French.

By 1945 Spears was arguing that 'the greatest possible goodwill towards France would not justify' upsetting the Anglo-Arab relationship.[1] This public advocacy of Arab over French interests by the British representative in Syria and Lebanon must be viewed in the context of the fact that Spears, the lifelong Francophile, had been sent by Churchill to the Levant precisely because of his close and intimate past history with the French (it had been Spears who alone had accompanied de Gaulle on his escape to England after the fall of France).

Spears' open hostility to the French ally resulted in his recall home from duty in December 1944, and he returned to England with the firmly held conviction that Arab friendship was the vital component of all future British success in that region. Time and again throughout these years Spears repeated his view that 'peace and tranquillity in the Middle East are essential to British interests ... we cannot have them except through peace and friendship with the Arab peoples',[2] and that 'the friendship of the Arab world is vital to the British Empire'.[3]

Spears went as far as telling a prestigious audience at the Royal Institute of International Affairs (also known as Chatham House, hereafter, RIIA), that had assembled in curiosity, in February 1945, to hear the views of this controversial former British representative, that 'I would propound at the outset my view that the Middle East is the key to the whole structure of the Empire, second only in importance to this Island itself.'[4] Spears was optimistic about the future because he believed that the British relationship with the Arabs coming out of the war was better than it had been for decades and that it was vital that Englishmen worked to protect this hard-earned position.[5] For as Spears warned, 'The friendship we enjoy today, is but a flower of recent growth and like all things requires careful tending. It is entirely based on the belief that we are in sympathy with Arab aspirations.'[6]

It was this belief that made him despair at the thought of British support for Zionism. For the prevention of a Jewish state in Palestine was the objective that united the whole of the Arab world. As he told readers of the *Daily Telegraph*, in February 1945: 'it is impossible to exaggerate the strength of Arab feeling on the subject of Palestine'.[7]

Spears developed this argument throughout his public statements during these years. In January 1946, during his evidence before the Anglo-American Committee of Inquiry on Palestine (hereafter, the Anglo-American Committee or the AACIP: the most important international forum on the Palestine problem in the post-war era, established to examine the Palestine problem in relation to the position of Jewish refugees in Europe made homeless during the war), he said: 'I have met many, many Arabs of all kinds, and I have not met one single one who was not of one mind on this subject of Palestine.'[8] He reiterated this view again towards the end of his evidence emphasising that 'there is no subject on which all Arabs ... feel so strongly and so completely unanimously as they do on Palestine'.[9]

Thus for Spears future British success 'largely depends on the future of Palestine'[10] and 'a solution to the Palestine problem is essential to peace in the Middle East'.[11] If Spears was prepared to sacrifice Britain's relationship with France for Arab friendship over the Levant it is not surprising that he cared little about the loss of support for Britain among Zionists over the Palestine issue. From the time he returned to Britain from his Levant duties he began a public crusade to promote the Arab cause in England through press, platform and parliament.

Spears was not alone within the British Arabist and foreign policy community in believing that a close and friendly relationship with the Arab states was impossible if Britain supported or was believed to be supporting the creation of a Jewish state in Palestine. There are numerous examples during these years, and much later, of British statesmen, diplomats, parliamentarians and observers of the Middle East, who held the same attitude as Spears. Men of renown such as Harold Beeley at the Foreign Office, the academic Professor Hamilton (H.A.R.) Gibb and the soldier and head of the Jordanian Arab Legion, Lieutenant-General Sir John Glubb all shared Spears' belief that it was primarily on the Palestine issue that Britain had let down the Arabs.[12]

Where Spears differed from these other Arabists was in his practical efforts to stand up and lobby for the Arab cause and to take the lead in the anti-Zionist movement in England at this crucial time in the battle over Palestine. During an interview with *al-Ahram* newspaper (whose London editor Kenneth Williams would play a central role in the CAA), at the end of 1944, shortly after his return from the Levant, Spears openly spoke of his desire 'to help the representatives in London of the Arabic-speaking states to form a united front on their problems'.[13] As such, in February 1945, Spears founded the Middle East Parliamentary Committee (hereafter, the MEPC), within parliament.

Despite Spears' insistence that this committee was founded to study events in the Middle East in general,[14] no one doubted that it was created specifically to present the Arab case over Palestine within the House. Ralph Beaumont MP, a staunch anti-Zionist and a member of both the MEPC and then the CAA, advised Spears that the MEPC should concentrate on 'presenting our point of view'.[15]

The *Jewish Chronicle*, the flagship paper of Anglo-Jewry, in commenting on the founding of the MEPC was of the view that Spears was the 'dominating personality' and that it was 'obvious' that Palestine 'will be the real central question in connection with which the committee formed'.[16] While *New Judea* (the paper of the World Zionist Organisation in London), was of the view that the MEPC 'includes most of the opponents of the Jewish National Home ... committee actively engaged against Zionist aspirations'.[17]

Whatever role Spears had envisaged for the MEPC under his chairmanship, his defeat in the 1945 Labour landslide election victory (he was a Conservative) meant that he needed to find another forum to promote the Arab cause. His response was to create the paramount British anti-Zionist body of the post-war era, the CAA. Spears founded this body with the help of the Arab Club in London, an elite group composed of himself and the representatives of the Saudi, Jordanian, Syrian and Egyptian governments in Britain. Meetings of this body were held at Spears' own home, and at one such gathering on 8 August 1945 the CAA, under Spears' chairmanship, was formed to present the Arab case in Britain.

The Arab Club agreed to finance the new committee from its own bank account, with each of the Arab governments represented in the Arab Club providing sufficient funds to cover the expenses accrued by Spears, and his secretary Miss Nancy Maurice, in the running of the CAA, the publication of pamphlets and the organising of meetings.[18] Such financial support enabled Spears to recruit members without asking them for donations to fund the committee, and also allowed Spears to turn down voluntary offers of monetary support from eager members.[19]

Given this central role in creating the new committee it is hardly surprising that the Arab ministers in London and the Arab League leadership in Cairo were kept fully informed of the efforts of the CAA. For example Spears provided the Arab legations with copies of the minutes of CAA meetings and of resolutions passed at those meetings, as well as information on the general efforts of the committee which were then communicated to the Arab League.[20] In these terms the CAA symbolises the close, almost intimate, relationship between the English Arabists and Arabs in London during these years of battle against Zionism.

But the CAA should also be viewed as an attempt by Spears to continue his pro-Arab efforts, lobbying for an independent unitary state in Palestine under Arab control, within the political establishment, after losing his seat in the 1945 election. As he told Brigadier Iltyd Clayton in August 1945, his real regret about losing his parliamentary seat was his loss of a platform from which to promote the Arab cause.[21]

The CAA was an answer to this. Certainly this was how the CAA appealed to other anti-Zionist politicians who had also lost their parliamentary seats in 1945, and were invited to join the body. Ralph Beaumont wrote to Spears to accept his invitation on the basis that 'the idea of forming a Middle East committee outside parliament is a very good one and it will enable us who have been flung out of the House to keep in touch with those who are still in, on the Middle East problem', a sentiment echoed by Henry Longhurst who had also lost his parliamentary seat in the 1945 election.[22]

For Spears the disadvantages of losing his position as an MP and chairman of the MEPC were somewhat compensated for by the fact that the new committee was an 'ad hoc body and as such has no strictly defined constitutional functions'.[23] As such, unlike the MEPC (which due to its parliamentary responsibilities had to have Zionist members), this new committee was not obligated to follow any specific parliamentary procedures or decorum. The CAA was a purely pro-Arab body, with Spears informing Lord Altrincham, formerly Sir Edward Grigg, who had replaced the assassinated Lord Moyne as British Minister resident in the Middle East, that the new body 'is intended to include those interested in the Arab side. In this it will be different from the Middle East Parliamentary Committee which included all shades of opinion.'[24]

One major difference between the two bodies was the CAA's deep involvement in pro-Arab propaganda over Palestine. The importance of fighting Zionism in the propaganda arena and actively facing up to what the commentator George Kirk at the time called the 'hundred-mouthed Sibylline cave whence issued the propaganda of Zionism',[25] had long been central to the anti-Zionist position. Indeed, long before the end of the Second World War Zionism had come to be defined primarily, if not purely, as a propaganda phenomenon.

Sir Ronald Storrs in his celebrated *Orientations*, written in 1937, compared the chance of the Arabs competing with Zionist propaganda as akin to the chance that the Dervishes had before Kitchener's guns at Omduran, i.e. none at all.[26] While George Antonius in his work *The Arab Awakening*, first published in 1938, which quickly came to be viewed as the seminal and pre-eminent statement of the pan-Arab and anti-Zionist cause, expressed the view that 'the most formidable obstacle to understanding, and therefore to a solution of the Palestine problem lies not so much with its inherent complexity as in the solid jungle of legend and propaganda which has grown up around it'.[27] Thus in both the Arab and English Gentile anti-Zionist mind it was propaganda that provided the momentum for the Zionist programme in Palestine. As such it was in the field of propaganda that the battle against future Zionist victories had to be fought.

Given this view and the belief in the importance of London in the immediate post-war era, there can be little doubt that the CAA was conceived by Spears and the Arab ministers (who along with Spears drew up a list of prospective members who would lend the necessary gravitas to the CAA),[28] with the aim of providing an organised forum for the leading anti-Zionists in presenting the Arab case in London.

The invitations that Spears sent out to prospective members show that the CAA was primarily intended to have a propaganda role in the battle over Palestine. Spears informed Major-General Sir George Jeffreys MP that 'it is extremely important now that the Palestine question is likely to assume such major importance that there should be a body of informed opinion aware of the Arab point of view'.[29] And this opportunity that the committee provided for offering an outlet for propaganda was its main appeal to prospective members.

The long-time Arabist and ambassador to Iraq, Sir Kinahan Cornwallis, though declining to join the CAA because of official duties, was very supportive and of the view that there was 'great scope' for such a body.[30] While Pierre Loftus, who like Spears, Longhurst and Beaumont, had lost his parliamentary seat in 1945 and who was constantly preoccupied with the 'great deal of extreme Zionist propaganda',[31] saw the committee as an opportunity, as he told Spears enthusiastically, to aid him in his plan to 'work by articles and letters in the press to help those causes in which I take a keen interest'.[32]

Spears not only enticed his prospective members with the opportunity of joining a committee that would actively engage in pro-Arab propaganda, but throughout the committee's existence he would tell correspondents that the CAA had a role in informing public opinion. For example, he reassured one such correspondent in 1946 not to worry about the future of the Middle East because he had formed a committee and one of its main functions was the 'education of public opinion in this matter'.[33]

Yet in reality the CAA was never a public body that openly announced its pro-Arab efforts, and it was agreed at the first meeting of the committee that it would not for the present seek publicity.[34] Spears justified this position on the basis that it took time for the committee to organise itself as a public propaganda body.[35] This had some credibility, but the primary reason for such a decision was the reluctance to be seen carrying out propaganda publicly and the belief in the importance of keeping the efforts of members quiet.

This is vividly illustrated by the actions of three of the leading members of the CAA. The journalist Nevill Barbour, the theologian and academic the Revd Dr Alfred Guillaume and Sir Ronald Storrs all eagerly accepted invitations to join the committee. However, they did so under the proviso that they were presented as members only of the cultural sub-committee of the CAA and that in dealings with the press or the public their names be given solely as members of that sub-committee.[36]

This hesitancy of leading members to be openly associated with the committee meant that the CAA itself did not receive very much public attention. It is in regard to the Anglo-Arab Association that one can see just how discreet the CAA was. The Anglo-Arab Association, an umbrella body for all Arabist efforts in England, was founded at a meeting of the CAA in July 1946. The CAA, with the blessing and financial support of the Arab legations, provided the inclination and manpower for this association. Indeed the entire membership of the CAA acted as a temporary council of the new body, and Spears, Lady Drower, Robin Maugham, Michael Ionides, Kenneth Williams, Colonel W.G. Elphinston and G.W.G. Baillie, in the role of honorary secretary, formed the executive with the task of setting the body up.[37]

One of the reasons that Spears and his fellow members felt it necessary to form this new group was to provide a popular forum for those who supported the Arab cause in England, or as a memorandum on the Anglo-Arab Association stated, 'to enlist in one body all those who wish to do something for the Arab cause'.[38] The memorandum also stated that this new body was to 'have an organisation which could be expanded indefinitely to undertake any form of activity in developing relations between Arab states and Great Britain and explaining the Arab point of view to the British public. Also to organise social functions, lectures, maintain contact with the House of Commons and the House of Lords.'[39] The CAA was very much an elitist body and saw its efforts, as shall be seen, as appealing to the upper strata of the English political nation. Thus the Anglo-Arab Association was a means of providing a forum for supporters of the Arabs who were not deemed of enough influence to warrant a place on the CAA. There are several examples of English supporters of the Arab cause writing to Spears to offer assistance, only to be turned down because the CAA was not the suitable forum for such efforts. As Spears told one correspondent, who had written offering to help in any organisation promoting the Arab cause, his own committee 'is not a large body and consists mainly of MPs and Middle East experts'.[40]

Great Britain and the East, a journal that under the editorship of John Bee was closely associated with the Arabist community and to which CAA members, including Storrs, Spears and Barbour, all contributed articles, never once referred to the CAA in its detailed coverage of events relating to the Arab world. Yet it did give coverage to the founding of the Anglo-Arab Association.

The journal set out the aims of the new body and noted its 'comprehensive range of Arab contacts' and the fact that under the leadership of Spears 'one could scarcely find anywhere gathered together more significant representatives of the various fields of interest which the Arab world has to offer'.[41] In commenting in such a way, this journal was responding to a request from G.W.G. Baillie, honorary secretary of the Anglo-Arab Association, who had written to the editor asking for coverage of the Anglo-Arab Association. Baillie also wrote to the *Daily Telegraph* requesting the same.[42]

Even the Anglo-Jewish press, that as a body never commented on or referred to the efforts of the CAA during these years although, as shall be shown, it had much to say about the anti-Zionist efforts of Spears and his contemporaries, also reported on the formation, under Spears' chairmanship, of the Anglo-Arab Association.[43]

However, one should not equate anonymity with inactivity because the CAA worked vigorously to promote the Arab cause in public, albeit surreptitiously. For example, in October 1945, Spears corresponded with Abd al-Rahman Azzam Bey, the secretary-general of the Arab League, who was in London meeting members of the government and working to build up the Arab Office. The correspondence was in regard to Spears' attempt, on behalf of the CAA, to get a book on the economic and industrial resources of the Arab states published in London, in the hope that the general reader would realise that the Arabs were just as able as Jews to develop the Middle East region.

This project was financed (as was every other facet of the committee's efforts) by the Arab legations in London through the Arab Club bank accounts. Spears was willing to pay the eventual author of this work £500 and was writing to Azzam Pasha to make sure that he understood that the committee's sponsorship of the book and the fact that it was funded by the Arabs should be kept secret. As Spears told Azzam Pasha, 'it is important the money should not come directly from an Arab source so as not to seem as direct propaganda'.[44]

Nor was this the only occasion that Spears devoted time and

effort to organising the publication of a book for the Arab cause. In 1946 he was approached by Dr Izzat Tannous, veteran Arab propagandist and at the time a member of the Arab Office, who asked him to help find a publisher for a manuscript on Palestine by one M.F. Abcarius.[45] Spears took up the challenge, and after having the manuscript refused by Messrs Luzac for being too political, he convinced Hutchinson's to take it on the basis that he would not only provide the foreword to the book, but also that he would personally revise the manuscript so that it would be more comprehensible to the native English speaker.[46]

The book that ultimately resulted from this effort by Spears was *Palestine: Through the Fog of Propaganda*, which became a classic example of Arab anti-Zionist propaganda.[47] The fact that Spears, chairman of the CAA, laboured so hard to get it published shows that both he and the committee saw propaganda as being of central importance. Indeed, Sir John Hope-Simpson, in writing to Spears in September 1945, was echoing the sentiment of the rest of the CAA membership, when he told his chairman that 'it is good to see that, at long last, some propaganda is being done on the Arab side'.[48]

Kenneth Williams is a good example of the fact that even when the CAA as a body was reluctant to fight Zionism publicly its leading members were constantly engaged in anti-Zionist publicity efforts. Williams, a professional journalist, and London editor of the Egyptian newspaper *al-Ahram*, played a central role in the propaganda efforts of the CAA. He was the committee's press officer, a member of the two-man sub-committee responsible for drafting a response to the Anglo-American Committee report that was published in May 1946, and he sat on the interim executive committee of the Anglo-Arab Association.[49]

But Williams was also a prolific writer of articles and had access to the media and many opportunities to present the Arab point of view publicly, both in his syndicated articles in the provincial press and for such journals of opinion as *Great Britain and the East* and the *Fortnightly*.[50]

Nevill Barbour was another member of the CAA held in high esteem as an expert on Middle Eastern affairs who had similarly excellent access to the media. He gave evidence to both the Royal Commission on Palestine in 1937 and the Woodhead Commission on Partition in 1938, and was awarded the Lawrence of Arabia Memorial medal by the Royal Central Asian Society in 1964, for his lifetime achievements in the field of Middle Eastern studies.[51]

He was the first editor of the BBC publication the *Arab Listener* and throughout these years held the mantle as the BBC's official in-house expert on the Middle East, retiring in 1956 as assistant head of the BBC Eastern Service.[52] As such he was responsible for drawing up internal memoranda at the BBC on the Palestine issue and reporting on such central events as the Anglo-American Committee hearings from Jerusalem.[53] And it was because of this professional involvement with every aspect of the Palestine problem that Barbour sought to keep his involvement in the anti-Zionist CAA quiet.

Torn between his need to appear unbiased and his desire to support and play a role in the CAA he overcame his dilemma by disingenuously accepting membership of the CAA 'to study conditions in the Middle East', telling Spears that 'I assume of course that this will not involve any activity of a propaganda nature, which would be inconsistent with the position I hold with the BBC.'[54]

As will be seen in the next chapter, Barbour, preoccupied as he was with 'Zionist pressure groups',[55] had a long history of involvement in promoting the Arab case against Zionism. And despite his efforts to convince himself that the CAA was not a propaganda body, he did not hesitate to provide both Spears and the Arab Office with information, material and advice gained through his work at the BBC.

During a 1945 meeting at the RIIA, for example, at which Edward Atiyah, secretary of the Arab Office, presented that body's plans for propaganda, Barbour informed him how best to use the BBC, telling him that the Arabs should concentrate on factual not emotional propaganda and that it should be stressed that the Arab world, through the Arab Office, was speaking with one voice.[56] He also provided information on Palestine to the CAA. On one occasion in 1947 he sent Spears material on the Zionist Congress, while the following year he forwarded photographs to his CAA chairman for what he termed 'propaganda purposes'.[57]

Nor was Barbour alone in providing Spears with information in the fight against Zionism. Sir Ronald Storrs would forward to Spears any material of interest on Zionism that he encountered, such as articles or Zionist letters in the press. In return Spears' office supplied Storrs with information he needed to write articles or letters to the press and responded positively to Storrs' requests for information needed to 'prime [him] for future assaults', as he liked to phrase it.[58] Storrs also wrote such letters attacking Zionism at the behest of Spears and on behalf of the CAA. On one occasion, after lunching with Spears, he agreed to the latter's request that he write to *The Times*, attacking a letter in the same paper by Ivan Greenberg, a former editor of the *Jewish Chronicle*, on the Palestine issue. After drafting his reply to Greenberg, Storrs telephoned Miss Maurice at Spears' office with the finished letter and she sent it to *The Times*.[59]

This interrelationship between Gentile anti-Zionists within the CAA stemmed from the close-knit nature of the Arabist community in London. Storrs often lunched with leading members of the CAA, such as the highly respected Dr Maude Royden-Shaw and the long-time Arabist, Colonel Stewart Newcombe.[60] Likewise, Newcombe and Storrs lunched with Thomas Reid MP (a leading opponent of Zionism within parliament, who served as a member of the Woodhead Commission of 1938 that opposed partition as a fair solution to the Palestine problem) on the day that he was to give an anti-Zionist speech to the Royal Central Asian Society, in an effort to give him some ideas and support.[61] Similarly Robin Maugham, another CAA member and the son of a former Lord Chancellor, based part of his 1947 book on Palestine on material supplied by Newcombe.[62]

As such the CAA provided this group of leading English Arabists with an organised forum through which concrete expression could be given to their anti-Zionist position. This can best be seen in the case of Sir John Hope-Simpson, the refugee expert and retired civil servant. In January 1946 he contributed an article to the *Fortnightly*, on the Palestine statement made by Foreign Secretary Ernest Bevin the previous November.[63] There was nothing new in Hope-Simpson writing an article in the general press on Palestine, in fact he had written one in the same journal in December 1944, which had argued that there was no credence in the Zionist call for a Jewish state.[64] However, the January 1946 article is of special interest because it was commissioned at the same time as the CAA had come into existence. As such Hope-Simpson (who, as we have already seen, viewed the CAA primarily as a body for the dissemination of Arab propaganda) looked to Spears for information and material for his article, telling the latter that 'I think this chance to present the Palestine case as it is today, should not be missed.'[65]

Naturally Spears supplied Hope-Simpson with the necessary information (which Hope-Simpson deemed to be 'invaluable').[66] As will be shown in chapter 5, this Hope-Simpson article was important as an example of the similarity of arguments used by Jewish and Gentile anti-Zionists in the post-war era. But in the context of discussing the role of the CAA as a propaganda body and its efforts to present the Arab case through use of the media and by means of propaganda one can see the direct relationship between Spears and other Gentile anti-Zionists who, acting as individuals, presented a position that had the backing and support of a committee funded by the Arab states.

The importance, to the CAA, of countering Zionist propaganda can be seen in an examination of three separate areas central to the battle over Palestine in these years: the Zionist propaganda of Walter Lowdermilk; the Anglo-American Committee hearings on Palestine and the Jewish problem that were held in London in January 1946; and the efforts of the CAA to influence parliament against Zionism.

THE LOWDERMILK ISSUE

In 1939 Walter Clay Lowdermilk, the American soil conservation expert, after extensive study of the soil and water potential in Palestine, publicly announced his belief in the possibilities of increasing the population of Palestine through effective use of the Jordan waters, primarily by proposing using the waters of the Mediterranean to provide energy and using the waters of the Jordan and its tributaries for irrigation purposes. In terms of the battle over Palestine this was important because his assessment favoured increased Jewish immigration on a scientific basis. He was, after all, assistant chief of the United States Soil Conservation Service and president of the American Geophysical Union.

But as well as being acknowledged as one of the world's foremost experts on soil conservation he was also a Gentile Zionist devoted to the idea of making Palestine viable as a Jewish state. Even before the war, during his time studying conditions in Palestine, Lowdermilk spoke passionately about political Zionism reclaiming the rightful home of the Jews as set down in the Bible. Lowdermilk gave a talk in 1939 on Jerusalem radio entitled 'The Eleventh Commandment', which was broadcast to the Jewish villages of Mandatory Palestine, during which he informed listeners that 'thou shalt inherit the earth as a faithful steward ...

thou shalt safeguard thy fields from soil erosion ... that thy descendants may have abundance forever'.[67]

Lowdermilk's commitment to the Zionist ideal, born partly out of religious belief and partly out of faith in his scientific findings, continued after he left Palestine. He appeared before the House of Representatives Foreign Affairs Committee, in support of a pending pro-Zionist resolution on Palestine. He also served on the board of the Palestine Survey Commission set up in 1943 and funded by Keren Hayesod (the Palestine Foundation Fund), to study proposals for increasing the population of Palestine. However, his greatest contribution to the Zionist cause was his book *Palestine: Land of Promise*, a work that provided the Zionist movement with one of its most valuable propaganda arguments in favour of Jewish settlement in Palestine.

The English edition of this book was published by Gollancz in London in October 1944, and received much critical acclaim.[68] It was immediately heralded in the Zionist press. The *Zionist Review* (the paper of the Zionist Federation of Great Britain and Ireland) called it the 'finest argument on record for a Jewish commonwealth in Palestine', while Ephraim Broido, a leading member of the World Jewish Congress,[69] writing in *New Judea*, praised the work in glowing terms as a 'significant' contribution towards solving the Palestine problem.[70]

The image of Palestine, as a land of promise was not new. It had been used in Zionist propaganda before the publication of the Lowdermilk book. For example, a film entitled *Land of Promise* had been shown to Zionist groups throughout England in 1940. But after the publication of the book, the slogan 'Palestine, Land of Promise' was to become the central battle-cry of Zionist publicity efforts in the post-war era. For example, in December 1944, the Zionist Federation held what it called an 'important public meeting' under the title 'Palestine, Land of Promise', while in the same month the Women's Mizrachi Society of London held a meeting to celebrate the 70th birthday of Chaim Weizmann under the heading 'Palestine, Land of Promise'.[71]

After the war, when the issues of immigration and land settlement in Palestine came once more to the fore, Lowdermilk continued to be an outspoken supporter of political Zionism's goals and a central figure in the post-war propaganda battle over Palestine. This culminated in his oral testimony before the Anglo-American Committee in Washington in 1946.

Despite the fact that Lowdermilk began his evidence before the Anglo-American Committee with the somewhat disingenuous claim that he was in no way connected to the Zionist cause or movement, his support for Zionist aspirations was greatly prized by the Zionist movement.

As such the attempt by Spears and the CAA to respond to what were perceived to be the damaging effects of Lowdermilk's public support for Zionism on the basis of his scientific studies shows how the committee, though not public, discreetly carried out propaganda against Zionism on issues deemed central to the whole debate.

One should not underestimate the importance attached to the public position of Lowdermilk in the anti-Zionist mind. The Lowdermilk issue is the one Zionist argument that appears, in order to be challenged, in all the anti-Zionist literature of the time. The Arab Office view that 'Dr Lowdermilk in his book *Palestine: Land of Promise* is a good illustration of how Zionists distort the conception of economic absorptive capacity for Palestine in order to serve their political aims' was echoed by all opponents of Zionism.[72] Indeed George Kirk, in his review of events in the Middle East during the war, written for Chatham House in 1950, was of the opinion that Lowdermilk was 'symbolical of the affinity between the American and the Zionist enterprise',[73] an affinity that to Gentile anti-Zionists was the greatest obstacle to Arab success in preventing a Jewish state.

This attitude to Lowdermilk's pro-Zionist attitude was coupled to a belief in the danger of Lowdermilk, a Gentile who advocated maximalist figures for immigration into Palestine on scientific grounds. This danger must be seen in the context of CAA member G.R. Driver's view, set out both in correspondence with Spears and in an article in *The Spectator*, that Gentile scholars had lower estimates of the historical Jewish population in Palestine than Jewish scholars.

For anti-Zionists like Driver, a renowned Hebraist and professor at Oxford University, this meant that the Jewish figures had less credibility because they were not corroborated by Gentile opinion.[74] As such, when a non-Jew of Lowdermilk's reputation supported Jewish maximalist claims in the even more sensitive area than past population figures, that of future immigration and absorption possibilities, this was seen as very dangerous.

Stewart Newcombe would later express to Spears his view that 'the Gentile Zionists are in some ways more harmful and misleading than the Jew Zionists'.[75] Here the implication being that Gentile Zionists were more damaging to the anti-Zionist cause because they were not Jews and as such their support for a Jewish state was a great coup for Zionists as it gave credence to the Zionist position from what could be presented to the general public as a fundamentally disinterested and objective group.

Indeed, the publisher of the English edition of Lowdermilk's book, Victor Gollancz, in a work of his own of 1945, arguing in favour of a Jewish state, used the fact of Lowdermilk's 'Aryan' background to show the validity of his claims.[76] While Sir John E. Russell, who wrote the foreword to the same edition of *Palestine: Land of Promise*, stated in an article in the *Zionist Review* supporting Lowdermilk's claims, 'like myself he is not Jewish and can view the enterprise quite dispassionately'.[77]

Yet Lowdermilk was in no way a dispassionate observer of the Palestine issue. He directly involved himself in lobbying and publicly supporting Zionism, and in 1948, in the company of his wife who was also a committed Zionist, he spent six weeks promoting the cause in England.[78] Given the importance attached to Lowdermilk it was not surprising that showing him to be a Zionist dupe became an early objective of the CAA.

Spears in his writings never openly attacked Lowdermilk's work purely as part of the Zionist propaganda armoury, but he played down the potential usefulness of the Lowdermilk proposals and was of the opinion that even if his plan was workable 'it is obviously a long-term project', and as such was not an answer to the Jewish problem or a validation of the Zionist claim to Palestine.[79] However, Spears embodied the general anti-Zionist refusal to accept Lowdermilk's figures regarding Palestine's ability to support increased immigration, and this was coupled to a deep suspicion of his motives given that he had knowingly allowed himself to become a central plank of the Zionist propaganda platform.

In his private correspondence Spears set out the anti-Zionist view that Lowdermilk was a menace. He told Wing-Commander Skilbeck, the principal of the South-Eastern Agricultural College, who was a prospective anti-Lowdermilk pamphleteer for the committee, that it was necessary to set down a viable attack on Lowdermilk because the 'Zionists are sure to make play with [his] fairytales'.[80]

Similarly, a member of the public, the aptly named Donovan

Waters, who had written to Spears to take issue with an article he had written in the *Daily Mail*,[81] quoted Lowdermilk's view that Palestine could support a further one million Jewish and Arab farmers.[82] In response, Spears told Waters that in basing his support for Zionism on Lowdermilk's position he had been 'misled by Zionist propaganda', and he added that rather than Lowdermilk having credibility 'the figures you quote from Lowdermilk's book are pure flatcatching propaganda with no basis in reality'.[83]

As such Spears agreed with Newcombe, who wrote to him in November 1945 urging him to use the CAA to take up the challenge of Lowdermilk and stressing that 'Lowdermilk can be attacked.'[84] Spears had previously approached Sir John Hope-Simpson, in September 1945, with the plan of attacking Lowdermilk's 'extremely dishonest' book because the Zionists were 'making great play with [it]'.[85] Spears continued by asking if Hope-Simpson, a veteran anti-Zionist, felt 'inclined to counter-blast it', which, given his position as a leading land-settlement expert, Spears felt would lend 'considerable weight' to the attack.[86]

Hope-Simpson agreed with Spears on the need to counter Lowdermilk but refused to take on the task himself because of ill health. Perhaps in anticipation of Hope-Simpson's negative response, Spears had also approached Wing-Commander Skilbeck at the same time, telling him that 'I think it is important to get something out as it is really being taken for granted that Lowdermilk's effusion is a really constructive attempt to solve the Palestine problem and the case against it is going by default', and informing him that if he wrote the rebuttal the CAA would distribute it and attempt to get it published in a leading journal of opinion.[87]

Spears reported Skilbeck's agreement to take up the challenge at a meeting of the CAA in October 1945.[88] The importance that Spears attached to challenging Lowdermilk can be seen by his persistent pressure on Skilbeck to produce the anti-Lowdermilk work. Three days after the CAA meeting at which it was stated that Skilbeck had agreed to write against Lowdermilk, Spears wrote to him emphasising that 'the committee is very anxious to get something on Lowdermilk' and wondering 'have you been able to get around to this?' Again in early November Spears felt it necessary to write to Skilbeck: 'I am sorry to keep bothering you but I do think it is really important to have something to blast Lowdermilk.'[89]

But within three weeks of this appeal Spears had given up on

Skilbeck and had his secretary Miss Maurice write to him asking for the name of somebody else qualified to take on Lowdermilk for the committee.[90] Skilbeck suggested a Dr B.A. Keen of Rothasted research station.[91] However, Keen was also unable to take on the task and as the Anglo-American Committee hearings approached in January 1946, Spears, aware of the importance of a rebuttal of Lowdermilk, became increasingly anxious that he had not been able to find someone qualified to write it.

As such the CAA decided to reissue an anti-Lowdermilk pamphlet that had been written by Dr H.F. Khalidi, the former Mayor of Jerusalem and a leader of the Palestinian Arab Reform Party. Khalidi's pamphlet was 14 pages of detailed attack on Lowdermilk's claims as 'nothing more and nothing less than cheap journalistic Zionist propaganda for the abolishment of the White Paper policy and the opening of the gates of Palestine for mass immigration'.[92]

The CAA, in a preface to Khalidi's pamphlet, claimed that the author had proved that Lowdermilk's claims were 80 per cent Zionist propaganda, and Spears, in his statement of evidence submitted to the Anglo-American Committee, recommended that the committee look to Khalidi's work as an antidote to the Zionist propaganda of Lowdermilk.[93] However, Spears was not content with the Khalidi pamphlet as the only counter to such important Zionist claims and continued in his search for an English rebuttal of Lowdermilk.

Ultimately, Spears turned to Michael Ionides, who had been director of Development in Transjordan, 1937–39, and whose report on water resources in Transjordan had been published in 1939.[94] Spears made contact with Ionides after reading his letter on water resources in the Middle East in *The Times*, in April 1946.

It is hardly surprising that on reading Ionides' letter Spears felt he had found someone both willing and able to attack Lowdermilk. In his 1939 report, published for the government of Transjordan, Ionides had called for the Jordan waters to be used internally within the boundaries of Jordan, and dismissed any claims that water could be channelled into Palestine to allow more Jewish immigration. And it was on these grounds that his 1946 letter in *The Times* was also harsh on Lowdermilk, referring to his plan for Palestine as 'science prostituted to politics' and concluding with the view that 'it is vital that the public should not be betrayed into accepting false premises in one of the most crucial issues of our times'.[95]

Spears wrote to Ionides immediately informing him that he had been trying 'for some time past without success' to find someone to write a pamphlet on Dr Lowdermilk's book 'which badly needs answering', and asked him to take up the challenge.[96] Ionides accepted and agreed to combine a lecture he was giving to the Royal Central Asian Society (hereafter, RCAS), with a pamphlet for the CAA. This pamphlet concentrated on attacking Lowdermilk on political rather than on technical grounds because Ionides felt that this would be more effective in reducing the power of his claims before a general audience.[97]

In the final account a case could be made that the anti-Zionist concerns over the influence of Lowdermilk's argument on the Anglo-American Committee members were much overstated. Recommendation 8 of the Anglo-American report welcomed Lowdermilk's Jordan Valley Scheme, as part of general support in principle for all large infrastructural projects to improve the region, but it was a weak endorsement of his plan as a means of increased Jewish immigration.[98] Even Ionides, writing in the immediate aftermath of the publication of this report, was of the opinion that the committee in its recommendations had not been deceived by Lowdermilk's claims.[99]

Nevertheless, Spears' attempts to find a credible counter to Lowdermilk, which culminated in Ionides' pamphlet for the CAA, highlights both the importance of Lowdermilk in the battle over Palestine and the efforts of this group of Englishmen to counter him.

THE CAA AND THE ANGLO-AMERICAN COMMITTEE OF INQUIRY ON PALESTINE

The Anglo-American Committee of Inquiry on Palestine was formed by the governments of Britain and the United States in November 1945. Made up of six members from each country, the committee's terms of reference were to examine conditions in Palestine as they related to the issues of Jewish immigration and settlement and to examine the position of Europe's Jewish population that had survived the Holocaust.[100]

Viewed as the crucial forum for deciding the fate of Palestine in this era it was fêted as such by the various Zionist and anti-Zionist constituencies at its hearings which were held in several locations (most notably London, Washington and Jerusalem), from late 1945 until March 1946. The Arab Office gave evidence to the body in Jerusalem in March 1946 and the Jewish Fellowship and leading members of the CAA gave evidence in London before the committee in the last week of January of that year.

Of all the testimony given by English anti-Zionists at the London sessions, Thomas Reid MP was the only leading anti-Zionist who was not a member of the CAA to give evidence. Spears, Royden-Shaw and Storrs were all CAA members, and other members, such as Driver and the University of London Professor of Old Testament, the Revd Dr Alfred Guillaume, applied to give evidence but were refused (Driver because he applied too late to be heard and Guillaume because his evidence was not deemed necessary).[101] Nevertheless, Driver and Guillaume as well as Hope-Simpson and Newcombe made written submissions to the committee.

Thus the CAA played no small role in putting forward the Arab case before what was perceived to be the vital commission on the Palestine problem in the post-war era. Spears, whose own evidence before the committee was warmly welcomed by Foreign Secretary Ernest Bevin,[102] was behind this effort to organise the Gentile anti-Zionist case, for example urging J.C.S. Reid MP to give evidence before the inquiry because 'the Zionists will be rolling up' to present their case.[103]

Likewise, Spears also encouraged the Arab legations in London to present evidence before the committee, telling Colonel Sayid Shakir al-Wadi of the Iraqi legation that it would be 'a thousand pities' if the five Arab ministers in London did not make the most of the hearings to oppose publicly Zionist aspirations.[104]

Given this belief in the importance of the Anglo-American hearings as an opportunity for the anti-Zionists to present their opposition to Zionist goals it is hardly surprising that Spears and his committee were determined to set out their subsequent opposition to the Anglo-American Committee's report that was published on 30 April 1946. The anger at the report was primarily due to the committee's recommendation that 100,000 Jewish refugees from Europe be allowed into Palestine as an interim humanitarian measure.[105] The issue of 'the 100,000' will be studied in detail in chapter 8, but the actual process by which the CAA organised a response to the report will be presented here in order to highlight the fact that the CAA, under Spears' leadership, was a pro-active body involved in propaganda against Zionism during these years.

Immediately on the publication of the committee's findings Driver wrote to Spears insisting that the CAA take action to fight the report.[106] Spears responded by convening a special meeting of the CAA.[107] At this meeting various options for attacking the report were discussed, including the possibility of publishing a resolution in the press, sending a small delegation to the prime minister and lobbying in parliament. The importance that the CAA attached to fighting the report can be seen in the fact that 26 members (out of a total CAA membership of 40) attended this meeting, while the next highest attendance at a meeting during the committee's entire existence was 15, and the average attendance at meetings from the time of the group's first meeting in August 1945 until the end of 1946, excluding the meeting on the Anglo-American Committee report, was 12.[108]

It was decided that the committee's first effort should be to try to influence parliament, and that the submission of resolutions or statements to the press should be postponed until the committee could assess its success in lobbying against the report within the House.[109] However, even at this stage Spears and other members believed that the report had to be opposed publicly, if not officially, by the committee. On the same day as the CAA decided to work within parliament to oppose the report, Spears wrote to both the Earl of Cromer (who was a member of the CAA) and Lord Altrincham (who was not, but who was a confidant of Spears),[110] informing them of his view that 'I feel it urgently necessary that an influential protest on the recommendations of the Anglo-American committee ... should be sent to the press.'[111]

In correspondence with two anti-Zionist members of the public during this month, Spears encouraged both men to write to the press to set out their opposition to the Anglo-American recommendations.[112] Nor was Spears alone. Sir Ronald Storrs was of the opinion that 'I truly believe our letter will strengthen the hand of the government' in standing up to the report.[113] Thus a letter opposing the Anglo-American Committee's recommendation that Palestine be opened to 100,000 Jewish refugees signed by Spears, Storrs, Driver, Hope-Simpson, Sir Reginald Wingate and Sir Frederick Sykes was published in *The Times* on 23 May 1946.[114]

At a second meeting of the CAA held to deal with the report, it was agreed to attack it openly by way of an official resolution issued to the press.[115] A draft resolution (that had been prepared in advance by a sub-committee of Ionides and Kenneth Williams, the press officer)[116] was sent to all committee members, who in turn were asked to give their comments by 6 June, so that the final agreed draft of the resolution could be delivered to the press. As Spears wrote in a letter to all members, 'the time had come' publicly to take a stand against the report.[117]

The enthusiastic, detailed and varied responses by numerous committee members as to the best way for the CAA to set out its resolution against the report show just how seriously the membership of the CAA took its role in opposing Zionist aspirations.[118] And it was in the light of this co-operative effort by the committee that Spears was, rather contentedly, able to inform the five Arab ministers in London on 11 June, that 'a resolution unanimously passed by my committee ... issued by the press today'.[119]

THE CAA AND PARLIAMENT

For Spears, the presentation of the Arab point of view in parliament was one of the most important tasks of the CAA. As he stated in his inaugural address to the body, 'I felt myself that there was a great need for a body which would co-ordinate and act as a liaison with MPs.'[120] Spears and the Arab ministers in London envisaged using the CAA to promote the position of the Arab legations, and hence the Arab governments, within parliament. As Spears told Sir Harold MacMichael, a former high commissioner of Palestine, in a letter written the day after the Arab Club meeting that founded the CAA, 'it is purely pro-Arab in tendency and might play a useful part as providing a link in parliament and with the Arab missions in London'.[121]

Spears also hoped that the committee, although outside parliament, would liaise with the pro-Arab bodies within the House.[122] Foremost among these bodies was the MEPC, which Spears himself had founded and chaired until his electoral defeat in the 1945 election. After this, chairmanship of the body passed to Richard Stokes, the Labour MP for Ipswich. Stokes, who became a member of the CAA, was after the 1945 election generally acknowledged as the leading anti-Zionist parliamentarian or as the *Manchester Guardian* phrased it, 'one of the keenest advocates of the Arab cause in the House'.[123]

Likewise Spears looked to work beside the pro-Arab

Parliamentary Committee, headed by Earl Winterton, who like Stokes was a determined opponent of Zionism at Westminster. As was the case with the MEPC, this body had also been formed in the wake of the war to give voice to the back-bench support for pro-Arab and anti-Zionist aspirations, and as a counter to the Palestine Committee, which presented the viewpoint of parliamentarians who supported the Zionist position.[124]

As has been seen, Spears saw the advantage of a committee providing a link between those within parliament and those outside, free from the political confinements of a committee of MPs, but with the influence that closeness to parliament conferred. As such the CAA was a non-party body and attempted to attract MPs of all political persuasions, the only criteria being that they supported the Arab cause and would lend themselves to the anti-Zionist effort of the CAA within parliament. In a letter to the Colonial and Foreign Office and to Downing Street, announcing the existence of the CAA, Spears was keen to stress the non-partisan basis of the CAA and the fact that it would work to inform the House on the Arab cause.[125]

Nor was Spears alone in believing in the value of being outside the House but having intimate access to it (when possible Stokes arranged that meetings of the CAA were held in the long committee room in Westminster).[126] Driver saw the value of the committee in the same terms, telling the influential Arabist Sir Reginald Wingate that information disseminated to MPs by the CAA should be presented as the work of 'non-political academic experts'.[127]

The importance of parliament in the committee's plans to oppose Zionist aspirations (as well as providing proof that the CAA was primarily interested in the Palestine issue to the exclusion of other issues affecting the Arab world) can be seen in the fact that at its first meeting it was agreed that the CAA would not meet again until after the parliamentary recess unless the situation in Palestine was dangerous enough to warrant an early meeting.[128] This decision was made because MPs would be in their constituencies during the parliamentary break and therefore not available to attend the meetings of the CAA.[129]

Yet it should not be forgotten that the CAA was ultimately a body that existed outside parliament and that many of its most active members in the fight against Zionism were not parliamentarians but men like Storrs, Hope-Simpson, Ionides, Newcombe and Spears himself. Even when the committee reached its largest membership of 40, the number of MPs on the CAA was never more than 12.[130]

However, the House of Commons was central to the efforts of the committee and as such at its first meeting it was decided that Stokes or M. Philips Price and E.H. Keeling or Kenneth Pickthorn should sit on the executive of the CAA representing the Labour and Conservative parties respectively. More than this, it was hoped that by working together within the CAA, members from both parties would be able to unite inside parliament to fight Zionist aspirations.[131]

Spears always placed the 'education' of MPs as central to the committee's efforts.[132] He did so because he believed the average MP was totally ignorant on the issue of Palestine and as such was likely to support Zionism almost by default. It was this belief that motivated Spears to ask General Sir Robert Haining, who had been commanding officer of British forces in Palestine and Transjordan (1938–39) and vice-chairman of the Imperial General Staff, (1940–41), to write a pamphlet for his fledgling committee that could be circulated amongst MPs who needed to be 'educated on this important matter'.[133] Haining declined, as he declined to join the committee, because he was unwilling to take sides on the Palestine issue.[134]

But Spears had more luck with others whom he approached and who agreed to contribute to this effort to educate parliament by means of the CAA. The first pamphlet commissioned and distributed by the CAA was written by Captain Henry Longhurst, the former MP, and was entitled *The British, the Arabs and the Jews*. It was sent to MPs and other influential people in October 1945 and just how low an opinion Spears had of the majority of MPs can be seen in the fact that he described the pamphlet, in correspondence with Maude Royden-Shaw, as a 'very simple … told the children leaflet', with the aim of educating MPs 'whose ignorance on the subject of Palestine is abysmal'.[135]

Professor Driver shared this view, and prepared a fact sheet on Palestine to be distributed by the CAA to MPs, motivated no doubt by his belief that parliamentary 'ignorance is appalling'.[136] Storrs also had a low opinion of the country's legislators. He believed that parliament, and especially the governing Labour Party, was 'utterly ignorant on Palestine', and went so far as to decline an invitation from the anti-Zionist MP Thomas Reid to address a meeting of Labour back-bench MPs because he felt it was impossible to find what he called a 'stable audience'.[137]

This attitude was somewhat understandable. The post-war parliament was dominated by a Labour Party that had many new members, the majority of whom could claim neither experience nor the inclination to get involved with the Middle East. Indeed, the *Manchester Guardian* welcomed the efforts of parliamentarians interested in the Palestine issue to educate their contemporaries as part of the necessary 'process of education' that was essential if the House was to be competent in debating vital issues.[138]

One has only to look at Richard Crossman who became embroiled in the debate over Palestine after being appointed by Foreign Secretary Bevin to the Anglo-American Committee, but who admitted that before this appointment he had little knowledge of or interest in the Palestine issue, and if anything had been pro-Arab.[139] This in itself contradicts the general anti-Zionist claim of the time that Zionism was winning by default because MPs in their ignorance instinctively supported it.

However, the fact that Spears and his contemporaries on the CAA held such a contempt for the knowledge of MPs on Palestine, shaped the committee's efforts in the propaganda sphere. Deadlines for the completion and publication of pamphlets came to be perceived in terms of needs within parliament. Spears justified his constant pressure on Wing Commander Skilbeck to produce his promised rebuttal of Lowdermilk because it was necessary to 'have something to blast Lowdermilk by the time of the Palestine debate in the House' and because 'I would really like to send a short brief summary to a few members who may be taking part in the debate.'[140] Similarly, Spears urged both Driver and Royden-Shaw (who wrote a pamphlet opposing continued Jewish immigration into Palestine) to finish their contributions to the committee in terms of the need to circulate their work within parliament before debates on Palestine.[141]

The CAA's determined response to the Anglo-American Committee report centred its primary efforts and hopes in opposing the recommendations through prompt and united action in parliament. At the committee meeting of 9 May it was decided that Labour and Conservative members of the CAA would consult each other and Lord Altrincham in an effort to 'thrash out a common basis' against the report, while those parliamentary members of the committee should also 'approach their colleagues in the House with the view of securing support for their actions'.[142]

Spears attached so much importance to this aspect of the

committee's efforts to oppose the Anglo-American report that he wrote to Philips Price MP, prior to the next meeting, to tell him that 'members are particularly anxious to hear how you MPs have been getting on' within the House.[143] One week later Kenneth Pickthorn MP was writing to Spears to inform him that both he and Stokes had made contact with several Labour MPs to promote opposition to the Anglo-American recommendations, and that he and Stokes together with another Labour MP, Harry McGhee, had written a reply to a letter by Crossman in *The Times*, that stated their opposition to the report.[144] At the second committee meeting convened to deal with the report it was Victor Raikes, a Conservative MP, who briefed the CAA on the efforts of the members within the House.[145]

The committee not only attempted to influence parliamentarians on issues such as the Anglo-American report or by sending literature to MPs at key times of debates, but Spears also used the CAA as a source of information for MPs. In his inaugural address to the committee he stated that the CAA was available to MPs who needed material to ask parliamentary questions or who wished to increase their knowledge on the Palestine issue. This offer was taken up by several MPs within the committee and also outside. Even before the CAA's first meeting, J. Henderson Steward MP (who ultimately declined to join the CAA)[146] looked to Spears for information on the issue of Palestine.

Other MPs who did join the committee, such as Stokes and Pickthorn, also looked to Spears to supply material needed to present the Arab case in the House. Indeed, it should be noted that during these crucial years in the debate over Palestine, it was men such as Pickthorn and Stokes, so intimately connected with the CAA, who led the parliamentary opposition to Zionism.[147]

For example in September 1945 five Labour MPs circulated an anti-Zionist memorandum within parliament. Of those five members, Stokes, Philips Price and Ernest Thurtle were members of the CAA (Harry McGhee and Thomas Reid were not). While in October of the same year it was Stokes who organised the appearance of Abd al-Rahman Azzam Bey, secretary-general of the Arab League, to speak to interested Labour MPs on the Palestine problem.

Yet Spears was not content solely with providing information to MP's, regardless of their anti-Zionist credentials. Rather, from the time of the founding of the CAA he used the committee as a means of continuing his own presence within the House, approaching sympathetic MPs with lists of subjects relating to Palestine which he felt needed to be raised in the House.

Thus, for instance, in November 1946, Spears asked Pickthorn to raise the issue of how many Jews wanted to leave Palestine and return to Europe which, as shall be seen in chapter 5, was a central anti-Zionist argument against a Jewish state in these years. Stokes, meanwhile, not only agreed to ask several questions on Palestine for Spears, but on one occasion he asked Spears to draft the question himself, and Spears even provided Stokes with a reserve question, about 'fanatic nationalist education given in the Jewish schools in Palestine', in case the first question could not be raised.[148]

The CAA's patronage of anti-Zionist propaganda such as the Abcarius book and the commissioning of pamphlets by members such as Henry Longhurst, Driver and Royden-Shaw and its efforts to disparage the pro-Zionist claims of Lowdermilk, show that the CAA was a propaganda body for the Arab cause on the Palestine issue. So too does its deep involvement in presenting the Arab case before the Anglo-American Committee, and then after the report of that body had been published, working to oppose it both in parliament and through the media. Last, but by no means least, its active anti-Zionism can be seen in the efforts of committee members inside parliament, through lobbying of MPs and supplying them with materials to oppose Zionism.

The committee purposefully appealed to an elite body of opinion and it was hardly known outside that sector. However, this does not mean that the CAA, under Spears' leadership, was either irrelevant or insignificant. As Spears correctly stated in the June of 1946, in the wake of the public attack on the Anglo-American report, the committee was 'quite an influential body'.[149]

More than this, it was a body that better than any other of the time symbolised the active anti-Zionist effort of a group of influential Englishmen and women who had access to the heart of the corridors of power in London. In these terms the CAA was the inevitable response of anti-Zionists to a challenge set out by Storrs in 1937 that 'extreme and logical anti-Zionists' would 'command more respect' if they organised themselves into some constituted public body 'prepared to devote time, brains and cash' to the Arab cause in Palestine.[150]

NOTES

1. Sir Edward Spears, 'Syria is Angry', *Sunday Express*, 28 January 1945.
2. Spears, 'Reply to Dr Parkes', in *Palestine Controversy: A Symposium*, Introduction by H.N. Brailsford, Fabian Colonial Bureau (London: Fabian Publications and Victor Gollancz, 1945), pp. 18–25, p. 24.
3. Spears, 'Our Duty to the Arabs', *Sunday Express*, 27 May 1945.
4. Spears, 'British Policy in the Middle East', lecture to General Meeting of RIIA, 15 February 1945, 8/1093, pp.1–33, p. 2.
5. 'The Future of Syria: An Interview with Major-General Sir Edward Spears', *Sunday Express*, 24 December 1944.
6. Spears, 'The Middle East and our Policy There', lecture to the RCAS, 7 February 1945, reprinted in *Journal of the Royal Central Asian Society* (hereafter, *JRCAS*), XXXII: 2 (April 1945), pp. 156–65.
7. Spears, 'What the Arabs States Expect of France and Ourselves: Future of Palestine, Sovereignty of Syria and Lebanon', *Daily Telegraph*, 8 February 1945.
8. Evidence of Spears before the AACIP, London, 29 January 1946, pp. 29–53, p. 30, ACC 3121/C14/30/4, ABD.
9. Ibid., p. 50.
10. Spears, 'Crux of the Palestine Problem: Arab and Jewish Claims Irreconcilable – The Case for the White Paper Policy', *Daily Telegraph*, 8 October 1945.
11. Evidence of Spears before the AACIP, p. 30.
12. See Harold Beeley's argument, 'The Middle East in 1939 and 1944', lecture to the RCAS, 4 October 1944, repr. in *JRCAS*, XXXII: 1 (January 1945), pp. 7–23, p. 19 and the view of Lieutenant-General Sir John Glubb set out before the same body at its annual lecture in 1959, 'Britain and the Arabs', 10 June 1959, reprinted in *JRCAS*, XLVI: 3 (July 1959), pp. 232–41, p. 232. Finally see the views of highly regarded commentators, H.A.R. Gibb, 'Towards Arab Unity', *Foreign Affairs*, 24: 1 (October 1945), pp. 119–29, p. 125; H.S. Deighton, 'The Arab Middle East and the Modern World', *International Affairs*, XXII: 4 (October 1946), pp. 511–20 and Arnold Toynbee's 'Britain and the Arabs: The Need for a New Start', *International Affairs*, XL: 4 (October 1964), pp. 638–46, p. 638.
13. Spears interview, *al-Ahram*, n.d., December 1944, Box 7/2, SPSP.
14. Spears to A. Abrahams, 19 April 1945, Box 4/6, SPSP.
15. Beaumont to Spears, 7 February 1945, Box 6/3, SPSP.
16. *Jewish Chronicle*, 2 March 1945, p. 8.
17. *New Judea*, February–March 1945, p. 72.
18. See minutes of the Arab Club meeting, 8 August 1945, Box 6/2, SPSP.
19. Hope-Simpson to Spears, 12 September 1945, Box 6/4, SPSP.
20. See minutes of the Arab Club, 8 August 1945, Box 6/2, SPSP.
21. Spears to Brigadier I. Clayton, 3 August 1945, Box 5/3, SPSP.
22. Beaumont to Spears, 15 August 1945, Box 6/3, SPSP; Longhurst to Spears, 21 May 1946, Box 6/4, SPSP.
23. Spears to Lady Drower, 26 June 1946, Box 6/3, SPSP.
24. Spears to Lord Altrincham, 16 August 1945, Box 6/3, SPSP.
25. George Kirk, *The Middle East in the War, 1939–1946*, Survey of International Affairs, (London: Oxford University Press, under the auspices of the RIIA, 1950), p. 344.
26. Storrs, *Orientations* (London: Nicolson & Watson, 1937, 3rd. edn), p. 422.
27. Antonius, *The Arab Awakening: The Story of the Arab National Movement* (London: Hamish Hamilton, 1938), p. 386. Antonius's work was heralded in Gentile anti-Zionist quarters precisely because it was seen as a response to Zionist propaganda. H.A.R. Gibb in a review of the book welcomed it as a much needed antidote to Zionist propaganda, 'The Case for the Arabs', *Spectator*, 25 November, 1938, p. 912. Indeed Spears considered writing the foreword to a new edition of Antonius's book republished by Hamish Hamilton in 1946, Box 9/1, SPSP. Also see Spears' recommendation to the Anglo-American Committee that its members should read Antonius's work as it was 'the best study of the Arab case that I know', evidence of Spears before the AACIP, p. 30. While Frances Newton called it a 'truly magnificent contribution to the Arab cause', *Fifty Years in Palestine*, p. 187.

28. Minutes of the Arab Club meeting, 8 August 1945, Box 6/2, SPSP.
29. Spears to Jeffreys, 29 August 1945, Box 6/4, SPSP.
30. Cornwallis to Spears, 16 August 1945, Box 6/3, SPSP.
31. Loftus to Spears, 20 September 1946, Box 11/1, SPSP.
32. Loftus to Spears, 13 August 1945, Box 6/4, SPSP.
33. Spears to Marjorie Hall, 24 March 1946, Box 4/6, SPSP.
34. See minutes of the CAA meeting, 22 August 1945, Box 6/2, SPSP.
35. Spears to Hope-Simpson, 30 August 1945, Box 6/4, SPSP.
36. See minutes of the CAA meeting, 22 August 1945, Box 6/2, SPSP and Storrs to Spears, 9 September 1945, Box 7/2, SPSP.
37. See minutes of the CAA meeting, 18 July 1946, Box 6/2, SPSP.
38. 'Memorandum on the Formation of the Anglo-Arab Society', July 1946, Box 6/2, SPSP.
39. Ibid. For the full correspondence pertaining to the setting up and running of the Anglo-Arab Association see files 1–4, Box 11, SPSP.
40. Spears to McGarvie, 27 May 1946; McGarvie to Spears, 29 May 1946, Box 4/6, SPSP.
41. 'The Anglo-Arab Association', *Great Britain and the East*, LXIII: 1769 (February 1947), pp. 51–2.
42. Baillie to Nancy Maurice, 26 November 1946, Box 11/2, SPSP; Baillie to editor of the *Daily Telegraph*, 2 January 1947, Box 11/2, SPSP.
43. See, for example, 'Anglo-Arab Relations', *Wiener Library Bulletin*, 1: 6 (September 1947), p. 3 and 'Anglo-Arab Association', *Jewish Chronicle*, 25 October 1946, p. 18.
44. Spears to Abd al-Rahman Azzam Bey, 25 October 1945, Box 6/3, SPSP. On this issue also see Spears to P.A. Wilson of the MESC, 24 October 1945, Box 7/2, SPSP.
45. Tannous to Spears, 20 February 1946, Box 15/5, SPSP.
46. Messrs Luzac to Spears, 10 July 1946, Box 15/5, SPSP; Spears to Walter Hutchinson, 15 and 19 July 1946, Box 15/5, SPSP.
47. M.F. Abcarius, *Palestine: Through the Fog of Propaganda* (London: Hutchinson, 1946). On Abcarius's book as an obvious example of Arab propaganda, see Paul Hanna's review in the *Middle East Journal*, 2: 1 (January 1948), p. 97.
48. Hope-Simpson to Spears, 24 September 1945, Box 6/4, SPSP.
49. See minutes of the CAA meetings, 30 May 1946 and 18 July 1946, Box 6/2, SPSP.
50. Articles written by Williams in the *Fortnightly* on the subject of the Middle East during this time include 'France and the Levant', CLVIII (July 1945), pp. 9–13; 'Persia, the Middle East and Russia', CLIX (February 1946), pp. 89–94; 'The Arab League', CLXIV (November 1948), pp. 302–6. Articles written by him in *Great Britain and the East* include 'We Cannot Neglect the Middle East', LXI: 1743 (January 1945), pp. 39–40; 'Are the British and Arabs in Step?', LXI: 1744 (February 1945), pp. 35–7; 'Light Needed on the Levant', LXI: 1745 (March 1945), pp. 41–2; 'Deserts That Are at Peace', LXI: 1746 (April 1945), pp. 38–40; 'Best Britons Wanted for the Arab World', LXI: 1748 (June 1945), pp. 41–2.
51. Sir William Dickson, president of the Society, awarded Barbour with the prestigious honour after he had given a speech, 'England and the Arabs', 15 December 1964, repr. in the *JRCAS*, LII: 2 (April 1965), pp. 102–15, p. 115.
52. Even after his retirement from the BBC Barbour remained very active. For example, between 5 March 1962 and 23 March 1966 he gave 16 talks on the BBC Arabic service, on issues relating to the Middle East, Box 2/3 BARB.
53. See Barbour, 'News Talk', BBC Home Service, 30 March 1946, Palestine Misc. Correspondence A–Z, 1939–48, BBCWAR.
54. Barbour to Spears, 18 August 1945, Box 6/3, SPSP.
55. Barbour, 'Memorandum on Palestine', 3 June 1948, Palestine Misc. Correspondence A–Z, 1939–48, BBCWAR.
56. Barbour speaking during the discussion after the lecture by Edward Atiyah, 'British Public Opinion and the Arab', Middle East Discussion Group, RIIA, 1 June 1945, 8/1176, pp. 12, 13.
57. Barbour to Spears, 26 February 1947, Box 4/6, SPSP; Barbour to Maurice, 20 September 1948, Box 6/3, SPSP.
58. MS Diary of Storrs, 17 April 1946, Box 6/7; 20 September 1945, Box 6/6, STOP; Storrs to Spears, 12 April 1946, Box 5/3, SPSP.

59. MS Diary of Storrs, 10 September 1948, Box 6/8, SPSP. This letter attacked Greenberg for his support for the Irgun, which Storrs believed his earlier letter seemed to imply. See Storrs' letter, *The Times*, 10 September 1948.
60. MS Diary of Storrs, 3 March 1944, Box 6/5; 5 June 1945, Box 6/6, STOP.
61. MS Diary of Storrs, 9 January 1946, Box 6/7, STOP. The Reid lecture at the RCAS was entitled 'Should a Jewish State be Established in Palestine?', 9 January 1946, repr. *JRCAS*, XXXIII: 2 (April 1946), pp. 161–77. It is interesting that Reid justified his opposition to Zionism at the beginning of this lecture on the ground that it was the duty of him and men like him who had access to influence and opinion to set out the Arab case (p. 173).
62. Maugham, *Approach to Palestine* (London: Falcon Press, 1947), p. 61.
63. Hope-Simpson, 'The Palestine Statement', *Fortnightly*, CLIX (January 1946), pp. 21–7.
64. Hope-Simpson, 'The Palestine Mandate', *Fortnightly*, CLVI (December 1944), pp. 341–9.
65. Hope-Simpson to Spears, 21 November 1945, Box 6/4, SPSP.
66. Hope-Simpson to Spears, 29 November 1945, Box 6/4, SPSP.
67. Lowdermilk, 'The Eleventh Commandment', Jerusalem, 1939, cited in *Zionist Review*, 5 May 1944, p. 3.
68. For examples of very positive reviews of Lowdermilk's book in highly regarded journals on both sides of the Atlantic, see Henry S. Gehman's review in the *Moslem World*, XXXV: 3 (July 1945), pp. 254–5; JFR, *International Affairs*, XXI: 2 (April 1945), p. 287 and Shlomo Bardin in *Jewish Social Studies*, VII: 2 (April 1945), pp. 174–6.
69. This was a pro-Zionist international Jewish organisation. It had been founded in 1936 in Geneva to replace the Comité des Délégations Juives, and its constituent members were primarily the governing federations of Jewish communities. It was presided over by the leading American Zionist Rabbi Stephen Wise until his death in 1949, when Nahum Goldmann succeeded him.
70. See 'Dr Lowdermilk's Jordan Valley Project', *Zionist Review*, 4 May 1944, p. 3; Ephraim Broidó, *New Judea*, May 1944, p. 128. The Lowdermilk argument was also introduced into Zionist publicity pamphlets. See *Keep Faith with the Martyrs of Israel* (London: ZF, 1945). See also Robert Nathan's *Palestine: Problem and Promise* (New York: American Council on Public Affairs, under the auspices of the American Palestine Institution, 1946).
71. See advertisements in *Zionist Review*, 29 December 1944, p. 10.
72. *Arab News Bulletin*, supplement to 43 (8 August 1947), p. 2. See also Nevill Barbour's attitude to Lowdermilk in *Nisi Dominus: A Survey of Palestine* (London: Harrap, 1946), p. 227 and Frances Newton's view in *Fifty Years in Palestine*, p. 270.
73. Kirk, *The Middle East in the War, 1939–1946*, Survey of International Affairs (London: Oxford University Press, under the auspices of the RIIA, 1950), p. 330.
74. Driver to Spears, n.d., Box 6/4, SPSP and 'A Plan for Palestine', *Spectator*, 19 October 1945, pp. 353–4. In this article Driver claimed that the tendency of Jewish scholars like Dr Salo Baron to inflate the numbers of Jews in Palestine, particularly in Jerusalem, was 'hardly credible'. Salo Baron, of Columbia University, was the author of the monumental 18-volume work *A Social and Religious History of the Jews* (New York: Columbia University Press, 2nd edn, 1952). He was also a founder of the journal *Jewish Social Studies* and is generally considered to be one of the leading scholars of Jewish history this century.
75. Newcombe to Spears, 9 July 1948, Box 7/1, SPSP.
76. Victor Gollancz, *Nowhere to Lay Their Heads: The Jewish Tragedy in Europe and its Solution* (London: Victor Gollancz, 1945), p. 21.
77. Sir John E. Russell, 'Land of Promise', *Zionist Review*, 8 September 1944, p. 3
78. For coverage of the Lowdermilk tour of England see reports in the *Palestine Information Bulletin*, 97 (10 March 1948), p. 4; 98 (17 March 1948), p. 3 and the *Zionist Review*, 19 March 1948, p. 11. Lowdermilk became special adviser to the Israeli government on soil erosion, 1951–52 and Professor of Soil Conservation at the Haifa Technion, 1954–57.
79. Spears, 'Reply to Dr Parkes', p. 24.
80. Spears to Skilbeck, 2 November 1945, Box 7/2, SPSP.

81. Spears, 'Palestine: Is there a Way out of the Morass?', *Daily Mail*, 23 March 1947.
82. Waters to Spears, 24 January 1947, Box 4/6, SPSP.
83. Spears to Waters, 31 March 1947, Box 4/6, SPSP.
84. Newcombe to Spears, 28 November 1945, Box 5/3, SPSP.
85. Spears to Hope-Simpson, 12 September 1945, Box 6/4, SPSP.
86. Ibid.
87. Spears to Skilbeck, 11 September 1945, Box 7/2, SPSP.
88. See minutes of the CAA meeting, 10 October 1945, Box 6/2, SPSP.
89. Spears to Skilbeck, 13 October 1945; Spears to Skilbeck, 2 November 1945, Box 7/2, SPSP.
90. Maurice to Skilbeck, 19 November 1945, Box 7/2, SPSP.
91. Keen was known to Spears from his time in the Levant as the author of a report on the agricultural development of the region for the Middle East Supply Centre in 1944. See Keen's *Agricultural Development of the Middle East* (Beirut: MESC, 1944), Box 6/1, SPSP.
92. H.F. Khalidi, *Reply to Dr Lowdermilk* (Jerusalem: 1945). Khalidi had also been a member of the Arab Higher Executive.
93. Spears, 'Suggestions for evidence to the Anglo-American Committee [AACIP]', Box 4/3, SPSP.
94. See M.G. Ionides and G.S. Blake, *The Water Resources of Transjordan and their Development*, published for the government of Transjordan by Crown Agents for the Colonies, 1939. For an assessment of both Ionides' and Lowdermilk's arguments see Aaron T. Wolf, *Hydropolitics Along the Jordan River: Scarce Water and its Impact on the Arab–Israeli Conflict* (Tokyo, New York, Paris: UN University Press, 1995), pp. 38–41. Also see Sara Reguer's 'Controversial Waters: Exploitation of the Jordan River, 1950–1980', *Middle Eastern Studies*, 29: 1 (January 1993), pp. 53–90.
95. Ionides, *The Times*, 1 April 1946.
96. Spears to Ionides, 3 April 1946, Box 6/4, SPSP.
97. Ionides to Spears, 6 April 1946; 2 May 1946 and 7 May 1946, Box 6/4, SPSP. The lecture at the RCAS that was turned into a CAA pamphlet was entitled 'Water Development in Palestine and Transjordan', 1 May 1946, repr. in *JRCAS*, XXXIII: 3 (July 1946).
98. See Cmd. 6808, *The Report of the Anglo-American Committee of Inquiry*, 30 April 1946.
99. 'Irrigation in Palestine: A Key to Economic Absorptive Capacity', *World Today*, III: 2 (April 1947), pp. 188–98. Even more than a decade later, in a book on the Arab world published in 1960, Ionides was still attacking Lowdermilk's work as a 'central strand of Zionist propaganda', Ionides, *Divide and Lose: The Arab Revolt of 1955–1958* (London: Geoffrey Bles, 1960), p. 83.
100. There are two main academic studies on the AACIP. Amikam Nachmani's *Great Power Discord in Palestine: The Anglo-American Committee of Inquiry into the Problems of European Jewry and Palestine, 1945–1946* (London: Frank Cass, 1986) and Alan H. Podet's *The Success and Failure of the Anglo-American Committee of Inquiry, 1945–46: The Last Chance in Palestine* (Lewiston and Queenston: Edwin Mellon Press, 1986). Also see the collection of documents edited by Michael J. Cohen, *The Rise of Israel. Vol. 35, The Anglo-American Committee on Palestine, 1945–1946* (New York, London: Garland, 1987) and his article on the committee as a symbol of the growing power of the United States in the Middle East, 'The Genesis of the Anglo-American Committee on Palestine, November 1945: A Case Study on the Assertion of American Hegemony', *Historical Journal*, 22: 1 (January 1979), pp. 186–207.
101. Spears to Driver, 1 February 1946, Box 4/6, SPSP; Spears to Guillaume, 3 February 1946, Box 6/4, SPSP.
102. See Joseph Heller, 'The Anglo-American Committee of Inquiry on Palestine (1945–1946): The Zionist Reaction Reconsidered', in Jehuda Reinharz and Anita Shapira (eds), *Essential Papers on Zionism* (New York: New York University Press, 1996), pp. 689–723, p. 696.
103. Spears to J.C.S. Reid, 21 January 1946, Box 5/3, SPSP.
104. Spears to Sayid Shakir al-Wadi, 14 January 1946, Box 4/3, SPSP. On 1 February 1946, a high-ranking Arab delegation did appear before the committee. Members of this delegation included Prince Faisal Ibn Abdul Aziz of Saudi Arabia, Farris Bey al-

The Committee for Arab Affairs and the Arab Cause 53

  Khoury, president of the Syrian Chamber of Deputies, and Hamid Bey Frangieyeh, the Lebanese Foreign Minister. For the Arab League's responses to the AACIP, see PRO/FO 371/2529.
105. Anglo-American Report, recommendation 2.
106. Driver to Spears, 3 May 1946, Box 4/6, SPSP.
107. The CAA meeting held on 9 May 1946 was called solely 'To Consider Action on the Report of the Anglo American Committee', see minutes of the CAA meeting, 9 May 1946, Box 6/2, SPSP.
108. For attendance figures and names of those who attended CAA meetings see minutes of those meetings, Box 6/2, SPSP.
109. See agenda and minutes of the CAA meeting, 9 May 1946, Box 6/2, SPSP.
110. Altrincham, formerly Sir Edward Grigg, was appointed Minister Resident in the Middle East in 1944. Because of his official position he was unable to join the CAA but was a staunch supporter of the group and acted as an adviser to Spears. For example, he attended the CAA's emergency meeting of 9 May 1946 held to discuss the committee's response to the Anglo-American report. See minutes of CAA meeting, 9 May 1946, Box 6/2, SPSP.
111. Spears to Earl of Cromer, 9 May 1946, Box 6/3, SPSP; Spears to Lord Altrincham, 9 May 1946, Box 6/3, SPSP.
112. Spears to F.S. Cragg, 16 May 1946, Box 6/3, SPSP; Spears to P. McGarvie, 29 May 1946, Box 4/6, SPSP.
113. MS Diary of Storrs, 10 May 1946, Box 6/7, STOP.
114. *The Times*, 23 May 1946.
115. See minutes of the CAA meeting, 30 May 1946, Box 6/2, SPSP.
116. Ionides to Spears, 15 May 1946, Box 6/4, SPSP.
117. Spears' letter to all members of the CAA, 30 May 1946, Box 6/2, SPSP.
118. For the diverse suggestions by committee members as to how the resolution on the Anglo-American report should be presented see Box 6/2, SPSP.
119. See Spears to Amr Pasha, the Egyptian Ambassador, 11 June 1946, Box 5/2, SPSP. Spears also sent a copy of the CAA resolution to the Foreign Secretary. See Spears to Bevin, 11 June 1946, PRO/FO 371/52529. For a copy of the resolution see Box 5/2, SPSP and for a discussion of the contents of this resolution see chapter 8.
120. Spears' inaugural address to the CAA, 22 August 1945, Box 6/2, SPSP.
121. Spears to MacMichael, 10 August 1945, Box 7/1, SPSP.
122. Spears to Haining, 13 September 1945, Box 6/4, SPSP.
123. *Manchester Guardian*, 18 October 1945. The *Zionist Review* kept track of Stokes' parliamentary anti-Zionist efforts throughout these years with articles such as 'Mr Stokes on the Warpath', 25 October 1946, p. 6. Indeed, in July 1948, the same paper interviewed this erstwhile opponent of Zionism in an effort to understand his devoted opposition to the Zionist cause, 'Facts Work Miracles', *Zionist Review*, 16 July 1948, p. 4.
124. See report in the *Glasgow Herald*, 17 October 1945 on the various bodies involved in the Palestine debate within parliament.
125. Spears to CO, FO and the Prime Minister's Office, 23 August 1945, Box 6/2, SPSP.
126. MS Diary of Storrs, 9 May 1946, Box 6/7, STOP.
127. Driver to Wingate, 26 October 1945, Box 5/3, SPSP.
128. See minutes of the CAA meeting, 22 August 1945, Box 6/2, SPSP.
129. Spears' inaugural address to the CAA, 22 August 1945, Box 6/2, SPSP.
130. At its peak the 12 parliamentary members of the CAA were Commander Peter Agnew, E.H. Keeling, Sir Peter MacDonald, Major Duncan McCallum, Kenneth Pickthorn, M. Philips Price, Captain Victor Raikes, J.C.S. Reid, Professor Savory, R.R. Stokes, Ernest Thurtle, R.M. Turton, Box 6/3, SPSP.
131. See minutes of the CAA meeting, 22 August 1945, Box 6/2, SPSP.
132. Spears to Hall, 24 March 1946, Box 4/6, SPSP.
133. Spears to Haining, 13 September 1945, Box 6/4, SPSP.
134. Haining to Spears, 20 September 1945, Box 6/4, SPSP.
135. Spears to Royden-Shaw, 8 October 1945, Box 7/2, SPSP.
136. Driver to Spears, 30 October 1945, Box 4/6, SPSP.
137. MS Diary of Storrs, 9 January 1946, Box 6/7, STOP.

138. *Manchester Guardian*, 18 October 1945.
139. Crossman, *Palestine Mission: A Personal Record* (London: Hamish Hamilton, 1947), pp. 12–16.
140. Spears to Skilbeck, 2 November 1945, Box 7/2, SPSP.
141. Spears to Driver, 2 November 1945, Box 4/6, SPSP; Spears to Royden-Shaw, 2 October 1945 and 7 November 1945, Box 7/2, SPSP.
142. See minutes of the CAA meeting, 9 May 1946, Box 6/2, SPSP.
143. Spears to Philips Price, 23 May 1946, Box 7/1, SPSP.
144. Pickthorn to Spears, 29 May 1946, Box 7/1, SPSP.
145. See minutes of the CAA meeting, 30 May 1946, Box 6/2, SPSP. Indeed, it was common for MPs to brief the CAA on parliament's position regarding Palestine. See, for example, the report of Philips Price's briefing of the CAA in minutes of the CAA meeting, 18 July 1946, Box 6/2, SPSP.
146. Henderson Steward to Spears, 15 August 1945, Box 6/4, SPSP.
147. For a copy of this 'Palestine Memorandum', see MSS Brit Emp.s. Box 176/3, Palestine Memoranda III, 1945, FCBA.
148. Spears to Pickthorn, 5 November 1946, Box 7/1, SPSP; Spears to Pickthorn, 29 July 1946, Box 7/1, SPSP; Spears to Stokes, 26 June 1946; Stokes to Spears, 2 July 1946; Spears to Stokes, 3 July 1946; Maurice to Stokes, 7 November 1946. All Box 7/2, SPSP. Spears also got sympathetic MPs outside the CAA to ask questions on his behalf. See Spears to Viscount Hinchinbrooke, 9 May 1946, Box 6/4, SPSP; Spears to Major-General Sir George Jeffreys, 15 May 1947, Box 4/6, SPSP.
149. Spears to Lady Drower, 25 June 1946, Box 6/3, SPSP.
150. Storrs, *The Memoirs of Sir Ronald Storrs* (New York: Arno Press, 1972, first published as *Orientations*, London, 1937), p. 402.

3 Zionist Responses to the English Anti-Zionist Constituency

In the post-war era, Zionist commentators in Britain were in no doubt that there existed an able group of men and women, holding a position of respect within their chosen field, who shared with Arab anti-Zionists an unflinching opposition to political Zionism and the creation of a Jewish state in Palestine. As dedicated Gentile Zionist publicist Mrs Edgar Dugdale, a niece of Lord Balfour and a confidante of Zionist leader Chaim Weizmann, stated in her weekly column in the *Zionist Review*, just two months after the Committee for Arab Affairs had been founded: 'the Arabs do not lack British sympathisers who speak with first-hand knowledge of their point of view'.[1]

The fact that the great majority of anti-Zionists challenged by Zionist publicists were to become members of the CAA underlines just how central this body, under Spears' leadership, was to the anti-Zionist effort in London. There were of course exceptions: the writer Freya Stark, whose 1943–44 North American lecture tour for the Ministry of Information was, as noted in the first chapter, condemned in Zionist circles as nothing but government-sponsored anti-Zionist propaganda; while Thomas Reid MP and Dr Cyril Garbett, Archbishop of York, were two other high-profile individuals who came under attack for their anti-Zionism but who remained outside the committee in these years. Of these, Reid refused to join the CAA only because he had 'not a loose moment even on Sunday',[2] and he worked closely with the CAA from the outside, attending meetings dealing with important issues such as the Anglo-American report.

But these individuals aside it was Sir Edward Spears, Dr Maude Royden-Shaw, Professor G.R. Driver, Nevill Barbour, Kenneth

Williams, Sir John Hope-Simpson, Richard Rapier Stokes MP, the Revd Dr Alfred Guillaume and Colonel Stewart Newcombe, all members of the CAA, who more than any others came under constant criticism for their public opposition to Zionism.

In January 1945 an editorial in the *Zionist Review* took issue with what it felt to be a widely held but false view (on this occasion expressed by George Orwell in the course of a review of Lowdermilk's *Palestine: Land of Promise*), that the Arab cause had no defenders of stature in England, by pointing to the efforts of 'those benighted gentlemen Storrs and [Hope-] Simpson'.[3] In doing so this paper was but reiterating the view of *New Judea*, which the previous August had argued in a similar editorial that the efforts of Hope-Simpson and Storrs proved that high-profile Englishmen did indeed work against Zionism.[4]

Zionist antipathy towards Hope-Simpson is not surprising considering the fact that he had for many years argued against Zionist aspirations in terms of two issues, land settlement and Jewish immigration into Palestine, that went right to the heart of the debate over the country's future. Without fail, Zionist attacks on Hope-Simpson began with the statement that the conclusions of his 1930 report on the future possibilities for land settlement and absorption of Jews into Palestine had been shown to be wrong in the proceeding years.[5]

This report, which was submitted to the Palestine administration in August 1930 and published in October of that year along with the Passfield White Paper on Palestine (which based many of its findings on Hope-Simpson's report), examined the issues of land settlement and agricultural development in Palestine in the context of the possibility of the land providing more opportunity for increased Jewish immigration.

The report was very negative on the effects of the Zionist endeavour on the Arabs of Palestine. It argued against the Zionist purchase of Arab land and called for a continuation of the traditional system of land tenure, rather than new methods introduced by the Zionists. The report was even more pessimistic regarding the future industrial development potential of the country. It concluded that there was not enough land in Palestine to maintain the existing Arab rural population at a decent standard of living and that the Arabs did not benefit from the increased development of the land by Zionists.

Not surprisingly this report, which opposed increased Jewish immigration, land settlement or development, became a staple in the anti-Zionist argument against the expansion of the Yishuv. But for Zionists it only went to prove the fallibility of those who opposed Zionism. In articles under headings such as 'They Were Wrong', Zionist publicists attempted to discredit all Gentile naysayers of Zionism by reminding readers that Hope-Simpson had been totally mistaken in 1930 and, because of this, his views on Palestine, and the views of those who shared his attitude, should be dismissed.[6] In the words of a *Zionist Review* editorial: 'Sir John Hope-Simpson has made it his business to oppose Jewish aspirations in Eretz Israel', and in doing so he was repeating nothing but the 'well-known distortions of anti-Zionist spokesmen'.[7] Likewise *New Judea* dismissed his article on Palestine in the *Fortnightly* of December 1944,[8] as valid only as an example of how a devoted opponent of political Zionism resorted to false arguments in an effort to hurt Zionist aspirations.[9]

There is little doubt that Hope-Simpson was a dedicated anti-Zionist and as such the objectiveness of his 1930 report must be questioned. Yet so widespread was this Zionist tactic that Sir Ronald Storrs took exception to and condemned the Zionist tendency to dismiss Hope-Simpson on the grounds that many of the claims of his 1930 report had been subsequently disproved.[10] However, this dismissal of Gentile anti-Zionist arguments by highlighting the divisiveness inherent in their claims was not confined to Hope-Simpson.

Nevill Barbour set out his anti-Zionist credentials in the years before the formation of the CAA. His 1936 pamphlet, *A Plan for Lasting Peace in Palestine*,[11] which was republished by the PIC in London, was warmly received by members of the Arab elite such as Jamal Husseini (who in the post-war years would lead the fight against Zionism) as an attempt at putting the Arab case before the English public.[12] Nor was it Arab leaders alone who welcomed Barbour's effort to present the Arab position in London. H.V. Hodson, editor of the journal the *Round Table*, wrote to Barbour after reading his pamphlet and asked him to contribute an article on Palestine to that journal because 'too little attention has been paid to the realities of sentiment, prestige and pride in the Arab outlook'.[13]

With the publication of the 1939 memorandum *Zionism, Palestine and the Jewish Problem* which called for a settlement of the Jewish problem outside Palestine,[14] it became the accepted view within the

Zionist community that Barbour was an anti-Zionist propagandist. For example, an article in the Jewish journal, the *Sentinel*, listed Nevill Barbour, in the company of leading pre-war anti-Zionists such as Frances Newton and Ernest Bennett of the PIC, among the main culprits responsible for defending, before the British public, the violence and 'bloody campaign' of the Arab revolt in Palestine in the years 1936–39.[15]

In the post-war world this view of Barbour as a leading apologist and propagandist for the Arab cause continued to grow. His book *Nisi Dominus*, published in 1946, though welcomed in Arab propaganda circles as the 'most penetrating study of the whole Palestine controversy',[16] was dismissed in the Jewish world. *New Judea* reviewed it together with Abcarius's *Palestine: Through the Fog of Propaganda* (which Barbour's CAA chairman Spears had been responsible for having published) under the heading 'Anti-Zionist Propaganda'.[17] While Aubrey (Abba) Eban, reviewing it in the *Zionist Review*, was contemptuous in his view that 'the literary world is graced with a book any man of conscience can feel deeply proud not to have written'.[18] Thus despite Barbour's attempts to conceal his membership of the CAA, for Zionists he was not a credible opponent. The *Jewish Chronicle* summed up this attitude when in 1946 it called him an 'uncompromising anti-Zionist' who precisely because of this 'need not be taken ... quite as seriously as he seems to take himself'.[19]

Both before and after the founding of the CAA Dr Maude Royden-Shaw was presented by the Zionist movement as an extreme Gentile anti-Zionist.[20] The *Zionist Review*, in response to an anti-Zionist article she wrote in the *Newsletter*,[21] stated that this Christian missionary 'did not disguise her animosity to Zionism'.[22] This paper continued to attack her for lending her reputation as a 'prominent figure in the Christian world and ... a distinguished Englishwoman' to Arab extremists.[23]

The *Jewish Chronicle* also joined this chorus of disapproval of Royden-Shaw's obvious anti-Zionism. After the paper had commented on two letters by Royden-Shaw on Palestine in the *Manchester Guardian* in January 1944, the editor, Ivan Greenberg, received much private correspondence from leading Zionists that stressed the view that Royden-Shaw lacked credibility in her fight against Zionism. Veteran publicist Samuel Landman congratulated the paper for its success in subjecting 'her credibility to ridicule'.[24] While Moshe Rosette (who as a member of the Jewish Agency information office in London, was directly involved in the propaganda battle over Palestine), in a letter later in the same month commended the leaderette on Royden-Shaw for showing her in her true light as an 'incorrigible' anti-Zionist.[25]

After the war's end the paper continued to undermine the validity of Royden-Shaw's position. In an editorial in October 1945 Royden-Shaw was referred to simply as the 'blindly fanatical pro-Arab and Zionist hater … who seems to have appointed herself advocatus diaboli against Zionism and to be carrying on her self-assured function with a zeal and persistency worthy of a better cause'.[26] Other CAA members such as Captain Henry Longhurst and G.R. Driver, both of whom, like Royden-Shaw, produced pamphlets for the CAA, and both of whom were public in their opposition to Zionist aspirations, were also dismissed by the Zionists. In late 1944 Longhurst, in an article in the *Observer*, had reported on a recent tour he had made of the Middle East, and praised Arab efforts in the region, while ignoring the endeavours and achievements of the Jewish National Home. This was held up as an example of the bias of certain public figures in the debate over Palestine.[27]

The attack by Hamabit (pseud.) on a letter by Driver in *The Times* (a letter that the *Jewish Chronicle* called a classic example of the 'White Arab' mentality)[28] clearly disparaged the professor's claims on the grounds of extremism and bias with the following words:

> Within a few short paragraphs he ingeniously disposed of the oracles of the Jewish God, of Jewish history and of the Jewish people itself. With more cynicism than professional accuracy, and more malice than fact he denied the Jews any right to Palestine.[29]

Thus the Zionist attitude to Gentile anti-Zionists was a contradictory mixture of anger – because of their virulent opposition to Jewish aspirations; fear – because of the reputations of those leading anti-Zionists; and dismissal – because of a belief that the extreme nature of their anti-Zionism reduced their credibility and thus their harm. This is illustrated by another correspondence between Moshe Rosette and Ivan Greenberg. In discussing the anti-Zionist editorial policy of the provincial paper the *Eastern Daily Press*, Rosette distinguished between the danger of the commentator J. Hampden Jackson whose 'subtle twists' in writing against Zionism 'give the impression he is favourably disposed' to a Jewish state and the syndicated articles by future CAA member Kenneth Williams, published in the same paper, that were less damaging to Zionism because 'his views are well known'.[30]

The issue of credibility in defining the Zionist attitude to the Gentile anti-Zionists can be seen most clearly in regard to Sir Edward Spears and Sir Ronald Storrs, two figures central to both the CAA and the Zionist belief that the Arab cause did have a vocal and highly placed body of support in England.

SIR EDWARD SPEARS AND ZION

The Jewish world paid close attention to the position of Sir Edward Spears on the Palestine issue. The daily press surveys of the Jewish Agency information office (London), the reports of the Palcor News Agency and the bulletins of the Jewish Telegraphic Agency all reported on Spears' various public pronouncements on Palestine.

The *Jewish Chronicle* also presented Spears as the defining personality in the anti-Zionist camp. From the time of his return to England in December 1944 from his post as minister plenipotentiary in the Levant, this newspaper paid close attention to Spears, the 'disgruntled ex-Francophile' and the 'Pickwickian fatboy' enslaved to the Arab cause.[31] Indeed, as early as August 1945 (the month that the CAA was founded), it was the editorial view of the *Jewish Chronicle* that Spears was the most open, obvious and public 'advocate of the Arab cause'. By March of the following year it was this paper's view that the failure of the general public to understand the Palestine situation from a Jewish perspective was due to the efforts of the Arabs who were 'under the brilliant inspiration, telepathically communicated ... by Sir Edward Spears'.[32]

The Zionist press also presented Spears as the ultimate example of a pro-Arab, anti-Zionist Englishman. For Mrs Dugdale, Spears was a man 'prepared to defend the point of view of the extreme Arab nationalist against all comers, and apparently at any sacrifice'.[33] Later in the same year (1945), in an article in the *Daily Telegraph*, she referred to 'Spears and the Arabs for whom he speaks'.[34] Indeed for Dugdale the only appealing thing about Spears was that one was able to learn the true Arab position from his comments for 'he must be credited with close contact with the views of the personalities of the Arab League'.[35]

This was a pet theme of Dugdale's and during the discussion after Spears' lecture at Chatham House, in February 1945, she asked him to elaborate on the Arab attitude on certain issues, presenting her request in terms that left nobody in attendance unaware of her belief that Spears was but a mouthpiece of the Arab extremists.[36] Again, when commenting on Spears' evidence before the Anglo-American Committee, the only point she was willing to concede to this 'out-and-out British protagonist of the Arab point of view' was that he spoke from 'personal knowledge' when he stated the Arab position.[37]

This Zionist conviction that Spears was the leading spokesman of the Arab opponents of a Jewish state in Palestine resulted in a tendency to view him as the paramount symbol of Gentile anti-Zionism in England, which led to considerable wariness in dealing with him. Thus for example, in May 1945, Spears had written to Professor Selig Brodetsky, president of the Board of Deputies of British Jews, member of the Jewish Agency executive, and the leading British Zionist of the time, asking for information on the Zionist claims to Palestine.[38] In his reply Brodetsky laid down conditions that had to be followed if Spears was to receive any material, specifically that the information should not be quoted out of context and that it should not be used as part of a 'demolition of the case which I have made'.[39]

More than this, Spears entered the Zionist psyche as a benchmark of anti-Zionism in these years. Zionist writers, in articles and reviews used comparisons to Spears to emphasise the anti-Zionism of someone. For example, Herbert Freeden in a review of Brigadier John Glubb's book on the Arab Legion, attacked it for its 'line of argument familiar to those who read General Spears's articles'.[40] Likewise, a contributor to *New Judea* attacked an anonymous article in the Chatham House publication the *World Today* by comparing the author's claim that the 1937 Royal Commission on Palestine did not imply a Jewish state with Spears' position, concluding that *even* Spears was of the opinion that the Balfour Declaration was an implicit, albeit unlawful, offer of a Jewish state.[41]

Yet even towards this paragon of anti-Zionism there was a tendency to dismiss his position, just as other Gentile anti-Zionists like Hope-Simpson, Royden-Shaw and Barbour were dismissed, because of a lack of credibility. For Zionists, Spears was disruptive and had little constructive to contribute to the debate over Palestine. During his tour of the Middle East in 1946 a Jewish Agency spokesman in Jerusalem summed up the general Zionist attitude to Spears when he dismissed his views on the future of Palestine not as an attempt to find a solution but 'to egg on the Arabs and cause trouble'.[42]

Indeed Spears' central thesis that Arab friendship and Arab unity were the central components of Britain's future strategic strength in the Middle East was derided by the Zionists as an example of how Spears was determined to appease the Arabs at all costs, which indicated his blind subservience to Arab interests, that further reduced his credibility.

Lord Strabolgi, founder of the Jewish Dominion League,[43] for example, was of the opinion, after listening to Spears talk about the importance of British–Arab friendship that 'I did not know we could find so eloquent and able an advocate of appeasement.'[44] While S.S. Hammersley, an active Zionist and MP until the 1945 election, publicly dismissed Spears' general arguments on the Middle East on the basis that appeasement of the Arabs was his underlying motivation.[45]

The Zionists presented their English opponents, of whom Spears was the leader, as being motivated by a twisted romantic notion of the Arab that warped their ability to distinguish between right and wrong. Leading Zionist publicists such as Israel Cohen consistently singled out the English infatuation with the Arab as a prime factor responsible for support for Arabs and the correspondent opposition to Zionist aspirations.[46] Likewise, *New Judea* in articles entitled 'The Flourishing Cult'[47] and 'Reflections on Liking Arabs',[48] mused on the curious relationship that had evolved between the Arab and a certain type of Englishman partial to anti-Zionist feelings.

Those English in question (primarily those who had come into contact with the Arabs through government service or missionary work in the region) had developed a relationship of mutual adoration and infatuation because it was in Arab lands that they had reached a status and position that had never been available to them in England. Glubb Pasha was the most obvious case of this, but Spears, in his wartime post as plenipotentiary extraordinary in the Levant, was also a classic example. Similarly, the adoration was based on a misguided conception of what the Arab world actually symbolised, a way of holding on to a lost past and of defying the modernisation that was occurring in the west where they lived.

In Zionist eyes this misconceived view resulted in an inability to view the Middle Eastern situation in an impartial or even realistic light. Mrs Dugdale in an article, in her column in the *Zionist Review*, appropriately enough on the issue of Spears' anti-Zionism, was embodying the general Zionist attitude on the issue when she put down the devoted English support for the Arab to the 'atmosphere in these regions' which distorted one's ability to look rationally at the Middle Eastern situation.[49] Thus for Zionists, Gentile opponents like Spears lacked credibility because, to borrow from the poetry of Walter de la Mare, the 'spell of Arabia … had stolen their wits away'.[50]

There was credence in the Zionist claim that support for the Arabs was really a romantic infatuation with one type of Arab, the Bedouin, that had nothing to do with the realities of modern Palestine. Storrs noted in his diary the danger of Englishmen allowing what he termed 'the Jew–Arab business' to be treated on the 'Bedouin thesis of the Arab' rather than on the basis of the long-settled Arabs of Palestine.[51] While Michael Ionides, who had come into contact with the Arab world when working for the government in Transjordan, must have been talking with his experience of the CAA in mind when in later years he recalled that it was the 'sentimental pro-Arabs' who had been at the forefront of opposition to Zionism.[52]

Indeed, Spears made an effort to get a book written on behalf of the CAA (and with committee funds) that would portray the Arabs in a romantic light. Norman Callan, of the University of London, was asked to write an Arabian anthology, using extracts from English literature that dealt with the Arab lands, and was informed by Spears' secretary that 'the object is to produce an attractive popular anthology which would show the contribution of Arabia as a source of inspiration'.[53]

The project never came to fruition because Callan, though willing to undertake the work, wanted to write it in Middle English, and Spears, understandably, felt that this defeated the goal of a book that was after all a propaganda exercise and as such was intended to have popular appeal.[54] Regardless of the fact that the book was never written, the whole episode is of interest because it shows that Spears, on behalf of the CAA, was attempting to tap into and foster the romantic image of the Arab, in the hope of gaining support for the Arab position on Palestine.

This incident is also of note because in the month prior to Spears' attempt to recruit Callan, the Arab Office in London had attempted to put to rest the romantic presentation of the Arab world as a desert full of Bedouin princes, and to present it instead as a modern and historically valid entity. This was set out in no uncertain terms when it stated that 'most people in England, when they hear the word Arab or the phrase Arab world, imagine a Bedouin living in a tent or riding a camel in the desert'.[55] The pamphlet went on to call this a 'misapprehension' created by the literary efforts of British writers and the more modern efforts of Hollywood, and the Arab Office would renounce this romantic presentation of the Arab in further writings.[56]

It is hardly surprising that the mostly middle-class, educated, urban intellectuals who staffed the Arab Office were keen to present a less clichéd image of the Arab world, if for no other reason than that there was a belief that the Arabs' best hopes in London lay with the Left currently in power, and that the romantic image of Arabia was not a credible argument with which to woo this political constituency.

But the fact that the Arab Office felt it necessary to correct the impression that the Arab world was a place of Bedouin princes at the same time as Spears was attempting to have a book promoting this image published, does emphasise just how much of a part the romanticised image of the Arab played in Spears' whole attitude to the Arab world. Indeed, Spears continued to try to get an Arabian anthology produced, and he entered into protracted discussions with both Professor R. Hewitt, of University College Nottingham, and Dr R.B. Sergeant, of the School of Oriental and African Studies in London, as to the possibility of taking up this project.[57]

Coupled with Spears' exaggerated romantic image of the Arab world, which in a sense enabled Zionists to present him as lacking credibility, was the fact that he was so openly hostile to Zionism. The editors of *The Palestine Controversy*, a symposium organised by the Fabian Colonial Bureau in 1945 (an organisation that by no means shared the aspirations of political Zionists regarding the future of Palestine), felt it necessary to modify Spears' claim in his article that the Jews had attacked the British throughout the war, with a footnote stating that despite the fact that Spears had not mentioned it in his contribution, all the official Jewish representative bodies led by the Jewish Agency had deplored and condemned terrorist acts.[58] This extremism did not go unnoticed by readers of the symposium, and a Sergeant Bartleman wrote to Rita Hinden, secretary of the Fabian Bureau, to complain of Spears as 'somebody approaching fascist'.[59]

Spears' attack on Jewry's wartime record is a good example of an issue where his unbridled anti-Zionism resulted in him overstepping the boundaries of acceptable criticism, which in turn reduced his credibility. In his evidence before the AACIP he claimed that during the war the British had been forced to station a large number of troops in Palestine to ensure that the Jews were kept in order, and also stated that although the Jewish industries in Palestine had contributed to the war effort they did so only by charging high prices for their services and thus profited very nicely from their efforts. These claims brought expressions of surprise from AACIP members Richard Crossman and Sir John Singleton.[60] They were also condemned by Major Wellesly Aron, who appeared before the committee during its Jerusalem hearings. Aron attacked the 'aspersions' that Spears had cast upon the Jewish contribution to fighting the Nazis, and took particular offence at his claim that Jewish industry in Palestine was motivated in its productiveness by the profit factor. Aron went even further, informing the committee that Spears' evidence was an example of 'the sort of thing that we are trying to end by Zionism'.[61]

Two of the AACIP members most sympathetic to Zionist aspirations, Richard Crossman and the American Bartley Crum, in memoirs of their time as members of the committee (both published in 1947) emphasised the extremist nature of Spears' evidence. Crossman, who became a committed supporter of Zionism at this time, was of the view that Spears was the 'only witness ... of any nationality who did not trouble to conceal a clearly unsympathetic point of view about the Jews'.[62] He was even more scathing in private, noting in his diary that Spears' evidence had been 'nauseating'.[63] And though Crossman's reliability as a source has been questioned by later historians, in the context of Zionist perceptions of anti-Zionism, his opinion is as good as any other.[64] Crum echoed Crossman's view of Spears, calling his evidence 'the most vehement attack so far upon Jews of Palestine ... he had nothing but evil to speak of the Jews ... startling allegations'.[65]

The Zionist community back in England did not have to wait for the publication of these memoirs to come to a similar view of the extremist nature of Spears' Anglo-American evidence. *New Judea* called his testimony 'the most fantastic allegations'.[66] Mrs Dugdale noted in her private diary that his evidence was 'really disgusting' and was of the opinion that 'his statements were so bad that they did us more good than harm'.[67] While the *Jewish Chronicle*'s response to Spears' evidence most tellingly reiterated this view when it referred to his 'hysterical outbursts against Zionism ... the very wildness of his statement and the obvious fierceness of his prejudice that seemed to inspire it could only have been more helpful than harmful to the Zionist cause'.[68] The disgust at the content of this testimony before the AACIP, coupled with the view that his extremism reduced his credibility as a witness, resulted in a tendency to belittle Spears' statements. The Jewish Telegraphic Agency reported with glee the fact that Spears' answers to questions posed by committee member Frank Buxton drew laughter from the audience, the implication being that one could not expect anything credible to come from the mouth of someone so openly hostile to Zionist aspirations.[69]

Yet even before his evidence at the Anglo-American hearings had crystallised and shown him to be the most implacable of Gentile anti-Zionists, the Zionists were denigrating him for his lack of credibility. In the summer of 1945, in the run-up to the general election, Spears had made a speech in his Carlisle constituency during which he claimed that 'the Arabs have been friends largely [owing] to my efforts ... thirty million Arabs will be watching with keen interest – even anxiety – the result of the election in Carlisle'.[70]

Mrs Dugdale, writing in her weekly column in the *Zionist Review*, taunted Spears for this claim and used it to argue once again that Gentile anti-Zionists were detached from reality because of a twisted relationship with the Arab world. Next to the Dugdale article was a mocking cartoon of a group of Arab Sheikhs standing on a hill looking at Spears through binoculars while he spoke to his Carlisle constituency. Beside this cartoon was the caption:

> Millions of Arabs will be dejected,
> If Brigadier Spears isn't elected,
> So come on Carlisle face the problem,
> Dare we upset a single Moslem?[71]

Spears' claims regarding the importance attached by the Arab world to the election result in Carlisle did not go unnoticed in the general press either, with Maurice Webb in the *Sunday Express* nominating him for the 'award for the most pontifical announcement of the whole election'.[72] However, this incident is of great interest in helping to understand the Zionist attitude to Spears. The offensive nature of his anti-Zionist claims, coupled with what was believed to be his political appeasement of the Arabs and his romanticised notion of the Arab world, made him in Zionist eyes almost a parody of what was perceived to be a Gentile anti-Zionist.

This is not to say that he was not considered a threat to Zionist aspirations. Spears was regarded as the central figure in the Gentile anti-Zionist effort to hurt Zionism in England, and his access to the general press and his deep antipathy to Zionism were of great concern (the constant coverage of his anti-Zionist efforts in the Jewish press highlights this preoccupation). Indeed, Dr Paul Riebenfeld, a commentator on Jewish affairs and a leading adherent of Zionist revisionism, saw the efforts of 'Spears, Storrs and six of their friends' to attack publicly the AACIP report in May 1946 as a great danger to Zionism precisely because of the reputation and access to the public that men like Spears had. (It is interesting, and highlights the discretion of the CAA, that Riebenfeld still attributed this effort to a group of individual anti-Zionists, 'Spears and six friends', rather than a conscious propaganda effort of the CAA.)[73]

But it was the extremist, open and obvious manner of his anti-Zionism that made Spears more disliked than feared. This can be seen in a 1947 review by Israel Cohen in the *Jewish Chronicle* of (appropriately enough) Abcarius's *Palestine: Through the Fog of Propaganda*. Cohen began his review by noting that 'the fact that it has an introduction by Sir Edward Spears leaves nobody in doubt as to its nature and purpose',[74] comment which in itself should leave nobody in doubt as to the fact that the Zionist attitude to Spears centred to a large extent on the issue of credibility.

SIR RONALD STORRS AND ZION

Just how central the issue of credibility was for Zionists when fighting anti-Zionist efforts can be seen in regard to another leading member of the CAA, Sir Ronald Storrs. Storrs was perhaps the most intellectually adroit of all the members of the CAA. Like many other members of the committee he had a long record of public service in colonial government, but he was best known for his position as governor of Jerusalem in the years following the Balfour Declaration.[75]

One should not underestimate the symbolism and mystique attached to the post of governor of the holiest city in the holiest of lands at a time when attachments to the Bible were widespread at all levels of British society. Storrs directly benefited from this perception. As the Arabist Harry St John Philby noted, Storrs had 'succeeded Pontius Pilate', while Edward Keith Roach, who himself succeeded Storrs as governor (district commissioner) of Jerusalem, was even more forthright in his view that Colonel Storrs was 'basking in Pilate's seat'.[76]

Spears and Storrs had known each other before the establishment of the CAA, and Storrs had been a guest of Spears in Lebanon during a tour of the region in 1943.[77] Their relationship was never close, Storrs describing it in his diary as 'cordial', and even at one point (after attending a dinner at the Arab Club hosted by Spears) noting that 'I feel [Spears] to be less friendly to me than he was in Beirut.'[78] But whatever Spears' personal view of Storrs was, there is no doubting that he saw him as a valuable ally in the battle against Zionism.

The former governor's role in the CAA was as a somewhat esteemed adviser and strategist. Spears had a high view of his capabilities and believed his reputation was a vital asset in the arsenal of the CAA. His correspondence with Storrs throughout these years is full of compliments over the latter's ability and value in presenting the Arab case. References to Storrs' letter-writing ability ('I envy your ... inimitable pen' and 'magnificent reply') were coupled with praise for his 'first-class articles' on the Palestine issue.[79] Indeed, as has been seen, it was Spears who prompted Storrs to use his prodigious writing ability for the benefit of the CAA by getting him to write anti-Zionist letters to the press.

Spears was not alone in his high opinion of Storrs as an expert on Palestine. Throughout these years Storrs was widely presented as a leading expert on the subject. In 1939 a caption beside an article he had written in the *Evening Standard* stated categorically that Storrs was 'one of the best men qualified to speak on Palestine'.[80] Almost a decade later this public presentation of Storrs as a great authority on the Middle East was no less apparent. In a preface to a Storrs article, 'The Dream that Turned into a Nightmare', in the *News of the World* in May 1948, Storrs was introduced by reference to T.E. Lawrence's view that 'the first of us was Ronald Storrs … the most brilliant Englishman in the Middle East'.[81]

Thus, not surprisingly, Storrs, the 'eminent authority and great British diplomat',[82] as one correspondent to the *Birmingham Jewish Recorder* referred to him in 1946, would receive mail in these years from admirers, one such correspondent, Hallburton Stretton, evoking the general view of Storrs when he wrote in a private letter that 'you write with perhaps greater authority than any other man'.[83]

Storrs fostered this view, and on returning from a trip to Africa, the Middle East and the Mediterranean in the first half of 1945 he was of the opinion that the tour's worth 'does exist, not of course in cash earned, but in real enhancement of my value as a knower of the Mid East and as a commentator'.[84] Storrs, 'the knower of the Mid East', passed on his knowledge in many varied ways. He gave radio talks on the Middle East,[85] at one time presiding as chairman of a much-publicised and controversial debate on Palestine between Sir Wyndham Deedes (who presented the Zionist case) and Dr Maude Royden-Shaw (who represented the Arab position).[86]

He also gave innumerable presentations of his lecture 'Palestine' to diverse groups, schools and clubs throughout the United Kingdom. This talk was based on chapter 15 of his autobiography *Orientations*. First published in 1937, this book also added greatly to Storrs' prestige as an expert on the Near East and its popularity can be seen in the fact that there were two reprints in 1937 alone. Even more indicative of Storrs' high profile than his success in filling up parish halls in small provincial towns were the requests that he write the forewords to books on the Middle East, such as those for Humphrey Bowman's *Middle East Window* and Albert Hyamson's *Palestine: A Policy* (both published in 1942).[87]

Then there was his popularity as a reviewer of recently published books on the region. For example, the *Observer*, the *Sunday Times*, the *New Statesman* and *Time and Tide* all asked Storrs to review the much-anticipated *East is West* by Freya Stark in 1945.[88] Likewise Storrs, in a letter to Spears in 1946, spoke of being in the process of reviewing simultaneously four books all directly related to the issue of Palestine and the Near East.[89] The four books in question were the autobiography of Edward Atiyah, secretary of the Arab Office, two works by another Arab Office member, Albert Hourani, and George Antonius's *The Arab Awakening*, reissued by Hamish Hamilton in 1946.

Storrs was aware of the value of this access to the press, allowing as it did the presentation of his own views on the material under review. Indeed, after reading *Jews and Arabs in the Near East*, published by the Labour Zionist movement (Poalei Zion), Storrs was of the opinion that it was 'very tendentious stuff' and that 'somebody should review and expose each of these books as they appear'.[90]

Storrs' position as an expert on the Palestine issue and the Near East in general, coupled with his wide access to the media, was similar to the position of Spears, Hope-Simpson, Barbour and Kenneth Williams, but caused much more concern amongst Zionists. For Storrs presented himself as a neutral observer, writing in his 1937 memoirs that in regard to the battle over Palestine 'I am not wholly for either, but for both.'[91]

Within Zionist circles Storrs' claims of impartiality were not taken seriously. The Zionist view of Storrs as an anti-Zionist can be traced back long before his membership of the CAA or the post-war battle over Zionism had begun. Christopher Sykes has noted how Zionists were suspicious of Storrs during his time as governor of Jerusalem, but argues that 'nothing was ever even faintly proven against him'.[92]

Perhaps the most blatant example of these attacks on Storrs came from Richard Meinertzhagen (chief political officer in Palestine, 1919–20), in his *Middle East Diary, 1917–1956*.[93] Of particular interest is the author's 1942 observation that although Storrs had been 'for twenty years paying lip-service to Zionism ... playing a double game ... it had taken all these years for Weizmann to find out'.[94]

This highlights very well both the perception in the 1940s that Storrs' attempts to appear neutral were part of his anti-Zionist strategy, and also shows the gradual awakening of the more moderate Zionists (such as Weizmann) to the fact that Storrs was indeed an opponent of their goals. By 1940, the Jewish Agency in London, after viewing a copy of his short work *Palestine and Zionism*,[95] and being invited by Storrs to comment on it, was of the opinion that 'your point of view and our own on these matters diverge so considerably that it is not possible to bridge the gap'.[96]

But in the context of the post-war battle over Palestine, the Zionist view of Storrs as an anti-Zionist publicist, rather than an impartial expert, can be traced back to 1943–44. In these years two articles written by Storrs on the practices of the Histadrut, the

General Federation of Jewish Labour, a significant institution within Palestine which played a major role in the political, economic, social and educational life of the Jewish population, and Solel Boneh, the contracting arm of the Histadrut, were published in the *Sunday Times*.

These articles resulted in legal action by the Histadrut against Storrs and the *Sunday Times*. This legal action was taken specifically over the claim that the Histadrut had promoted strikes with the aim of forcing independent companies out of business enabling them to be taken over.[97] Rather than defend the allegations in court the paper and Storrs issued a joint apology.[98]

This whole episode gained much attention in the Anglo-Jewish press. The *Sunday Times* apology was reprinted in full in the *Zionist Review* and both the *Jewish Chronicle* and *New Judea* commented on it in great detail.[99] Storrs was very well aware of the reaction to the Histadrut affair in the Jewish world. The articles had been written while he was in Jerusalem and on a subsequent visit he quickly realised the unpopularity of his claims; a note in his diary from Jerusalem, after the two articles were published, states simply, 'bitter criticism of my articles ... about time I cleared out', while in the wake of the apology he once again confided in his diary, 'I must await the Jewish press, which I shall doubtless receive marked, full and free.'[100] Indeed Storrs' private papers do contain numerous cuttings from the Jewish press on the incident including an editorial in *Ha-Boker*, the Hebrew daily, entitled 'Anti-Zionist Propaganda', and a copy of his apology to the Histadrut from the *Palestine Post* of March 1944.[101]

Despite his awareness that the Zionists had seized on his articles to portray him as an anti-Zionist, Storrs was still greatly angered by the Jewish response. This was partly due to the fact that he felt wronged over the whole incident. It was his contention that he had published the articles in good faith and that not only had he followed the Foreign Office guidelines but that the Labour department of the Palestine administration and Sir Harold MacMichael, the High Commissioner, had vetted the articles and found nothing wrong with them, only to find that in the aftermath of the legal battle he had been 'left to bear the brunt alone'.[102]

Regardless of where the actual blame for this incident lay, the Zionist movement did not hesitate to try to use Storrs' articles as proof of his anti-Zionism. In April 1943 *Ha-shomer Ha-tzair* set the tone when it stated that although Storrs may claim to be a friend of

Jews, 'the enemies of Zionism are not the friends of the Jews, whatever their intentions'.[103]

In August 1944, in the wake of the *Sunday Times* apology, the *Zionist Review* in an article entitled 'Sir Ronald Storrs Again' attacked Storrs' claims of admiration for Jewish achievements in Palestine. His compliments were dismissed as nothing but a tactic whereby Storrs was attempting to present himself as a neutral observer of Zionism, for although 'this sounds very impartial and helps win the confidence of the reader', in reality 'there can be no compromise between the Zionist conception of the future of the Middle East ... and that of Sir Ronald Storrs'.[104]

Similarly, *New Judea* in the same month was equally forthright in its attack of Storrs' criticism of the call for unlimited Jewish immigration in the election platforms of both the Democratic and Republican parties in the United States. Storrs, the journal argued, was an ingenious enemy of Zionism who dressed up his opposition to Jewish aspirations with praise, and the article continued 'though a man of many talents, he has not the gift of disguising curses when bestowing blessings on the tent of Israel'.[105]

Even before the controversy over his *Sunday Times* articles Storrs had been of the view that he was an undeserving victim of Zionist fury. In his 1937 memoirs he stated that he had been 'pogromed in their [Jewish press] as have few other goys and with less cause'.[106] Later he was of the view that he had been 'comically traduced as the originator of British anti-Zionist policy' in Van Passen's book *Our Forgotten Ally*,[107] and was offended by the 'half a dozen comic slanders against myself' in William Ziff's *The Rape of Palestine*, which he thought a prime example of the 'pointless mud slung by Yank Zionists'.[108] Even at the time of Israel's founding in May 1948, as well as later, Storrs was still publicly arguing in the press that the British reward for its efforts in Palestine had been 'written in a frenzy of hatred and calumny of the world Zionist press' and that anyone (meaning himself) who took issue with Zionism, regardless of his 'pro-Jewish record', was 'liable to be pilloried as an anti-Zionist'.[109]

Despite the fact that throughout these years Storrs portrayed himself as the undeserving victim of Zionist vilification there is no doubt that he was opposed to Zionist aspirations, and indeed in a private letter to an American journalist he stated categorically that he was 'avowedly and openly anti-extreme Zionism'.[110] His membership of the CAA, in itself, showed that he was motivated to take an active part in supporting the Arab cause, and he contributed to the committee's publications. For example, he wrote to Spears in September 1945 offering his own material on Palestine to Henry Longhurst who was in the process of drafting a pamphlet on the Palestine situation to be distributed by the CAA.[111]

But Storrs also took a subtly anti-Zionist stance in his public pronouncements on the Palestine issue. In his talk for the Current Affairs for Schools series on the BBC Home Service, he concluded a review of the situation in Palestine with what was to all intents and purposes an emotional appeal to the listener. 'Can anybody', he asked, 'be surprised at the Palestine Arab for being, first frightened, then indignant, at the thought of being overwhelmed by countless streams of immigrants ... in a country which has been their home for 1300 years?'[112]

The Zionist anger at Storrs was not so much directed against what were perceived to be his anti-Zionist statements. There were others such as Hope-Simpson and particularly Spears who held similar anti-Zionist views to Storrs. What was different about Storrs, and what most angered Zionists, was not his anti-Zionism but his claims of impartiality on the issue. It was bad enough that he used the press, the platform and the radio to oppose Zionism, but to do so under the guise of a disinterested observer was infuriating. In the Zionist mind it would have been far preferable if he had come out openly and stated his opposition to Zionism, thereby opening himself to direct attack. *New Judea* summed up this position when it stated that 'from our view avowed opposition would be preferable to this insidious friendship'.[113]

In this context it is not surprising that when Storrs was presented as the neutral chairman of a much-heralded radio debate on Palestine between Sir Wyndham Deedes (a dedicated and highly respected Gentile Zionist, who had been won over to Zionism while chief secretary of the Palestine Administration, 1920–23) and Dr Maude Royden-Shaw, it became too much for Zionists to bear.

The BBC not only asked Storrs to chair the talk but also asked him to select the guests. He chose Royden-Shaw over Brigadier Stephen Longrigg (another member of the CAA) because she was 'best known' to the public and he chose Deedes because he was '110% Zionist'.[114] Yet the fact that both Storrs and Royden-Shaw were members of the CAA should have suggested to Storrs that he was not best suited to chair the talk. Indeed, at the same time that Storrs was supposed to be adjudicating this radio debate, Spears had commissioned Royden-Shaw to write a pamphlet on the injustice of further Jewish immigration into Palestine, for a committee of which Storrs was a leading member.[115]

Storrs was well aware that his chairmanship might arouse suspicion in Zionist circles, and even noted in his diary after being asked to chair the talk that Sir Wyndham Deedes 'on this topic I should say [is] suspicious of me'.[116] The day that the radio debate was to take place an editorial in the *Jewish Chronicle* called on Deedes not to partake in the debate because he would be outnumbered by both Storrs and Royden-Shaw and he could not win.[117] Not surprisingly the Zionist reaction to Storrs in the wake of the radio debate was harsh. The *Zionist Review* commented on 'the biased attitude adopted by Sir Ronald Storrs' and asked whether he 'forgot or deliberately disobeyed the established rule that the chairman of the debate ought to be completely impartial'.[118]

An examination of the transcript of the radio debate does seem to show that Storrs did refrain from out-and-out condemnations of political Zionism in his role as chairman, and his promotion of partition as a possible solution during his concluding remarks is to his credit considering he never supported partition as a just solution. Nevertheless, he did lend support to Royden-Shaw on many of the key issues that separated Zionists from anti-Zionists. He claimed that the debt of the Balfour Declaration had been repaid in full and he opposed increased Jewish immigration into Palestine on the grounds that the country was unable to take more refugees.[119]

Another episode that highlights the Zionist desire to expose Storrs as a malevolent anti-Zionist, in contradiction to the general view of him, occurred just two months after the radio debate. Following a lecture in Hull on Palestine, where Storrs had attacked Lord Strabolgi and the Jewish Dominion League, Ivan Greenberg passed on to Lord Strabolgi the news of Storrs' verbal attack on him.

Strabolgi confronted Storrs, warned him that he regarded his statements as libellous, and wrote to Greenberg to tell him that after being confronted Storrs was 'very much taken aback'. Strabolgi also asked Greenberg, the editor of the *Jewish Chronicle*, if he had any direct evidence other than verbal reports over Storrs' allegations as 'I would like to force him to make a public denial and apology.'[120] Greenberg was unable to provide evidence of Storrs' libel, but the incident once again illustrates both the Zionist efforts to 'out' Storrs and their frustration with his attempts to cast aspersions on Zionism and its leaders, while hiding behind the mantle of a neutral expert.

The fact that Storrs was called as an expert witness before the AACIP without having requested to be heard, goes to emphasise how far his reputation as an authority on Palestine travelled. He had not intended to speak at the hearings, but while attending as an observer, committee chairman Singleton had seen him in the audience and had called on him to 'bear witness'.[121] In his evidence he set out the central anti-Zionist arguments that the Jewish National Home had already been established in Palestine, that partition was not a fair solution and that Palestine was not a refugee problem.[122]

It is hardly surprising that the Zionist press in reviewing his evidence presented it as a classic piece of anti-Zionist rhetoric.[123] Of course Storrs was not the only witness called before the AACIP who opposed a political Zionist solution to the Palestine problem. But Storrs, as has been said, was perceived differently by the Zionists because it was believed that he purposefully presented himself as an unbiased expert, simply giving his detached opinion as an experienced observer rather than an active opponent of Zionism.

At least Spears made no secret of his involvement with the Arab cause and nobody was in doubt as to where his tendencies lay. Indeed, he began his statement before the AACIP with the words:

> I am chairman of the Committee for Arab Affairs ... founded to promote good relations between the Arab states and Great Britain. I have kept in close touch with the Arab heads of mission in London and have seen many Arab leaders from all states, members of the Arab League, as well as leading Palestine Arabs who have come to England during this period.[124]

Storrs' reluctance to declare openly his support for the Arab cause made him dangerous in Zionist eyes precisely because it gave him credibility. One must recall Crossman's view that Spears was not taken very seriously by the AACIP because he was so openly anti-Zionist and pro-Arab. In these terms it is enlightening to note that the *Jewish Chronicle* (often a harsh critic of Storrs) only referred to his evidence by saying that the ex-governor of Jerusalem was 'an unexpected witness', and one must compare this with its claims in the same issue that Spears' evidence had been 'hysterical' and almost beneficial to the Zionists.[125]

This varying attitude to two men who in substance shared the same position was due to their differing styles of presentation rather than the content of their argument. Indeed, the same night as he gave evidence to the AACIP, Storrs, the perceived neutral expert, attended a dinner given by the Lebanese legation in London, at which he sat at the head table beside Spears and Azzam Pasha, secretary-general of the Arab League.[126]

It was only when Storrs allowed his name to be used in the public letter by the CAA members opposing the Anglo-American report for being pro-Zionist, that the Jewish press believed that at last Storrs had declared his true position. The *Jewish Chronicle* dismissed this letter, published in *The Times* on 23 May 1946, in the harshest terms. The letter was called a 'typical Arab League effusion over the names of a group which included such notorious Jew haters as Ralph Beaumont, Storrs, Hope-Simpson, and of course, the tireless Sir Edward Spears'.[127] The following week the paper was forced to retract the claim that these men, all members of the CAA (although once again this was not mentioned), were indeed 'Jew haters', and especially noted the fact that Spears and Storrs could not be defined by this 'inadvertent epitaph'.[128]

Nevertheless, Storrs by openly attacking the report in the company of Spears and other noted anti-Zionists had at last shown his true colours and regardless of the retraction in the *Jewish Chronicle*, the Zionists felt that finally his position as a virulent anti-Zionist could no longer be denied. The *Zionist Review* responded to this affair in an article entitled 'Thank You Sir Ronald'. In the title of this piece one can sense the feeling of satisfaction, even the palpable relief, amongst Zionists that at last Storrs had come out from behind his veneer of objectivity and admitted his true position:

> In the course of many years [Storrs] has paraded as a friend of Jewry and an impartial expert on Palestine. Two years ago he had to offer a public apology for misleading statements on the Histadrut in the *Sunday Times*. Last year he acted as chairman of the BBC discussion on Zionism ... Sir Ronald's biased chairmanship on that occasion aroused the indignation of many listeners. But he still continued to appear as an expert on Palestine trying his best to be fair to both sides in the

controversy. Sir Ronald has now allied himself openly with the anti-Jewish side. Now at least he will no longer be able to claim impartiality in a case in which he is the prejudiced champion of one party to the dispute.[129]

By 1947 even Storrs himself was beginning to reflect on just how neutral he was on the Palestine issue. After chairing a debate in May of that year between Edward Atiyah of the Arab Office and the Zionist, the Revd Bernard Cherrick, at the Streatham branch of the United Nations Association, he noted in his diary that his concluding remarks following the debate had been 'assailed by Zionist accusations of unchairmanlike partiality'. With hindsight Storrs was of the opinion, 'looking back, I perceive [these accusations] to have been not altogether without substance ... I must in future be more judicial in the chair.'[130]

Even after the birth of Israel, Storrs never modified his anti-Zionist position. In 1949 he was still fighting Zionism in the press and was continually on the lookout for 'a good loophole for riposte' to Zionist articles and letters.[131] And in 1951 Norman Bentwich, a moderate Zionist who had known Storrs while both were members of the Palestine administration, was even driven to write privately to Storrs to say he was 'disturbed by [your] continuing anti-Zionist statements'.[132]

Throughout the battle over Palestine in the final years of the British Mandate the Zionists viewed those such as Spears, Royden-Shaw, Hope-Simpson and Storrs, in short members of the CAA, as their major Gentile opponents. That the Zionists concentrated on these individuals, almost to the exclusion of all others, highlights the fact that the CAA included the leading anti-Zionists of the era. However, the differing approach and attitude of the Zionists to those like Hope-Simpson and Spears, who were deemed to be openly anti-Zionist and hence, though dangerous, were viewed as having a credibility problem, and to Storrs, who was believed to be more of a threat because he professed neutrality, show that for the Zionists the key to their view of their opponents was credibility.

And it was this issue of lending credibility to Gentile opponents of Zionism that came to be at the heart of the Zionist attitude towards the Jewish Fellowship. For it will be argued in the following chapter that the Jewish anti-Zionist body, the Jewish Fellowship, was not feared by Zionists as a credible threat to Zionism because of its position or efforts within Anglo-Jewry, but because it was believed, and feared, that it gave credence to the arguments of men like Spears, Hope-Simpson and Storrs in the non-Jewish world.

NOTES

1. Mrs Edgar (Blanche) Dugdale, 'Some Aspects of Publicity', *Zionist Review*, 12 October 1945, p. 3. Throughout this period Blanche Dugdale wrote a weekly column, 'Thru Gentile Eyes', in the *Zionist Review*, and produced propaganda pamphlets for the Zionist cause. See, for example, *The Balfour Declaration: Origins and Background* (London: JA, 1942). On Dugdale see Norman Rose's *The Gentile Zionists: A Study in Anglo-Zionist Diplomacy, 1929–1939* (London: Frank Cass, 1973).
2. Reid to Spears, 30 January 1946, Box 7/1, SPSP.
3. *Zionist Review*, 12 January 1945, p. 1.
4. *New Judea*, August 1944, pp. 166–7.
5. Cmd. 3686 *The Hope Simpson Report on Immigration, Land Settlement and Development*, October 1930. See the Jewish Agency's memorandum submitted to Hope-Simpson at the time of his report, *Palestine, Land Settlement, Urban Development and Immigration* (London: JA, 1930).
6. See for example David Horowitz, 'They Were Wrong', *Zionist Review*, 12 May 1944, p. 1.
7. 'Putting Back the Clock', *Zionist Review*, 15 December 1944, p. 1.
8. Hope-Simpson, 'The Palestine Mandate', pp. 34–9. This article was reissued by the CAA as a pamphlet in 1946, see Box 4/3, SPSP.
9. *New Judea*, December 1944, pp. 34–5. On Hope-Simpson's anti-Zionism see Evyatar Friesel's article on Sir John Chancellor 'Through a Peculiar Lens: Zionism and Palestine in British Diaries, 1927–1931', *Middle Eastern Studies*, 29: 3 (July 1993), pp. 419–44, p. 436 and Hope-Simpson's letter to Colonel Elphinston of the CAA, at the time of the Anglo-American Committee hearings, 27 January 1946, file 6, YOUNG.
10. Storrs, *Notes on the Emergence of the Jewish Problem*, Box 6/15, STOP.
11. Barbour, *A Plan for Lasting Peace in Palestine* (Jerusalem: 1936).
12. See Jamal Husseini to Barbour, 7 September 1936 and R. Nashashibi to Barbour, 8 September 1936, Box 2/3, BARB.
13. Hodson to Barbour, 29 September 1936, Box 2/3, BARB. Barbour agreed and the article 'Palestine: The Commission's Task' was published anonymously in the *Round Table*, XXVII: 105 (December 1936), pp. 79–94.
14. Barbour, *Zionism, Palestine and the Jewish Problem* (Jerusalem: 1939), pp.1–11, p. 10.
15. The *Sentinel*, 1: 7, 17 March 1939, p. 5. See also two similar letters by Rabbi L. Miller attacking Barbour in the same terms in the *North-Eastern Daily Gazette*, 18 February and 30 March 1937.
16. Albert Hourani, *International Affairs*, XXIII: 1 (January 1947), pp. 132–3. For another glowing appraisal of Barbour's book see 'Palestine in Asia: A Plea for a Broader Perspective', *Round Table*, XXXVIII: 151 (April 1948), pp. 643–8.
17. 'Anti-Zionist Propaganda', *New Judea*, October–November, 1946, p. 19.
18. Aubrey Eban, *Zionist Review*, 15 November 1946, p. 10.
19. *Jewish Chronicle*, 18 October 1946, p. 11. See a similar view in the *Wiener Library Bulletin*, 1: 2 (January 1947), p. 4.
20. 'A Reply to Dr Royden', *Zionist Review*, 17 March 1944, p. 4.
21. Royden-Shaw, 'Arab Palestine', *Newsletter*, 7: 8 (August 1944), pp. 233–6.
22. 'Two Articles', *Zionist Review*, 1 September 1944, p. 1.
23. Mrs E. Dugdale, 'Some Aspects of Publicity', *Zionist Review*, 12 October 1945, p. 3.
24. Landman to Greenberg, 3 January 1944, MS150 AJ 110/5, GREEN.
25. Rosette to Greenberg, 19 January 1944, MS150 AJ 110/5, GREEN.
26. 'Another Disputation', *Jewish Chronicle*, 26 October 1945, p. 10.
27. 'An Observer Article', *Zionist Review*, 1 June 1945, p. 1.
28. 'Arab League's War of Nerves', *Jewish Chronicle*, 5 October 1945, p. 10.
29. Hamabit (pseud), 'History Distorted', *New Judea*, 7 October 1945, p. 7.
30. Rosette to Greenberg, 12 February 1945, MS150 AJ 110/8, GREEN.

31. *Jewish Chronicle*, 9 February 1945, p. 12; 16 February 1945, p. 11.
32. *Jewish Chronicle*, 10 August 1945, p. 5; 1 March 1946, p. 12.
33. Mrs E. Dugdale, 'The Time Has Come', *Zionist Review*, 23 February 1945, p. 5.
34. Mrs E. Dugdale, 'Palestine Problem: A Conflict of Right and Right', *Daily Telegraph*, 10 October 1945.
35. Mrs E. Dugdale, 'London Fog', *Zionist Review*, 23 November 1945, p. 3.
36. Mrs E. Dugdale speaking after Spears' lecture at the RIIA, 'British Policy in the Middle East', p. 31.
37. Mrs E. Dugdale, *Zionist Review*, 8 February 1946, p. 3.
38. Spears to Brodetsky, 15 May 1945, Box 4/6, SPSP.
39. Brodetsky to Spears, 5 June 1945, Box 4/6, SPSP.
40. Review by Herbert Freeden of Glubb's *The Story of the Arab Legion* (London: Hodder & Stoughton, 1948), in the *Zionist Review*, 30 August 1948, p. 15.
41. 'The Chatham House Gallimaufrey', *New Judea*, March–April 1945, pp. 115–16 (emphasis added). It is doubtful whether Spears did accept that the Balfour Declaration was an implicit offer of a Jewish state. He denied this during an interview with the *Arab News Agency*, 15 August 1945, and in his evidence before the AACIP, p. 34. Similarly the Zionist press attacked a pamphlet by Dr Walter Zander, secretary of the English Friends of the Hebrew University that criticised the Zionist leadership, on the grounds that it had been 'widely quoted by such enemies of Zion as General Spears', *Gates of Zion*, 2: 3 (April 1948), p. 32.
42. Palcor News Agency report, 16 October 1946, p. 2.
43. The Jewish Dominion League under the chairmanship of Lord Strabolgi, formerly Commander Joseph M. Kenworthy, wanted Palestine to become a self-governing state on both sides of the Jordan river with the status of a dominion within the British Empire. See the group's pamphlet *Palestine and the British Commonwealth of Nations* (London: Jewish Dominion League, 1945).
44. Strabolgi expressed this view after Spears' RIIA lecture 'British Policy in the Middle East', p. 20.
45. Hammersley, *Daily Telegraph*, 20 February 1945.
46. For an example of Cohen arguing in this vein see his comments during the discussion after a lecture by Elizabeth Monroe at the RIIA in 1948, 'The Interests of the Great Powers in the Middle East', 25 May 1948, 8/1545, pp. 10, 11. Also see his article in the *Jewish Chronicle*, 18 December 1936, pp. 19–20 and his autobiography, *A Jewish Pilgrimage: The Autobiography of Israel Cohen* (London: Vallentine Mitchell, 1956), pp. 347–63.
47. Brian Stone, 'The Flourishing Cult', *New Judea*, January–February 1948, pp. 73–4.
48. 'Reflections on Liking Arabs', *New Judea*, June 1948, p. 5.
49. Mrs E. Dugdale, 'The Time Has Come', *Zionist Review*, 23 February 1945, p. 4.
50. *Arabia*, originally published in 1912 in his collection *The Listeners and Other Poems*, republished in *The Complete Poems of Walter de la Mare* (London: Faber & Faber, 1969), p. 119.
51. MS Diary of Storrs, 9 November 1944, Box 6/5, STOP.
52. Ionides, *Divide and Lose*, p. 54.
53. Maurice to Callan, 31 December 1945, Box 6/3, SPSP.
54. Spears to Ifor Evans, 7 January 1946, Box 6/3, SPSP.
55. *The Arab World and the Arab League* (London: AO, 1945), p. 1.
56. See for example Atiyah's 'The Arab League', *World Affairs*, 1: 1 (January 1947), pp. 34–7, p. 34.
57. See Spears to Hewitt, 28 November 1945, Box 6/4, SPSP; R.B. Sergeant to Spears, 21 August 1946; Spears to Sergeant, 28 August 1946, Box 7/2, SPSP. Ultimately Sergeant, though keen to write the book, was unable to guarantee completion until 1948, and Spears felt that this was too long to wait for a propaganda work.
58. See Spears' 'Reply to Dr Parkes', p. 25, fn 1.
59. Bartleman to Hinden, 1 January 1946, MSS Brit Emp.s. 365, Box 176/6, FCBA.
60. See their comments during Spears' evidence before the AACIP, p. 42.
61. Evidence of Major Wellesly Aron, MBE before the AACIP, Jerusalem, 25 March 1946, *Public Hearings of Anglo-American Committee, Jerusalem* (Jerusalem: 1946), pp. 16–27, p. 23.

62. Crossman, *Palestine Mission: A Personal Record* (London: Hamish Hamilton 1947), p. 68.
63. Private Diary of R.H. Crossman, January 1946, file 2, CROSS.
64. Ritchie Ovendale, *Britain, the United States and the End of the Palestine Mandate, 1942–1948* (Woodbridge: Boydell Press/Royal Historical Society, 1989), p. 115. See also Michael Cohen's view that Crossman's *Palestine Mission* was 'blatantly tendentious', *Palestine and the Great Powers, 1945–1948*, p. 101. For a study of Crossman's actual role and influence during the Anglo-American hearings see Amicam Nachmani, *Great Power Discord in Palestine: The Anglo-American Committee of Inquiry into the Problems of European Jewry and Palestine, 1945–1946* (London: Frank Cass, 1986), pp. 77–9.
65. Crum, *Behind the Silken Curtain* (New York: Simon & Schuster, 1947), pp. 66–7. Another American member of the Anglo-American Committee favourable to Zionism was James G. McDonald. He later became the first US Ambassador to Israel. See his account of his time in that post, *My Mission in Israel, 1948–1951* (London: Victor Gollancz, 1951).
66. *New Judea*, January–February 1946, pp. 65–6.
67. Diary of Mrs E. Dugdale, 29 January 1946, cited in Norman Rose (ed.), *Baffy: The Diaries of Blanche Dugdale, 1936–1947* (London: Frank Cass, 1973), p. 230.
68. *Jewish Chronicle*, 8 February 1946, p. 10.
69. 'Anti-Zionists Testify before the Committee of Enquiry', *Jewish Telegraphic Agency Bulletin*, 30 January 1946, p. 3.
70. Egremont, *Under Two Flags*, cited p. 271.
71. Mrs E. Dugdale, *Zionist Review*, 20 July 1945, p. 3.
72. Maurice Webb, *Sunday Express*, 15 July 1945.
73. Riebenfeld, 'The Politics of the Unpolitical Zionists', *Jewish Forum*, 1: 1 (October 1946), pp. 34–46, p. 45.
74. Cohen, *Jewish Chronicle*, 14 February 1947, p. 11.
75. Sir Ronald Storrs (1881–1955) was Oriental Secretary in Cairo, 1907–17. He served as Military Governor of Jerusalem, 1917–20 and Governor of Jerusalem and Judea, 1920–26. He was Governor of Cyprus, 1926–32 and then Governor of Rhodesia, 1932–34.
76. H. St J.B. Philby, *Arabian Days* (London: Robert Hale, 1948), p. 127; Edward Keith Roach, *Pasha of Jerusalem: Memoirs of a District Commissioner under the British Mandate* (London: Radcliffe Press, 1994), p. 53.
77. MS Diary of Storrs, 10 February 1943, Box 6/5, STOP.
78. MS Diary of Storrs, 17 January 1945, Box 6/6; 19 September 1946, Box 6/7 STOP.
79. Spears to Storrs, 13 September 1948; Spears to Storrs, 11 November 1948; Spears to Storrs, 31 May 1948, Box 5/3, SPSP. The Storrs article that Spears was praising was 'The Dream that Turned into a Nightmare', *News of the World*, 16 May 1948.
80. Storrs, 'Stand Firm on Palestine', *Evening Standard*, 20 July 1939.
81. Storrs, 'The Dream that Turned into a Nightmare', *News of the World*, 16 May 1948. For the original reference see Lawrence's *Seven Pillars of Wisdom: A Triumph* (London: Jonathan Cape, 1935), p. 56.
82. See letter of V.M. Green, *Birmingham Jewish Recorder*, September 1946, p. 20.
83. Stretton to Storrs, 27 January 1949, Box 6/10, STOP.
84. MS Diary of Storrs, 22 May 1945, Box 6/6, STOP.
85. For example see Storrs' 'The Middle East Revisited', BBC Home Service, 29 July 1945, Palestine Misc. Correspondence A–Z, 1939–48, BBCWAR and 'The Problem of Palestine' Current Affairs for Schools, BBC Home Service, 10 October 1945, Box 5/3, SPSP.
86. 'The Future of Palestine', BBC Home Service, 26 October 1945, repr. in *The Listener* XXXIV: 877, 1 November 1945, pp. 479–95.
87. See Humphrey Bowman's *Middle East Window* (London: Longman, Green, 1942) and Albert Hyamson's *Palestine: A Policy* (London: Methuen, 1942).
88. MS Diary of Storrs, 4 September 1945, Box 6/6, STOP.
89. Storrs to Spears, 24 June 1946, Box 5/3, SPSP.
90. MS Diary of Storrs, 21 May 1944, Box 6/5, STOP.
91. Storrs, *Memoirs*, p. 358.

92. See Sykes' *Crossroads to Israel* (London: Collins, 1965), pp. 39–40.
93. Meinertzhagen, *Middle East Diary, 1917–1956* (London: Cresset Press, 1959), pp. 22, 82, 160.
94. Ibid., p. 187.
95. Storrs, *Palestine and Zionism* (London: Penguin, 1940).
96. Jewish Agency (London) to Storrs, 26 February 1940, Box 6/10, STOP.
97. The Storrs articles that Histadrut took legal action over were 'Wartime Problems in Palestine: Economic and Labour Peril', *Sunday Times*, 7 March 1943 and 'Wartime Problems in Palestine: Racial and Economic', *Sunday Times*, 21 March 1943.
98. The Storrs apology appeared in the *Sunday Times*, 27 February 1944.
99. See 'Sir Ronald Storrs and the Histadrut: An Apology', *Zionist Review*, 3 March 1944, p. 3; *Jewish Chronicle*, 1 March 1944, p. 2; *New Judea*, February 1944, p. 71.
100. MS Diary of Storrs, 28 February 1944, Box 6/5; 15 April 1944, Box 6/5, STOP.
101. *Ha-Boker*, 29 March 1943; *Palestine Post*, 3 March 1944.
102. MS Diary of Storrs, 10 February 1944, Box 6/5, STOP.
103. *Ha-shomer Ha-tzair*, 11 April 1943.
104. The comments were in response to Storrs' article in the *Evening Standard*, 7 August 1944. See 'Sir Ronald Storrs Again', *Zionist Review*, 11 August 1944, p. 1. Also see earlier attacks on Storrs in the same paper, 'Sir Ronald's Report', 26 March 1943, p. 1 and 'Sir Ronald's Political Game', 16 April 1943, pp. 1–2.
105. *New Judea*, August 1944, pp. 166–7.
106. Storrs, *Memoirs*, p. 358.
107. MS Diary of Storrs, 2 July 1944, Box 6/5, STOP.
108. See Storrs to Spears, 16 December 1946, Box 5/3, SPSP and MS Diary of Storrs, 11 November 1946, Box 6/7, STOP.
109. See Storrs, 'Palestine: The Dream that Turned into a Nightmare', *News of the World*, 16 May and his letter in *The Times*, 10 September 1948.
110. Storrs to Benevisti, 30 November 1946, Box 5/3, SPSP.
111. Storrs to Spears, 9 September 1945, Box 5/3, SPSP.
112. Storrs, 'The Problem of Palestine', Current Affairs for Schools, BBC Home Service, 10 October 1945, Box 5/3, SPSP.
113. *New Judea*, June 1943, p. 130.
114. MS Diary of Storrs, 5 October 1945, Box 6/6, STOP.
115. Minutes of the CAA meeting, 10 October 1945.
116. MS Diary of Storrs, 5 October 1945, Box 6/6, STOP.
117. 'Another Disputation', *Jewish Chronicle*, 26 October 1945, p. 10.
118. 'People and Events', *Zionist Review*, 2 November 1945, p. 8.
119. See 'The Future of Palestine', *The Listener*, p. 494.
120. Strabolgi to Greenberg, 13 December 1945, MS150 AJ 110/5, GREEN.
121. MS Diary of Storrs, 31 January 1946, Box 6/7, STOP; Storrs to Spears, 16 December 1946, Box 5/3, SPSP.
122. See evidence of Storrs before the AACIP, London, 31 January 1946, pp. 35–57, ACC3121/C14/30/5, ABD.
123. See *New Judea*, January–February 1946, p. 85 and the supplement to the *Zionist Review*, 8 February 1946, p. 2.
124. Evidence of Spears before the AACIP, p. 29.
125. *Jewish Chronicle*, 8 February 1946, p. 17.
126. MS Diary of Storrs, 31 January 1946, Box 6/7, STOP.
127. *Jewish Chronicle*, 24 May 1946, p. 10.
128. *Jewish Chronicle*, 31 May 1946, p. 12.
129. 'Thank You Sir Ronald', *Zionist Review*, 31 May 1946, p. 6.
130. MS Diary of Storrs, 5 May 1947, Box 6/7, STOP.
131. MS Diary of Storrs, 3 May 1948, Box 6/8.
132. Bentwich to Storrs, 26 January 1951, Box 6/10, STOP.

4 The Jewish Fellowship and the Battle over Zionism in Anglo-Jewry

THE FELLOWSHIP ENTERS THE FRAY

On 7 November 1944 Lord Moyne, British Minister resident in the Middle East, was assassinated by Zionist extremists in Cairo.[1] On the same day the Jewish Fellowship officially entered the battle over Palestine by holding a press conference to announce its public existence. It is ironic that these two events occurred on the same day, because despite the fact that the mainstream Zionist movement in Britain was shocked by the Moyne assassination and condemned it vigorously,[2] the Fellowship saw the assassination of Lord Moyne, by Jews in the name of Zionism, as symbolic of the perversion of Judaism inherent in Zionist statist aspirations and the spiritual decay within Jewry.

For the Fellowship, the campaign of political Zionist Jews for a Jewish state in Palestine raised issues that struck at the heart of Jewish existence in the Diaspora such as with whom should the loyalty of Jews lie: with their country of birth or with the Zionist nationalist movement and, ultimately, if it ever came into being, the Jewish state. A Jewish state would severely strain, if not destroy beyond repair, the great strides that the Jews as members of a religious community had made since being granted citizenship. For this new perception of Jews as a nation in waiting was bound to increase the level of anti-Semitism in the Gentile world that, understandably (in the Fellowship's eyes), could not be expected to comprehend this altered state of the Jews.

Therefore, political Zionism was inextricably linked both to the moral decay within Jewry and the changing perceptions of Jewry in the Gentile world. And only when a strong and vibrant Jewish community based on religious rather than political principles existed and was inhabited by 'people of the book' and 'Shema Jews', as opposed to the 'Hatikva Jews' who supported political Zionism, could the claims of the political Zionist movement be shown to be false.[3]

The writer Joseph Leftwich, who to many was the literary heir of Israel Zangwill within Anglo-Jewry, was a founding member of the Fellowship. Like other Anglo-Jewish intellectuals, such as Cecil Roth,[4] Leftwich's instinctive response to the Holocaust was to look critically at the state of Judaism in those communities that had survived Hitler's onslaught. As such, as a member of the first council and executive of the Fellowship, he sincerely hoped that the Fellowship would provide an answer to the spiritual poverty of Judaism that threatened to engulf post-Holocaust Jewish life.[5]

But Leftwich was also very aware of the antipathy to Zionism fundamental to the Fellowship position and he feared that this aspect would come to dominate the body, which in turn would nullify any moral force it had. Writing in a private letter of August 1944, Leftwich summed up this fear and concluded that 'the Jewish Fellowship is useless unless it can be lifted out of an atmosphere of suspicion and hostility'.[6]

However, as this chapter will argue, the Fellowship was never able to lift itself out of 'an atmosphere of suspicion and hostility' within the community of Jewry. Rather it came to be isolated within the community. This was for two reasons. Firstly, the Zionists were successful in presenting the Fellowship's opposition to Zionism not as an inherent part of the body's attempt to rejuvenate Jewish life but to try to destroy it. Secondly, by openly opposing Zionism in the non-Jewish world, the Fellowship alienated much of the Jewish community and provided credibility to the Zionist claims that it was indeed betraying Jewry in the outside world.

ZIONIST RESPONSES TO THE FELLOWSHIP

The Zionist movement had always deemed it vital to present Zionism as a philosophy representing all of Jewry. As early as the opening session of the second Zionist Congress of 1898, Max Nordau was proclaiming that the 'Zionists are not a party, they are Jewry itself.'[7] This was an attempt to elevate Zionism from the position of just another faction within Jewry, thus lending gravitas to its principles and objectives. In the case of England the realisation of Nordau's ambitious claim was not achieved quickly. In 1916, one year before the Balfour Declaration, Samuel Landman, a Zionist publicist, was candid enough to admit in a Zionist pamphlet that English Jews were by and large 'more English than Jews ... cannot see any reason to become adherents of the Zionist organisation'.[8]

However, by 1945 the Zionists could claim with much credence that the great mass of Jewry was in support of, or at least in sympathy with, Zionist aspirations. The introduction of the Palestine White Paper of 1939 and the Zionist victory in the 1943 communal elections to the Board of Deputies of British Jews, the representative body of British Jewry, marked an increase in support for Zionism within Jewry. This was followed by the horror of the Holocaust which, more than any other factor or event, increased the average member of Jewry's sympathy towards Zionism as a pro-active answer to the troubles that Jewry faced.

The Zionist attitude to the Fellowship as anathema to the rest of Jewry must be viewed in the context of the time. It was distasteful enough that a body like the Fellowship should choose to make its public appearance in the wake of the White Paper, the Zionist capture of the Board of Deputies and especially the Holocaust. But to do so at a time when the crucial decisions over Palestine's future would be made, and to oppose Zionism in the non-Jewish world, where the appearance of Jewish unity on Palestine was particularly important, presented Zionism with a direct challenge to its claim that all of Jewry was united behind the goal of a Jewish state in Palestine.

Added to this was the fact that there had always existed a willingness in the Zionist mind to view Jewish anti-Zionism as nothing but a branch of Gentile anti-Zionism. An anonymous report, written during the war and circulated among the Zionist leadership, claimed that after the war a 'group of leading and influential British Jews' would work with Gentile anti-Zionists against Zionism and would attack the Zionists as 'unpatriotic foreign-born Jews' and 'label all such Jews as Jewish Nazis'. This memorandum ended with a warning that these Jews, with the co-operation of Gentile allies, would attempt to replace the Zionist leadership of Anglo-Jewry with a 'pure British–Jewish community'.[9]

In itself this memorandum means little as an historical

document (it was anonymous and named neither the Jews nor Gentiles that it suspected of planning this strategy), but it does show how the Zionist activists viewed future Jewish anti-Zionism as part of a conspiracy with Gentiles. It is in the context of this perception that one should view the Zionist response to the Fellowship.

From the time of its public mobilisation, the Zionists continually and at every opportunity presented the Fellowship as a political body attempting to oppose Zionism in the non-Jewish world, rather than as a religious body motivated by a desire to enrich Jewish life. Dr Ernst Cohen, writing in 1945, accused the Fellowship of using 'the Jewish creed ... [to] weaken the Jewish fight for Palestine'.[10] Zionists continued to argue in this way until the body's demise, with the *Zionist Review*, in an editorial in November 1948, stating that although the Fellowship had claimed that its main goal was to strengthen the religious life of all sections of Jewry 'the real purpose of its establishment was, of course, to conduct anti-Zionist propaganda on a high level behind a religious camouflage'.[11]

Councillor Emanuel Snowman encapsulated the general Zionist position when he warned the political session of the north-west London regional conference of the Zionist Federation, in November 1945, of 'the need to consolidate against fifth columnists ... they are small in number and supported by only a very tiny number of our community, but our enemies are using them for their anti-Zionist purposes'.[12]

As such, Zionist disgust at the efforts of Jewish anti-Zionists was much greater and much harsher in tone than it was in regard to Gentile anti-Zionists like those on the CAA. Though individuals like Spears and Storrs were held in disdain there was an underlying acceptance, perhaps even an understanding, on the part of Zionists that these men, so under the spell of Arabia and owing nothing to Jewish aspirations, were supportive of the Arab cause.

But for Jews to oppose a Jewish state in Palestine at this time of crisis, and in so doing to give credence to Gentile anti-Zionists, was unacceptable. A Joint Palestine Appeal (JPA) supplement, distributed with the *Zionist Review* in the wake of the Anglo-American Committee hearings, summed up this attitude when it stated: 'We could take in our stride the threats and slander [of non-Jewish anti-Zionists] ... but the protracted testimony of gentlemen of the "Jewish Faith" was more than the long-suffering Jews and humane non-Jews could bear with equanimity.'[13] Thus, in the words of Walter Pinner, a leading figure of provincial Zionism, the battle against Jewish anti-Zionists became 'our most distasteful task'. Pinner also argued that it was impossible to prevent such Jews from 'dissociating themselves from Jewry', and in doing so he was expressing an opinion that other leading English Zionists, such as Labour MP Barnett Janner, would also set out.[14]

This presentation of Jewish anti-Zionists as a distinct, separate and isolated group within Jewry became a central part of the Zionist attack on the Fellowship. *New Judea*, in an early article on the body, was of the opinion that

> The concept of *kol yisrael chaverim* has an historical significance. It means comradeship of all Israel; it means true solidarity, sharing Jewish suffering, ideals, aspirations and hopes for the future. The Fellowship reject this concept and real meaning of kol yisrael, yet presume to take the name of the Jewish Fellowship.[15]

There was also an attempt to analyse why this alienation from the rest of Jewry had occurred. At the most superficial level the existence of such a body was put down to social position and wealth, with the statement in *New Judea* that 'those Jews who do not support Zionism [come] from the wealthy class' embodying this view.[16] But this was too much of a generalisation to be accepted as the definitive reason for what was perceived to be such anti-Jewish behaviour.

Thus Zionist commentators delved deeper into what motivated Jews such as those that made up the Fellowship. For example, in a 1947 article, Zionist publicist Harry Sacher asked why certain Jews attempted to fight their heritage by taking sides with the Christian majority.[17] Though undoubtedly a piece of Zionist propaganda it should also be seen as an example of Jewish bewilderment at the actions of certain co-religionists.

Barnet Litvinoff, another Zionist commentator, looked to 'Self-Hatred Among Jews', the pioneering work of the American social psychologist Kurt Lewin, to explain the attacks on Zionism by Rabbi Dr Israel Mattuck, spiritual leader of the Fellowship. Litvinoff saw in Mattuck an 'interesting example of self-hatred'. But more generally he also saw in the Fellowship's role within Jewry a perfect example of Lewin's analysis of leaders from the periphery, those influential Jews, who, ashamed of their religion, attempted to limit the action of their co-religionists by taking a position of leadership within the community as a way of silencing the vast majority of Jews with whom they disagreed.[18]

In the Zionist use of arguments such as this, one begins to see that there existed a tendency to view those members of Jewry who made up the Fellowship, as separate from the majority of Jews, not only in their position over Zionism, but in fundamental and irreconcilable respects. Maurice Cohen, honorary secretary of the Zionist Federation, speaking in the aftermath of the publication of the Anglo-American report, stated that there was no possibility of compromise with Jews who opposed Zionism because 'their aims are essentially different to ours'.[19] This view was reiterated constantly throughout these years, most notably in an editorial on the Fellowship at the time of the body's winding up in 1948, which concluded with the observation 'the difference between them [the Fellowship and the Zionists] is in quality and kind'.[20]

In these claims one sees the implications of what Freya Stark had referred to in her Scylla and Charybdis metaphor of 1943. For the Fellowship came to be viewed as the concrete expression of a lack of Jewish self-respect that was believed to be at the heart of the division between Zionist and anti-Zionist Jews. It was in these terms that the anti-Zionist statements of Julian Franklyn, the secretary of the Fellowship, were dismissed because 'for every self-respecting Jew his views are beyond contempt'.[21] Similarly, the 1947 Fellowship 'Memorandum on the Jewish Problem', sent to the Foreign Secretary and to ambassadors at the Court of St James, stressed Jewish loyalty to the nations in which they lived and vigorously attacked political Zionism. This prompted the Zionist response 'could spiritual servility and lack of dignity go further?'[22] As the Zionist columnist Zakan (pseud.) asked rhetorically: 'Take our Jewish Fellowship ... can any other people boast of such strange growths? Of course not, because among other peoples self-respect would not allow a man to deprecate his own spiritual inheritance.'[23]

THE JEWISH FELLOWSHIP AND LIBERAL JUDAISM

There is a certain credence in the above Zionist claims, especially in regard to the 1947 'Memorandum on the Jewish Problem' that was sent to the Foreign Office. Even Bernard Burrows of the Foreign

Office, writing to Basil Henriques to acknowledge receipt of this document, saw the Fellowship's actions as overly deferent, informing Henriques that 'it is not of course necessary for your organisation to seek permission to communicate this memorandum'.[24]

However, the Zionist portrayal of the Fellowship as a body motivated by a lack of self-respect was primarily a continuation of the age-old Jewish (adopted by the Zionist movement) accusation that Jews who looked away from Jewry and into the non-Jewish world did so out of Jewish self-hate.[25] What made the case of the Fellowship an interesting variation on this theme was the use of the intimate connection of that body with the progressive Jewish movement in Britain to emphasise its betrayal of Jewry and to nullify it as a valid alternative to Zionism within Jewry.

Progressive Judaism, most commonly divided into Reform and Liberal Judaism, had its roots in Germany in the early years of the nineteenth century and emerged in response to changes in the political, social and cultural conditions brought about by the emancipation of the Jews. It manifested itself in different forms in various countries. But in general terms the progressive movement differed from Orthodox Judaism in its belief that it was legitimate to make changes in the formulations of Jewish belief or in the codification of Jewish law. This resulted most noticeably in an attempt to adapt the synagogue service to the modern world, which saw a shortening of the liturgy and the presentation of sermons, and even some prayers, in the vernacular rather than Hebrew.

Reform Judaism, was first introduced into England in 1840, with the formation of the West London Synagogue. But during the latter part of the nineteenth century, the British variety of Reform developed along conservative lines and kept many of the traditions of Orthodoxy. Liberal Judaism, which espoused a more radical reinterpretation regarding both Orthodox theology and practice, grew out of Reform and first appeared in England with the formation of the Religious Union in 1901 and the formation of the Liberal Synagogue in 1911.[26]

Religious leaders of both of these branches of Judaism in Britain, such as Rabbi Curtis Cassell, the Revd Dr Harold Reinhart (senior minister of West London Synagogue) and Rabbi Gerhard Graf (minister at Bradford and Sinai Synagogue, Leeds), were all avid anti-Zionists in these years and lent support to the Fellowship and its spiritual leader, Rabbi Dr Israel Mattuck. Reinhart was a member of the Fellowship council. Rabbis Graf and Cassell contributed anti-Zionist articles to the fellowship paper the *Jewish Outlook*.

Mattuck, the Rabbi of the Liberal Synagogue and the religious head of the Liberal movement, came to symbolise the domination of the Fellowship by progressive Jews, with the leading Zionist publicist Paul Goodman describing the Fellowship as 'a number of English men of Jewish faith inspired by the leader of a Synagogue [Mattuck]'.[27]

The most vocal lay leaders of the Fellowship were also closely involved in the British progressive Jewish movement. In 1945 Colonel Louis Gluckstein became president of the Liberal Synagogue, while the following year Colonel Robert Henriques became chairman of the Association of Synagogues of Great Britain, the umbrella body for all Reform synagogues in the country, and held the position until 1952. Lord Justice Cohen, Fellowship president Sir Jack Brunel Cohen, and Fellowship secretary Julian Franklyn all served on the council of the West London Liberal Synagogue. While Leon Rees, treasurer of the Fellowship, and Ben Moss (a leading Fellowship spokesman at the Board of Deputies) were leading members of the St George's Settlement Synagogue.

Fellowship chairman Basil Henriques was both founder and warden of this settlement synagogue and it was he who more than any other of the lay leaders of the Fellowship symbolised the close relationship between Liberal Judaism and anti-Zionism. Indeed, one of the few things that Zionists and anti-Zionists seemed to agree on was the central position held by Henriques within the Fellowship. Both Selig Brodetsky, in his memoirs, and Colonel Louis Gluckstein, in a letter to Sir Edward Spears, described Henriques' role in exactly the same words: 'the moving spirit behind the Fellowship'.[28]

This close connection to progressive Judaism of the leading and most publicly known Fellowship members was significant because there existed a great schism between Orthodox and progressive Judaism within Jewry at this time (which exists up to this day). The vast majority of the Anglo-Jewish community (regardless of their actual level of religious observance) identified with the traditional form of Orthodoxy. And in turn this engendered a deep suspicion of the progressive section of the community.

The divide within Jewry was not disputed by the progressive movement. For example, in October 1945 the *Synagogue Review*, the organ of the Association of British Synagogues, acknowledged this cleavage in an editorial that admitted that the 'orthodox party has been overwhelmingly superior in both numbers and organisation'.[29] At the annual meeting of the Liberal Synagogue in June 1945, at which Gluckstein was appointed president, an official complaint was made in regard to the bad relationship that existed between Liberal Jewry and the rest of the community.[30] While Colonel Robert Henriques writing in 1946 on this divide in Jewry was of the view that 'so called orthodox Jewry has denounced the so called progressive movement in Judaism as a festering sore to be excised, or an evil tumour to be rooted out'.[31]

Zionist polemics concentrated on this seemingly intimate relationship between the Fellowship and the progressive leadership as a way of isolating the Fellowship from the mainstream of Jewry. The *Zionist Review* in an article on the founding of the Fellowship, in December 1944, stated 'it is gratifying that Zionists and representatives of religious Jewry, except members of the Liberal Synagogue, have not found it possible to join Mr Henriques's organisation'.[32]

Indeed, through these years a central part of the propaganda battle against the Fellowship became an attack on progressive Judaism, the 'deformed congregation [Reform congregation]',[33] rather than on anti-Zionist Jews who happened to be Reform or Liberal Jews. The *Zionist Review* was consistently derogatory towards the Liberal Jewish movement, which it termed as 'the cold theology so foreign to living Judaism'.[34]

Particular animosity was directed towards the Bernard Baron Settlement, not coincidental considering that it was the section of the Liberal movement personally associated with Basil Henriques. In 1943 the paper had claimed that Henriques was 'only Jewish in name' and that the Jewish children under his care were under threat.[35] It continued in this vein throughout the post-war era, condemning Henriques' attempts to make 'gentlemen out of little Yiddish boys' by means of indoctrinating them with the belief that 'in Liberal Judaism and anti-Zionism lay the future happiness of the Jews'.[36]

Harry Sacher was even more specific, accusing Henriques of being a Liberal Jewish anti-Zionist with the aim of Christianising, and hence destroying, Judaism.[37] This view of Henriques was also emphasised in the *Jewish Chronicle* in 1945 when he was referred to as an 'extreme anti-Orthodox ... whose anti-Orthodox activities are abhorrent to the vast majority of Jews in this country'.[38]

But perhaps the most potent example of Zionist propaganda

devoted to attacking the Fellowship as a Liberal entity and the Liberal movement as an anti-Zionist entity, was the *Gates of Zion*, the quarterly review of the Central Synagogue Council of the Zionist Federation, under the editorship of Paul Goodman. This paper continually attacked the Fellowship's links with the Liberal movement as proof of its lack of Jewishness and its isolation from the rest of Jewry. The first editorial of the first issue attacked the 'British Israelites' (a common and derogatory term denoting anti-Zionist Liberal Jews) and highlighted the failure of the Fellowship to gain support within the Orthodox community, a fact that was reiterated and deemed 'highly significant' in the paper's subsequent attacks.[39] Raphael Loewe, a Fellowship leader and Reader in Rabbinics at the University of Cambridge, was constantly preoccupied with the need to counter this aspect of Zionist propaganda and to show that the Fellowship represented Orthodoxy.[40]

The Fellowship as a body shared Loewe's concerns, and it was Fellowship policy to present its principles and objectives from an Orthodox perspective in both its literature and public appearances. For example, in the first educational pamphlet published by the Fellowship, *What is Judaism?*, Basil Henriques presented the Fellowship argument from the Liberal perspective and Dr Alfred Marmorstein, Professor of Talmud, Midrash and Liturgy at Jews' College, presented the traditional position.[41] Secondly, the Fellowship also attempted to counter the Zionist accusation that it was only a body of progressive Jews, by stressing that some of its leading members were also leading members of Orthodox Jewry.

The most obvious example of this was that both the president Sir Robert Waley Cohen and vice-president, the Hon. Ewen Montagu, of the governing body of the majority of Orthodox synagogues, the United Synagogue, were founding members of the Fellowship. Indeed, the Zionist attacks on Waley Cohen at this time were so strong precisely because his ranking position on the United Synagogue gave credence to the Fellowship claim that it represented the Orthodox tradition within Jewry.[42] For example, Mr H. Grunis, writing in the *Jewish Chronicle*, called on Waley Cohen to resign from the Fellowship because of his position on the United Synagogue. While a similar letter in the same paper by Mr J. Mendel, a member of the United Synagogue council, called on Waley Cohen, Montagu, Henry Gledhill and Frank Samuel, all honorary officers of the United Synagogue, to resign from the Fellowship council.[43]

Indeed, the size of the Fellowship's delegation (15 members) to the Anglo-American Committee, which included Ewen Montagu, vice-president of the United Synagogue, A. Alan Mocatta, warden of the Spanish and Portuguese Congregation, and Revd Bueno de Mesquita, retired senior minister of the Sephardi community, must be primarily seen as an effort to stress (as Brunel Cohen informed the committee) that the Fellowship 'represents every shade of Orthodoxy, members of the United Synagogue, the Liberal Synagogue, Reform and Sephardic'.[44] Indeed Basil Henriques wrote to the *Jewish Chronicle* after the Fellowship appearance to stress that the delegation had been represented by many leading Orthodox members.[45] This claim was rejected in further correspondence by both Joseph Nabarro, who denied that the Sephardi community *en masse* supported the Fellowship, and J. Mendel, who denounced Henriques for trying to pretend that the Fellowship delegation represented the United Synagogue.[46]

In May 1947 the *Jewish Outlook* condemned the attacks on the Fellowship in the Zionist press as 'malicious', precisely because 'its intention is to traduce the Jewish Fellowship and convey the impression that the Jewish Fellowship is simply an accretion to Liberal Judaism', adding that up to 75 per cent of the Fellowship membership was Orthodox.[47] In the same month Harold Soref, chairman of the AJA's publications committee and editor of the AJA journal the *Jewish Monthly*, also took up this issue. Soref, a staunch anti-Zionist, represented the Liberal Synagogue at the Board of Deputies and although he was not a member of the Fellowship he supported and advised the body and attended Fellowship executive meetings.[48] He especially attacked the *Gates of Zion* for its 'heresy hunt' and 'sordid and unseemly tactics' against Liberal Judaism.[49]

More than this, the Fellowship attacked the Zionist claims on the Liberal issue as hypocritical, coming as they did from a movement that counted among its public spokesmen individuals such as Professor Lewis Namier. Namier, Professor of Modern History at the University of Manchester (1931–57), who had served as political secretary of the Jewish Agency in London (1929–31), was a fierce critic of Jewish anti-Zionists, whom he referred to as 'the judeocentric assimilationists'.[50] However, he was also a man who had married outside the Jewish religion not once but twice, and on the second occasion had been baptised into the Russian Orthodox Church. Thus the *Jewish Outlook* wondered how apostate Zionists such as Namier as well as Zionist atheists could have the gall to attack them for their close connection with Liberal Judaism, asking 'if this of their leaders, what of the rank and file?'[51]

Regardless of the validity of these claims – and it should be noted that Namier defended this seemingly contradictory position with the argument that although the 'charge of irreligion is sometimes levelled against Zionists ... the Jew who works for the Return, and still more the one who effects it, bears the truest testimony to his faith',[52] the overriding impression within Jewry throughout these years was that the Fellowship was an anti-Zionist body motivated in part by its relationship with Liberal Judaism. As George Weber, a commentator on Jewish affairs, soberly stated in a 1946 review of Anglo-Jewry, 'the lay and religious leaders of Progressive Judaism are hostile to the Jewish National Home and play a decisive part in the Jewish Fellowship'.[53]

The Zionist attack on the Fellowship as a Liberal body was first and foremost a propaganda tactic that played on the prejudices that existed within the community to make real the Zionist claim that 'the Jewish Fellowship ... excludes the overwhelming part of Anglo-Jewry'.[54]

Undoubtedly, there was reason to believe that the progressive movement was indeed anti-Zionist. In 1946, for example, prominent Fellowship leaders Basil Henriques, the Revd Harold Reinhart, Ben Moss, Lilly H. Montagu and Rabbi Israel Mattuck all attended the World Congress of Progressive Judaism. And at this conference the Liberal Rabbi M.C. Weiler called on Liberals to eliminate the anti-Zionist element as it prevented the Liberal movement from gaining the support of the masses.[55]

However, there was no unanimity on the issue of Zionism within the progressive movement, even within the Liberal section. Weiler, a Liberal Rabbi from South Africa, was himself a leader of Zionism. So were other leaders of progressive Jewry, especially Rabbis Silver and Wise in the United States.

The same held true for England. This can clearly be seen in an illuminating report in the *Synagogue Review*, on a meeting of the weekly discussion group at the Liberal Synagogue. The report stated that during the discussion a Miss Henriques had defended the right of the Fellowship to be heard at the Anglo-American Committee. This view was opposed by the Revd Goldberg who stated that the Fellowship was well aware that the majority of Jews both Liberal and Orthodox were 'diametrically opposed' to its appearance before the Anglo-American Committee.[56] While Basil

Henriques writing a decade later admitted that although in his view there were very few ardent Zionists who were Liberal Jews, the Liberal movement never took an official position either for or against Zionism.[57]

Yet the Zionist success in instilling the view of the Fellowship as an un-Jewish Liberal body within Jewry cannot be overemphasised. For example, in a report in the *Jewish Chronicle* on a Fellowship meeting in Yorkshire in 1946 the correspondent reported that throughout the evening 'we were told we should spread the gospel of the Jewish Fellowship, "gospel" being the right word', and continued 'I cannot remember whether the meeting concluded with the sign of the cross or the double cross'.[58]

While a letter by Harold Morris in the same paper condemning Rabbi Mattuck's position on Palestine is only one of a myriad of letters written to the 'Organ of Anglo-Jewry' in these years that highlight the Zionist success in presenting anti-Zionism, Liberal Judaism and the Fellowship as one and the same, sharing a common isolation from Jewry: for Morris, 'one thing is quite certain ... In their rejection of Palestine as a Jewish state ... Liberal Jews have forfeited all rights to be part of Jewry at all.'[59]

Such was the effect of this argument in isolating the Fellowship that even members of Agudath Yisra'el, a body opposed, like the Fellowship, to the creation of a Jewish state, could not support the Fellowship or even condone it, because of the overriding perception that it was a Liberal assimilationist body lacking halakhic validity and outside the community of Israel. This was demonstrated by a letter, sent in the wake of the AACIP report, signed simply 'Agudist'. The letter stated:

> As an Agudist of many years standing ... it seems to me interesting that the only two Jewish bodies ... really pleased with the report of the Anglo-American Committee ... Agudah and the Fellowship ... [and yet] ... we find it difficult to cooperate with you because we do not consider most of your members Jews.[60]

THE FELLOWSHIP IN THE NON-JEWISH WORLD: MEMORIES OF 1917

The Fellowship made no attempt to conceal the fact that it was greatly concerned with setting out its position, which to Zionists meant its anti-Zionist position, in the non-Jewish world. A list of Jewish Fellowship aims drawn up at a meeting of the executive in March 1944 stated that the body looked to

> Co-operate with fellow citizens of other creeds in strengthening the influence of religion in the life of the nation, in bearing the responsibility of citizenship and national loyalty and in promoting the highest standards of honour and service in public and private life.[61]

Joseph Leftwich (who opposed the politicisation of the Fellowship) called for this 'loyalty and honour' clause to be removed as it 'savoured of apologetics'. But rather than taking his advice the executive agreed with Brunel Cohen that this section was very important and decided to re-emphasise this goal once more at the end of the document.[62]

The Fellowship also made a conscious decision to oppose Zionism in public. Brunel Cohen in an early speech admitted that the Fellowship's opposition to the Jewish state policy 'entails the necessity to combat propaganda'. This objective was reiterated by other Fellowship leaders, defended in editorials in the *Jewish Outlook* and endorsed by way of resolution at Fellowship annual meetings.[63]

In September 1944 Brunel Cohen and Colonel Robert Henriques sent letters to *The Times* stating their opposition to the creation of a Jewish Brigade (a military formation of Jewish volunteers within the British army).[64] Brunel Cohen's letter, which he signed in his capacity as president of the Fellowship, can be viewed as the first official effort of this organisation to make use of the media in order to fight Zionism, something that Brunel Cohen admitted in his address to the Fellowship council after the publication of the letters.[65]

Within the Zionist movement there had always been a sensitivity to what was perceived to be anti-Zionist Jews using the general press to oppose Zionist aspirations. As early as 1917 Leon Simon argued against an essay by the influential Jewish anti-Zionist, Lucien Wolf, in the *Edinburgh Review*,[66] primarily in terms of the damage that his article could do by misleading an uninformed non-Jewish readership that was unaware of the 'ignorance and half-truths' of the Jewish opponents of Zionism.[67]

Given this belief, it is not surprising that the Zionist response to the Henriques and Brunel Cohen letters was both immediate and fierce. Barnett Janner MP urged Jews 'not to rush into print' with views that they knew to be contrary to the wishes of Anglo-Jewry,[68] while there was a rally at the Glasgow Jewish Institute condemning the letters within a week of their publication.[69] An editorial in the *Jewish Chronicle* gave expression to the prevalent Jewish attitude to the letters when it condemned the introduction of the Fellowship to 'public cognisance … in a non-Jewish paper' and added that it was 'tragic that even before its existence [was] announced in the Jewish press or world it used *The Times*'.[70]

The Fellowship's decision to hold a press conference to announce its existence at a London hotel in November 1944, just a few months after the publication of these letters, fostered the belief that it was appealing primarily to a non-Jewish constituency through the use of the press. This had a basic truth to it, despite the fact that the Moyne assassination occurred on the same day as the press conference, and thus, as the Fellowship admitted, the press conference received 'only meagre publicity' and was 'crowded out of the papers'.[71]

Likewise, a *Jewish Chronicle* report on a meeting, held by the Fellowship in May 1946 at Harrogate Synagogue Hall (in the wealthy Jewish community of Harrogate, Yorkshire), noted that Basil Henriques had invited non-Jewish reporters to the talk despite being asked by the Synagogue not to do so, and as such the Synagogue refused to allow the press men into the meeting when they arrived.[72]

Apart from appealing to the non-Jewish world as a way of fighting Zionism, the Fellowship's use of the non-Jewish media was inevitable given its leadership's conviction that it was unable to receive an objective hearing in the Jewish press. The *Synagogue Review*, which under editorial guidance was fiercely anti-Zionist during these years, argued in 1945 that 'the whole orientation of these papers [the Jewish press]' was Zionist and criticised the fact that 'Palestine propaganda tends to monopolise the Jewish reader's eyes'.[73] This was a view reiterated by Brunel Cohen who informed the Anglo-American Committee that anybody who studied the Jewish press 'might come to the conclusion that there was simply no other point of view [than Zionist]'.[74]

This use of the non-Jewish press as a response to the lack of support for the Fellowship's position in the Jewish media highlights just how isolated the body was within Jewry. But this was of little comfort to English Zionists because the Fellowship's use of the general press to oppose Zionist aspirations evoked memories of the notorious letter to *The Times* sent in 1917 by leading anti-Zionist Jews opposed to the British government's support for what would ultimately be the Balfour Declaration.[75]

This letter was issued by the heads of the Board of Deputies Conjoint Committee[76] without permission from the leadership of either the Board or the AJA, and both bodies subsequently censured the signatories. Nevertheless, the Zionist movement was united in its belief that the letter had been harmful to Zionist aspirations and that its really damaging effects had not been within Jewry, for if anything this letter marked the beginning of the process of Zionists gaining a foothold in the communal institutions, especially the Board of Deputies.[77]

Rather, the letter's real harm had been in its effect on Gentile opinion. As David Vital argues, the decision of the leaders of the Conjoint Committee to go public in *The Times* was 'an effort to meet the publicists and polemicists of Zionism on the ground where they had been evidently making the most progress: among members of the non-Jewish social and political elite'.[78] As such this decision was a watershed not so much because of the contents of the letter but because it was sent at all. For it was believed that this intervention in *The Times* had raised in the Gentile mind the possibility that a prestigious and significant section within Jewry opposed Zionist aspirations, and as such was the prime reason that the Cabinet decided to water down the original wording of the Balfour Declaration.

Chaim Weizmann, recalling this incident in his memoirs, was of the view that although active Jewish opposition to Zionism was very small 'it was capable of working great harm'.[79] And in 1942 Lavy Bakstansky (secretary of the Zionist Federation and a leading Zionist at the Board of Deputies) appealed to Louis Gluckstein not to oppose Zionism in public, reminding him that '25 years ago people like you attempted to kill the Balfour Declaration …[you] failed but managed to change its formulation … which cost many lives'.[80] And an article in the *Zionist Review* entitled 'Remember 1917', written shortly after the publication of the Brunel Cohen and Henriques letters in *The Times*, concluded with the view that 'the result of the intervention by notables of British Jewry was disastrous'.[81]

Despite the fact that Fellowship leaders would denounce this Zionist portrayal of the events of 1917, specifically Weizmann's recollection of the affair in his memoirs, as 'grotesquely untrue and unjust',[82] there was much credence placed in the Zionist interpretation of events in 1917, even by anti-Zionists. For example, Sir Ronald Storrs, writing in 1937, was of the opinion that the two most formidable opponents of the Balfour Declaration were those British Jews who preferred to remain 100 per cent 'Englishmen of the non-conformist persuasion' and the India office under its Jewish secretary of state, Edwin Montagu.[83]

The Arab Office in a 1945 pamphlet on the Balfour Declaration stated that its importance was 'above all' the fact that 'a large body of eminent British Jews and leading representatives of Jewry' opposed it publicly. The pamphlet continued, under the heading 'Anti-Zionist Jews', to recount the efforts of men such as Montagu, Lucien Wolf and Sir Lionel Abrahams to block the Balfour Declaration.[84] Twenty years later this was still the view, with an Arab League pamphlet of 1967 stating the opinion that the Jewish anti-Zionists of 1917 led by Montagu 'put up a strong fight that led to the watering down of the original draft'.[85]

If the end of the First World War had provided the backdrop for the Balfour Declaration, then all agreed that the end of the Second World War was a prelude to a permanent decision on the future status of Palestine. It is in this context that the emergence of the Fellowship and its propaganda efforts in the non-Jewish world must be seen. For the shadows of 1917 still clouded Zionist aspirations and the momentous events of 1917, the issuance of the Balfour Declaration and the efforts of group of important Jews to oppose it, became the benchmark for the actions of the Fellowship in the post-war world.

Moshe Rosette in a private letter in January 1944 summed up the Zionist fear when he stated that 'I believe a conflict in Jewish life is coming which will make 1917 look like a dress rehearsal.'[86] Thus it is hardly surprising that the same man, speaking in his capacity as a member of the Board of Deputies (Montague Road Beth Hamidrash), during a debate in April 1945, attacked the Fellowship for going outside the community and using the non-Jewish press to fight Zionism, arguing that this would result in great harm to Zionism and the Jewish people.[87]

Rosette's view was echoed by the *Zionist Review* which condemned the Fellowship for 'using methods of propaganda which are nothing but a menace to the community',[88] arguing that 'the worst possible thing' Jews could do was to oppose each other in the British press, because this was a direct threat to Jewish defence.[89] Indeed, the Board's defence committee (responsible for ensuring the security of the community) did examine the Fellowship's threat to communal safety after being contacted by Isaac Dartle, an indignant member of the community, who made an official complaint after attending a meeting of the Paddington branch of the Fellowship.

The committee also sent a report on the Fellowship to Ivan Greenberg, in his capacity as editor of the *Jewish Chronicle*, to make him aware of the Fellowship's public statements.[90] Dartle also contacted the *Jewish Chronicle* and had a letter published attacking what he termed the Fellowship's 'campaign of abuse' in the Gentile world against the majority of Jewry, and concluding that this effort was 'earning them, and rightly, the contempt not only of the community but of the non-Jews whose favours Mr Henriques and his fellow members so obsequiously pursue'.[91]

THE *JEWISH CHRONICLE* AND THE JEWISH FELLOWSHIP

The extent of the Fellowship's isolation within Jewry can be seen in the attitude of the *Jewish Chronicle*, the flagship paper of Anglo-Jewry, to this body. Throughout these years the Zionist leadership in Britain viewed the *Jewish Chronicle* as an obstacle to Zionist aspirations, and leading Zionists were continually corresponding with Ivan Greenberg (editor, 1937–46)[92] about the perceived anti-Zionist position of the newspaper.

Councillor Abraham Moss (representative of the Council of Manchester and Salford Jews on the Zionist Federation) wrote to Greenberg in 1944 pleading that the *Jewish Chronicle*, because of 'its prestige', had to support the Zionist goals.[93] While Moshe Rosette, writing in the same month, informed Greenberg that he was 'astonished to think' that the *Jewish Chronicle* could be opposed to Zionist aspirations.[94]

Greenberg took offence at what was termed the 'smear campaign' against the paper in the Zionist press.[95] He also insisted that he shared the same objectives and the same enemies as the Zionists but that he felt that the Zionist obsession with total dominance of the community was hurting not helping the movement. As such he stood by his editorial position on the basis that it was the duty of a non-party paper to provide a forum for all elements within Jewry to set out their positions.[96] Yet even after Greenberg had resigned in the summer of 1946 (ironically, he was replaced by his assistant editor John Shaftesley, because it was felt he was too sympathetic to Zionist extremists in Palestine), the paper continued to be attacked as 'the mouthpiece of the Order of Trembling Israelites'.[97]

The Zionist attack on the *Jewish Chronicle* was presented primarily in terms of the impact that this paper's opposition to Zionism would have on the non-Jewish world, where it would be a 'Godsend to the enemies of the Jewish national revival'.[98] Yet despite the Zionist claims that the *Jewish Chronicle* was anti-Zionist, and that this was having a devastating effect in the non-Jewish world, the reality was that on the truly defining benchmark of Jewish anti-Zionism – attitudes to the Fellowship – this newspaper held a position very close to that of the Zionists.

The *Jewish Chronicle* was extremely harsh on the Fellowship both in its editorial comments and in its reports on the body's activities. Its first editorial on the Jewish Fellowship, following the letters by Robert Henriques and Brunel Cohen in *The Times* on the Jewish Brigade, attacked both Brunel Cohen and Henriques personally, stating that the Henriques letter 'would make every self-respecting Jew blush' (like the Zionist polemics, equating Jewish anti-Zionism with a lack of self-respect), and continued by accusing him of 'indulging in a disloyal impertinence to Jewry'.[99]

This same editorial concluded with a statement that was to encapsulate the isolated position of the Fellowship within Jewry throughout its existence, when it stressed that the Fellowship did not appeal to the Orthodox Jew, the AJA or the Board of Deputies, and that 'whether intended or not ... [the] avowedly anti-Zionist movement ... seems to have started off on a somewhat strange course of anti-everything, for a body which has chosen the nice chummy sounding title of Fellowship'.[100]

In the first half of 1946, a time when tension was rising in anticipation of the publication of the Anglo-American report (which was followed by the arrest by the British army of Yishuv leaders), the *Jewish Chronicle* continued to present the Fellowship in the harshest terms. A correspondent who attended and reported in detail on two Fellowship meetings at this time was damning of the Fellowship and its position.

Reporting on a February meeting he was of the view that some of the claims by the Fellowship speakers were 'so wickedly libellous of Jews as to be unfit to print' and described the Fellowship as a non-humanitarian, anti-Zionist, assimilationist body, and as if to emphasise the damaging nature of these three characteristics he concluded his report with these lines from Shakespeare: 'Mine eyes were full of tears, I could not see, and yet salt water blinds them not so much but they could see a sort of traitor here.'[101] In his next report in May 1946 he was equally appalled and could only muster the strength to say 'I cannot sufficiently emphasise how distressing the whole thing was'.[102]

One must put these denunciations into their proper context. They were made despite the Zionist claims that the paper was anti-Zionist.[103] They were also made despite the private efforts of Fellowship leaders to influence Greenberg into taking a positive view of their organisation.

Joseph Leftwich, whom Greenberg admired, lobbied the editor in the early days of the Fellowship and sent him copies of the confidential minutes of Fellowship executive meetings, in an attempt to prove that it would be possible for him, if given the opportunity and encouragement, to lead the Fellowship away from its negative (anti-Zionist) inclinations and towards its positive (religious) principles.[104]

In the wake of the publication of the Brunel Cohen and Henriques letters in *The Times*, and undoubtedly sensing that their publication was a miscalculation in terms of the response they evoked within the community, Fellowship chairman Basil Henriques wrote a personal letter to Greenberg (who was himself a strong supporter of the Jewish Brigade proposal), informing him that he was 'desperately keen that the Jewish Fellowship should not be wrecked over the letters to *The Times*'. Henriques continued by arguing that the religious goals of the Fellowship would be hurt if the body was condemned in the paper and concluded with the plea 'Don't let your momentary anger overcome your vision of what the Jewish Fellowship can achieve.'[105]

However, as has been seen, the *Jewish Chronicle*'s anger with the Fellowship was not 'momentary', and the paper ignored both the general appeals by Leftwich and Henriques' specific plea regarding the letters in *The Times*. Indeed, so aggressive was the editorial attack on Henriques in response to his letter that the paper had to retract its remarks and apologise in the following issue.[106] In short, under the editorship of both Greenberg and then Shaftesley, the 'Organ of Anglo-Jewry' was no supporter of the Fellowship, something which once more highlights the isolation of the body within Jewry.

DANIEL LIPSON: MP AND PUBLIC ANTI-ZIONIST

The Fellowship saw in Daniel Lipson, the outspoken anti-Zionist Jewish MP, one of its greatest assets in the public fight against Zionism. The *Jewish Outlook*, applauded Lipson as 'the one voice and one voice only speaking as a Jew [who] saved the Anglo-Jewish community from total misrepresentation', maintaining that this 'has won him [the] grateful admiration of thousands of Jewish people'.[107]

The majority Jewish view of Lipson was in fact totally different. The *Jewish Chronicle* in an editorial in June 1945, reflecting on the achievements of Jewish MPs in the outgoing parliament, concluded that although Lipson had 'undoubtedly grown in parliamentary stature [he has] been from the specifically Jewish point of view [of] no assistance whatsoever ... if anything the reverse'.[108] Moreover, an editorial in March of the following year fiercely attacked the 'nauseating role' of Lipson and the 'snivelling contemptible meanness' of his position on Zionism, adding that his isolation could be seen by the lack of support he received from other Jewish MPs.

Indeed more often than not it was Jewish members, like Barnett Janner, who rose to condemn Lipson in the House. Perhaps the most striking example (to the great satisfaction of the Zionist press) was when Lieutenant-Colonel Harry Morris, MP for Sheffield Central, responded to a Lipson speech attacking Zionism with the words, 'I know the honourable gentleman very well. I know his background ... I know his family ... his father would turn in his grave if he could have heard his son speak as he did in this House.'[109]

Apart from the disgust at Lipson's open opposition to Zionism in the House (Paul Goodman called him the 'Ma Yuphis Id' of the House of Commons),[110] his real danger was in his efforts in the non-Jewish world. Hamabit (pseud.) attacked Lipson's anti-Zionism not because of the threat it posed within Jewry because 'from a Jewish point of view his opinions are of no account', but in terms of the false impression that he created in the non-Jewish world.[111]

Moshe Rosette recalled in a 1961 interview that it would have been 'an exaggeration' to say that the Jewish anti-Zionists had any effect on the Jewish community and added that the 'small lunatic fringe – the Jewish Fellowship – were never very effective ... never an effective counterblast to good Zionist propaganda'. However, he was less sure when discussing the effects of Lipson's anti-Zionism on the non-Jewish world. For, although he was of the opinion that Lipson was 'not an important man ... a reactionary man', he also recalled that because Lipson so openly acknowledged his Judaism in his attacks on Zionism it was natural for people to think that he 'represents Jews no less than any other fellow'.[112]

It is in this context that one must view the Zionist call, in response to Lipson's highly publicised anti-Zionist article published in the *Spectator* in November 1945, that although he was entitled to his views (he claimed that Jewry was a religious community not a nation and that political Zionism was an illegitimate creed opposed by the majority of Jews)[113] 'he must be honest enough to admit that he has no right to be a Jewish spokesman'.[114] The *Jewish Chronicle* in an editorial also in response to Lipson's article was even more specific in the opinion that 'all he does is give anti-Zionists in this country another opportunity of gloating over the vastly exaggerated division in the Jewish community on the Zionist issue, although Lipson and his clique represent a very small proportion of Jewry'.[115]

THE JEWISH FELLOWSHIP AND THE BOARD OF DEPUTIES

In 1917 Edwin Montagu, the Jewish anti-Zionist secretary of state for India, wrote to two of his cabinet colleagues, Lords Robert Cecil and Robert Milner, to take issue with their claim that his outspoken anti-Zionism was the position of but a small minority of English Jews. In his letter Montagu stated that in response to this claim by his esteemed colleagues he had 'set out to discover whether the Zionists are in a large minority as regards the Jews of the United Kingdom'.[116]

In Montagu's account, his investigations on this issue led him to the Board of Deputies, which 'I am told Zionists and non-Zionists alike would regard ... as the one body whose resolutions may be quoted as representing with some degree of correctness the opinion of the community as a whole'. The letter concluded with an example of the lack of support for Zionism among Board members, which enabled Montagu to conclude 'it is on this ... that the best claims to a statement that the majority of British Jews are Zionist can be based'.[117]

The Montagu letter is of interest in the context of the post-war era because it shows how the Board of Deputies was perceived to be a benchmark of whether or not the Jewish community was in support of Zionist aspirations. This belief in the importance of the Board engendered a debate within the community, not only among Zionist, non-Zionist and anti-Zionist Jews, but within the Zionist movement also.

This was defined primarily in terms of how best to use the Board to fight the claims and influence of those Jews opposed to Zionism. Selig Brodetsky, president of the Board of Deputies,[118] believed that the Zionists should use the Board to give legitimacy to Zionism, telling Alexander Easterman, the leading member of the British section of the World Jewish Congress, in 1942 that 'our duty as well as our interest as Zionists is to keep this organisation [the Board] in being and not destroy it ... we should use it'.[119]

When the Zionists achieved a majority at the Board in the communal elections of 1943, the internal debate intensified. Lavy Bakstansky, the influential secretary of the Zionist Federation, wanted the Zionists to use their majority to purge the anti-Zionist elements from the Board. This was opposed by Brodetsky who believed that it was to the advantage of Zionists that those opposed to Zionism remained inside the Board, and he called for the co-opting of leading non-Zionists and anti-Zionists on to the main committees of the Board (especially the executive, Palestine and foreign affairs committees).[120]

Regardless of the disagreements within Zionist ranks as to how best to make tactical use of their majority at the Board, all agreed that after the 1943 election it was impossible for anyone to claim that the community of Anglo-Jewry, as represented by the Board of Deputies, was opposed to the Zionist programme. In November 1944 the Board voted in favour of a statement on Palestine supporting the main goals of political Zionism and taking the unprecedented step of endorsing the Zionist call for a Jewish state or commonwealth in Palestine.[121] In Zionist eyes this symbolised the fact that the community of Anglo-Jewry was wholeheartedly in support of Zionist aspirations for a Jewish state. *New Judea* welcomed the Board's statement as 'an unequivocal endorsement of the Zionist claim by so important a representative body' and the

Zionist Review was of the view that the Board statement 'indicates clearly where British Jewry stands on the question of Palestine'.[122]

This paper took care to stress continually that the representative nature of the Board indicated the support for Zionism within Jewry. In 1944 it argued that there was 'no question that the masses of Anglo-Jewry fully recognise the representative character of the Board'; two years later it was reminding readers that 'never before in its long history was the Board so representative of the community'. While in 1948 readers were once more reminded that 'never in its history has the Board been so representative'.[123]

The importance that the Zionist leadership attached to the Board of Deputies' support for its programme can be seen by the fact that leading Zionists in England such as Joseph Linton, the political secretary of the Jewish Agency in London, were in constant communication with Board officials during these years, lobbying the Board's leadership to give support for Jewish Agency initiatives.[124]

The Fellowship refused to accept the Zionist assertion that its control of the Board of Deputies meant that it was representative of Jewry's stance on the Palestine issue and Zionism. Rather it blamed the existence of a 'Zionist caucus' that controlled the Board but had no right to pretend it represented the Jewish community *en masse*.[125] The Fellowship's central argument was that the Board had forfeited its right to claim that it represented the community because it had stopped acting in the interests of Anglo-Jewry when it had been taken over by an international Zionist movement which had no interest in representing British Jews, but rather saw the Board as a vehicle for its Jewish state policy.[126]

The Fellowship presented the Board as nothing but a tool of the Zionist movement or, as the *Jewish Outlook* called it, 'a branch of transatlantic and Middle Eastern political organisations' and 'a letter box of Great Russell Street [headquarters of the Zionist movement and the Jewish Agency in London]'.[127] For the Fellowship, the Board's support for the Jewish Agency's Palestine policy was the most obvious proof that it was nothing but a rubber stamp for international Zionism in all its guises (the Jewish Agency, the World Jewish Congress and the World Zionist Organisation).

Especially galling was the Board's tendency to stress in all its communications with the government that on the issue of Palestine it acted in support of the Jewish Agency. For example in a letter to George Hall, the colonial secretary in 1945, Sidney Salomon, the

Board's executive and press officer, after requesting that Jewish terrorist suspects in Palestine be given a hearing before deportation, stated that 'I am directed to add that this request is made with the knowledge of the Jewish Agency for Palestine'.[128] Given this it is hardly surprising that the Board's decision to refuse an invitation to the Palestine conference of 1947 unless the Jewish Agency first agreed to attend was presented in the Fellowship paper as proof that the Board's policy was being 'dictated by extremist leaders from abroad'.[129]

Others within Anglo-Jewry, most notably leading members of the AJA, such as Percy Cohen and Neville Laski, were also very critical of the Board's domination by political Zionists. The AJA had been the biggest loser when the Zionists gained control of the Board in 1943. The Zionist victory resulted in the disbanding of the Joint Foreign Committee (Conjoint), which had been regarded as the pre-eminent committee at the Board (it was made up of AJA and Board representatives), and thus removed much of the AJA's ability to influence the policy of the Board.[130]

This marked the beginning of a fraught and at times openly hostile relationship between the Zionist-dominated Board, the English Zionist movement and the AJA leadership. This in turn resulted in the direct appeal to the government by the AJA on issues relating to Palestine, and the organisation of a 'New Group' of AJA-oriented deputies at the Board to oppose Zionist dominance, which in turn developed into a co-ordinated attempt to challenge the Zionist majority, particularly the dual position of Professor Selig Brodetsky who was both president of the Board and the leading Zionist in England.

The 'New Group' as it was called, was chaired by its founder Neville Laski KC, who had been president of the Board of Deputies from 1933 to 1940. In its inaugural resolution it claimed that its objective was to restore the independence of the Board as a representative institution of Anglo-Jewry. This culminated in the orchestrated attempt by Laski to have Selig Brodetsky removed from his position at the head of the Board, a motion that was defeated resoundingly by 227:35 votes in March 1948.

Members of the Fellowship played a prominent role in the 'New Group'. For example, Colonel Gluckstein was on the *ad hoc* committee of the 'New Group' while the chairman and secretary of the permanent committee of the 'New Group' were respectively Fellowship members Robert Henriques and Robert Carvahlo.[131]

Nevertheless the Fellowship's relationship with the AJA was complex. One of the reasons the Fellowship came into being in the first place was that it was felt that the AJA was not representing the view of those anti-Zionist Jews clearly or forcefully enough, and throughout its existence it looked to the AJA for moral and practical support and attempted to achieve what was described as 'an understanding' with the body.[132]

However, as was stated in the Introduction, the AJA under its president Leonard Stein never did come to 'an understanding' with the Fellowship. As will be seen in the next chapter, Stein was not only unwilling to co-operate with the Fellowship but was hostile to the body's public attacks on Zionism in the non-Jewish press and he made every effort in public to distance himself from the body. For example, in a 1946 letter to the *Jewish Chronicle*, Stein stated that although the previous week the paper had printed a statement by Basil Henriques, in which the Fellowship leader had quoted a statement by Stein to support his own opposition to Zionism, he wanted to make clear that he was not in agreement with Henriques and that any opposition to Zionism he had was, unlike Henriques', not based on 'abstract conceptions' but 'actual facts'.[133]

The refusal of the AJA to lend official support to the Fellowship position (the AJA refused the Fellowship's request that the AJA represent it before the Anglo-American Committee) added to the latter's isolation within the community because the AJA was the pre-eminent unelected body within Jewry with a history of service to the community and eminent leaders.

Undoubtedly there was an overlap between members of the AJA and the Fellowship (in 1948 Alan Mocatta, Basil Henriques, Albert Hyamson, Lord Swaythling and Samuel Isidore Salmon sat on both the Fellowship and AJA councils) and Zionist polemics often tended to blur the distinction between the two groups and the 'challenge thrown out by the AJA and the Jewish Fellowship'.[134] However, while there was never official support from the AJA for the Fellowship's anti-Zionist position, there was a divide within the AJA as to whether or not the body should support the Jewish Agency in its Palestine policy.[135]

The Fellowship's relationship with the Board was also different from that of the AJA. Ultimately the AJA withdrew from its position as a constituent member of the Board in an effort to offer itself as a viable alternative to the Board, albeit a minority one, for those Jews who agreed with its Palestine policy.[136]

The Fellowship, in contrast, was not in a position to take a similar course and offer itself as a functioning alternative to the Board. It was only a new body, and was limited in its actions by the fact that it presented itself as an organisation primarily concerned with the religious revival of Anglo-Jewry. Indeed, the Fellowship was not even a constituent member of the Board (which meant that it had no right to send members as delegates to the Board). This, however, did not mean that it had no role within the Board or could not oppose Zionism from within the Board.

Leading Fellowship members such as Louis Gluckstein, Ben Moss and Basil Henriques sat on the Board as representatives of synagogues and communal institutions that were constituent members of the Board and also participated in the Board's various committees.

In 1946, for example, Gluckstein represented the Board on behalf of the Liberal Synagogue, while Basil Henriques and Ben Moss represented the St George's Settlement Synagogue and Robert Henriques represented the West London Synagogue. In the same year, Leon Rees, treasurer of the Fellowship, was on the Board's charities registration committee. Robert Henriques was on both the defence committee and the Palestine committee, while both Ben Moss and Basil Henriques were appointed in May 1946 to the special committee investigating the baptism of Jewish children.[137] Yet the efforts of these men to oppose Zionism from inside the Board highlight just how marginalised the Fellowship position was within Jewry.

Colonel Louis Gluckstein was the most vociferous of the Fellowship leaders in attacking Zionism from his position as a member of the Board of Deputies, and his long-time efforts in this respect had come under repeated attack from Zionists. In 1942 Lavy Bakstansky began a heated correspondence with Gluckstein after the latter, a member of the Board's foreign affairs committee at the time, had publicly attacked Zionism in a speech. Bakstansky asked him to refrain from such public statements in future. Gluckstein in reply took 'strong exception' to the 'dictatorial pretensions' of Bakstansky's letter.[138]

This was hardly surprising as Palestinian-born Bakstansky was the apotheosis of what the Fellowship saw as the Board's domination by international Zionists. The Fellowship's paper referred to him, for example, as the '*Palestinian* official of the Zionist Organisation on the *so-called* Board of Deputies of British Jews'.[139]

But Bakstansky persisted and in further correspondence informed Gluckstein that he deserved 'severe criticism if not censure' for his actions.[140] Gluckstein was unfazed by these threats and continued openly to attack the Board. So much so that in October of the same year Brodetsky in a letter to D.I. Sandelson, a leader of the Leeds Jewish community and one of Brodetsky's closest advisers, stated that he was getting very tired of the anti-Zionist efforts of Gluckstein, who had not been elected as MP for Nottingham 'to intervene with the government on Jewish questions or to represent Jewish interests in public'.[141]

Gluckstein was not alone in his opposition to the Board's Zionist stance. As has been mentioned this opposition resulted in the creation of the 'New Group' in 1947, but it was his stubborn refusal to bow to the Zionist majority at any point in the debate over Palestine that marked him apart from the general group opposed to the Zionist domination of the Board. This singular opposition resulted in Gluckstein experiencing the wrath of Zionist members of the Board, with deputy Dr John Mack on one occasion attacking his anti-Zionist obstructions as an attempt to purchase immunity from anti-Semitism.[142]

The perception of Gluckstein as the leader of the anti-Zionist group within the Board, which had infuriated Bakstansky and Brodetsky so greatly during the war, increased in the post-war era, so much so that Barnett Janner MP, during the Board's debate on the government's Palestine statement of November 1945, found it natural to call on 'Gluckstein and those few who were with him' to halt their opposition to the Board's Palestine policy.[143]

However, it was Gluckstein's evidence before the Anglo-American Committee on behalf of the Fellowship that most outraged the Board. In his evidence Gluckstein stated that both he and Basil Henriques, the other main Fellowship spokesman to give evidence, had long been members of the Board of Deputies, but that the Board had 'ceased to be a representative body of all types of Jews and denominations of British Jews'. Gluckstein continued to inform the committee that it was because 'many of us felt that the Board no longer represents the voice of Anglo-Jewry that the Fellowship was formed', finishing off his tirade against the Board with the claim that the Fellowship 'represents much more properly the great unheard and unspeaking masses of British Jewry'.[144]

In response to these claims Alexander Easterman, the chairman of the Board's Palestine committee, informed deputies that the

Anglo-American Committee would be furnished with a statement showing the composition of the Board, as well as the method of election and the general procedure, to re-emphasise the representative and democratic nature of the Board. The Board also passed a motion, proposed by the Palestine committee, condemning Gluckstein on the grounds that, as one of its members, he had told the Anglo-American Committee that the Board was 'not representative of Jewry'.[145]

This condemnation of Gluckstein was of particular and unusual ferocity, even by the standards of the battle between the Zionists and anti-Zionists. Harold Reinhart, who had been a member of the Fellowship's delegation to the Anglo-American Committee, described the Board's attack on Gluckstein as 'beastly'.[146] The correspondent of the *Jewish Chronicle* who attended the Board's censure of Gluckstein was of the opinion that the latter was totally isolated at one of the most highly attended and 'boisterous' meetings of the body that he had known.[147] This view was echoed in a letter to the same paper by David Brotmacher (Board deputy for Vine Court) who noted the 'astonishing unanimity' of the condemnation of Gluckstein at the Board and justified it on the basis that Gluckstein's attacks on the Board's representative nature 'cast before a non-Jewish body, caused grave harm to Jewry and Zionism'.[148]

In part, the ferocity of the Zionist attack was an attempt to gain revenge on Gluckstein for his long-time public opposition to Zionism, which Brodetsky informed a correspondent in 1942 had been 'agitating us now for years'.[149] Gluckstein had always disregarded the Zionist attacks on his position. In the heated exchange of letters with Bakstansky in 1942 he had ended the correspondence with the statement that he was 'entirely indifferent' to the abuse heaped upon him by Zionists.[150]

Nor did he bow to the Zionist censure of his Anglo-American Committee evidence. Gluckstein's response to the condemnation was that the Board could do whatever it wished, it would not injure him in the slightest – an attitude that other Fellowship leaders wholeheartedly supported, with Rose Henriques (wife of the Fellowship chairman and herself a leading member of the body), recalling the episode in later years, admiring Gluckstein wholeheartedly because 'right forcefully and persistently did he stick to his Fellowship guns'.[151]

Yet despite Gluckstein's stoicism in the face of recurrent attacks and condemnations from the Zionists at the Board, his efforts only go to highlight the fact that both he and the Fellowship were little more than a nuisance to the Zionist-dominated Board. One has just to look at the manifold resolutions passed at various annual meetings of diverse Jewish bodies to see how much support the Board had amongst the synagogues and communal institutions of Anglo-Jewry in these years.[152]

The Zionists also were quick to use the fact of the Fellowship's ineffectiveness at the Board to dispel any claims that it made about representing Jewry. The *Zionist Review* dismissed what it saw to be the Fellowship's efforts to speak for Jewry on the issue of Zionism by reminding readers that 'when Henriques and friends put their view against a Jewish state before the Board on November 5th 1944 ... they got 18 out of 159 votes and only a few of the 18 shared the extreme anti-Zionist views of the Fellowship'.[153]

Indeed, the Fellowship activists never gained credible support for their efforts at the Board. Gluckstein's proposed amendment to the Board resolution on Bevin's Palestine statement (with its conciliatory call for an equitable solution to the Jewish problem and support for the creation of the AACIP) received only 15 votes of support. While the motion to refer back the Board's resolution on not attending the Palestine conference in London, unless the Jewish Agency attended, was defeated by 123 votes to 14. Similarly, the motion to refer back the Board's official statement on the United Nations Special Committee on Palestine (UNSCOP) report, a motion proposed by Ben Moss and seconded by Gluckstein, was defeated by 126 votes to 17.[154]

And it was with votes like this in mind that Selig Brodetsky, in his capacity as president of the Board, was able to state in a letter to the *Yorkshire Post* attacking the Fellowship's claims to speak for the community that 'I think not even five percent of the members of the Board would have anything to do with the Fellowship.'[155]

THE FELLOWSHIP: SUPPORT WITHIN ANGLO-JEWRY?

As has already been seen, Jewish anti-Zionists such as Edwin Montagu had traditionally used the Board of Deputies' opposition to Zionism to show how Zionism was a minority position within Jewry. After the Zionist success in gaining a majority at the Board elections in 1943, the argument that the Board of Deputies opposed

Zionism and therefore Zionism did not represent Jewry lost much of its credibility.

For example, during his evidence before the Anglo-American Committee, Thomas Reid MP was questioned by committee member James McDonald about the claim in his memorandum that political Zionists were but 'a tiny fraction of the Jews in the world'. Reid replied that his statement was based on Jewish sources and stated that 'British Jewry from the start including ... the Board of Deputies have all opposed it'. McDonald in turn responded that 'the policy you have just mentioned in regard to the position of the Board of Deputies is not a policy of today is it? It was a policy of some time ago was it not?', to which Reid, fully aware that this was in fact the case, could only answer, 'it was the policy of the start'.[156]

This exchange highlights just how the argument that the Board opposed Zionism had lost its potency in the post-war era. The Fellowship, aware of this, took the second most effective course: yes the Board supported Zionism, but in doing so it did not represent the masses of Anglo-Jewry. This had been Gluckstein's argument before the Anglo-American Committee, and it had been how Basil Henriques had responded during his talk before the MEPC, when challenged over the fact that the Fellowship's position had been overwhelmingly defeated at the Board of Deputies.[157]

The Zionists were aware that the Fellowship, lacking even the most minute support at the Board, had no right to claim to speak on behalf of Anglo-Jewry, and that such claims would not gain any foothold within Anglo-Jewry. The *Zionist Review* in commenting on the appearance of Brunel Cohen and Basil Henriques before the MEPC was of the opinion, 'Could there be a greater farce? The Jewish Fellowship represents but a tiny section in the Jewish community, repudiated by the whole of the Jewish press and all sections of Anglo-Jewry.'[158] *New Judea*, in a scathing attack on the Fellowship's AACIP evidence, condemned the body in similar terms primarily because it had 'the temerity to assert that they represented the views of the greater part of Jewry'.[159]

There is no doubt that the Fellowship did indeed attempt to present itself as speaking on behalf of Anglo-Jewry. *The Times* reported that Colonel Robert Henriques, in his speech to the first annual meeting of the Fellowship, was confident that 'the overwhelming majority of British Jews could unite within the Fellowship'.[160] Throughout its entire existence the Fellowship did not hide its belief in the importance of having a large membership. It was the 'main task',[161] and Basil Henriques continually urged other Fellowship leaders to concentrate on attracting new members.[162] He even made the Fellowship's success in attracting members the benchmark to be used in considering whether or not the body was speaking for the Jews of England.[163]

Throughout 1945 and 1946 the Fellowship claimed that membership was increasing to a 'marked degree', and a meeting of the Fellowship executive in September 1946 was informed that membership was rising steadily and satisfactorily.[164] Much of the basis for this optimism was due to the establishment of local Fellowship groups in areas of large Jewish populations in London and the provinces. By 1947 within the greater London area there were groups in Bayswater, Paddington, Hampstead, South London and the Thames area.[165]

But although the creation of these local groups was an achievement of sorts, and the determined efforts of the Fellowship leaders such as Julian Franklyn and Basil Henriques to visit these groups to speak and motivate them show the commitment of Fellowship leaders, the reality was that there were never more than ten local groups in England, just as there were never more than 2,000 members of the Fellowship.

Yet even after the birth of the State of Israel the *Jewish Outlook* persisted in claiming that it represented the views of the majority of Jews (even the name the *Jewish Outlook* implies that the Fellowship view was the only right one) when it stated 'while the Zionists are rejoicing, the bulk of the community is stunned and bewildered by the speed of events'.[166]

At certain times Fellowship leaders admitted that the body had failed to achieve much support within Jewry, Julian Franklyn in a 1947 article admitting that support for the Fellowship was 'at present but a trickle'.[167] A 1948 'Private and Confidential Memorandum' even admitted that the Fellowship position was 'not held by the majority of Jews in England'.[168]

Overall, however, the Fellowship's constant claim was that it represented the majority of Jewry. The delusion inherent in this shows that the group though sincere in its opposition to Zionism was not always logical or rational. In October 1945 Mattuck and Gluckstein met Professor Selig Brodetsky in a private meeting to discuss the Board's position on the issue of Zionism. Mattuck warned Brodetsky that the Liberal Synagogue's position as a constituent of the Board would be jeopardised 'if the Board's policy and attitude continued to be so diverse from that of the majority of the Board'.[169]

In making this threat Mattuck was providing credence to the Zionist claims that Liberal Judaism and anti-Zionism were one and the same. But this statement also seems to imply a certain contradiction. For what was the Board's policy, if not that decided by a majority of the Board members, and as such how could Mattuck claim logically that this policy was opposed by the majority of the Board? The answer is of course that he could not, and the confusion inherent in Mattuck's statement was apparent in much of the claims by Jewish anti-Zionists in these years, desperate to show that they, and they alone, spoke for the majority of Jewry on the issue of Zionism.

Robert Abrahams in a letter to the *Jewish Outlook* typifies this attitude. It was his view that 'we [anti-Zionist Jews] must stress that decisions reached by various Jewish organisations outside the Fellowship are not necessarily representative of the true opinion of Jewry'.[170] In other words, while the position of the Fellowship was the legitimate position of Jewry, the stance of other, much larger communal bodies was not.

Yet, however the Fellowship's membership was able to delude itself, it failed to gain credible support either at the Board or in the wider community of Jewry by way of a large membership. It failed to prevent itself from being perceived as a Liberal anti-Zionist conspiracy against the Jewish community and its lack of success in appealing to other Jewish bodies, even those such as the AJA or Agudath Yisra'el that were not political Zionist in orientation, enabled the Zionists to feel secure in the belief that this body of anti-Zionist Jews was of no consequence within the community of Anglo-Jewry. Its danger in the non-Jewish world was, of course, a different matter.

NOTES

1. Lord Moyne had been colonial secretary 1941–42 and deputy minister of state in Cairo, 1942. For a full but somewhat dramatised account of his assassination see Gerold Frank's *The Deed: The Assassination of Lord Moyne* (London: Jonathan Cape, 1964). For a more academic study see Bernard Wasserstein's 'The Assassination of Lord Moyne', *Jewish Historical Society of England, Transactions*, XXVII (1978–80), pp. 72–83.
2. See statement by the president of the Board of Deputies of British Jews, 8 November 1944 and the minutes of the meeting of the Board of Deputies, 19 November 1944, ACC3121/C14/21/1, ABD.

3. See Fellowship secretary Julian Franklyn argue in these terms in 'Israel: State or Religion?', *Contemporary Review*, CLXXI: 979 (July 1947), pp. 35–9, p. 36. Franklyn points out in this article that it was former Chief Rabbi Hertz who, speaking in a different context, had originally made this distinction in 1936.
4. See Roth's pessimistic view in a letter in the *Jewish Chronicle*, 12 January 1945, p. 5, where he stated that 'the community itself is facing disaster' and also his article 'The Collapse of Anglo-Jewry', *Jewish Monthly*, 1: 4 (July 1947), pp. 11–17. Roth was so deeply pessimistic on this issue that after meeting Sir Ronald Storrs, the latter noted in his diary that Roth was 'despairing ... sees no future for Jews anywhere', MS Diary of Storrs, 1 December 1945, Box 6/6, STOP.
5. Leftwich, 'Are we a Philistine Community?', *Jewish Monthly*, 1: 9 (December 1947), pp. 11–23.
6. Leftwich to Greenberg, 21 August 1944, MS150 AJ 110/5, GREEN.
7. See Michael Heymann's 'Max Nordau at the Early Zionist Congresses, 1897–1905', *Journal of Israeli History*, 16: 3 (autumn 1995), pp. 245–56, p. 249.
8. Samuel Landman, *Zionism: Its Organisation and Institutions* (London: ZO, 1916), pp. 19, p.6.
9. See the memorandum 'Report on Post-War Plans of Jewish Anti-Zionists', n.d, MS119 AJ3 278–83, BROD.
10. Cohen, 'The Errors of the Jewish Fellowship', *Synagogue Review*, XIX: 11 (July 1945), pp. 82–4, p. 84. Also see 'Misrepresenting the Jewish Case', *Zionist Review*, 9 March 1945, p. 1.
11. 'The Jewish Fellowship', *Zionist Review*, 19 November 1948, p. 1.
12. Snowman's statement to the north-west London regional conference of the Zionist Federation, 28 October 1945, reprinted in *Zionist Review*, 2 November 1945, p. 9.
13. 'Brief Encounter', JPA supplement to *Zionist Review*, 14 March 1946, p. 2.
14. Pinner, 'Our Future Tasks', *Zionist Review*, 26 January 1945, p. 7. For example see Barnett Janner MP, speaking at the political session of the north-west regional conference of the Zionist Federation, 26 October 1947, reprinted in *Zionist Review*, 31 October 1947, pp. 10–11.
15. *New Judea*, February–March 1945, p. 72.
16. *New Judea*, November 1945, p. 19.
17. Sacher's article 'The Study of Jewish History' first published in *New Judea* in 1947 can be found in his *Zionist Portraits and Other Essays* (London: Anthony Blond, 1959), pp. 291–6.
18. Litvinoff, 'Fanaticism and Fantasy', *Zionist Review*, 19 July 1946, p. 9. Lewin's 1941 essay 'Self-Hatred Among Jews' can be found in Gertrud W. Lewin (ed.), *Resolving Social Conflicts* (New York: Harper & Row, 1948), pp. 186–200. Also see Miriam Lewin Papanek's 'Psychological Aspects of Minority Group Membership: The Concepts of Kurt Lewin', *Jewish Social Studies*, XXXVI: 1 (January 1974), pp. 72–9.
19. Maurice Cohen speaking at a meeting of the East London branch of Poalei Zion, 4 April 1946, reprinted in *Zionist Review*, 19 April 1946, p. 11.
20. 'Life and Language', *Zionist Review*, 26 November 1948, p. 8.
21. Beyond Contempt', *Zionist Review*, 20 April 1945, p. 2.
22. 'Scandalous Document', *Zionist Review*, 6 February 1948, p. 1.
23. Zakan (pseud.), 'The Order of Trembling Israelites', *Zionist Review*, 28 June 1946, p. 10.
24. See Burrows to Henriques, 9 December 1947, PRO/FO 371/61759.
25. For a fascinating analysis of this see Sander L. Gilman's *Jewish Self-Hatred: Anti-Semitism and the Hidden Language of the Jews* (Baltimore, London: Johns Hopkins University Press, 1986), see especially 'The Development of Self-Hatred', pp. 206–308.
26. For a contemporary study of Liberal Judaism by someone directly involved in both the Liberal movement and the Fellowship see Rabbi Dr Israel Mattuck's *The Essentials of Liberal Judaism* (London: Routledge, 1947). See also Solomon B. Freehof's *Reform Jewish Practice and its Rabbinic Background*, Vol. II (Cincinatti: Hebrew Union College Press, 1952); Gunther Plaut, *The Rise of Reform Judaism* (New York: World Union for Progressive Judaism, 1963). Finally see Anne J. Kershen and Jonathan A. Romain's *Tradition and Change: A History of Reform Judaism in Britain*

27. Goodman, 'Our Own Effort', *Zionist Review*, 26 January 1945, p. 6.
28. See Brodetsky, *From Ghetto to Israel* (London: Weidenfeld & Nicolson, 1960), p. 243; and Gluckstein to Spears, 6 March 1945, Box 4/6, SPSP.
29. *Synagogue Review*, XX: 2 (October 1945), p. 9.
30. See Shabtai Rowson's report on the meeting, *American Jewish Yearbook, 5705, 1944–45* (Jewish Publication Society of America), p. 192.
31. Henriques, 'Unity and Expedience', *Jewish Monthly*, 1: 2 (May 1947), pp. 9–15, p. 11.
32. 'Capturing Youth', *Zionist Review*, 22 December 1944, p. 1.
33. 'The Unmentionable', *New Judea*, June 1948, p. 148.
34. 'High Festivals', *Zionist Review*, 19 September 1947, p. 11.
35. *Zionist Review*, 17 December 1943, p. 6.
36. 'Guiding the Young', *Zionist Review*, 20 August 1948, p. 8.
37. Sacher, *New Judea*, April 1945, p. 98.
38. *Jewish Chronicle*, 9 November 1945, p. 6.
39. See Paul Goodman, 'Mount Zion or Mount Gerizim?', *Gates of Zion*, 1: 1 (September 1946), p. 3 and 'Zion and the United Synagogue', 1: 2 (January 1947), p. 1.
40. On Loewe's concerns on this issue see Leftwich to Greenberg, 21 August 1944, MS150 AJ 110/5, GREEN. Also see the report on Loewe's speech to Fellowship members at Harrogate Synagogue, 4 October 1946, TBJSBH, 3/34,1945–47, MS132 AJ 195, HENP.
41. Henriques and Marmorstein, *What is Judaism?* (London: JF, 1945). See also *The Religion of the Jew* by the same authors (Leicester: Newry Welsey, n.d.).
42. See for example, *Gates of Zion*, 2: 3 (April 1948), p. 2.
43. See Mr H. Grunis, 27 April 1945, p. 15, and Mr J. Mendel, 18 May 1945, p. 15. Both in the *Jewish Chronicle*.
44. See evidence of the Jewish Fellowship before the AACIP, London, 30 January 1946, pp. 38–66, p. 39, ACC3121/C14/30/5, ABD.
45. Henriques, *Jewish Chronicle*, 15 February 1946, p. 14.
46. Both Nabarro's and Mendel's letters were published by the *Jewish Chronicle*, 22 February 1946, p. 16.
47. *Jewish Outlook*, 1: 12 (May 1947), p. 2. See also Rabbi Curtis Cassell's article 'The Gates of Zion: A Criticism', in the same paper, 1: 9 (January 1947), p. 8.
48. See for example his comments at the executive meeting of March 1944, in minutes of the Jewish Fellowship executive, 9 March 1944, MS150 AJ 110/5, GREEN. For an exposition of Soref's strong anti-Zionist position see his article 'They were Ringing the Bells', in the *Jewish Monthly*, 1: 11 (February 1948), pp. 8–18. The Fellowship's paper claimed that Soref should receive the 'blue riband of Jewish journalism' for this piece. See 'Knell of Pell', *Jewish Outlook*, 2: 8 (March 1948), p. 5.
49. See Harold Soref's review of the *Gates of Zion* in *Jewish Monthly*, 1: 2 (May 1947), pp. 65–6, p. 65.
50. See Namier's attack on Mattuck in these terms, *Manchester Guardian*, 16 December 1943. Also see a longer argument on similar lines in his essay 'The Jewish Question', in *Facing East* (London: Hamish Hamilton, 1947), pp. 142–50.
51. *Jewish Outlook*, 2:1 (June 1947), p. 14.
52. Namier, 'The Jewish Question', *Facing East*, pp. 142–50, p. 148. For a highly interesting account of Namier's complicated relationship with Zionism see Norman Rose's *Lewis Namier and Zionism* (Oxford: Clarendon Press, 1980).
53. Weber, 'The Present Position of Anglo-Jewry', *Jewish Forum*, 1: 1 (October 1946), pp. 75–85, p. 80.
54. *Zionist Review*, 5 September 1947, p. 3.
55. See report on the conference, *Jewish Chronicle*, 2 August 1946, p. 15.
56. *Synagogue Review*, XX: 7 (March 1946), p. 59.
57. See Henriques, 'The Attitude to the State of Israel and Jewish Nationalism' in Israel Mattuck (ed.), *Aspects of Progressive Jewish Thought* (London: Victor Gollancz, 1954), pp. 115–20, p. 115.
58. 'A Performance in Yorkshire', *Jewish Chronicle*, 22 February 1946, p. 8.

59. Harold Morris, *Jewish Chronicle*, 19 July 1946, p. 15. For other examples of attacks on the Fellowship in the letters pages of this newspaper see J.H. Sieff, 16 February 1945, p. 15; Cecil Nash, 1 March 1946, p. 18; Barnett Hyman, 8 March 1946, p. 14; Corporal A. Berkovitch, 29 March 1946, p. 15; H. Grunis, 26 April 1946, p. 15.
60. 'Agudist', *Jewish Outlook*, 1: 2 (May 1946), p. 13.
61. See *Aims of the Jewish Fellowship*, 9 March 1944. The other aims were to (1) uphold the principle that Jews were a religious community; (2) strengthen the religious life of Jewry; (3) support and assist Jews in other lands.
62. See minutes of the Fellowship's executive meeting, 9 March 1944, MS150 AJ110/5, GREEN.
63. See Brunel Cohen's *Address to the Fellowship Council*, p. 4, and Basil Henriques' speech to a meeting of the executive and council on 15 February 1946, TBJSBH, 3/34, 1945–47, MS132 AJ 195, HENP. Also see editorials in *Jewish Outlook* including 'Progress and Future Activities', 1: 3 (June 1946), p. 7; 1: 11 (March–April 1947), p. 13; 2: 7 (February 1948), pp. 6–8 and 'Spreading the Message', 2: 9 (April 1948), p. 5.
64. See Henriques' letter in *The Times*, 21 September 1944 and Brunel Cohen's letter, ibid., 23 September 1944.
65. Brunel Cohen, *Address to the Fellowship Council*, p. 3.
66. See Wolf's essay 'The Jewish National Movement', *Edinburgh Review*, 225: 460 (April 1917), pp. 1–17.
67. Simon, *The Case Against the Anti-Zionists*, (London: ZO, 1917), p. 17.
68. Janner, *Zionist Review*, 29 September 1944, p. 2.
69. See report in *Jewish Chronicle*, 6 October 1944, p. 13.
70. *Jewish Chronicle*, 29 September 1944, p. 8.
71. See Brunel Cohen's *Address to the Fellowship Council*, 20 June 1945, pp. 1–7, p. 3 and *Some Information for You: Confidential Memorandum* (London: JF, 1945), p. 4.
72. *Jewish Chronicle*, 24 May 1946, p. 15.
73. *Synagogue Review*, XIX: 5 (January 1945), p. 35.
74. See evidence of the Fellowship before the AACIP, p. 41. Also see Basil Henriques' speech to the first annual meeting of the Fellowship, 14 October 1945, TBJSBH, 3/34, 1945–47, MS132 AJ 195, HENP, and his speech to the Paddington group of the Fellowship reported in the *West London Chronicle*, 29 March 1946.
75. The letter was published in *The Times*, 24 May 1917.
76. The Joint Foreign Committee (Conjoint) of the Board of Deputies was founded in 1878 by the Board of Deputies and the AJA with the aim of merging the overseas work (charity, protection of Jewish rights, etc.) of the two bodies. It developed into the pre-eminent committee at the Board of Deputies concerned with international affairs.
77. The Board of Deputies was the governing body of Anglo-Jewry. For a history of this body see Aubrey Newman's *The Board of Deputies of British Jews, 1760–1985: A Brief Survey* (London: Vallentine Mitchell, 1987). For a discussion of the gradual change in leadership within the Jewish community see Stuart Cohen's 'The Conquest of the Community?: The Zionists and the Board of Deputies in 1917', *Jewish Journal of Sociology*, XIX: 2 (December 1977), pp. 157–84, and his *English Zionists and British Jews: The Communal Politics of Anglo-Jewry, 1895–1920* (Princeton, New Jersey: Princeton University Press, 1982); Eugene C. Black, *The Social Politics of Anglo-Jewry, 1880–1920* (Oxford: Basil Blackwell, 1988), especially chapter 13 'Zionism in the Ascendant', pp. 356–88 and Israel Finestein's 'Changes in Authority in Anglo-Jewry since the 1930s: A Critical View', *Jewish Quarterly*, 32: 2 (1985), pp. 33–7.
78. See Vol. 3 of Vital's history of Zionism, *Zionism: The Crucial Phase* (Oxford: Clarendon Press, 1987), p. 276. For a concise argument that supports this view see Geoffrey Alderman's *Modern British Jewry* (Oxford: Clarendon Press, 1992), pp. 247–248. Also see Mark Levene's 'Anglo-Jewish Foreign Policy in Crisis, Lucien Wolf, the Conjoint Committee and the War, 1914–1918', *Jewish Historical Studies, Jewish Historical Society of England, Transactions*, XXX (1987–88), pp. 179–97. Finally see Mayir Verete, 'The Balfour Declaration and its Makers', *Middle Eastern Studies*, 6: 1 (January 1970), pp. 48–76; Isaiah Friedman's 'The Response to the Balfour Declaration', *Jewish Social Studies*, XXXV: 2 (April 1973), pp. 105–24 and Leonard

Stein's *The Balfour Declaration* (London: Vallentine Mitchell, 1961).
79. Chaim Weizmann, *Trial and Error* (London: Hamish Hamilton, 1949), pp. 254–7.
80. Bakstansky to Gluckstein, 11 June 1942, MS150 AJ 110/8, GREEN.
81. 'Remember 1917' *Zionist Review*, 27 October 1944, pp. 1–2.
82. Henriques, *Sir Robert Waley Cohen, 1877–1952* (London: Secker & Warburg, 1966), p. 266.
83. Storrs, *Memoirs*, p. 362.
84. *The Secret History of the Balfour Declaration and the Mandate* (London: AO, 1945).
85. Rasheen M. Busteen, *Edwin Montagu and the Balfour Declaration* (London: Arab League, 1967).
86. Rosette to Greenberg, 18 January 1944, MS150 AJ110/5, GREEN.
87. Rosette's statement, Board of Deputies debate, 15 April 1945, reported *Jewish Chronicle*, 20 April 1945, p. 5.
88. 'An Outrage', *Zionist Review*, 23 March 1945, p. 2.
89. 'Vicious Propaganda', *Zionist Review*, 13 April 1945, p. 1.
90. Chairman of the defence committee to Greenberg, 3 April 1946, MS150 AJ 110/4, GREEN.
91. Isaac Dartle, *Jewish Chronicle*, 12 April 1946, p. 15.
92. See David Cesarani's *The Jewish Chronicle and Anglo-Jewry* (Cambridge: Cambridge University Press, 1994), especially chapter 6 'Ivan Greenberg and the Crisis Years, 1937–1946'.
93. Moss to Greenberg, 2 February 1944, MS150 AJ 110/5, GREEN.
94. Rosette to Greenberg, 18 January 1944, MS150 AJ 110/5, GREEN. See also Brodetsky to Greenberg, n.d., MS119 AJ3 208, BROD; Bakstansky to Greenberg, 1 July 1942, MS150 AJ 110/5, GREEN.
95. 'Zionist Isolationists', *Jewish Chronicle*, 11 May 1945, p. 8.
96. Greenberg to Brodetsky, 13 July 1943, MS119 AJ3 205, BROD.
97. *Zionist Review*, 13 September 1946, p. 1.
98. 'A New Campaign', *Zionist Review*, 18 May 1945, p. 1. See a similar argument in the *Zionist Review*, 6 September 1946, p. 2.
99. 'Fellowship or Free for All ?', *Jewish Chronicle*, 29 September 1944, p. 8.
100. Ibid., p. 8.
101. 'A Performance in Yorkshire', *Jewish Chronicle*, 22 February 1946, p. 8.
102. *Jewish Chronicle*, 24 May 1946, p. 15.
103. See Brodetsky to Greenberg, 20 June 1945, MS150 AJ 110/4, GREEN.
104. Leftwich to Greenberg, 20 March 1944, MS150 AJ 110/7, GREEN.
105. Henriques to Greenberg, 25 September 1944, MS150 AJ 110/5, GREEN.
106. See the retraction and apology, *Jewish Chronicle*, 20 October 1944, p. 10.
107. 'Anglo-Jewish Honour Vindicated: D.L. Lipson Speaks Up', *Jewish Outlook*, 1: 4 (August 1946), p. 1. Other sources indifferent to Zionist aspirations also acknowledged Lipson as the lone sane Jewish voice amongst Zionist fanatics. See George Kirk, *The Middle East, 1945–1950*, Chatham House Survey of International Affairs (London: Oxford University Press, under the auspices of RIIA, 1954), pp. 247–8.
108. *Jewish Chronicle*, 22 June 1945, p. 10.
109. *Jewish Chronicle*, 1 March 1946, p. 10. See Palestine debate, 21 February 1946, Parliamentary Debates, Vol. 419, 11 February–1 March 1946, p. 1394.
110. Goodman, *Gates of Zion*, 1: 1 (September 1946), p. 3.
111. Hamabit (pseud.), 'Badge of …', *New Judea*, October–November 1947, p. 6.
112. Moshe Rosette, Interview, 8 February 1961, p. 16; 15 February 1961, p. 13. These interviews were part of the Oral History project of the Hebrew University of Jerusalem's Institute of Contemporary Jewry, Project 2 'Management of the Jewish Agency in London, 1938–1948'.
113. Lipson, 'Is Jewry a Nation?', *Spectator*, 2 November 1945, pp. 403–4.
114. *Zionist Review*, 9 November 1945, p. 1.
115. 'Their Jewish Friends', *Jewish Chronicle*, 9 November 1945, p. 10.
116. Edwin Montagu to Lords Cecil and Milner, 4 September 1917, PRO/CAB 24/27.
117. Ibid.
118. Selig Brodetsky (1888–1954), an immigrant to England as a child, had risen from

The Jewish Fellowship and the Battle over Zionism in Anglo-Jewry 119

humble origins to become Professor of Mathematics at Leeds University and the dominant symbol of the Zionisation of Anglo-Jewry and of the new era of Jewish communal leadership. See his autobiography *From Ghetto to Israel*, published posthumously in 1960. There has been much written on Brodetksy's position and importance within Anglo-Jewry during these years. For varying interpretations of his role see two articles in the *Jewish Journal of Sociology*. Gideon Shimoni's 'Selig Brodetsky and the Ascendancy of Zionism in Anglo-Jewry, 1939–1945', XXII: 2 (December 1980), pp. 125–62 and Stuart Cohen's 'Selig Brodetsky and the Ascendancy of Zionism in Anglo-Jewry: Another view of his Role and Achievements', XXIV: 1 (June 1982), pp. 25–38.

119. Brodetsky to Easterman, 7 May 1942, MS119 AJ3 126, BROD. He reiterated this view in a letter the following year to Easterman's superiors at WJC headquarters in New York, Brodetsky to Wise, Goldman, Perlzweig, 11 January 1943, MS119 AJ3 173, BROD.
120. Bakstansky to Brodetsky, 15 September 1943, MS119 AJ3 214, BROD; Brodetsky to Bakstansky, 23 September 1943, MS119 AJ3 217, BROD.
121. See Board of Deputies of British Jews, *Statement on Palestine* (London: 1944).
122. *New Judea*, October–November 1944, p. 3; 'The Voice of Anglo-Jewry', *Zionist Review*, 10 November 1944, p. 1.
123. *Zionist Review*, 10 November 1944, p. 1; 12 May 1944, p. 1; 10 May 1946, pp. 1–2; 2 January 1948, p. 1.
124. For examples of such correspondence between Linton, veteran Zionist civil servant, appointed to the position of political secretary of the Jewish Agency, London in 1940, and such Board officials as executive and press officer Sidney Salomon in these years see ACC3121/C14/11/5, ABD.
125. *Jewish Outlook*, 1: 2 (May 1946), pp. 4–5.
126. Ibid., 1: 7 (November 1946), pp. 1–2.
127. Ibid., 1: 3 (June–July 1946), p. 13.
128. See Salomon to Hall, 6 September 1945, ACC3121/C14/28, ABD.
129. *Jewish Outlook*, 1: 6 (October 1946), p. 13.
130. The Zionist resolution proposing the disbanding of the Conjoint Committee was supported by a majority of 154 to 148 Board deputies. As such it did not have clear-cut support. For correspondence and material on the disbanding of the Joint Foreign Committee see ACC3121/C11/10, ABD.
131. For the Fellowship's public support for the AJA efforts see *Jewish Outlook*, 1: 12 (May 1947), p. 2.
132. See minutes of Fellowship executive meeting, 9 March 1944, MS150 AJ 110/5, GREEN.
133. Stein, *Jewish Chronicle*, 19 July 1946, p. 15.
134. 'Anglo-Jewry Backs the Agency', *Zionist Review*, 19 July 1946, p. 1.
135. For example, Zionist members of the AJA organised to submit a memorandum to the colonial secretary in March 1945 stating their support for the Jewish Agency's Palestine policy. For a copy of this memorandum see ACC3121/C14/28, ABD.
136. On the AJA decision to leave the Board see minutes of the meeting between representatives of the AJA and the Board of Deputies, 18 July 1947, ACC3121/C11/10, ABD.
137. On Fellowship members who were also on the Board of Deputies see *The Board of Deputies of British Jews Annual Reports* (1944–49).
138. See Bakstansky to Gluckstein, 11 June 1942, MS150 AJ 110/8; Gluckstein to Bakstansky, 19 June 1942, MS150 AJ 110/8, GREEN.
139. *Jewish Outlook*, 1: 4 (August 1946), p. 3 (emphasis added).
140. Bakstansky to Gluckstein, 26 June 1942, MS150 AJ 110/8, GREEN.
141. Brodetsky to Sandelson, 13 October 1942, MS119 AJ3 151, BROD.
142. Mack was speaking at the debate on the Board's Palestine statement, 5 November 1944 and his claim was reprinted in the *Zionist Review*, 10 November 1944, pp. 4–5. See also a similar editorial attack on Gluckstein in 'Contortions', *Zionist Review*, 10 January 1947, p. 1.
143. See Janner's statement during Board's debate on Bevin's Palestine statement, 18 November 1945, reported in the *Jewish Chronicle*, 23 November 1945, pp. 6, 15.

144. See evidence of the Fellowship before the AACIP, p. 41.
145. The condemnation of Gluckstein took place at the Board meeting, 24 February 1946.
146. Reinhart to Henriques, 25 February 1946, MS171 AJ 240 92, REIN.
147. *Jewish Chronicle*, 1 March 1946, p. 7.
148. David Brotmacher, *Jewish Chronicle*, 15 March 1946, p. 15.
149. Brodetsky to Sandelson, 13 October 1942, MS119 AJ3 151, BROD.
150. Gluckstein to Bakstansky, 30 June 1942, MS150 AJ 110/8, GREEN.
151. Rose Henriques, 1 March 1946, TBJSBH, 3/34, 1945–47, MS132 AJ 195, HENP.
152. For example, the annual conference of the Synagogues, Societies and Institutions of East London passed a resolution at its annual meeting, 25 February 1945, that 'expresses its accord with the policy of the Board of Deputies in regard to Palestine'. A similar resolution was passed at the North Middlesex Communal Conference, 11 February 1945, and at numerous other communal conferences and meetings during these years. For various examples of this form of communal support see ACC3121/C14/28, ABD.
153. *Zionist Review*, 9 March 1945, p. 1. *New Judea* presented the vote in exactly the same way (October–November 1944), p. 3.
154. For details of these debates see reports in *Jewish Chronicle*, 23 November 1945, pp. 6, 15; *Zionist Review*, 20 September 1946, p. 9, and 25 July 1947, p. 8.
155. Brodetsky, *Yorkshire Post*, 15 January 1946.
156. Evidence of Thomas Reid before the AACIP, pp. 1–28, p. 17, ACC3121/C14/30/4, ABD.
157. In the March of 1945 at the invitation of committee chairman Sir Edward Spears, Basil Henriques and Sir Jack Brunel Cohen spoke on the subject of Zionism before the MEPC. See the Jewish Telegraphic Agency's *Daily News Bulletin*, 12: 56, 8 March 1945, p. 2. Also see William Frankel's report on the meeting in the *American Jewish Yearbook, 5706, 1945–46* (Jewish Publication Society of America), p. 344.
158. 'Misrepresenting the Jewish Case', *Zionist Review*, 9 March 1945, p. 1.
159. *New Judea*, January–February 1946, p. 66.
160. *The Times*, 15 October 1945.
161. Brunel Cohen, *Address to the Fellowship Council*, p. 5.
162. Henriques to Reinhart, 27 October 1945, MS171 AJ 240 92, REIN.
163. Henriques, *Statement to Fellowship Members*, 1 February 1946, p. 4.
164. See *Some Information for You*, p. 6; *Jewish Outlook*, 1: 3 (June 1946), p. 7 and the report on the Fellowship executive meeting, *Jewish Outlook*, 1: 6 (October 1946), p. 13.
165. Brunel Cohen in his presidential address to the second annual meeting of the Fellowship, 10 December 1945, stressed the importance of these local groups. For the abridged version of Brunel Cohen's speech see *Jewish Outlook*, 1: 9 (January 1947), p. 5.
166. See *Jewish Outlook*, 2: 11 (June 1948), p. 8.
167. Franklyn, 'Israel: State or Religion?', *Contemporary Review*, CLXXII: 979, p. 39.
168. *Private and Confidential Memorandum* (London: JF, 1948), p. 3.
169. See minutes of a meeting between Rabbi Mattuck, Gluckstein and Brodetsky, 22 October 1945, ACC3121/C14/28, ABD.
170. Abrahams, *Jewish Outlook*, 1: 6 (October 1946), p. 15.

5 Common Arguments, Common Goal: Anti-Zionist Arguments against the Creation of a Jewish State

From the time that the publication of the Balfour Declaration awoke outspoken opposition to Zionism from Jews and non-Jews alike, there developed a tendency amongst Gentile anti-Zionists to use Jewish opposition to Zionism as part of their own propaganda. In 1923 the *Daily Mail* journalist, J.M.N. Jeffries, who as we have seen was a central anti-Zionist of the early Mandate era, and a founding member of the PIC in London during the 1930s, argued that Zionism 'is not supported by oriental Jews, spiritual Jews and the Yishuv', adding that both the Board of Deputies and the AJA had 'refused to accept the programme of political Zionism'.[1]

That Jeffries felt confident in relying on the existence of a vibrant Jewish opposition to political Zionism is hardly surprising given the fact that in 1923, as in 1917 when Edwin Montagu made the same arguments, these claims had much credibility. But even in the post-war era when Zionism had made much progress in gaining support within Jewry, anti-Zionists continued to argue in these terms, with Stewart Newcombe's description of Zionists as an 'articulate, organised and vociferous minority within Jewry' a position adhered to publicly by all anti-Zionists.[2]

Similarly, anti-Zionists argued that they were motivated in their staunch opposition to Zionism in part out of concern for the damage that Zionism caused to Jewry. Leading English anti-Zionists such as Spears and Thomas Reid MP were continually arguing that if a Jewish state was created, it would be the Jews who would be the 'biggest sufferers' and 'would suffer most' and because of this Zionists were 'the greatest foes of Jewry'.[3] This view was echoed by William Hocking, the American academic and anti-Zionist, who declared in 1945, in the immediate aftermath of the destruction of European Jewry by the Nazis, that political Zionism was 'the chief enemy' of world Jewry.[4] Nor was the Arab Office slow in arguing against Zionism in these terms (or setting out the likely consequences for the Jewish communities in the Arab lands if a Jewish state came about).[5]

The Zionist movement was sceptical of the claims that opposition to Zionism was born out of a concern for the welfare of Jews, and that Jews in Arab lands had indeed become a vulnerable minority only with the rise of Zionism. But Gentile anti-Zionists did not confine themselves to these simplistic and obvious arguments, but also entered into more subtle Jewish arguments (those arguments against a Jewish state that originated in the Jewish world and that were argued in Jewish terms and given credibility because they were arguments used primarily by Jews) in their opposition to Zionist aspirations.

JEWRY: A RELIGIOUS COMMUNITY

A central argument of assimilationist Jewish anti-Zionists in their opposition to Zionism was that Jews were not a nation that had been scattered into an artificial Diaspora in biblical times. This argument against a Jewish state on the grounds that Jewry was primarily a religious community was certainly a legitimate issue and, as shall be seen in this chapter, one to which the Zionists were concerned to respond, but it was also utilised for propaganda purposes by both Jewish and Gentile anti-Zionists in these years.

Nevill Barbour, in the preface of his book, *Nisi Dominus*, was of the view that 'the religion of Judaism is today the most obvious link between various Jewish communities in the world'.[6] And he continued with the view that the Zionist claim for a Jewish state was

> Based on the doubtful theory that the link which binds together Jews of ... Polish, North African, South Arabian or Negro provenance is a common racial or Palestinian origin, not adherence to a common religion.[7]

The Arab Office also argued in identical terms against a Jewish state in Palestine. In an editorial in the *Arab News Bulletin*, in what may be seen as a last-ditch effort by the Arab Office to convince the British not to recognise the new State of Israel, it was argued that

> A state should be a unique entity ... membership should entail a common nationality ... what do we find in the so-called state of Israel? Its subjects have no common nationality, they belong to all the nationalities and races of the world.[8]

These statements by Barbour and the Arab Office could easily have been from a speech by a Fellowship leader, or from an editorial in the *Jewish Outlook*. Indeed one such editorial challenged the 'untruth' that the Jews 'were the members of an ancient so-called Jewish race which had become dispersed in every part of the world', echoing Barbour when it stated that

> These widely scattered people, all of the Jewish faith, have the same religious belief but do not constitute a Jewish race, their belief in Judaism being the only tie which they can have in common with each other ... religious beliefs do not ever determine racial origins.[9]

Just how interrelated the Gentile and Jewish anti-Zionist position on this issue was can be seen in the case of Sir John Hope-Simpson. Writing in 1944 in the *Fortnightly*, Hope-Simpson stressed that the Jews were not a national body and that the Zionist movement, as opposed to Judaism, was 'definitely the urge of political nationalism'.[10]

The following year, in an article in *International Affairs*, Hope-Simpson took issue with a statement made by the Gentile Zionist Revd Dr James Parkes, in the same journal, regarding Hitler's effort to 'wage war against the Jews'. Hope-Simpson was offended by this statement because it seemed to imply that the Jews were a nation rather than a religious community. For, in his opinion, 'only metaphorically can Hitler's treatment of the Jews be described as waging war, and the assumption that ... Jewry on which he waged war is a nation is devoid of basis'.[11]

Parkes in his *International Affairs* article had not actually claimed that the Jews were a nation,[12] and indeed in a detailed exposition elsewhere as to whether the Jews were a nation, a race, or a religious community he concluded that 'the best description is to say that Jewry is a civilisation'.[13] Nevertheless, Hope-Simpson, in exactly the same way as the Fellowship, made the argument that Jewry was not a nation central to his anti-Zionist position.

In doing so he echoed the letters by Brunel Cohen and Robert Henriques to *The Times*, which had caused such an outcry within the Jewish community, and which had opposed the creation of a Jewish Brigade precisely because it would make it appear that Jews were fighting Hitler as a nation rather than as members of a religious community. This similarity in argument was not lost on Hope-Simpson, and in his *International Affairs* attack on Parkes he referred to these two letters to support his own claim.[14]

In a later article in the *Fortnightly*, Hope-Simpson quoted from the article by Daniel Lipson MP that had appeared in the *Spectator* in November 1945. This was a seminal statement of the position of Jewish anti-Zionists, and in setting out Jewish opposition to Zionism primarily on the grounds that Jewry was a religion not a nation, Lipson was following in the footsteps of earlier Jewish anti-Zionists of the Liberal-assimilationist school, most notably C.G. Montefiore. As Lipson stated:

> Many Jews, of whom I am one, deny that the Jews are a nation, and are opposed to the agitation of the Zionists to set up a Jewish state in Palestine. We regard ourselves as members of a world wide religious community. As such we are citizens in the countries in which we live, with the same rights and responsibilities as our fellow citizens of other creeds ... we claim that it is only in religion that we differ from our fellow citizens.[15]

By quoting this passage from Lipson's article in such detail and concluding his own article with the view that 'this seems to me the sound view, accepted by the vast majority of Jewish citizens in the world',[16] one can again see how Gentile anti-Zionists claimed that Jews were in the majority anti-Zionist, as part of their own argument against Zionism. This is all the more so when one considers that Hope-Simpson on being requested by the journal to write the above article saw it solely as a propaganda opportunity to present the anti-Zionist case, and he wrote to Spears requesting information and material for his article, which the latter duly provided.[17]

Nor was Hope-Simpson alone amongst CAA members in viewing Lipson's *Spectator* article as vital to the general anti-Zionist argument. Newcombe wrote to Spears, requesting that he send a copy of the article to influential people outside the CAA such as Sir Reginald Wingate.[18]

Spears was able to comply with Newcombe's request due to the fact that already in December 1945 he had arranged for the Lipson article to be issued and distributed by the CAA as a pamphlet. Thus within a few months of the founding of this Gentile anti-Zionist committee, the fundamental arguments of the Fellowship were republished in pamphlet form under the auspices of the CAA. This in itself shows the importance that Gentile anti-Zionists attached to the Jewish argument against Zionism.

In an editorial following the publication of Lipson's *Spectator* article, the *Jewish Chronicle*, under the revealing title 'Their Jewish Friend', attacked Lipson for his article, speculated that it was nothing more than an effort to win plaudits from the influential 'white Arabs', and concluded sarcastically that if Lipson tried even harder he might eventually qualify for this category himself.[19]

In another editorial later in the same month the paper continued its attack on the Lipson article, but this time noted the fact that this 'effective anti-Zionist propaganda' had been circulated in parliament by the Arab Office under the direction of Spears.[20] The *Jewish Chronicle* was incorrect in crediting the Arab Office with the distribution of the pamphlet (which underlines the tendency, shown in chapter 7, of the Jewish press to view Spears as a leader of the Arab Office, as well as its failure to see the role of the CAA in the propaganda sphere). But these editorials do emphasise the fact that an impression existed within Jewry that Jewish anti-Zionists were providing non-Jews with ammunition to use against Zionist claims.

THE BIBLICAL, RACIAL AND HISTORICAL ARGUMENTS AGAINST ZIONISM

Throughout the Mandate era the Zionist movement attached much importance to the biblical argument in arguing its case. One notable example was Nahum Sokolow's monumental *History of Zionism, 1600–1919*. Published in the wake of the Balfour Declaration, this work was written very much with the objective of appealing to English sensibilities, and the first volume especially devotes much emphasis to the biblical aspect of the Zionist endeavour.[21]

As such, support for Zionism on the basis of the belief that Jews had a biblical right to Palestine greatly concerned Gentile anti-Zionists. Storrs called this support for a Jewish state on biblical grounds 'the Abrahamic Declaration', implying in his own sardonic way that just as the Balfour Declaration had given political credibility to Zionist aspirations, the Bible had given religious credibility to the Zionist claims at the expense of the Arabs who lived in Palestine.[22] Maude Royden-Shaw reiterated this view when she stated during the course of a radio discussion on Palestine that support for a Jewish state was due to the fact that 'the average Englishman gets all his knowledge of Palestine out of the Bible'.[23]

It is interesting how devout Christians such as Royden-Shaw (and Frances Newton) overcame their natural inclination to accept the literal meaning of the Bible when it clashed with their anti-Zionist stance. Indeed Royden-Shaw was asked to comment on this apparent contradiction during her evidence before the Anglo-American Committee. Her response, which was original if hardly credible, was that her opposition to Zionism did not contradict her belief in God as set out in the Bible because some of the most ardent Zionists were communists who did not believe in God.[24]

Sir Edward Spears was less concerned with the niceties of Christianity in opposing Zionism than was the missionary Royden-Shaw; but he also argued that support for Zionism was due to some biblical appeal, when, in the foreword to Abcarius's *Palestine: Through the Fog of Propaganda*, he declared that

> The average well-meaning citizen ... his biblical memories generally as vague as his knowledge of geography, ... [feels] that somehow Palestine is or should be a Jewish land. How the Jews came to leave it he does not remember, if he ever knew. The Jews were promised Palestine in the Bible ... there must be something to be said for their return to it.[25]

Spears expounded much effort in his attempt to find a credible refutation of Zionist claims on biblical grounds. He wrote to Selig Brodetsky in the summer of 1945 asking him for information on Zionist claims and specifically inquiring as to whether 'any of the claims [were] based on biblical prophecy'.[26] Earlier in the same year he had written to the Rt Revd W.H. Stewart, Bishop of the Church of England in Jerusalem. In this letter Spears requested a 'refutation on biblical grounds of the Jewish claim to Palestine' and informed the Bishop that the Zionist agitation was 'very successful owing to the fact that the public is most abysmally ignorant of biblical matters but doesn't like to confess it'.[27]

The Bishop (who, like Spears, would appear as a witness before the Anglo-American Committee),[28] though stating his reluctance to put a 'theological oar into deep political waters', gave a detailed exposition on the difficulties of using the theological argument in the battle against Zionism, warning of the futility of trying to argue against Zionism on biblical terms because every argument against the biblical right of Jews to Palestine could be countered by an equally convincing argument in favour (and vice versa).[29]

Spears' intense desire to deny Zionism its biblical claim to Palestine can be seen by his encouragement of the Revd Dr Alfred Guillaume to present a theological refutation of political Zionism's claims to the AACIP.[30] Guillaume, a Professor of the Old Testament, though the most qualified member of the CAA to speak on this subject, was never called by the AACIP to give evidence. Nevertheless, both he and Spears were determined to set out the anti-Zionist position on this issue, and Spears arranged for the Arab Office to make Guillaume's biblical argument against Zionism into a pamphlet.[31]

Guillaume's attempt to show that the Zionists had no valid biblical claim was considered to be of the utmost importance in fighting Zionism. Lord Altrincham, one of those who received a copy of Guillaume's pamphlet, saw it as 'a shattering repudiation of the *fundamental attitude* of the Jews'.[32] While Lord Lloyd, a former high commissioner to Egypt and the Sudan (1925–29) and colonial secretary (1940–41), felt that Guillaume's pamphlet 'supplied a long felt need'.[33]

There was a tendency for both the Jewish and Gentile anti-Zionist constituencies to mix together the biblical, historical and racial arguments against Zionism. An example of this can be seen in one article in *The Jewish Outlook* entitled 'The Jewish Race: Anthropological, Geographical and Historical Facts to Defeat Political Zionist Theory'.[34] This compression of so many complex issues together was an effort to find a winning argument against Zionist claims that it was believed were deeply ingrained in the public consciousness.

For example, Izzat Tannous, the veteran Arab propagandist and a member of the Arab Office (London), who had written to Spears to ask for his help to get the manuscript by M.F. Abcarius published, vouched for the book's worth primarily in terms of its attack on the Jewish historical claim to Palestine.[35]

This aspect of Abcarius's work no doubt appealed to Spears, for the previous year the CAA had issued a pamphlet, written by Professor G.R. Driver, entitled *Palestine: The Historical Background*. This began with the Abrahamic era and continued up to modern times to show that 'much of the land that the Jews have acquired ... and much that they claim, was in no sense or hardly in any sense theirs in previous history'.[36]

This kind of historical argument against Zionism was closely related to the racial one. In the run-up to the Anglo-American Committee hearings in London, Hope-Simpson sent Spears a memorandum he had written arguing against Zionism on the basis that

> The immigrants [Jewish immigrants to Palestine] in ... no sense [are] returning to their homeland ... they have in them not one drop of Hebrew blood ... [They are] descended from pagans who converted to Judaism many centuries ago.[37]

Spears adopted this argument in his evidence before the Anglo-American Committee, referring to Hope-Simpson's memorandum to support his own claim that 'the great majority of immigrants ... [have] no racial connection to Palestine even in the distant past ... [and are] not descendants of the Israelites who migrated to Palestine from Egypt'. He concluded that only 4,000 of the 400,000 Jews returning to Palestine could claim that they were returning to the home of their ancestors in Israel and Judea.[38]

What both Spears and Hope-Simpson were arguing was that the majority of East European Jews who wanted to go to Palestine had no historical or racial connection to the Jews of biblical Israel but were descended from the pagan tribes of Europe. This was most popularly known as the 'Khazar theory', an intriguing and curious aspect of Jewish history.[39]

The Khazars had been a pagan people of Turkish stock who appeared in Europe during the fifth century. In about AD 740, the King of the Khazars and his ruling elite converted to Judaism, and Judaism became the state religion of the Khazar people. The Khazar empire did exist and prospered until it fell victim to the hordes of Ghengis Khan in the thirteenth century, during which time Khazar communities scattered from their home in the Caucasus into what are now Russia and Poland.

Both Gentile and Arab anti-Zionists used this fascinating argument to deny the Jews a state in Palestine on historical and racial terms. Faris al-Khouri made the Khazar theory a central part of his public argument against a Jewish state during the special session of the United Nations in 1947; while Jamal Husseini, leader of the Arab Higher Committee, giving evidence before the United Nations Special Committee on Palestine in 1947, opposed Zionist claims on the basis that 'Western Jews known as Askenazim are descendants of the Khazars who were converted to Judaism'.[40]

In using this argument to deny the Zionists an historical or biblical link to Palestine, non-Jewish anti-Zionists were echoing another primarily Jewish argument against Zionism. The most striking example of this occurred in the United States and in relation to the efforts of Benjamin Friedman, a wealthy American Jewish businessman and a devoted opponent of Zionism who had formed the League for Peace with Justice in Palestine and spent large sums on anti-Zionist publicity primarily in the New York press.[41]

Cecil Hourani, of the Washington Arab Office, claimed in his autobiography that it had been Friedman who had convinced Arab leaders, particularly Jamal Husseini, of the value of the Khazar theory as an argument against Zionism.[42] And Hourani's claim is given credence by internal British official diplomatic reports on meetings with Friedman which also refer to this.[43] Back in London the Khazar argument was also a central component of the Fellowship argument, the *Jewish Outlook* challenging the Zionists' claims to Palestine because Palestine was 'a country with which the Khazars in all their history had neither geographical nor ethnic association'.[44]

DUAL LOYALTY

The post-war Jewish anti-Zionists of the Jewish Fellowship argued that to support political Zionism was to call into doubt one's loyalty to Britain. This attitude was partly due to a (false) belief that English Jews in their support for Zionism were not condemning terrorist actions in Palestine. But it was also due to an acceptance of the view that Jews, in return for receiving citizenship, had certain obligations to Britain. For the Jews had received citizenship as a religious community and the Zionist claim that the Jews were a nation in exile meant that the Jewish right to citizenship was under threat from Zionism.

This idea that Jewish citizenship was born out of a contract with Gentiles created during the era of emancipation in the nineteenth century had been an argument in early Jewish polemics against Zionism. Edwin Montagu, in a last-ditch effort to obstruct the Balfour Declaration, declared that Zionism was 'untenable ... inconsistent with British citizenship'.[45]

This view was echoed in the following year in a pamphlet by Basil Henriques and Claude Montefiore. This pamphlet called for the Jew to be

> A citizen of England and a Jew by religion ... not merely in a legal sense ... this loyalty [is] owed to England by the Jews ... one's blood boils if these great gifts are not answered by a single and undivided and complete allegiance.[46]

Thus the Fellowship's argument against Zionism on the ground of dual loyalty was very much a continuation of a long-held and central Jewish anti-Zionist argument. For example, Rabbi Mattuck in a lecture on Judaism arranged by the B'nai B'rith First Lodge of England in 1945 expressed much the same conception of loyalty to Britain as Henriques and Montefiore had done in 1918 when he stated that British Jews were an integral part of the British nation, integral not only by loyalty of citizenship but also through a spirit of nationality.[47]

The standard Zionist response to these claims had been made by Harry Sacher in his 1917 pamphlet *Jewish Emancipation: The Contract Myth*.[48] However, this issue took on an increasing significance after the Biltmore Declaration of 1942 when the official policy of Zionism became the creation of a Jewish state. Colonel Gluckstein, for example, seconded the motion to remove all references to a Jewish state or commonwealth from the Board of Deputies statement on Palestine in November 1944, because to support the creation of a Jewish state 'means that we are pleading guilty to the charge of dual loyalty'.[49]

The Jewish Fellowship abhorred the fact that a Jewish state was being openly supported by British Jews, born, raised and educated in Britain in a climate of freedom born out of citizenship rights. As an article in the *Jewish Outlook* entitled 'Abuse of Freedom' stated: 'A Jewish citizen has for more than a hundred years been accepted here as a full citizen professing the Jewish religion, and so long as he attempts to uphold his religion England will continue to accept him.'[50]

Daniel Lipson MP on more than one occasion during these years used the floor of the House of Commons to fight Zionism on the grounds of the dual loyalty issue, and in terms of the contract theory. In a 1942 debate Lipson was of the opinion that Zionists could not have it both ways: they could not belong to a separate people and also claim all the advantages of citizenship in their countries of residence. Again, in the course of a speech in the House in 1946, in the wake of the arrest of Zionist and Jewish Agency leaders in the Yishuv, Lipson informed the House that 'not all Jews in this country have forgotten the debt they owe to Britain'.[51]

Just how intensely Lipson thought of the Jewish position within Britain in terms of a contract can be seen in his important 1945 article in the *Spectator* (published by the CAA as a pamphlet). His first paragraph is replete with words such as 'citizen', 'patriotism', 'better citizen', 'loyalty' and 'responsibilities'.[52]

This determined effort to try to show that Jews, as opposed to Zionists, were in no way guilty of dual loyalty did not go unnoticed. Newcombe in a letter to Spears was of the opinion that 'all members [of parliament] except Lipson classify Jews as Zionists who put Palestine first and use every other country as best they can for their own objectives'.[53] Indeed the dual loyalty charge was repeated by the Gentile anti-Zionist community.

Even before the Biltmore programme of 1942, Gentile anti-Zionists were very concerned lest Zionism would bring about dual loyalty amongst Jews. Sir John Hope-Simpson, speaking at the RIIA in 1938, was of the opinion that the efforts of the Jewish Agency to spread Zionism throughout the world would inevitably detach the Jews from their 'local loyalty'.[54] In the same year Newcombe, in a pamphlet written for the PIC, raised the issue of dual loyalty and argued that from the Jewish perspective it was one of the fundamental points of the whole debate on Palestine.[55]

Once Spears embroiled himself in the debate over Palestine in the post-war era, he also claimed that Zionism would result in a dual loyalty amongst English Jews. At a talk on the future of the Middle East at the RCAS in February 1945, he informed those present that he did not want to dwell on the issue of Zionism, and then proceeded to raise the issue of dual loyalty, asking his audience:

> Do these Jews who form part of our body politic ... aspire to another nationality? ... would they not fear and dread anything that might in any way cast doubt on the intangibility of their oneness with the other citizens of the land of their birth?[56]

Spears raised this issue again during his evidence before the AACIP, while in March 1948 he wrote to *The Times* with his opinion that 'there can be no doubt' that a Jewish state would create a dual loyalty, concluding 'I have warned against this danger for a long time'.[57]

Such was Spears' preoccupation with this issue that he wrote to Kenneth Pickthorn MP, a month before the creation of Israel, about the need to call a meeting of the CAA, saying: 'we might well discuss the question of the dual loyalty of British Jews'.[58] Spears never said why a committee supposedly concerned with general Arab affairs felt the need to meet to discuss the loyalty of British Jews. He did, however, on an earlier occasion comment on the Arab position on the issue of dual loyalty, and was of the opinion that 'this aspect did not interest the Arabs at all'.[59] Here Spears is indicating that the Arabs in their fight against Zionism saw no reason to involve themselves in an issue that was primarily a concern of Jews and their adopted countries.

However, in as much as dual loyalty was an issue to be used against Zionism, the Arab Office was very interested in addressing it. In articles under headlines such as 'Zionism and Dual Allegiance', the *Arab News Bulletin* argued against a Jewish state because it 'would inevitably create a divided allegiance'.[60] In other articles it was less sure of the inevitability of this happening, but argued that even if dual loyalty did not occur, non-Jewish citizens would still think it had, and the negative effect on Jewry would be the same.[61]

Thus the Gentile anti-Zionists saw the issue of dual loyalty as both an opportunity to threaten Jewry, with warnings of what their fate would be if a Jewish state were created, while also using this argument as a reason for Gentiles not to support a Jewish state. Perhaps even more than the argument that Jews were a religious community, the Jewish acceptance of the validity of the dual loyalty charge gave credibility to Gentile claims. For if this was the view of Jews, many of whom occupied a leading position both inside and outside Anglo-Jewry, who were Gentiles to disagree?

For example, Storrs writing in 1947 referred to Jewish concerns about dual loyalty, to confirm his own fears, and was of the opinion that the dual loyalty that eminent Jews such as Claude Montefiore had prophesied had occurred in the post-war era.[62] And CAA members continued publicly to air this apprehension even after Israel had been created. Stephen Longrigg in a 1949 review of Chaim Weizmann's *Trial and Error* was of the view that

> it would obviously be over-optimistic or merely foolish ... to expect more than a certain degree of 'loyalty' to Great Britain, its policies and its people from immigrant foreigners of alien blood, background and ambitions such as are the foreign-born Jews to whom HMG so readily accords the privilege of British nationality.[63]

As far as the Zionists were concerned, the fact that the Jewish opponents of Zionism provided much of the credibility for Gentile anti-Zionists on the above issues was unforgivable. They refused to accept that the Gentile anti-Zionist opposition to Zionism on Jewish grounds was sincere, and believed that Jewish arguments against Zionism were only adopted as a way of adding credibility to their own positions.

There was much credence in this. For example, Maude Royden-Shaw, like her contemporaries, was always careful in her public statements to claim that 'the immense majority of Jews are non-Zionist'.[64] Yet only months before this claim she had informed Storrs in a private correspondence, that while a non-Zionist solution to the Palestine problem would appeal to those Jews who did not support political Zionism, 'there are such Jews, though perhaps not many'.[65]

Similarly, there was a touch of hypocrisy in the continual claims of Spears and his contemporaries that Zionism was causing dual loyalty amongst Jews. For as will be seen in chapter 8 the call by Spears and the CAA for the British government to open England to more Jewish refugees was made, not in a belief that this was in the interest of England but because it was seen as essential to the Arab argument against opening up Palestine to Jewish immigration. Thus on this issue the members of the CAA were putting what they deemed to be the interests of Arabs before what they believed to be best for their own country.

During a dinner in Beirut, held in his honour in 1946, Spears informed the guests that, although a proud Briton, he was also 'a citizen of Syria and Lebanon'.[66] And despite being technically correct, having been awarded honorary citizenship of Beirut by the city's municipality in recognition of his services to Lebanon in 1944, Spears would have undoubtedly condemned this as an example of dual loyalty had it been a Jew talking about his relationship with Zionism and Palestine. Moreover, at the same time as Spears attacked Zionists for showing dual loyalty in their verbal attacks on Britain, he was welcoming even more anti-British attacks from Albert Hourani.

Hourani, a leading member of the Arab Office, was also a British subject, born and raised in Manchester. He was vehement in his hostility to what he saw to be the British betrayal of the Arabs in these years. In one lecture at the RIIA, that Spears and many other CAA members attended (nine of the 40 people in the audience were members of the CAA), Hourani condemned Britain and said that he felt 'completely wrong' in advocating Anglo-Arab friendship in the past and believed that in doing so he had 'cheated his Arab friends'.[67]

As such it is understandable that the Zionists saw Gentile anti-Zionists arguing in Jewish terms as primarily a propaganda tactic to give their anti-Zionism credibility. This is not to say that the Zionists dismissed issues such as dual loyalty and whether or not the Jews were a religion or a nation as of no importance. Within Jewry there existed an awareness that the subject of whether Jewry was a religious community or a national body was important and deserved to be debated in the post-war era. The Board of Deputies, in a 1944 memorandum entitled 'Questions Asked at Meetings', and intended to help Jews to answer some of the more awkward questions posed to them by non-Jews, stated that 'there is probably no problem that provides so many answers as this one'.[68]

Likewise Zionist publicists, recognising the complexities inherent in the debate on whether Jews were a nation or religion, did not trivialise the issue. Joseph Heller in one of a series of Zionist educational pamphlets admitted that the question of whether the Jews were a nation was not academic but important.[69] Nor did Zionists dismiss the debate on the racial antecedents of Jewry, from which the Khazar theory flowed. For example, Abraham Poliak's 1943 work, *Kazaria: History of a Jewish Kingdom in Europe*, was debated and given serious consideration within Zionist and Jewish intellectual circles.[70] Ignaz Zollschan, one of the leading Jewish authorities on race, who had begun writing on the subject at the beginning of the twentieth century in Vienna in the company of other Viennese intellectuals such as Sigmund Freud, Ludwig Wittgenstein and Otto Rank, writing in the Zionist publication the *Jewish Forum* in 1946 went so far as to claim that the racial argument was becoming 'the strongest argument against Jewish immigration into Palestine'.[71]

Yet regardless of the validity of these issues, as issues that needed to be seriously debated, the Zionists still viewed the racial/national argument first and foremost as a propaganda tactic on behalf of anti-Zionists. And it was the fact that members of Jewry were providing credence for such propaganda arguments in the wake of the Holocaust and at such a critical time in the life of Palestine, not the debate on the issues *per se*, that angered the Zionists. As an article in *Gates of Zion* attacking the Fellowship stressed, 'those who annihilate us do not enter into the subtleties of the word nation'.[72]

Similarly the Zionists, while denying the validity of the dual loyalty claim, were sensitive to the fact that it was a legitimate issue for concern, especially since British Jews in promoting Zionism were clashing with their own government, the Mandatory power for Palestine. As Selig Brodetsky told the 1946 Zionist Congress, where the efforts of British Zionists had been criticised by delegates as somewhat lacklustre, 'there was no other Jewish community that had fought its own government over 25 years on the subject of Palestine'.[73]

In 1944 Mrs Dugdale addressed the position of British Jews who wanted to support Zionism, but who were wary of giving support to political Zionism if it affected their relationship with Britain. Rather than dismissing this as nonsense, she called it an 'extremely honourable scruple'.[74] Indeed, the Zionist response to the claim of dual loyalty was not to deny that Jews held a special place for Zionism and Palestine but to state that there was room for loyalty of many types. What the Zionists would not tolerate was the use of the dual loyalty issue as a weapon against Zionist aspirations. And this is how Zionists saw the Fellowship's position on the issue, with Harry Sacher rejecting Fellowship claims of dual loyalty as part of its 'ill-conceived propaganda in their opposition to the Zionist ideal'.[75]

This was the attitude of the Zionists to the common arguments that both Jewish and non-Jewish anti-Zionists used against

Zionism. For the Zionists these shared arguments proved beyond doubt that the Jewish Fellowship was betraying Jewry by giving credibility to the Gentile enemies of Zion. That this view came to be shared throughout Anglo-Jewry can be seen in regard to other shared arguments against Zionism: arguments that were even more emotive in the context of the time and which isolated the Fellowship even more within Jewry.

REHABILITATION OF JEWRY IN EUROPE

The Jewish Fellowship supported the argument that the surviving Jews of Europe should be rehabilitated in their native lands and partake in rebuilding the destroyed continent. In doing so it presented the resettlement of Jews in Germany and Poland as both a viable and acceptable solution to the Jewish problem. For example, Rose Henriques always maintained that during her time in Germany most of those she met wanted to remain in that country and rebuild their congregations.[76]

Henriques' claims on this issue carried a certain amount of weight. She was chairman of the German department of the Jewish Committee for Relief Abroad, 1945–52. In June 1945 she led a team of 12 (the first Jewish relief team from Britain) to Belsen, and in 1947 she went to the British zone in Germany as a special investigator for the same committee. Indeed, her involvement in helping Jewish displaced persons (DPs) was noted when she attended the Anglo-American Committee hearings in London as a member of the Fellowship delegation, and the committee members asked her for advice on the issue of DPs.[77]

The Fellowship paper welcomed the re-establishment within Germany of 'Germans of Jewish Faith' and gave individual examples of Jewish rehabilitation in Germany, which were presented as proof of German repentance and remorse.[78] It also attempted to show, in articles entitled 'Enlightenment Enters Poland' and 'Reliable News From Poland' that Poland was safe for Jews to return to and thrive in.[79]

One of these articles reported that 'every effort is being made to resettle Polish Jews in Poland and make them happy and free and fearless citizens'. The same issue of the paper also contained photographs of Jewish children under the heading 'Jewish Life in Poland Today' and one of the captions accompanying the photographs read, 'Jewish children are safe, happy and well cared for in a crèche, while parents work or receive training in new trades'.[80] There was also an attempt to show that in this new climate anti-Semitism had virtually disappeared and that those anti-Semitic incidents that did occur had their roots outside Poland.[81]

One should view this encouragement of Jewish resettlement in Germany and Poland, and the parallel enthusiasm in claiming that anti-Semitism in these countries was at an end, in the context of the destruction of European Jewry that had just taken place. There were other groups within Jewry such as the Central British Fund, the Jewish Committee for Relief Abroad and the Chief Rabbi's Religious Emergency Council who worked to improve the quality of life of Jewish refugees in Europe.

However, no other body in Anglo-Jewry in these years promoted rehabilitation in Poland and Germany (the two countries most identified with the Holocaust) so keenly or took it upon itself to speak up for the moral rejuvenation of Polish or German society. Rabbi Dr Solomon Schonfeld, executive director of the Chief Rabbi's Religious Emergency Council (and by no means a Zionist),[82] on his return from a visit to Poland in 1945 as a delegate of the United Jewish Relief organisation, stated categorically that no Jews wanted to remain in Poland and that while he saw hope for Jewish children in other parts of Europe, the same could not be said about Poland.[83]

Likewise, no paper in the community presented rehabilitation in these two countries in such an appealing light as the *Jewish Outlook*. The *Jewish Chronicle* analysed the position of Jews in Poland during these years under headlines such as 'Pogrom in Poland', where it asked 'is there any sense, let alone justice or mercy, in preaching to the Jews about re-establishing themselves on this hate and blood-sodden soil?'[84]

Similarly, the *Jewish Monthly*, the paper of the Anglo-Jewish Association, the leading non-Zionist body in Anglo-Jewry, was unwilling to present a picture of a rejuvenated Germany or Poland. In June 1947 it was of the opinion that the 'Jewish outlook [in Germany] is by no means favourable', while the following month it was of the opinion that 'there was little pleasant to report from Germany'.[85]

Nor was this simply the view of the Anglo-Jewish media and community elite removed from the positive realities of Polish and German life, who felt a reflexive post-Holocaust need to attack these countries. For at exactly the same time a memorandum to the Foreign Office, from the British Embassy in Warsaw, reported the position of Jews in Poland as presented to it during a meeting with the Chief Rabbi of Poland. The Rabbi's evaluation was in total contradiction to the optimistic picture painted by the Fellowship.

The official Jewish population, according to the Chief Rabbi, was 93,000, and of the 150,000 Polish Jews recently repatriated from Russia 'practically none' stayed in Poland, preferring DP camps in Germany. Similarly the Chief Rabbi explained that those Jews who remained in Poland did so due to the fact that very few Jews were being allowed out of the country (which was perhaps the real reason for what the *Jewish Outlook* called the 'cessation of unorganised and wild emigration from Poland').[86] The memorandum concluded with the Chief Rabbi's assessment that 'the attitude towards the Jews has taken a turn for the worse'.[87]

While the Fellowship's stance on rehabilitation and the rejuvenation of Jews in Germany and Poland found no support amongst any section of Anglo-Jewry it did find an equally vigorous promotion among Gentile anti-Zionists at this time. In November 1945 Foreign Secretary Bevin had set out the fundamental argument in favour of rehabilitation of Jews in Europe when he stated that 'We cannot accept the view that the Jews should be driven out of Europe and should not be permitted to live again in these countries without discrimination and contribute their ability and talent towards rebuilding the prosperity of Europe.'[88] The Gentile anti-Zionist community agreed with Bevin (some even asked how Jews could be called refugees if they were still in their own countries of birth!), using Jews who supported this position to back up their arguments. For example, in November 1945 one Dr Emil Leimdoerfer, in a letter to Spears, proposed the settlement of Jews outside of Palestine through rehabilitation, as a solution to the Jewish problem.[89] Spears replied enthusiastically to the proposal on the grounds that 'I feel myself that if a body of persons of Jewish faith advocated a solution along the lines you suggest there would be a great deal more chance of it being considered.'[90] Spears' reply to Leimdoerfer shows just how much importance he attached to such arguments, coming as they did from Jews.

Thus, in a letter published in the *Manchester Guardian* in 1946, Spears recounted in great detail the contents of a letter that he had received from a Viennese Jew who opposed Zionism and who had a plan that would enable Jews, like himself, who supported rehabilitation to stay in Europe. Spears emphasised that 'my correspondent states that there are many thousands of Jews like himself who do not wish to go to Palestine'.[91] Not surprisingly Zionists saw this letter by Spears purely as an attempt to use Jewish opposition to Zionism to back up his own efforts against Zionism. Thus Professor Lewis Namier's response to Spears ended with a sarcastic attack on this tactic: 'I feel that it was not his purpose [in writing] merely to restate the thesis that some Jews do not wish to go to Palestine and none should be allowed to do so.'[92]

Spears and his contemporaries not only argued that those Jews still in Europe should remain there, but that a substantial number of Jews who were in Palestine wanted to return to Europe. In October 1945 five anti-Zionist MPs, three of whom (Pickthorn, Philips Price and Stokes) were members of the newly formed CAA, circulated an anti-Zionist memorandum in parliament arguing, among other things, that by December 1944 over 35,000 European Jews had applied for permission to leave Palestine after the war.[93]

Spears also argued this as part of his support for rehabilitation in Europe. In his prolific writings on Palestine he set out his belief that many thousands of Jews would return to Europe from Palestine if allowed to do so.[94] Spears was so interested in this aspect of the Palestine issue that he even asked Kenneth Pickthorn to ask a question in the House, during question time, as to just how many Jews intimated to the government their desire to leave Palestine, and told the MP that in his opinion the number was 35,000.[95] The Arab Office would also continually claim in both its paper and its pamphlets that Jews wanted to leave Palestine and return to Europe if 'the dictatorship of the Jewish Agency and terrorists would allow them'.[96]

This argument had very little basis in fact. At the same time as Spears and the group of anti-Zionist parliamentarians associated with the CAA were arguing that 35,000 Jews wanted to leave Palestine, C.V. Shaw, the chief secretary of Palestine, was of the view that 'there is as yet no sign of any "backflow" on a large scale', and added that speculation of even 15,000 Jews wanting to leave 'was a considerable exaggeration'.[97] But it is of interest to note, and highlights the considerable influence of anti-Zionist arguments at the time, that Shaw had been requested to give his opinion on this issue by J.M. Martin of the Colonial Office because 'we have heard a good deal recently [as an] argument used against immigration into Palestine'.[98]

The real appeal of this argument was the fact that it was a Jewish argument and a highly symbolic example of Jewish opposition to the creation of a Jewish state – for what was more damning to political Zionist claims than thousands of Jews already in Palestine desperately attempting to leave? Hope-Simpson, in a letter to Spears in September 1945, broached this issue of Jews in Palestine who wanted to return to Europe. He referred to an article in the *Central European Observer*, entitled 'No Backers',[99] and told Spears that after reading this article and having corresponded on the subject with Emile Marmorstein (an Iraqi-born Jew who worked at the BBC Near Eastern Service), he was of the view that 'this aspect of the problem [is] both encouraging and unpublicised'.[100]

Both the correspondence with Marmorstein, a member of the Fellowship council, and the article in the *Central European Observer* must have made a great impression on Hope-Simpson, for he would return to this issue in the article he wrote for the *Fortnightly* in January 1946. In this article he commented on the Jewish desire for repatriation from Palestine (thus giving this 'unpublicised' issue some publicity) and quoted from the 'No Backers' article (written by an anonymous 'Jerusalem correspondent'), to back up his claims.[101] Indeed, this same article aroused the interest of another member of the CAA, Major G.W.G. Baillie, who was so taken with this alleged Jewish desire to leave Palestine that he forwarded a copy of the 'No Backer' article to his committee chairman, Spears.[102]

Not surprisingly, the Zionists responded aggressively to the argument that Jews should stay in Europe and help to rebuild the continent, rejecting outright the claims that Jews wanted to leave Palestine *en masse* but were prevented from doing so by the Jewish Agency. Moshe Rosette epitomised the Zionist attitude, when in response to the claim that Jews were needed in Europe to ensure the moral recovery and post-war reconstruction efforts, he answered 'we refuse to become the mercury of the moral thermometer of Europe'.[103]

Zionists believed that the call for rehabilitation was but an anti-Zionist tactic to block Zionist efforts to gain immigration into Palestine and was intricately connected to an opposition to Zionism and a Jewish state, rather than a concern for what was best for either Europe or the Jews.[104] As such Zionists treated the Jewish support for rehabilitation with contempt, and some of the most severe criticism of the Fellowship came over the group's public support for the rehabilitation of Jews in Europe.

In 1944 Mr A. Reiss, speaking in Leeds at a meeting of the Jewish Labour Committee, ridiculed those Jews who called for rehabilitation in Europe, asking rhetorically, 'Go back to where? To Lublin, full of the remains of slaughtered Jews?'[105] While in response to a speech given by Daniel Lipson to a Fellowship gathering in London, the *Zionist Review* quoted his call for Jews to return to their former homes to build them on better and juster foundations, asking, 'Why do not Mr Lipson and his friends set an example to the present-day refugees by returning to their countries of origin, for, say, five years of service, in order to help them rebuild on better and juster foundations?'[106] And the same paper described as 'rubbish' a speech by Julian Franklyn, secretary of the Fellowship, in which he gave numerous examples of German Jews who had been persecuted by the Nazis, but who yearned for their home in Germany.[107]

The Zionist anger at the Fellowship's position on rehabilitation is understandable. For at one stage, in February 1947, the *Jewish Outlook* admitted that although in November 1946 it had published reports that suggested life for Jews in Poland was returning to normality, unfortunately news had reached it from relief workers in Poland that these earlier reports were somewhat optimistic. Nevertheless, rather than playing down the attractiveness of rehabilitation in the light of this information, the paper was of the opinion that the answer was even more 'relief and rehabilitation'.[108]

It was this seemingly irrational pleading on behalf of Germany and Poland, and the failure to relate what had happened in the war to the post-war environment, that disgusted the Zionists. They were less harsh in attacking Gentile anti-Zionists in their call for rehabilitation of Jewry and the subsequent claim that many Jews in Palestine wanted to return to Europe. In one such article, Hannah Stein, the president of the Federation of Zionist Youth, in England, quoted Spears' arguments for rehabilitation and asked readers of the *Zionist Review*, 'Can we allow this view to go unchallenged?'[109]

Of course the answer was no, but the fact that it was an argument propounded by Jews themselves made it harder to attack the Gentile anti-Zionist efforts to block a Jewish state by supporting rehabilitation, and all that the Zionists could do was to note these efforts by Gentiles such as Spears and dismiss them. And the Jewish commentator C.C. Aronsfeld did exactly this in an article sarcastically entitled 'The Captivity of Zion' when he attacked Spears, 'the notorious anti-Zionist and champion of Arab feudalism', for an article in the *Daily Mail* in which he claimed that many Jews in Palestine wanted to leave and would do so if they were provided with the means to go.[110]

However, the Fellowship's eager support for rehabilitation in the immediate aftermath of the Holocaust and in the face of all other accounts of the existing situation was too much for Zionists to bear. Thus it is hardly surprising that in response to the Fellowship's congratulations to 'Germans of Jewish Faith' for rebuilding their lives in Germany, the *Zionist Review* was driven to say, 'it brings one to the point of vomiting to read such stuff. Six million Jews were massacred and the Jewish Fellowship can still talk about Germans of Jewish Faith.'[111]

Nor was this an extreme Zionist reaction to the Fellowship. In supporting and enthusiastically promoting rehabilitation in Germany and Poland the Fellowship was very quickly becoming beyond the pale within Jewish, not simply Zionist, circles. A letter by the Revd Leslie Hardman to the *Jewish Chronicle* in 1947 encapsulated the general view within Jewry when he condemned the 'attempt to convince [an] uninformed public … to establish remnants in blood-sodden places', and asked, 'are we to read into these utterances a subtle attempt to support the anti-Zionist bloc?'.[112]

Hardman was not writing out of Zionist motive, for he had been a forces chaplain attached to the British 8th Army Corps headquarters in Germany and had worked in Belsen. In a private letter to Ivan Greenberg, editor of the *Jewish Chronicle*, written more than a year before the above letter was published in the paper, he told Greenberg that, since his Belsen experience, 'nothing is important in my life except to save these people'.[113]

Thus even those Jews, like Hardman, apathetic to the communal battle between Zionists and anti-Zionists and dedicated to relieving the suffering of Jewish survivors of the Holocaust, found it hard to promote Germany or Poland as viable homes for Jewry *en masse* in 1946 and 1947, and perceived Jewish efforts to do so as part of an attempt to support Gentile anti-Zionists. As such, the promotion of rehabilitation brought Jewish anti-Zionists closer to the position of Gentile anti-Zionists and gave credence to Gentile claims on the issue, but at the cost of pushing them further from the mainstream of Anglo-Jewry.

ZIONISM IS NAZISM

The historian Yaacov Shavit has stated the view that the main question debated within Jewry in the wake of the Holocaust was 'was Nazism an inherent feature of the European essence or was it a diverted characteristic, an historical accident?'[114] Jewish anti-Zionists were able to support the rehabilitation of Jews in Europe precisely because they viewed Nazism as more of a 'diverted characteristic, an historical accident', than the 'real face of Europe'.

It was also the contention of anti-Zionist Jews that political Zionism and the Jewish state policy should be viewed as a result of and a reaction to Jewish suffering at the hands of the Nazis. Colonel Gluckstein told the Anglo-American Committee that

> I think it is pertinent to ask the question: does anybody really believe that if Hitlerism had not appeared, if six million Jews had not been slaughtered you would today be sitting here faced with the question of a Jewish state and all that goes with it?[115]

On one level this was but an attempt to oppose Zionism by reiterating the commonly held view that the Nazi treatment of Jews, and that alone, had created the momentum for a Jewish state as a way of dealing with the Jewish refugee problem. And it must be stated that although the Zionist movement was anxious not to be perceived as a refugee movement, and was adamant that even if the Nazi persecution of the Jews had never occurred there would eventually have been a Jewish state, it did attempt to capitalise on whatever humanitarian sympathy could be gained as a result of the Holocaust.

However, on another level Gluckstein's statement to the AACIP can be seen as part of the Jewish Fellowship's belief that those Jews who had suffered at the hands of the Nazis and were subsequently involved in the efforts to gain a Jewish state acted as they did because they had become somewhat deranged by the whole Nazi experience.

Gluckstein spelt this out later on in his evidence when he told the AACIP that DPs' and camp survivors' own views regarding travelling to Palestine should be discounted as they were not 'mentally or physically fit to form a judgement'.[116] In part this was the view that the Nazi terror had caused some mental imbalance in Jewry best symbolised by those who resorted to terrorism to gain a Jewish state. Basil Henriques, writing in the *Star* on political Zionism and terrorism, stated his belief that

> Many of those who perpetrated them [terrorist acts] suffered in concentration camps ... nearly all have relatives in Europe ... they feel that they have nothing to lose by what they do. They are too unhinged in their mental outlook to be able to see the appalling consequences.[117]

If the Fellowship had left its analysis of the relationship between Zionism and Nazism as an explanation of the motivations of those who carried out terrorism (regardless of whether it was the correct diagnosis of the mental state of Jewish terrorists), it would have been harder for Zionists to criticise the Fellowship. Many within mainstream Zionism and Anglo-Jewry as a whole would not have disagreed with the *Jewish Outlook*'s claim that 'the fanaticism of some Jews in Palestine ... can only be understood by those who realise how their hearts bleed for their loved ones ... they have completely lost their sense of reasoning'.[118]

But the Fellowship went further and portrayed Zionism itself, Jewish nationalism, the Jewish state policy, and all those Zionist Jews, whether they had been directly involved in the suffering in Europe or not, as being under a delusion brought about by Nazism. Julian Franklyn, a veteran communal worker, who before becoming secretary of the Fellowship had been the Board of Deputies organiser for outdoor speaking campaigns against anti-Semitism, was of the opinion that the real ailment that the Jewish community was suffering from was not Zionism *per se*, but the 'traumatic effect of the Nazi attack', which had made Zionism appear as an appealing option.[119]

Another Fellowship leader, the Revd Harold Reinhart, wrote to *The Times* to give his view that Zionism which had gathered momentum in the Nazi era was 'bred on despair and disillusion – naked nationalism – contrary to the whole Jewish tradition'.[120] After the publication of this letter, Reinhart received much supportive correspondence from other Fellowship members, including Basil Henriques and Albert Hyamson, the Jewish historian and a founding member of the Fellowship, who wrote to tell him that his letter in the press encapsulated 'the true Jewish view'.[121]

Indeed, Henriques in an earlier letter to Fellowship members after the hearings of the AACIP, argued along the same lines as Reinhart when he stated that

> It is only the deterioration in the status of the Jews arising

from Nazi doctrines of race, and the consequent appalling persecution ... which is responsible for the spread of the fallacious doctrine of Jewish nationhood and a Jewish state.[122]

More than this, it was the view of Jewish anti-Zionists that those Jews who supported the creation of a Jewish state were not only victims of Nazism who, blinded by the trauma of Nazism, had forgotten the true meaning of Judaism but were also enemies of Jewry. For by subscribing to the theories of a Jewish race and a Jewish state they had become the torchbearers of the Nazi-inspired doctrines, and hence had to be viewed as the propounders of the Nazi philosophy in the post-war world.

Gluckstein, for example, informed the Anglo-American Committee that 'to believe that this [Jewish suffering] is a justification for Jewish separatism and Jewish nationalism seems to me the adoption of the Hitler doctrine'.[123] While *The Jewish Outlook* echoed this in an editorial that claimed 'the conception of a Jewish race can only stand if we are prepared to accept the Nazi conception of a Nordic race'.[124]

Julian Franklyn was even more outspoken when he stated the view that 'many of us are supporting Hitler's racial theory with which he has scourged us, and are repeating his blood and soil slogan ... in the idea that we are asserting destiny'.[125] In another article, published in the *Contemporary Review* in July 1947, Franklyn again explained clearly why the Jewish anti-Zionists believed there to be a direct link between the Nazi creed and the Jewish support for a Jewish state:

> [the] degeneration of Jewish affairs has been brought about mainly by the rise of Hitlerism ... Hitlerism ... making its 'anti-Semitic international' not a religious, but a racial and political issue ... the Zionists with short-sighted opportunities succumbed to the challenge, since the ultimate development of the philosophy of blood and iron was Nazism, it is not surprising that modern Zionism's definition of Israel is racial and national.[126]

Thus Nazism had artificially created, through propaganda, the belief that Jewry was a race and a national entity rather than a religion. By promoting the Jews as a race, and a sub-human one at that, rather than a religion, the Nazis had attempted to present Jewry as a nation.

This in turn provided other nations with a reason to refuse to help Jewry when it faced the Nazi persecutions. For once Jewry was perceived as a national entity, it became a legitimate casualty of the war. As Franklyn continued to say in his *Contemporary Review* article:

> When the Jewish outlook was that of a religious community devoid of egocentric political consciousness, the Christian countries of the world in the name of religion ... [were] ready to receive victims of the Pogroms ... [but] Hitlerism reversed all that making [Jewry] ... not a religious but a racial and political issue.[127]

According to the Fellowship, the Zionists continued to propagate this myth in order to achieve their objective – a Jewish state. In the process they had become the imitators of the Nazis and heirs to the Nazi mantle.

Gentile anti-Zionists also echoed this Jewish anti-Zionist argument. Perhaps the best-known comparison of Zionism to Nazism was made by Arnold Toynbee, Professor of History at the University of London and director of studies at the RIIA, 1925–56, in the eighth volume of his monumental *A Study of History*. This analogy was born out of his view of the similarity in the way that the Zionists treated Palestinians during and after the 1948 war with the way that the Nazis had treated the Jews in Europe.[128]

Toynbee's claims in this work relating to Jews and Judaism caused great controversy and he was accused of being an anti-Zionist who was motivated in his opposition to a Jewish state by ideological anti-Semitism.[129] However, the Toynbee argument was neither the first nor the most outspoken on the subject, and in the immediate post-war world Gentile opponents of political Zionism rapidly adopted the Nazi–Zionist comparison as part of their anti-Zionist arguments.

As early as January 1945 Sir Edward Grigg (Lord Altrincham), speaking at a press conference in Cairo, referred to 'the establishment of a kind of Nazi gangsterism in the Holy Land'.[130] Similarly, CAA members such as Robin Maugham and M. Philips Price lost no opportunity to argue that Zionism had evolved into a Nazi movement. In a 1946 talk at the RIIA, Maugham was of the opinion that 'many Jews have become fascist', and in a speech the following year to the same body he set out in even greater detail the

Anti-Zionist Arguments against the Creation of a Jewish State 147

similarities between Zionism and Nazism. For Maugham 'the stare of hatred ... the patriotic songs ... the pride and confidence ... are all the same as in the Germany of Hitler', and with this he concluded, 'fascism has come to Palestine'.[131]

Likewise Philips Price had noted during a trip to Palestine in January 1946 that 'Zionism is acquiring ... the characteristics of the Nazis.' On his return home he continued in this vein, attacking Zionists in the Commons for 'adopting the tactics of their persecutors the Nazis'.[132] This presentation was to continue after the creation of Israel, with Storrs so preoccupied with the Nazification of the Zionist movement that in 1949 he even considered revising his *Orientations* to write about this phenomenon.[133]

The Arab Office (London) also compared Zionism to Nazism extensively during these years, both in private and in official propaganda writings. Edward Atiyah, in both a pamphlet written for the Arab Office in 1945 and in his autobiography published the following year, made this comparison and implied that Zionism was the Nazism of the Middle East.[134] Even in his last public speech before his death in 1964 Atiyah was still propounding this view and talking of the Zionist 'doctrines of racial exclusiveness and a policy and technique not easily distinguishable from Nazism'.[135]

Several other Arab Office pamphlets and editorials in the *Arab News Bulletin* made similar claims.[136] As one surveys the paper's editorial position one notices that as the Arab objective of preventing a Jewish state became less likely during 1947, culminating in the UN support for the partition of Palestine, Zionism was increasingly portrayed as a Nazi movement. In July 1947 it was claimed that 'Zionists are employing Nazi methods'. By September 1948 when partition had been established and a war raged in Palestine the paper's view was that 'Deir Yassin was a true expression of Zionist ideology and techniques, as Lidice was of Nazi ideology and technique, the murdering of Count Bernadotte as the slaughtering of the Jews in the Gas Chamber.'[137] By November 1948, in the last months before the Arab Office closed down, it was argued that the Zionist 'spirit ... techniques ... aims are almost indistinguishable from those of the Nazis'.[138]

But once again it was Spears who best highlighted the Gentile use of the Zionist–Nazi analogy as part of the opposition to Zionism. Already, before the war's end, he did not hesitate to inform correspondents that 'political Zionism as it is manifested in Palestine today preaches very much the same doctrines as Hitler'.[139]

In his evidence submitted to the Anglo-American Committee he expanded on this claim stating his view that

> Zionist policy in Palestine has many features similar to Nazi philosophy ... the politics of Herrenvolk ... the Nazi idea of Lebensraum, is also very much in evidence in the Zionist philosophy ... the training of youth is very similar under both organisations that have designed this one and the Nazi one ... [for] the intimidation of their own people.[140]

In making this claim Spears was deeply influenced by the Jewish anti-Zionist advocacy of this position. His comparison of Zionism to Nazism in terms of *Herrenvolk* policy echoed the claim made by Lipson in his *Spectator* article that the CAA had published as a pamphlet. And in notes made in preparation for his evidence before the AACIP he set out the argument against Zionism as a Nazi creed on the same page as he set out the Fellowship's position against Zionism.[141] Given this connection in Spears' mind, it is of note that immediately after informing the AACIP of the similarities between Zionism and Nazism, he called upon it to hear evidence from the Fellowship.[142]

The Zionist leadership dismissed the Nazi–Zionist analogy as not worthy of reply. Moshe Shertok, speaking at the United Nations in 1947, represented the general Zionist attitude when he said 'I will not attempt to refute this charge because it refutes itself.'[143] But English Zionists were aware that this comparison of Zionism to Nazism was a dangerous, insulting and endemic tendency in the post-war years.

It is of note that the anonymous wartime memorandum on the post-war strategy of Jewish anti-Zionists (referred to in chapter 4) predicted that Jewish and Gentile anti-Zionists in co-operating against Zionism in the post-war era would present Zionists as 'Jewish Nazis'. This became such a common part of anti-Zionist polemics that as early as March 1945 James Parkes, the Gentile Zionist commentator and theologian, was lamenting that it was an argument 'which I have heard too often'.[144] Indeed the following year, in his evidence before the AACIP, Parkes specifically rejected Spears' comparison of Zionism to Nazism, and argued that not even the most extreme branches of Zionism could be compared to the Nazis.[145]

Twice during these years at meetings at the RIIA, Mrs Dugdale challenged Gentile comparisons of Zionism to Nazism. In the discussion that followed a speech by Lieutenant-Colonel E.H.R. Altounyan (a surgeon of Armenian descent who had served in British intelligence in the war and who was a highly regarded member of the British Arabist community) she challenged the speaker's implicit claim that the Zionist argument was based on the theory of *Herrenvolk* and asked him just who stated that this was the Zionist position.[146] One year later Mrs Dugdale challenged Elizabeth Monroe, who in a talk at the same body had compared the Haganah to the Nazi SS, and asked her to clarify in what way the two bodies were similar.[147]

Interestingly, Altounyan, whose view of Zionism can be seen in his observation that 'Palestine Jewry represents a hysterical clot of humanity whose malady has been deliberately exacerbated by a band of politically bankrupt leaders',[148] responded to Dugdale with the claim that his comparison of Zionism to Nazism was valid because 'it is an argument often used'.[149]

This is hardly a credible defence of such a serious allegation, but it does show how this argument, that Zionism was the new Nazism, was a propaganda tactic given legitimacy because of its common use rather than its intrinsic merit. And it is in this context that one should view the Jewish response to the Fellowship on the issue. For the Fellowship's use of the Zionism–Nazism comparison brought it even closer to the Gentile anti-Zionist position. But in doing so it increased the isolation of the Fellowship within Jewry.

Julian Franklyn, the Fellowship's most vocal proponent of the belief that Zionism was a Nazi creed, was viewed as a pariah within the community. He felt that it was his duty to present publicly the Jewish view on such issues as this, telling the Revd Harold Reinhart that he undertook the task as 'I do not know anybody better qualified', but that if there was someone else who would do the job 'I shall only be to happy to take a backseat and remain mute.'[150]

The Zionists, unmoved by this selfless sacrifice to duty, responded to his comparisons of Zionism to Nazism with the view that he had gone 'completely mad'.[151] Leonard Stein, in his capacity as head of the AJA, the most important non-Zionist body within Jewry, was less willing to view Franklyn's statements as a consequence of insanity. In April 1945 he discussed the Fellowship's, especially Franklyn's, attempt to discredit Zionism in public by labelling it a Nazi creed, with the editor of the *Jewish Chronicle*, Ivan Greenberg. Stein was in no doubt as to 'the damage that may be done by this kind of talk' and urged Greenberg to 'take up this issue' in his paper.[152] Less than a week later Stein once more informed Greenberg just how 'objectionable' he found this Fellowship 'scandal' to be.[153] Greenberg heeded Stein's opinion and in an editorial condemned Franklyn as 'a lamentable propagandist ... lacking a sense of decency'.[154]

This abhorrence of the Fellowship's argument against Zionism on the basis that it was a Nazi creed can be seen as a Jewish rather than a purely Zionist attitude. And it can be best summed up by reference to a letter by a correspondent to the *Zionist Review* written in the aftermath of a claim by Franklyn in the *Streatham News* that Zionism was a Nazi, fascist creed. As far as this member of Jewry was concerned:

> The attempt by one or other of their worthy brotherhood [the Fellowship] to compare the ideals of Zionism with the revolting theories of Nazism (nay even to pronounce the two names in the same breath) is a scandal ... the so called Fellowship, what a misnomer, for there can be no kind of Fellowship between that body and the rest of Jewry.[155]

NOTES

1. See Jeffries' *The Palestine Deception* (London: *Daily Mail*, 1923), p. 18.
2. Newcombe, 'The Arab Countries', lecture to RIIA, 17 September 1942, 8/860, p. 5. Also see Freya Stark, *East is West* (London: John Murray, 1945), p. 100.
3. Spears, 'The Middle East and our Policy There', *JRCAS*, XXXII : 2 (April 1945), p. 156 and the *Daily Telegraph*, 24 November 1945. While Thomas Reid called Zionists 'the greatest foes of Jewry' in his evidence before the AACIP, London, 29 January 1946, pp. 1–28, p. 16, ACC3 121/C14/30/4, ABD.
4. William Hocking, 'Arab Nationalism and Political Zionism', *Moslem World*, XXXV: 3 (July 1945), pp. 216–23, p. 223.
5. See Arab Office evidence before the AACIP, Jerusalem, 25 March 1946, *Public Hearings before the Anglo-American Committee of Inquiry* (Jerusalem: 1946), pp. 96–132, p. 101.
6. Barbour, *Nisi Dominus: A Survey of Palestine* (London: Harrap, 1946), p. 5.
7. Ibid., p. 6.
8. *Arab News Bulletin*, 69 (13 August 1948), p. 1.
9. 'The Jewish Race: Anthropological, Geographical and Historical Facts Defeat Political Zionist Theory', *Jewish Outlook*, 1: 11 (April 1947), p. 6.
10. Hope-Simpson, 'The Palestine Mandate', *Fortnightly*, CLVI (December 1944), p. 36.
11. Hope-Simpson, 'The Jewish World since 1939: A Comment on Dr James Parkes' Paper', *International Affairs*, XXI: 1 (January 1945), pp. 100–5.
12. Parkes, 'The Jewish World since 1939', *International Affairs*, XXI: 1 (January 1945), pp. 87–100.
13. Parkes, *Palestine, Yesterday and Tomorrow* (London: British Association of the Jewish National Home, 1945), p. 2.
14. Hope-Simpson, 'The Jewish World since 1939', p. 100.
15. Lipson, 'Is Jewry a Nation?', *Spectator*, 2 November 1945, pp. 403–404, p. 403.

Anti-Zionist Arguments against the Creation of a Jewish State 151

16. Hope-Simpson, 'The Palestine Statement', *Fortnightly*, CLIX (January 1946), p. 27.
17. Hope-Simpson to Spears, 21 November 1945, Box 6/4, SPSP.
18. Newcombe to Spears, 18 January 1946, Box 5/3, SPSP.
19. 'Their Jewish Friend', *Jewish Chronicle*, 9 November 1945, p. 10.
20. 'Anti-Zionist Article', *Jewish Chronicle*, 30 November 1945, p. 5.
21. Nahum Sakolow, *History of Zionism, 1600–1919* (New York: Longmans, Green, 1919). On this issue see also Mayir Verete 'The Restoration of the Jews in English Protestant Thought', *Middle Eastern Studies*, 8: 1 (January 1972), pp. 3–50, and Barbara Tuchman's *Bible and Sword: How the British Came to Palestine* (London: Papermac, 1988).
22. MS Diary of Storrs, 27 January 1945, Box 6/6, STOP.
23. 'The Future of Palestine', *The Listener*, p. 480.
24. See Royden-Shaw's evidence before the AACIP, London, 29 January 1945, pp. 54–70, p. 63, ACC3121/C14/30/4, ABD. For Newton's argument on this issue see *Fifty Years in Palestine*, p. 306. Also see Jacob Sarna's letter to the *Jewish Chronicle* attacking Royden-Shaw's use of the 'communist bogey' in her Anglo-American evidence, 8 February 1945, p. 15.
25. See Spears' preface to Abcarius's *Palestine: Through the Fog of Propaganda* (London: Hutchinson, 1946), p. 9.
26. Spears to Brodetsky, 15 May 1945, Box 4/6, SPSP.
27. Spears to Rt Revd W.H. Stewart, 26 March 1945, Box 4/6, SPSP.
28. On Bishop Stewart's evidence see *Public Hearings before the Anglo-American Committee of Inquiry* (Jerusalem: 1946), pp. 1–4. For the Jerusalem diocesan involvement in the Palestine debate see file 3, Box LXVII, JEMP.
29. Stewart to Spears, 7 April 1945, Box 4/6, SPSP.
30. Spears to Guillaume, 23 January 1946, Box 6/4, SPSP.
31. Spears to Guillaume, 5 February 1946 and 23 February 1946, ibid. See Guillaume's *Zionism and the Bible: A Criticism of the Establishment of an Independent Jewish State in Palestine as Prophesied in the Holy Scriptures* (London: AO, 1946).
32. Altrincham to Spears, 3 April 1946, Box 6/3, SPSP (emphasis added).
33. Lloyd to Spears, 8 April 1946, Box 6/4, SPSP.
34. *Jewish Outlook*, 1: 11 (April 1947), p. 6. Also see G.R. Driver's memorandum *Considerations on Palestine*, circulated in 1946, which also argued against Zionism on biblical, historical and racial grounds, Box 4/7, SPSP.
35. Tannous to Spears, 20 February 1946, Box 15/5, SPSP.
36. See Driver's *Palestine: The Historical Background* (London: CAA, 1945). Storrs, for one, was of the opinion that Driver's argument was an 'an excellent summary of Jewish history', MS Diary of Storrs, 30 October 1946, Box 6/6 STOP.
37. Hope-Simpson to Spears, 18 January 1946, Box 4/3, SPSP.
38. Evidence of Spears before the AACIP, pp. 34, 37.
39. On the Khazar issue see Poliak's *Kazaria: History of a Jewish Kingdom in Europe* (Tel Aviv: Bialik–Masada Foundation, 1943); D.M. Dunlop, *The History of the Jewish Khazars* (Princeton, NJ: Princeton University Press, 1954). Also see Bernard D. Weinryb, 'Origins of East European Jewry: Myth and Fact', *Commentary* (December 1957), pp. 509–18. Arthur Koestler, whom Ronald Storrs ironically referred to as that 'half Jew Magyar writer', also wrote on this issue in *The Thirteenth Tribe: The Khazar Empire and its Heritage* (London: Hutchinson, 1976). For a critical analysis of Koestler's work on the Khazars see Robert Blumstock, 'Going Home: Arthur Koestler's Thirteenth Tribe', *Jewish Social Studies*, XLVIII: 2 (1986), pp. 93–104.
40. Jamal Husseini's statement to UNSCOP was reprinted in the *Zionist Review*, 3 October 1947, p. 4.
41. For an example of one of Friedman's full-page exorbitant adverts see the *New York Herald Tribune*, 2 May 1946.
42. See Cecil Hourani's *An Unfinished Odyssey: Lebanon and Beyond* (London: Weidenfeld & Nicolson, 1984), p. 61.
43. See letter from T.E. Bromley of the British Embassy, Washington to Sinclair of the British Consulate in New York, 7 September 1946, PRO/FO 371/52557.
44. 'The Jewish Race', *Jewish Outlook*, 2 :1 (June 1947), p. 12. For other Fellowship arguments against Zionism on the grounds that the Jews were not a race with links

back to biblical Palestine see Robert Henriques' letter in the *Jewish Chronicle*, 25 October 1946, p. 13; the report on Gluckstein's speech to the Jewish Literary Society in 1945 attacking the non-existent racial claim of Jews to Palestine, *Jewish Chronicle*, 10 June 1945, p. 10 and *Some Information for You*, p. 4. For another Jewish anti-Zionist argument calling on the Khazar theory see Alfred Lilienthal's *What Price Israel?* (Chicago: Henry Regnery, 1954), pp. 219–28. Also see Milton Himmelfarb's attack on Lilienthal's 'excursus on the Khazars' in 'Anti-Zionism as Ideology', *Commentary*, 17: 2 (November 1954), pp. 194–6, p. 195.

45. See Montagu's memorandum on Zionism, 23 August 1917, PRO/CAB 24/24.
46. Henriques and Montefiore, *The English Jew and His Religion* (London, 1918), p. 6. See also Montefiore's *Race, Nation, Religion and the Jew* (Keighley: Rydal Press, 1918).
47. Mattuck's speech was reported on in the *Jewish Chronicle*, 12 January 1945, p. 11.
48. Harry Sacher *Jewish Emancipation: The Contract Myth* (London: ZF, 1917).
49. Gluckstein, speaking at the Board of Deputies' Palestine debate, 5 November 1944, reported in *Zionist Review*, 10 November 1944, pp. 4–5.
50. 'Abuse of Freedom', *Jewish Outlook*, 2: 4 (September–October 1947), p. 2.
51. See Lipson's speeches, 3 December 1942, Parliamentary Debates, vol. 385, 11 November–17 December 1942–43, p. 1384 and 1 July 1946, Parliamentary Debates, vol. 424, 18 June–5 July 1945–46, p. 1894.
52. Lipson, 'Is Jewry a Nation?', p. 403.
53. Newcombe to Spears, 3 July 1946, Box 5/2, SPSP.
54. Hope-Simpson, 'The Refugee Problem', lecture to RIIA, 28 June 1938, 8/547, pp. 17, 20.
55. Newcombe, *The Future of Palestine* (London: PIC, 1938), p. 2.
56. Spears, 'The Middle East and our Policy There', p. 157.
57. Evidence of Spears before the AACIP, p. 30 and his letter in *The Times*, 15 March 1948.
58. Spears to Pickthorn, 21 June 1948, Box 7/1, SPSP.
59. Spears, 'The Middle East and our Policy There', p. 157.
60. 'Zionism and Dual Allegiance', *Arab News Bulletin*, 65 (18 June 1948), p. 2.
61. See the supplement to the *Arab News Bulletin*, 43 (8 August 1947), p. 4. Also see Albert Hourani's *Is Zionism the Solution to the Jewish Problem?* (London: AO, 1946), p. 3.
62. MS Diary of Storrs, 29 May 1947, Box 6/8, STOP.
63. Stephen H. Longrigg, review in *Arab World* (October 1949), p. 12.
64. Royden-Shaw, 'Arab Palestine', *Newsletter*, 7: 8 (August 1944), p. 236.
65. Royden-Shaw to Storrs, 3 April 1944, Box 6/15, STOP.
66. See report on Spears' Middle East visit, *Jewish Chronicle*, 25 October 1946, p. 19.
67. Hourani, 'Palestine after the Report', lecture to Middle East Group, RIIA, 17 May 1946, 8/1332, p. 6.
68. *Memorandum on Questions Asked at Meetings* (London: Board of Deputies, 1944), pp. 3, 11, ACC3121/C14/21/1, ABD.
69. Heller, *The Zionist Idea* (London: ZF, 1944), p. 3
70. See, for example, the review by Dr J. Litvin, secretary of the Central Zionist Synagogue Society, of Poliak's book which welcomed the research, *Gates of Zion*, 1: 3 (April 1947), pp. 39–43. A harsher response to Poliak's book can be seen in Joshua Starr's sceptical review in *Jewish Social Studies*, VII: 1 (January 1945), pp. 65–7.
71. I. Zollschan, 'The Arabian Race of Palestine: The Facts', *Jewish Forum*, 1: 1 (October 1946), pp. 46–51, p. 46. On the issue of Jews and race see Sander L. Gilman's *Smart Jews: The Construction of the Image of Jewish Superior Intelligence* (Lincoln, NB, London: University of Nebraska Press, 1996) and John M. Efram's, *Defenders of the Race: Jewish Doctors and Race Science in Fin-de-Siècle Europe* (New Haven, CT, London: Yale University Press, 1994), especially see chapter 6, 'Zionism and Racial Anthropology', pp. 123–74.
72. *Gates of Zion*, 2: 3 (April 1948), p. 32.
73. Brodetsky's speech to the 1946 Zionist Congress was reprinted in *New Judea*, December 1946–January 1947, pp. 52–3.
74. Mrs E. Dugdale, 'Double Loyalties', *Zionist Review*, 5 May 1944, p. 3.
75. Sacher, *Zionist Review*, 30 January 1948, p. 8.
76. For Rose Henriques' view on this see TBJSBH, 3/34, 1945–47, MS132 AJ 195, HENP.

Anti-Zionist Arguments against the Creation of a Jewish State 153

77. Evidence of the Jewish Fellowship before the AACIP, p. 47.
78. *Jewish Outlook*, 2: 10 (May 1948), p. 12; 'Professor F.M. Heichelheim Honoured by Germans', 2: 9 (April 1948), p. 1. Heichelheim who after the war became Professor of Greek and Roman History at the University of Toronto was also a supporter of the American Council for Judaism (the American equivalent of the Fellowship) and he wrote an endorsement for the cover of Rabbi Elmer Berger's anti-Zionist tract *Who Knows Better Must Say So* (New York: Praise Books, 1955).
79. *Jewish Outlook*, 1: 12 (May 1947), p. 6; 2: 1 (June 1947), p. 13.
80. *Jewish Outlook*, 1: 12 (May 1947), pp. 6–7.
81. 'Reliable News From Poland', *Jewish Outlook*, 2: 1 (June 1947), p. 13. See also 'Confirmation Regarding Poland', *Jewish Outlook*, 2: 3 (August 1947), p. 11.
82. Schonfeld was Rabbi of the Adath Yisroel Synagogue in North London and president of the Union of Orthodox Hebrew Congregations.
83. For Schonfeld's assessment of the situation in Poland see report in *Jewish Chronicle*, 30 November 1945, p. 15.
84. 'Pogrom in Poland', *Jewish Chronicle*, 12 July 1946, p. 10. Also see editorials such as 'Mass Exodus Empties Poland of Jews', 23 August 1946, p. 8 and in regard to the position in Germany, 'Whither German Jewry?', 24 October 1947, p. 11.
85. See *Jewish Monthly*, 1: 3 (June 1947), p. 58 and 1: 4 (July 1947), p. 49. The Zionist paper the *Jewish Forum* was equally pessimistic. See, for example, 'The Terror in Poland', 1: 1 (October 1946), p. 7.
86. 'Reliable News From Poland', *Jewish Outlook*, 2: 1 (June 1947), p. 13.
87. See John Russell to Robin Hankey, 2 December 1947, PRO/FO 371/61759.
88. Bevin's 'Palestine Statement', 13 November 1945.
89. Leimdoerfer to Spears, 4 November 1945, Box 4/7, SPSP. Leimdoerfer's proposal was entitled 'Memorandum on Suggestions for a Practical Solution to the Jewish Refugee Problem'.
90. Spears to Leimdoerfer, 7 November 1945, Box 4/7, SPSP.
91. Spears, *Manchester Guardian*, 18 March 1946.
92. Namier, *Manchester Guardian*, 21 March 1946.
93. 'Memorandum on Palestine', MSS Brit. Emp.s. 365, Box 176/3, FCBA.
94. Spears, 'What the Arabs Expect of France and Ourselves', *Daily Telegraph*, 8 February 1945; 'Crux of the Palestine Problem', *Daily Telegraph*, 8 October 1945.
95. Spears to Pickthorn, 5 November 1945, Box 7/1, SPSP.
96. *Arab News Bulletin*, 60 (9 April 1948), p. 3, and 32 (7 March 1947), p. 7. See also *Palestine: The Solution* (London: AO, 1947), p. 4. This view was reiterated by journals supportive of the Arab cause. For example, see 'Returning Jews', *Great Britain and the East*, LXII: 1762 (July 1946), p. 45.
97. Shaw to Martin, 7 October 1945, PRO/FO 371/ 52600.
98. Martin to Shaw, 25 September 1945, PRO/FO 371/52600.
99. 'No Backers', *Central European Observers*, 21 September 1945.
100. Hope-Simpson to Spears, 24 September 1945, Box 6/4, SPSP.
101. Hope-Simpson, 'The Palestine Statement', pp. 25–6.
102. Baillie to Spears, n.d., Box 6/3, SPSP.
103. Rosette, 'Moral Recovery in Europe', *Zionist Review*, 9 March 1945, p. 5.
104. *Zionist Review*, 28 March 1947, p. 1.
105. A. Reiss, speaking at Jewish Labour Committee, Leeds, 3 September 1944, reported in the *Zionist Review*, 8 September 1944, p. 2.
106. *Zionist Review*, 15 February 1946, p. 6.
107. 'An Outrage', *Zionist Review*, 23 March 1945, p. 2.
108. 'Poland', *Jewish Outlook*, 1: 10 (February 1947), p. 11.
109. Stein, 'Wishful Thinking', *Zionist Review*, 8 March 1945, p. 8.
110. C.C. Aronsfeld, *Gates of Zion*, 2: 2 (January 1948), p. 28.
111. *Zionist Review*, 26 February 1948, p. 1.
112. Leslie Hardman, *Jewish Chronicle*, 24 January 1947, p. 17.
113. Hardman to Greenberg, 23 September 1945, MS150 AJ 110/5, GREEN.
114. Shavit, ' "The Glorious Century" or "The Cursed Century": *Fin-de-Siècle* Europe and the Emergence of Modern Nationalism', in George L. Mosse and Jehuda Reinharz (eds), *The Impact of Western Nationalisms* (London, New Dehli: Sage

Publications, 1992), pp. 199–221, p. 202.
115. Evidence of the Jewish Fellowship before the AACIP, p. 42.
116. Ibid., p. 43.
117. Henriques, 'British Jewry and the Terrorists', *Star*, 13 January 1947. This view was also shared by Newcombe, who was of the opinion that 'people brought up in Poland with the things they have seen, heard and been taught are scarcely blameable if they are fanatics and don't see right. Anyway one can't cure mental disease.' See Newcombe to Spears, 9 July 1948, Box 7/1, SPSP.
118. *Jewish Outlook*, 1: 3 (June–July 1946), p. 3.
119. Franklyn, 'Jewish Defence and the Jewish Fellowship', *Synagogue Review*, XIX: 9 (May 1945), pp. 66–7, p. 66.
120. Reinhart, *The Times*, 23 September 1947.
121. Hyamson to Reinhart, 23 September 1947, MS171 AJ 246 122, REIN.
122. Henriques, *Statement to Fellowship Members*, p. 2.
123. Evidence of the Jewish Fellowship before the AACIP, p. 60.
124. 'Cannibal Scientists', *Jewish Outlook*, 2: 9 (January 1948), p. 6.
125. Franklyn, 'Jewish Defence and the Jewish Fellowship', p. 66.
126. Franklyn, 'Israel: State or Religion?', *Contemporary Review*, CLXXII: 979 (July 1947), p. 38.
127. Ibid., p. 37. Also see 'Fascism Fertilises Fascism', *Jewish Outlook*, 12 :1 (June 1947), p. 14.
128. Arnold Toynbee, *A Study of History*, Vol. 8 (London, New York, Toronto: Oxford University Press, under the auspices of the RIIA, 1954), pp. 288–92.
129. For example, see Nathan Rotenstreich's 'The Revival of the Fossil Remnant – Or Toynbee and Jewish Nationalism', *Jewish Social Studies*, XXIV: 3 (July 1962), pp. 131–43; Harry Sacher, 'Dr Toynbee and the Jews', *Jewish Chronicle*, 19 March 1956, p. 6 and especially Oskar K. Rabinowicz's *Arnold Toynbee on Judaism and Zionism: A Critique* (London: W.H. Allen, 1974). Toynbee defended his position in the face of this severe criticism. See his reply to critics, *A Significant and Important Essay*, published in pamphlet form (London, 1955) and his article 'Jewish Rights in Palestine', *Jewish Quarterly Review*, LII: 1 (July 1961), pp. 1–11. Not all Jewish commentators were negative about Toynbee. See for example Jacob B. Agnus, 'Toynbee's Epistle to the Jews', *Commentary*, 32: 3 (September 1961), pp. 239–41 and Hans Liebeschurtz's 'Arnold Toynbee', *Leo Baeck Year Book*, XXI (1976), pp. 289–93.
130. *Jewish Chronicle*, 12 January 1945, p. 6.
131. Maugham, 'Impressions Gathered in a very Recent Tour of Egypt, Palestine and the Levant States', lecture to the Middle East Group, RIIA, 15 March 1946, 8/1325, pp. 5, 10, and 'The Middle East Revisited', lecture to the Middle East Group, RIIA, 17 April 1947, 8/1475, pp. 7, 10.
132. Diary of Philips Price, 4 January 1946, Diary of Travels in Palestine, Box 1/3, PPP; Palestine debate, 1 July 1946, Parliamentary Debates, Vol. 424, 18 June–5 July, 1945–46, p. 1896.
133. MS Diary of Storrs, 2 September 1948, Box 6/8, STOP.
134. Atiyah, *Arab Rights and the British Left* (London: AO, 1945), p. 8 and *An Arab Tells His Story: A Study in Loyalties* (London: John Murray, 1946), p. 203.
135. *Bulletin of the Republic of Iraq*, 5: 2 (November–December, 1964), p. 8.
136. See, for example, *Palestine: The Solution*, p. 3; *Partition* (London: AO, 1947), p. 8; and Walter Stace's *The Zionist Illusion* (Washington: AO, 1947), p. 11. This was originally published in the *Atlantic Monthly*, in February 1947.
137. See *Arab News Bulletin*, 41 (11 July 1947), p. 3; 72 (24 September 1948), p. 1.
138. *Arab News Bulletin*, 76 (19 November 1948), p. 5.
139. Spears to Skinner, 27 March 1945, Box 4/7, SPSP.
140. Evidence of Spears before the AACIP, p. 41.
141. Spears, 'Suggestions for Evidence to the AACIP', Box 4/3, SPSP.
142. Evidence of Spears before the AACIP, p. 43.
143. Shertok's speech to the UN ad hoc committee, 17 October 1947, was reprinted in full in *New Judea*, October–November 1947, pp. 15–17.
144. Parkes made this comment during a talk to the Manchester Jewish Forum on the subject 'The Jewish Conception of Chosen People', 7 March 1945. For a copy of the

talk see MS150 AJ 110/7, GREEN.
145. See Parkes' evidence before the AACIP, London, 30 January 1946, pp. 3–38, p. 14, ACC3121/C14/30/5, ABD.
146. Mrs E. Dugdale speaking after lecture by Lt.-Col. E.H.R. Altounyan 'Policy in Palestine', RIIA, 29 November 1946, 8/1345, p. 6.
147. Mrs E. Dugdale speaking after lecture by Elizabeth Monroe 'Impressions of Palestine', RIIA, 19 December 1947, 8/1447, pp. 9, 11.
148. Altounyan to Lionel Curtis, 22 July 1946, PRO/FO 371/52624.
149. Mrs E. Dugdale speaking after Altounyan's RIIA lecture, 'Policy in Palestine', p. 6.
150. Franklyn to Reinhart, 23 March 1948, MS171 AJ 246 24, REIN.
151. 'Beyond Contempt', *Zionist Review*, 20 April 1945, p. 2.
152. Stein to Greenberg, 19 April 1945, MS150 AJ 110/5, GREEN.
153. Stein to Greenberg, 23 April 1945, ibid.
154. *Jewish Chronicle*, 27 April 1945, p. 10.
156. F. Polishuk, *Zionist Review*, 27 April 1945, p. 5.

6 The Failure to Co-operate: Sir Edward Spears, the CAA and the Jewish Fellowship

In the July and August of 1937 talks took place in London between Arabs, including Izzat Tannous (head of the Arab Centre in London at the time and future Arab Office member), Gentile English anti-Zionists, including Stewart Newcombe (then treasurer of the PIC and future member of the CAA), and Albert Hyamson (future council member of the Jewish Fellowship), who represented those prominent English Jews opposed to the creation of a Jewish state in Palestine.

The most notable result of these informal talks, as far as co-operation between Jewish and Gentile anti-Zionists is concerned, was the drafting of a plan in August–September 1937 by Hyamson and Newcombe which was intended to provide a basis for the settlement of the Palestine problem on non-Zionist lines. The plan envisaged the founding of a sovereign independent state in Palestine where all Palestinian nationals had equal rights and where complete autonomy existed for all communities, including complete municipal authority for all Jewish towns, villages and districts. However, the plan also made clear that there could be no possibility of the creation of a Jewish state in any part of Palestine at any time in the future.[1]

The plan was rejected by the Zionist leadership, with David Ben-Gurion in a letter to Judah Magnes dismissing the plan as a 'deception' and a 'plot of the Mufti and his supporters in England'.[2] Nevertheless, it is of interest because it was a conscious and active attempt by Newcombe and Hyamson to provide a non-Zionist Jewish–Gentile alternative to political Zionism. In the year following this proposal, Nevill Barbour, speaking in front of the RCAS, began a lecture on Palestine with the statement 'in the first place I would like to discuss what the ultimate objective of the Jewish people is in regard to Palestine', and added later that 'in estimating ... the objective of the Jewish people in Palestine we must consider the views of all groups, both those who favour the idea of a Jewish state ... and those who repudiate it'.[3]

Sir Ronald Storrs, who chaired Barbour's RCAS meeting, also defended the rights of those Jews opposed to political Zionism to present their position publicly, reminding readers in his foreword to Hyamson's 1942 book on Palestine that 'It would be a strange and hard paradox for Jewry ... that a Jew could be assailed by Jews for recording the objective truth with his honest opinions ... while facts are sacred comment is free.'[4] In the same year Newcombe, in a speech at a general meeting at the RIIA, also defended Hyamson's book in terms similar to Storrs', telling his audience that 'in this country Hyamson's book ... indicates a means of Jew–Arab co-operation'. Newcombe followed this up with the observation that 'the influential but retiring non-Zionists can help by co-operating'.[5]

The importance that Newcombe, Storrs and Barbour attached to Jewish anti-Zionists presenting their position in a constructive and co-operative way was echoed by Freya Stark. As has been seen, in 1943–44 she travelled to North America to present, on behalf of the Ministry of Information, the Arab–British position over Palestine, in an effort to reduce American anti-British feeling that had been rising, with the help of Zionist agitation, since the introduction of the Palestine White Paper of 1939.

Indeed, because of the situation in which Stark found herself, with the task of setting out the case against Zionism in the most ardently Zionist of countries, she really had to think during her time in the United States and Canada as to the best way of fighting Zionism. To all intents and purposes Stark was a professional anti-Zionist during her tour of North America. As such her extensive correspondence with Elizabeth Monroe[6] provides a great insight into Gentile anti-Zionist thinking (it was in these months that Stark employed the Scylla and Charybdis metaphor to describe the position of anti-Zionist Jews).

There were two constant themes in Stark's letters to Monroe: the power of Zionist propaganda, and the value of securing co-operation from Jewish opponents of political Zionism. As her biographer Caroline Moorehead has noted, 'within days of arriving [in the United States on her tour] Freya began contacting anti-Zionist Jews'.[7] And time and again in her letters to Monroe she set out her belief in the importance of working with these Jews, stating at one stage that 'I still believe that the moderate Jews, who are being threatened by the Zionist idea, are the best field for our efforts.'

Ten days later she informed Monroe that she believed that 'these non-Zionist Jews are the only people here who could be actively inspired to help us, because they are the only people interested in the combat of Zionism'. Six months later, in April 1944 after a conversation she had with the seasoned Arabist William Hale of the State Department, she was surer in this view than ever, informing Monroe that her conversation with Hale 'bears out what I have been saying all along: the best line is to weaken the Zionists by getting at other Jews'.[8]

It could be argued that Stark was concerned solely with the American situation and as such her views have no validity in the English context. Yet this would be wrong. All the reasons that she gave for her beliefs on this issue were as relevant, if not more so, to the situation in England as to the United States or Canada. For anti-Zionist Jews in England as in North America perceived themselves to be the biggest losers if the Zionists gained a state in Palestine, and for Stark this awareness was the primary motivation for Jews to cooperate with Gentiles.

Gideon Shimoni, in writing on the Fellowship, has stated the view that it was much weaker than its American counterpart the American Council for Judaism (hereafter, the ACJ).[9] There is no doubt that in terms of longevity and persistence the American body did prove more resolute than the Fellowship, continuing its agitation against Zionism long after the Fellowship had dissolved. But as Thomas Kolsky, an historian who has written in great depth on the ACJ has shown, by 1948 the majority of support for the ACJ was Gentile rather than Jewish. Indeed as Kolsky points out, by the time of its fourth annual meeting in January 1948, the ACJ was unable to find any Jewish speakers to be guests and had to rely on Gentiles to address the conference.[10]

Thus it was the support that the ACJ received from Gentiles that provided the extra momentum for the American body that enabled it to continue long after the Fellowship had foundered. Outside the context of the Jewish–Gentile relationship the Fellowship was more than equal to the ACJ. It could boast members of the House of Lords (Lord Swaythling, Viscount Bearsted) and one present MP, Daniel

Lipson, among its staunchest supporters. The ACJ could make no similar claim in terms of representation in the highest institutions of government in the United States.

The Fellowship also included men and women who had attained the highest positions of authority both inside and outside the community of Anglo-Jewry. Brunel Cohen and Gluckstein were both former MPs. Lord Justice Cohen was the first Jewish Lord of Appeal. Robert Waley Cohen was the President of the United Synagogue, the foremost Orthodox religious body in England, and Rabbi Dr Israel Mattuck was the leader of Liberal Jewry in England.

The Fellowship also had an advantage over the ACJ in the fact that it was led, with the exception of Mattuck, by laymen. Apart from its president, Lessing Rosenwald, it was Liberal Rabbis that provided the core leadership of the ACJ. This meant that there existed within the Fellowship a level of practical experience with government, administration, the military and the media that the ACJ did not possess.

Albert Hyamson, one of the most active Jewish anti-Zionists in the post-war era, is an example of this. Hyamson began his public life as a supporter of the Jewish National Home concept only to become a fierce critic of political Zionism as the Mandatory era progressed. He had been an early editor of the *Zionist Review*, and in the company of Leon Simon and Harry Sacher was central to the early Zionist propaganda efforts, contributing to and editing such Zionist pamphlets as *Zionism and the Jewish Future* in 1916. From 1917–19 he was the officer in charge of the Jewish branch of the Ministry of Information, and in 1919 he was sent by the Foreign Office to Paris as secretary of the Zionist mission to the peace conference.

Thus it is hardly surprising that in 1920 a confidential Foreign Office report talked of Hyamson as having a 'personal knowledge of Zionism'.[11] He was appointed to the Palestine administration during Sir Herbert Samuel's time as High Commissioner and spent 14 years in the immigration department of the Palestine administration. This gave him both a first-hand experience of the workings of the Palestine bureaucracy and politics and also, as will be seen, a close relationship with leading Gentile anti-Zionists, most notably Storrs and Newcombe.

As such the Jewish anti-Zionist community in England, in objective terms, had far more experience and potential influence, both outside and inside the community of Anglo-Jewry (and we saw how meagre that was) than did the American body headed by the retail magnate Lessing Rosenwald. Amikam Nachmani, for example, in his study of the Anglo-American Committee, cites an entry in the private diary of commissioner James McDonald, that the Fellowship delegation unlike the ACJ's leadership were 'distinguished and [had] impressive records of public service'.[12]

Similarly, Richard Crossman came into contact with both American and English Jewish anti-Zionist bodies while a member of the Anglo-American Committee. He had little respect for the Fellowship, noting in his diary after the appearance of its delegation, that Gluckstein who represented the 'Pukha Sahib anti-Zionist Jews' was a very 'unpleasant' character.[13] But on reflection Crossman had to admit that the Fellowship was much more of a force in the British context than the ACJ was in the United States, and declared that 'it was obvious that Colonel Gluckstein, who spoke for the anti-Zionists, had greater influence among British Jewry than his American counterpart Lessing Rosenwald'.[14] The Fellowship was diametrically opposed to Crossman's Zionist position but agreed with him on this issue, and during a review of his book *Palestine Mission* in the *Jewish Outlook* referred to this claim by Crossman regarding the Fellowship's superiority to the ACJ with some satisfaction.[15]

In April 1945 Newcombe, Barbour and Ralph Beaumont MP drew up a document entitled *A Constitution for Palestine*.[16] This was in part a logical outcome to the Gentile belief in the need to present an alternative to the Zionist solution to the Palestine problem. As has been seen, both Barbour and Newcombe had written pamphlets in the 1930s setting out a solution to the Palestine problem on non-Zionist grounds. In 1940 Newcombe again took up this issue. He wrote to Barbour, in anger over the seeming impotency of the government in the face of Zionist pressure, asking his anti-Zionist contemporary 'how do we overcome this?', and suggesting that perhaps what was required was 'some very logical and moderate plea written in a matter of fact and convincing way'.[17]

The *Constitution* was an attempt to provide 'a moderate plea' in a 'convincing way' by showing that Jews, Arabs and Christian Englishmen were agreed on a solution to the Palestine problem. This aspect of the document was emphasised in its introduction which stated that

> The following pages are the joint work of a small body of Christians, Muslims and Jews ... last January they formed themselves into a committee to see if they could work out a plan which they could recommend as a fair settlement from the point of view of the communities to which they severally belong.[18]

The document essentially reiterated the Hyamson–Newcombe proposals of 1937 and called for an independent Palestinian state where the different communities had complete control over their municipal institutions. However, what was important was not the details of the plan, but the fact that Jews, Arabs and Englishmen were seen to be co-operating. Indeed, Newcombe in separate letters to both Spears and Storrs emphasised that the document was important precisely because 'three Jews, three Arabs and three Englishmen worked on the committee to compile it ... it shows that the three parties can co-operate'.[19] Newcombe's view was echoed by Nevill Barbour who, in recalling the *Constitution*, stated that it was 'memorable for one reason ... unanimously agreed by [a] body of Jews, Arabs and Christians ... almost unique'.[20]

What is even more interesting is the fact that the three Jews who participated in drawing up the *Constitution* were Albert Hyamson, Emile Marmorstein and Rabbi Dr Israel Mattuck – avid opponents of political Zionism and members of the Jewish Fellowship council. Thus, as close to the formation of the CAA as April 1945 (when the *Constitution* was published), contemporaries of Spears, leading anti-Zionists in their own right, and future members of the CAA, were working with leading members of the Jewish Fellowship in an effort to provide a non-Zionist answer to the Palestine problem.

On 7 March 1945, one month before the publication of the *Constitution*, Brunel Cohen and Basil Henriques, president and chairman of the Jewish Fellowship respectively, presented the Jewish anti-Zionist case before the MEPC, a body chaired by Sir Edward Spears, who was at this time still a member of parliament. Zionists viewed this Fellowship appearance before the committee as proof that men like Spears used the existence of Jewish anti-Zionists to give credibility to their own position. *New Judea*, for example, saw the invitation as an attempt to 'make the committee strictly kosher'.[21]

It had never been the intention of this meeting to give the impression that both Jewish and non-Jewish anti-Zionists were embarking on a platform of co-operation against Zionism. Rather, the intention had been to keep the meeting private and unpublicised. However, as Brunel Cohen recalled in a report to the Fellowship's council in the aftermath of the meeting, his and Henriques' appearance before the MEPC had been leaked to the Jewish press.[22]

Although the identity of the mole was never officially acknowledged, Spears had a good idea who was 'responsible for the indiscretion',[23] and it seems probable that the guilty party whom Spears suspected was S.S. Hammersley, Conservative MP for East Willesden and chairman of the pro-Zionist Parliamentary Palestine Committee until he lost his seat in the 1945 election. Hammersley was one of the Zionist minority on the MEPC and his attack on Henriques and Brunel Cohen during the meeting was heralded in the Zionist press.[24]

Once knowledge of the Fellowship appearance before the MEPC became public there was uproar in Zionist circles. The *Zionist Review* professed amazement that the MEPC had called on Cohen and Henriques and stated that it 'must be made aware how unrepresentative are the spokesmen whom they invited'.[25] Spears even received letters from Zionists such as Rabbi Kopul Rosen (future leader of the Federation of Synagogues and at the time religious leader of the Glasgow Jewish community) attacking the Fellowship appearance.[26]

But it was Hammersley, acting as a representative of the Zionists, who tried to put right any damage the Fellowship speakers had caused before the committee by asking Spears to allow Professor Selig Brodetsky to respond to the Fellowship by presenting the Zionist case before a meeting of the MEPC. While defending the Fellowship's appearance, Spears told Hammersley that he was not keen to hear the Zionist representative. It was only after numerous letters from Hammersley and a letter from the Chief Rabbi vouching for Brodetsky, and a final agreement by Hammersley that the meeting would be kept private, that Spears acquiesced and allowed Brodetsky to talk to his committee.[27]

Spears had defended his refusal to hear Brodetsky on the grounds that he was not familiar with this Zionist representative and would much prefer to hear the views of the Chief Rabbi or his representative.[28] However, this argument has little credibility. For Spears himself had been unfamiliar with both the Fellowship and its members before the appearance of the group's delegation in front of the MEPC. Indeed Colonel Louis Gluckstein MP, a member of the MEPC (as was Daniel Lipson), had to send Spears some information on Henriques, Brunel Cohen and the Fellowship organisation before the meeting, so that Spears could acquaint himself with the body, its goals and the backgrounds of its representatives.[29]

Thus Spears' unwillingness to hear Brodetsky was not due to the latter's anonymity but an attempt to adhere to the advice given to him by E.H. Keeling MP, a future member of the CAA, who in respect to the MEPC, had informed Spears that while it could not exclude Zionist MPs 'there is no point having Zionists address us'.[30]

The persistent rebuttal by Spears of Hammersley's efforts to get the MEPC to hear Brodetsky gave the impression to the Zionists that Spears was conspiring with the Fellowship. In the wake of this incident the Zionist suspicions seemed to be confirmed both by the similarity of the arguments used by the Fellowship and Spears, and the fact that Spears in his public pronouncements openly endorsed the Fellowship.

For example, in June 1945 Spears wrote to Brodetsky asking him to supply some information for an article he was writing, and added that he was also asking the Fellowship to provide him with information on its Palestine position.[31] While in the most public of forums over Palestine, Spears called on the Anglo-American Committee to hear evidence from the Fellowship, making his support for the body obvious with the statement that

> I don't know whether the Jewish Fellowship is going to give evidence before the committee. They gave it before our committee in the House ... we found it very interesting ... I only hope they will have the opportunity of testifying before the committee.[32]

One must remember that the Anglo-Jewish press had already presented Lipson's 1945 *Spectator* article 'Is Jewry a Nation?', and Spears' subsequent reissuing of it as a pamphlet, as a prime example of Jewish and Gentile anti-Zionist co-operation.

In the light of this, and Spears' open plea for the Fellowship before the AACIP, it is not surprising that leading Zionists viewed Jewish and Gentile anti-Zionists as working together. Philip Wigoder, a leading member of the Manchester Jewish community, in letters to both the *Zionist Review* and the *Jewish Chronicle* used the phrase 'strange bedfellows' to describe the relationship between the Fellowship and the non-Jewish anti-Zionists led by Spears.[33]

Hamabit (pseud.), writing in *New Judea*, not only used exactly the same words as Wigoder to describe the relationship between Jewish and non-Jewish anti-Zionists, but went further and specifically accused Gluckstein of 'taking crafty counsel against the Jewish people' by working with Spears and others in opposing Zionist aspirations.[34]

Gluckstein took offence at this article and demanded, under threat of legal action, that *New Judea* retract these accusations. The paper did apologise and accepted that Gluckstein 'has never combined with these persons or any others against the Jewish people'.[35] However, this apology should in no way be viewed as an indicator of a change in attitude, and the reality was that Hamabit's view continued to be paramount within Jewry. For example, F.M. Landau, a member of the Board of Deputies, in a private letter to the *Jewish Chronicle* defended his support of the Board's condemnation of Gluckstein for his Anglo-American evidence on the grounds that 'there had been complete unanimity on the part of the Jewish Fellowship, Royden-Shaw, Storrs, Spears, Communist party, Arab League'.[36]

In August of the same year Julian Franklyn felt compelled to write to the *Jewish Chronicle* to take issue with a statement made in the 'Sermon of the Week' column, because he believed it included an implicit attack on the Jewish Fellowship. The passage is worth quoting because it shows just how sensitive the Fellowship's leadership was to accusations that they conspired with non-Jews to betray Jewry. The column stated:

> Zion should have a faithful city – loyal to its true self, to the Jewish national ethos, to the Jewish God idea. But with strange, perverted humility we honoured the alien, but disrespected ourselves; we served other people's interests and did the greatest disservice to our own cause. To this day there are some who call this attitude Fellowship. Though it spells nought but disunity and disruption in the Jewish midst.[37]

The fact that Franklyn felt it necessary to respond (to what was after all an indirect rather than obvious charge against the Fellowship) in such a defensive manner with the words 'it is with a clear conscience that we of the Jewish Fellowship can say that that sin is not ours and we have never encouraged it',[38] gives an insight into the overwhelming awareness that those in the Fellowship must have had about the general view within Jewry that they did indeed conspire with the enemies of Zion.

Franklyn's pleading would have carried very little weight within the community because, even before the outcry he had caused by publicly and continuously comparing Zionism to Nazism, he had very little credibility. For example, in 1943 he had written to the *New Statesman* defending an earlier correspondent who had accused Jewry of black-marketing and hoarding wealth during the war. Sidney Salomon, executive and press officer of the Board of Deputies, embodied the general attitude to Franklyn's letter with the view that Franklyn really was a 'pitiful' character in his defence of Gentile attacks on Jewry.[39] And a Mr H. Newman, after discussing the subject of Zionism with Franklyn in 1945, wrote to the *Jewish Chronicle* to state his horror at Franklyn's views, and to ask whether in the light of Franklyn's example the Fellowship could even be classed as a Jewish body.[40]

However, the Zionists were wrong to view the Jewish and Gentile anti-Zionists as working together. Neither the use of Jewish arguments to oppose Zionism, nor the previous history of co-operation between prominent Fellowship and CAA members (which culminated in the publication of *A Constitution for Palestine* in April 1945), nor even the appearance of Brunel Cohen and Basil Henriques before the MEPC in the dignified surroundings of the House, resulted in real co-operation between Jewish and Gentile anti-Zionists in these years. Rather, the appearance before the MEPC marked the high point in co-operation between these bodies who shared a common enemy, political Zionists, and a common goal – the prevention of a Jewish state in Palestine.

A prime reason for this can be found in the position of Sir Edward Spears himself. As has been seen, Spears was the leading force in the Gentile anti-Zionist movement during these years. He was the founder, chairman and most devoted member of the CAA. Other leading members of the committee, veteran anti-Zionists, directly approached Spears about the possibility of working with the Fellowship, to no avail. In September 1945 Spears had requested Sir John Hope-Simpson to draft some proposals which the CAA could use as the basis for its opposition to political Zionism.[41] Hope-Simpson responded by suggesting that the CAA should work with the Fellowship, telling Spears, his chairman, that

Any constructive proposals should be the result of discussion with representatives of different schools of thought. For instance is it possible that the Jewish organisation (anti-political Zionism) headed by Sir Brunel Cohen might have some useful ideas as a way out of the existing impasse?[42]

This call by Hope-Simpson for co-operation with the Jewish Fellowship in setting out an anti-Zionist alternative to a settlement in Palestine on a Zionist basis went unanswered by Spears. However, Sir Ronald Storrs, like Hope-Simpson, was interested in the position of Jewish anti-Zionists in the debate over Palestine.

Storrs kept himself well informed of the efforts of Jewish anti-Zionists in both England and the United States. He corresponded with one Siegfried Aufheuser, a Jewish refugee in New York, whom he had known in London, and who kept him informed of the efforts of the ACJ. Aufheuser even sent him a copy of Lessing Rosenwald's infamous *Life* magazine article, which became the definitive exposition of the Jewish anti-Zionist position in America (something akin to Lipson's 'Is Jewry a Nation?' article in the *Spectator*).[43]

Closer to home, Storrs also had a long relationship with the Jewish anti-Zionist Albert Hyamson, which began when both were serving in the Palestine administration during the 1920s. They continued to keep in contact after they returned to England, Storrs for example sending Hyamson an inscribed copy of his 1935 work on T.E. Lawrence. As has already been seen, Storrs, despite his dislike for unpaid toil, also provided the foreword to Hyamson's 1942 book on Palestine.

Both men corresponded on the Palestine issue throughout these years, and even after the creation of Israel, Storrs was seeking out Hyamson's opinion on the subject, meeting him for lunch at his club in 1949 so that Hyamson could comment on his draft review of Weizmann's *Trial and Error* (of which, according to Storrs, he 'warmly approved').[44] As late as 1954, the year of his death, Hyamson was sending Storrs information about the continued efforts of Jewish anti-Zionists in both England and the United States.[45]

Storrs spent much time socially with other members of what could be termed the anti-Zionist element within Jewry, and he used these contacts to distribute CAA pamphlets and propaganda that he felt would be 'useful in Jewish parts of the world'.[46] He paid frequent social visits to one Mrs Loebl, whom he himself described as 'a Jewish acquaintance and an anti-Zionist Jew'.[47]

And it was with this Mrs Loebl that he dined in 1947, at the height of the battle over Palestine, with Rabbi Dr Israel Mattuck, the spiritual leader of the Fellowship, during which both men discussed the efforts of anti-Zionist Jews in opposing Zionism.[48] Storrs also paid close attention to Mattuck's public offerings on Zionism, and his private papers include copies of Mattuck's letters to the press on Zionism and articles that the Rabbi wrote on Jewish issues in relatively obscure journals such as the *Liberal Jewish Monthly*.[49]

Storrs had a high view of the individual Jews who over the years had spoken out against Zionism. He was of the opinion that Edwin Montagu, the archetypal Jewish anti-Zionist,[50] was 'in some ways almost a saint',[51] and his view of more contemporary Jewish anti-Zionists was also high. For example, Storrs was full of admiration for Lipson's efforts to oppose Zionism, especially through his outspoken statements in the Commons.

Storrs went further than praising Lipson's oratorical skills in debates, and in November 1947 he took it upon himself to defend him in public. He was angered by a letter in *The Times* by Robert Waley Cohen that had attacked Lipson in no uncertain terms for his intransigent 'destructive' anti-Zionism.[52] Despite being a member of the Fellowship council, and in the face of severe Zionist criticism, Waley Cohen appears to have lost much of his anti-Zionist resolve and faith in the Fellowship in these years. For example, in June 1945 he wrote to Basil Henriques to express his opposition, as head of the United Synagogue, to the Fellowship's increased involvement in politics.[53]

A month after this Waley Cohen entered into a heated correspondence with Emile Bustani (a member of the Arab trade delegation in London who was a close associate of Spears) because Bustani refused to attend a Palestine Corporation luncheon because there would be Zionists present. After Waley Cohen had admonished Bustani for his position, Bustani responded 'you make us think and lead us to decide that after all you do sympathise with the Zionists against the Arab cause'.[54]

Storrs wrote to defend Lipson from Waley Cohen's attack in *The Times*, and his high regard for the man's anti-Zionist efforts can be seen in this letter, where he stated that he had 'nothing but admiration for the courage of Mr Lipson and other loyal British

Jews in expressing their conviction'.[55] And although this letter was not published in *The Times* it does go to show how a leading Gentile anti-Zionist like Storrs valued and respected the position of Jewish contemporaries of a similar disposition to his own.

Newcombe, who like Storrs had first come to know Albert Hyamson while serving in Palestine, and like Storrs had continued to correspond and consult with him over the Palestine issue,[56] was another leading Gentile anti-Zionist who took an interest in the Jewish anti-Zionist position.

In a letter accompanying his memorandum to the Anglo-American Committee, he informed the chairman that 'I have worked with non-Zionist Jews and with Arabs ... especially since 1936 up to now'.[57] Newcombe not only corresponded with anti-Zionist Jews on the Palestine issue, but was of the opinion that their views were of value to the CAA precisely because they were Jews. For example, in the course of sending some notes on the Palestine problem to Spears, he wrote in a covering note that 'Dr Jamal gave me these; being the views of a Jew they may be of help.'[58]

Newcombe would reiterate this belief in the value of co-operating with Jews throughout his correspondence with Spears in these years. In one letter he informed Spears that 'there are very large numbers of non-Zionists [Jews] who will co-operate in the USA and Britain ... directly we open the door'.[59] In other words, like Hope-Simpson, Newcombe not only saw the value of co-operating with Jewish anti-Zionists but envisaged doing so. Interestingly, in this letter Newcombe also specified which Jews he had in mind to co-operate with when he gave Spears examples of 'the best type' of Jew and included Colonel Gluckstein of the Fellowship in his list.

Newcombe even went as far as setting out what, in his view, the exact relationship between the CAA and Jewish anti-Zionists should be in the event of co-operation, informing Spears that it was his belief that 'we must take the lead. *Not* the non-Zionist Jews, for tactical reasons.'[60] Newcombe did not expound as to what these 'tactical reasons' were, but there is a strong case to be made that one of the primary reasons that he believed that Gentile anti-Zionists should take the lead was because he felt that Jewish opponents of Zionism were unable to speak out due to their weak position within Jewry. Thus it was up to non-Jewish anti-Zionists to create an environment where Jews would feel comfortable in openly opposing Zionist aspirations in tandem with Gentiles.

Newcombe's belief that Jewish opponents of Zionism were too afraid to speak up was a theme he repeated over a number of years. In a lecture at the RIIA in 1942 he stated his view that 'most non-Zionists [Jews] will not come into the open to express their beliefs'.[61] While in his letter to the chairman of the Anglo-American Committee he claimed that although Jews in Palestine were afraid to speak out, in private some had told him that they wanted to work with the Arabs and did not favour the goals of political Zionism.[62] Thus by 1947 Newcombe was asking rhetorically, almost despairingly, why 'we ... follow the wishes of Zionists and ignore those ... numerous non-Zionist Jews who are less clamorous?'[63]

Like Newcombe, Jewish anti-Zionists made much of the intimidation they faced within Jewry during these years. The anti-Zionist Rabbi Curtis Cassell, writing in the *Synagogue Review* in August 1945, was of the view that 'woe to the Jew' who dares to stand up to the Zionists. While Brunel Cohen in a confidential memorandum to Fellowship members in the same year reported that the Fellowship, which had already been 'grossly mis-represented ... will probably be slandered and ridiculed' in the future, and he brought to the attention of the Anglo-American Committee the personal attacks the Zionists had poured on him.[64]

It will be recalled that Spears only became involved in the Palestine issue on his appointment to the Levant in 1942. As such, he differed from these other CAA members in his lack of a long-term relationship with Jewish anti-Zionists or experience of the Palestine problem. This was paralleled by a lack of interest in Jewish affairs.

Despite the Zionist view that Spears lacked credibility there were many within informed circles who perceived him as something of an expert on Palestine and the Jewish problem. For example, T. Drummond Shiels wrote to Spears on behalf of the Fabian Colonial Bureau, asking him to contribute to the Bureau's symposium on Palestine, telling him that 'I thought of you at once when I was consulted.'[65] Similarly, M.V. Seton Williams in her book *Britain and the Arab States* (which was attacked by the Zionists as anti-Zionist propaganda)[66] stated that she had based her views on Britain's problems in the Middle East on a series of articles that Spears had written in the *Daily Telegraph* in January 1947.[67]

There were also many ordinary men and women concerned with the Palestine problem who saw Spears as the leading expert on the issue and who asked his advice or sent him their opinion, with one E.W. Elsworth writing a letter to the *Yorkshire Post* (she forwarded a copy to Spears) in which she praised 'General Sir Edward Spears [who] has told the English people some of the truths about Palestine and the Jewish question'.[68]

Yet Spears, unlike many of his contemporaries, did not perceive himself as an expert on Zionism or the Jewish problem. In 1945 he received a request from one T.C. Skinner to comment on an article 'Anti-Semitism: Its Causes, Palliatives and Cures'.[69] However, Spears felt obliged to inform Skinner that 'I do not pose as an expert on the subject [Zionism and the Jewish problem] and am only interested in it as far as it affects the British position in the Middle East.'[70]

This statement by Spears is vital in any attempt to understand the reasons why there was not a closer relationship between Jewish and Gentile anti-Zionists in these years. For Spears was the central figure in the anti-Zionist movement at the time. He was the linkman between all anti-Zionist efforts to fight Zionism and was devoted to building up an organised coalition to present the Arab position in Britain, as can be seen by his use of the CAA as a base for founding the Anglo-Arab Association with the goal of providing an umbrella body for all pro-Arab groups in England. But as he admitted to Skinner, he had no interest in the Jewish aspect of the whole debate and he was resolute throughout these years in maintaining this lack of interest.

As has been seen, Spears' rejection of Hammersley's request that Brodetsky be heard before the CAA, on the basis that he was 'personally not familiar [with him] ... nor the hierarchy of the Anglo-Jewish community',[71] was partly an excuse to avoid having a Zionist speak before the MEPC. But the fact that Spears, chairman of the MEPC, had no compunction in stating his ignorance of who Selig Brodetsky was, sums up his total indifference to the affairs of Anglo-Jewry. For Brodetsky was not only a member of the Jewish Agency executive and the leading Zionist in England at the time, he was also the president of the Board of Deputies of British Jews, and as such the most senior representative of British Jewry on all communal and Jewish issues.

It is unthinkable that other anti-Zionists of Spears' stature could have been unaware of Brodetsky's position within Anglo-Jewry. Men like Storrs prided themselves on being very well-informed on just what position members of Anglo-Jewry took on the issue of Palestine. For example, on one occasion in 1944 after running into

Gordon Liverman, the Jewish communal worker, Storrs noted in his diary that he had met 'anti-Zionist Liverman'.[72] Thus Storrs, who was neither an acquaintance nor a friend of Liverman, was well enough informed of the situation in Anglo-Jewry to know both who the man was, and to have a view as to his stance on the Palestine issue.

Nor did the invitation to the Fellowship's leaders to speak before the MEPC result in Spears' knowing the anti-Zionist Jews any better than he did Brodetsky and the Zionists. This was not due to a lack of effort by the Fellowship. For it invited Spears to be special guest of honour at its first annual meeting, held on 14 October 1945. True, this decision can partly be seen as a return courtesy to Spears who as chairman of the MEPC had hosted Henriques and Brunel Cohen earlier in the year. But even more, this invitation must be viewed as the symbolic and practical acceptance by the Fellowship that in the post-war battle against political Zionism it shared the position of openly hostile Gentile enemies of Zionism, of whom Spears was the leading example.

However, Spears failed to see the opportunity that this invitation offered for the beginning of a working relationship between the Fellowship and the CAA. Nor did he comprehend the implications and the awkward position that anti-Zionist Jews were putting themselves in by extending this invitation. In his reply to Julian Franklyn, who had written inviting him to attend the meeting, Spears stated that

> I am in complete sympathy with your movement and if you deem it really important to attend I will ... but I have the feeling that it is much more a family party. The matters under discussion would probably be entirely strange to me and I even feel that a stranger might be a nuisance.[73]

If Spears had been unable to attend because of a prior commitment or for health reasons, that would have been one thing. But that was not why he did not attend, telling Franklyn, 'if you deem it really important to attend I will', and ending his letter 'if you really think it would be useful ... I will come'. But the lack of enthusiasm behind the words make the real reason that Spears did not want to attend clear. He did not believe that he would fit in and considered himself a 'stranger' to whom the proceedings would 'probably be entirely strange'.[74]

These few sentences epitomised one of the central reasons why there was not greater co-operation between Spears, the CAA and the Fellowship in these years. For implicit in Spears' words is the belief that, although the Fellowship may have been opposed to the creation of a Jewish state, and although its members may have been 'on the right lines', as he had earlier written to Basil Henriques,[75] in the final analysis the Fellowship was a Jewish body, its members were Jews and he had no interest in the Jewish aspect of the battle over Palestine.

Thus while Spears was 'in deep sympathy' with the Fellowship's efforts, he could not bring himself to attend a meeting marking the first anniversary of a body formed, as was his committee, to fight Zionism (and this refusal must also be viewed in the context of his acceptance of many invitations to dinners and meetings with Arab bodies in London during the same years).

Indeed Spears' reference in his letter to Franklyn to the Fellowship's annual meeting as a 'party' only goes to emphasise even more just how little he comprehended the actual position that the Fellowship saw itself to be in. The members of the Fellowship believed that they had the duty to bear the burden and responsibility of saving Jews from the curse of political Zionism which threatened, no less than Nazism, the survival of Jewry. There was little levity involved in the group's efforts.

Other anti-Zionists, close contemporaries of Spears, were aware of the strife that divisions over Zionism had caused within the Jewish community. Storrs, in his foreword to Hyamson's *Palestine: A Policy*, noted that the book 'may gall and provoke the complete ... Zionist [as] ... revulsion ... betrayal' and added that Hyamson in writing this book had not been 'afraid' to develop his belief that Zionism was out of step with Judaism.[76]

Storrs wrote this in 1942, a time when Jewry was still relatively united in the face of the Nazi menace and behind the war effort, and as such the hostile divide between Zionist and anti-Zionist Jews had not come into the open. But his comments show a sensitivity to the divisiveness of the Zionist issue in the Jewish world of which Spears, in the far more acrimonious climate of 1945, appears to have been unaware.

This is hardly surprising given Storrs' close relationship with men such as Hyamson. Indeed, in his Memoirs (published in 1937) Storrs recalled how he admired Hyamson during their time in the Palestine administration because, in his position in the immigration department, his adherence to duty in refusing entry into Palestine to those Jews who were not eligible made him one of the most unpopular figures amongst Zionists.[77] Even more to the point, Hyamson had written to Storrs before his 1942 book was published to tell him 'I am in for a bout of persecution.'[78] Hyamson even asked Storrs if he minded toning down his own foreword to the book because he was facing a rough enough time without Storrs' comments adding to the condemnation he received.[79]

Storrs acceded to this request and it obviously left a great impression on him. His letter to *The Times* in defence of Lipson in 1947 was expressed partly in terms of the courage that it took for Lipson and men like him in the face of 'loud severity from their co-religionists'.[80] And even after the Jewish state had been created and the battle was over, Storrs took the opportunity of a review of Weizmann's *Trial and Error* to raise this issue again and argue that

> The Zionist creed ... admits no compromise ... he that is not for me is against me; and the nearer he is in Jewish interest and sympathy – even though a Jew and otherwise the best type of Jew – the less excusable is his non-Zionism.[81]

As has been seen, Newcombe, like Storrs, was very aware of the condemnation that Jewish anti-Zionists faced within Jewry, and like Storrs he made an effort to keep up with news that emanated from the Jewish community. One on occasion he wrote to Spears saying, 'I suppose you saw Max Beloff's article in the *Jewish Chronicle* of January 9th ... a very sensible one.'[82]

This was a reference to an article written by Max Beloff, at the time Reader in Comparative Study of Institutions at the University of Oxford.[83] The article, which criticised political Zionism and the Zionist leadership in Palestine, caused an outcry in the Zionist press. Both Beloff and the *Jewish Chronicle* were attacked over the article. Zionist columnist Hamabit (pseud.), arguing, for example, that the Beloff article was 'nothing but an offensive attack on Zionism by a writer who has swallowed all the arguments used by Messrs. Stokes, Reid and Price in the House of Commons ... irresponsible assertions and distortions lifted from sources hostile to Jewish aspirations'.[84]

Spears had not seen the Beloff article and corrected Newcombe's presumption that he had.[85] But one can see in Newcombe's reference to Beloff a sense of being involved, or at least aware of, and interested in, the debate within Jewry, just as one can see in Spears' reply his indifference to events and opinions within the Jewish community. Nor did Newcombe limit his interest to the situation within Anglo-Jewry. In another letter to Spears, he informed his chairman 'I heard about Friedman [the American Jewish anti-Zionist referred to elsewhere] who is apparently devoting all his means and energies to anti-Zionist propaganda in the United States, more power to him.'[86]

In similar vein he wrote to Spears to tell him that 'I am getting a very good pamphlet ... from Melbourne written by Sir Isaac Isaacs and I'll send you a copy.'[87] Sir Isaac Isaacs was an Australian Jew who became chief justice and then served from 1931 to 1936 as the first Australian-born governor-general.[88] He was also a staunch anti-Zionist and the author of anti-Zionist tracts including *Political Zionism: Undemocratic, Unjust, Dangerous*, published in Australia in the 1940s. Indeed Norman Bentwich, one of the more moderate Zionist commentators, referred to him in his autobiography as 'inflexibly opposed to the Zionist idea and unwilling to accept the conception that Jews are a nationality as well as a religious community'.[89] This was a view shared by Rose Henriques, an anti-Zionist contemporary of Isaacs', who after a meeting with him noted his 'strong anti-political Zionist views'.[90]

One would not have expected Spears to have written to other Gentiles about his correspondence with Jewish anti-Zionists, and when Hyamson, the anti-Zionist Jew perhaps most closely involved with Gentiles, wrote to Spears, the correspondence was very formal. Hyamson began his letter with an introduction 'I should say that I am an English Jew',[91] which would have been unnecessary if he had been writing to Spears' contemporaries on the CAA such as Storrs or Newcombe.

Spears' reply to Hyamson was also very formal and although it expressed 'deep sympathy' for the position of Jews who opposed Zionism, it did not address any of the issues involved.[92] Indeed, Spears' consoling admission to Hyamson that he was 'in deep sympathy' with the position of anti-Zionist Jews was but a repetition of the words in his letter to Julian Franklyn, in which he declined the invitation to the first Fellowship annual meeting.

However, this 'deep sympathy' was not translated into co-operation with Jewish anti-Zionists. This was not because of Spears' belief that this body of Jewish anti-Zionists had no value in the battle against Zionism. On the contrary, like other Gentile anti-

Zionists, Spears used Jewish arguments to oppose Zionism and saw the value of Jewish opposition to political Zionism. In a lecture at the RCAS in February 1945, four months after the Jewish Fellowship had held a press conference to announce its existence and one month before the Fellowship's delegation spoke before the MEPC, Spears told his audience: 'I personally felt for a very long time that it would be a good thing if we could have a pronouncement from the great mass of Jews of the world on the subject of Zionism, especially militant Zionism.'[93]

Spears also promoted the Fellowship in his correspondence, telling one Dr Emile Leimdoerfer to make contact with the body 'who are opposed, as you are, to political Zionism'.[94] Nor can this be seen as a one-off response to a Jewish (as Leimdoerfer was) correspondent. Even in correspondence with Gentiles Spears stated his belief in the value of Jewish anti-Zionists, telling T.C. Skinner that 'I think ... encouragement should be given to the Jewish Fellowship.'[95]

Only one month after Spears had declined the invitation to attend the Fellowship's annual meeting as the special guest, he responded to an idea made to him by Royden-Shaw of setting up a council to safeguard the three religions in the Holy Land by agreeing with her as to the value of this enterprise and saying that 'I think the Jewish Fellowship ... could probably supply a religious Jew who feels as strongly anti-Zionist as you and I do.'[96]

Thus here we see that Spears, like Newcombe, Beaumont, Barbour, Stark, Royden-Shaw and Storrs, believed there was much to be gained by working with Jewish anti-Zionists and having Jews represented on an anti-Zionist committee. Yet this never materialised in regard to Spears' own committee. Indeed, Spears did not even bother to invite Lipson or Gluckstein, both of whom had been members of the MEPC (Lipson on the committee's executive), to join the CAA. This must be viewed in the context of his invitations to 26 of the other MPs who had been on the MEPC to join his new venture, many of whom had a far less active interest in the Palestine issue or Zionism than these two prominent Fellowship leaders.[97]

The furthest Spears himself got to working with the Fellowship in these years was to write to Colonel Gluckstein asking him for a short note, setting out the position of the Fellowship on the Zionist issue that he could use in his writings on Palestine. In doing so he was once again showing how Gentile anti-Zionists looked to use

Jewish anti-Zionist arguments as part of their own opposition to Zionism.[98]

Apart from this, the only other occasions that Spears initiated correspondence with the Fellowship were on matters incidental to the fight against Zionism. For example, on one occasion he forwarded to Basil Henriques a request for help he had received from a struggling Viennese Jew.[99] This not only shows (once again) how Spears was identified with Jewish affairs (or he would not have been approached in the first place), but also that Spears never really grasped the function of the Fellowship. It was at no time a body that existed directly to help refugees, and Franklyn replying on Henriques' behalf felt it necessary to inform Spears of this, telling him that the Fellowship 'has no organisation for this type of work', and as such had handed on the request to the relevant body within Jewry.[100]

Spears' lack of understanding of the functions of the Fellowship was coupled to a failure, despite his use of Jewish arguments, to come to terms with the fundamental premises on which Jewish anti-Zionism was based. This lack of comprehension as to the specifics of the Jewish Fellowship position can be seen in relation to the issue of whether or not Zionism was an inherent part of Judaism.

The Fellowship presented Zionism as a secular ideology unrelated to Judaism. For the Zionists this was nonsense. Selig Brodetsky, in the course of a private meeting with Mattuck and Gluckstein in 1945, responded to the claim that Zionism had nothing to do with Judaism with the view that Palestine was 'as much a matter of Judaism as Kashrut'.[101] But for Jewish anti-Zionists the words and actions of the Zionist movement seemed incompatible with their own concept of Judaism. Rabbi Mattuck, in a sermon at the Liberal Jewish Synagogue in June 1945, spelt out why Jewish anti-Zionists could not accept Zionism as part of Judaism. In his opinion, 'The adjective Jewish belongs to whatever shows a distinctive spiritual quality related to the Jewish religious outlook ... the adjective Jewish can therefore be appropriately applied only where the Jewish spirit is present.'[102] Zionism did not live up to this definition and as such it was separate from Judaism. Fellowship leaders used public forums to set out this view, with Colonel Gluckstein's effort to separate Zionism from Judaism during his evidence before the AACIP resulting in committee member McDonald asking him if he was trying to say that all

Zionists were 'Jewish atheists'.[103] This was also the editorial position of the *Jewish Outlook* which stated in no uncertain terms that Jews had to decide if they were Jews or political Zionists as 'Jews cannot be both'.[104]

It was one thing for Jewish anti-Zionists to promote this view but it was much more difficult to get others, especially Gentiles, to view Zionism and Judaism as separate entities. For Zionism had become ingrained in the public consciousness as a facet of Judaism (after all were not the Zionists fighting for a Jewish state!). Regardless of the difficulty in separating the two (which was blamed on the Zionist effort to make the two appear as one),[105] it was deemed essential that non-Jews, especially those in positions to influence the general attitude to Zionism, differentiated between Zionists and Jews. Brunel Cohen in his presidential address to the second Fellowship annual meeting stated that

> This meeting begs His Majesty's Government to distinguish clearly between political Zionism and Judaism ... and refrain from employing in Parliamentary debate, and in government-sponsored reports and similar publications the term Jew and Jewish.[106]

Thus when high-profile Gentiles did indeed take the trouble to differentiate between Jews and Zionism, the Fellowship warmly congratulated them. An article in the *Jewish Outlook*, a few months after the plea from Brunel Cohen, congratulated Kenneth Pickthorn MP, a member of the CAA, for performing a 'signal service' when he asked the prime minister 'to note the desirability of not referring to Jews in debates when discussing those who subscribe to Zionist ideology'.[107]

However, Spears never did manage to differentiate between Jews and Zionism. For example, in a letter to Selig Brodetsky in 1945 he informed the Zionist leader that he was thinking of 'preparing a pamphlet on the Middle East, and I want to be quite sure of understanding *Jewish claims*'.[108] Likewise, in a speech the same year he informed his audience that the Arabs 'contest the right of *the Jews* to the land'.[109]

Nor did this tendency of Spears go unnoticed. Richard Stokes MP wrote to him requesting a list of all Jewish MPs who were also Zionists. Spears replied with a list informing Stokes that all the Jews in the House were in the Labour Party and they were 'all Zionists'.

Stokes was unhappy with the list. He asked Spears to redo it, this time only including those Jews who 'are to your certain knowledge Zionists', reminding him that 'you will be aware as I am that not all Jews are Zionist'.

Spears obliged Stokes and rewrote the list, but Stokes was still unhappy with the inclusion of some MPs who although Jewish were not Zionists, and wrote once more that it was 'important that we should have these descriptions clear'.[110] But Spears did not heed Stokes' advice, and continued to refer to Zionists as Jews and to talk of Jewish claims to Palestine. So much so that in 1947 Albert Hyamson felt moved to write to Spears to correct him on this issue.

Hyamson was a leading campaigner against the tendency to equate Zionism with Judaism. In his book *Palestine under the Mandate: 1920–1948* (published during the early years of the State of Israel) he stressed that 'The reader will perhaps notice ... at times the terms Jew and Jewish, at times the word Zionist have been employed ... this has been deliberate ... the term Jew has hitherto been used too loosely to express both ideas.'[111] Thus it was no doubt a disappointment for him that he felt it necessary to write to Spears, the leading Gentile anti-Zionist of the time, to ask him,

> Would it be possible for you when opening or writing on the subject [of Palestine] to please call the proposal not a Jewish state – many Jews object very strongly to mixing Judaism with politics or nationalism – but a Zionist state which it is in reality.[112]

Spears replied that this was a 'good idea' and one that he would 'bear in mind'.[113] Yet the fact that two years after the Fellowship had first set out its position to Spears during its talk before the MEPC and after all the efforts in between to differentiate Zionists from Jews, and even in the light of his discussion on the issue with CAA members such as Stokes, Spears could only answer Hyamson that it was 'a good idea'.

This shows just how out of touch he was with the position of Jewish anti-Zionists. Nor did Spears 'bear in mind' Hyamson's appeal because in later correspondence he still talked of Zionist efforts as Jewish efforts, at one point commenting to a Palestinian Arab correspondent that he did not see 'how the Jews could hold out' in the battle over Palestine.[114]

It could be argued that Spears' persistent failure to differentiate between Zionism and Judaism was in line with the position of the majority of Gentiles (and all Zionists). Indeed, the public statements of other Gentile anti-Zionists also showed a failure to grasp this difference. Thomas Reid MP, during his evidence before the AACIP, was challenged by a committee member over what he meant when he referred to 'Jewish intrigues' in Palestine, and Reid attempted to correct this by saying that any remarks he had made of 'a critical nature ... were about political Zionist leaders and not about the Jews'.[115]

But Spears was neither Reid nor an average member of the public. He was a man at the centre of the battle against Zionism in these years and he had access to the Fellowship on this and many other issues if he had any desire to know the Jewish anti-Zionist position. As such his failure to differentiate between Jews and Zionists is an example of his lack of desire to grasp the fundamental principles on which the Fellowship was based.

Spears' refusal to attend the Fellowship's first annual meeting, and his reluctance to engage in practical co-operation with the Fellowship or take into consideration its position on such issues as Zionism and Judaism, is all the more interesting in the light of his response to another anti-Zionist body. In June 1948 Newcombe wrote to Spears suggesting that the CAA should co-operate with Kermit Roosevelt's newly formed anti-Zionist committee in the United States.[116] Spears immediately responded to this suggestion in a positive manner and informed Newcombe, just four days later, that 'I have written to him [Kermit Roosevelt] telling him we should very much like to co-operate with his committee.'[117]

The committee in question was the Committee for Justice and Peace in the Holy Land led by prominent church leaders and Protestant educators including Virginia Gildersleeve and Henry Sloan Coffin, former president of the Union Theological Seminary. It had been officially formed in March 1948 in an attempt to organise the various anti-Zionist efforts in the United States into one last-ditch concerted effort to prevent the creation of a Jewish state. This body was despised by the Zionists. Sir Leon Simon, a very moderate Zionist, wrote to Judah Magnes that the body was 'bitterly anti-Zionist ... some of them anti-Semitic ... at any rate anti-Jewish ... notoriously represent missionary and pro-Arab interests'.[118]

Spears' eagerness to co-operate with this new committee in the United States is very informative when compared with his reluctance to work with the Fellowship during the previous years, before Israel had been founded. But this incident is also of interest when one compares Roosevelt's relationship with Jewish anti-Zionists in America with Spears' contemporaneous relationship with English Jewish anti-Zionists.

Kermit Roosevelt, grandson of American president Theodore Roosevelt, a founding member of the Central Intelligence Agency and a life-long Arabist with a reputation as an expert on the Middle East, was perhaps the most active Gentile anti-Zionist in the United States during these years. As such he held a position similar to Spears in England.[119] For example, Freya Stark during her trip to the United States described Roosevelt as 'bubbling over with pro-Arab and anti-French feeling and might help'.[120] Pro-Arab and anti-French was exactly how Spears was described at the same time. And like Spears, Roosevelt used the existence of Jewish anti-Zionist arguments and Jewish opposition to Zionism as part of his own public argument against Zionism.[121]

However, unlike Spears he saw all anti-Zionist efforts as inextricably linked to Jewish anti-Zionism. As such he was one of the closest and most supportive allies of the American Council for Judaism (ACJ). He worked closely with this organisation in his efforts to prevent the implementation of the partition resolution at the United Nations, and on a more personal level he attended ACJ dinners throughout the United States promoting the position of Jewish anti-Zionists.

Roosevelt's co-operative efforts with the ACJ in opposing Zionism were charted in the *Council News* (the paper of the ACJ) and it is unthinkable, given the lack of co-operation between Spears and the Fellowship, to envisage a situation where the *Jewish Outlook* would have devoted its pages to the efforts of Spears in travelling around Britain speaking to Fellowship groups.[122]

As has been seen, Spears would not even attend the Fellowship's inaugural annual meeting, whereas in April 1948 Roosevelt was honoured by the ACJ at a dinner in San Francisco. While back in Washington, where the Committee for Justice and Peace had its headquarters, he spoke at rallies organised by the Washington chapter of the ACJ and shared the platform with leading Jewish anti-Zionists.[123]

Given this situation it is hardly surprising that Roosevelt in his role as executive director of the Committee for Justice and Peace attempted to involve the ACJ in the group's efforts. Rabbi Morris

Lazaron, Rabbi of the Baltimore Hebrew Congregation, 1915-49 and a co-founder and vice-president of the ACJ, represented the Jewish body on the committee's council. Other leading anti-Zionist Jews played a central role behind the scenes of the committee. For example, Rabbi Elmer Berger, a leading ACJ publicist, advised the committee's executive on issues of recruitment and publicity.

Indeed, for as long as the Committee for Justice and Peace in the Holy Land existed it co-ordinated its activities and kept in close touch with the ACJ.[124] Thus just as Spears' eagerness to co-operate with Roosevelt's new committee highlights his reluctance to co-operate with the Fellowship on an institutional level, Roosevelt's active co-operation with American-Jewish anti-Zionists highlights his (Spears') lack of co-operation with Jewish anti-Zionists in England on a personal level.

Nor was this in any way due to a reluctance on the part of Jewish anti-Zionists to work with Spears and his committee. The Fellowship was not worried about being seen sharing a common position with Gentiles over Zionism (it had eagerly attended a meeting of the MEPC, a body suspected of anti-Zionist motives).

This was due to its belief that Jews were 'Englishman of the Jewish Faith' who owed their political allegiance to England and who differed from their Gentile fellow citizens only in their religious practice. In this context the acceptance by Gentile anti-Zionists of their Jewish contemporaries as partners in the fight against Zionism would have been a vindication of the position of anti-Zionist Jews as loyal Englishman who happened to be Jews.

The most obvious example of the Jewish desire to be legitimised by their relationship with Gentile anti-Zionists was the invitation to Spears to attend the first Fellowship annual meeting as guest of honour. However, both before and after this invitation the Fellowship made an effort in diverse ways to appeal to the Gentile anti-Zionist constituency. The appearance of Brunel Cohen and Henriques before the MEPC and the sending of Fellowship pamphlets, copies of resolutions and reports on Fellowship meetings to leading anti-Zionists such as Spears, Storrs and the Archbishop of York is proof of this.[125]

Even after Spears had refused the invitation to attend the Fellowship's annual meeting, that body was still hopeful that there could be co-operation. Franklyn, for example, in writing to acknowledge Spears' decision not to attend the annual meeting did not hide the disappointment, telling Spears that although the

Fellowship would be 'very grateful for your presence, we feel it would perhaps be unfair to press for this', and concluded on the optimistic (or possibly naïve) note that 'perhaps on some future occasion you would come to attend a ... more public function'.[126]

Nor should Gluckstein's threat of legal action against *New Judea* for claiming that he conspired with Spears and others against Jewry be viewed as an attempt to distance himself from Gentile anti-Zionists (it had been Gluckstein who had organised the Fellowship's appearance before the MEPC), but rather as a riposte to the accusation that his anti-Zionist position was aimed at hurting Jewry in the first place.

Even in 1947, after Spears had made no effort to move towards co-operating with the Fellowship, leading Jewish anti-Zionists were still writing to him in a positive manner emphasising their support for his efforts and agreeing with his arguments against Zionism. Albert Hyamson, for example, wrote to Spears in February 1947 applauding his efforts and telling him how close their positions on Palestine were.[127]

Hyamson's effort to communicate with Spears is not surprising, given his earlier involvement in the 1937 Hyamson–Newcombe plan and his subsequent involvement in drawing up *A Constitution for Palestine* in 1945. Indeed, Joseph Leftwich was of the view that Hyamson was trying to make the Fellowship 'a sort of Ichud' – a body established in 1942 by Judah Magnes to promote Jewish–Arab co-operation in resolving the Palestine problem on the basis of a binational unitary state.[128] And it was in this vein that in 1946 Hyamson had two meetings with Harold Beeley of the Foreign Office on the possibility of non-Zionist Jews reaching an agreement with Arabs over Palestine and asking Beeley what the government's attitude to such an agreement might be.[129]

Thus it is impossible to avoid the conclusion that the lack of co-operation between the Fellowship and the CAA was to a large extent down to Spears himself, who was after all the driving force behind all CAA efforts. In these terms his refusal to co-operate with the Jewish Fellowship relates to one of the most fascinating and complex aspects of the Palestine problem: the extent to which anti-Zionism within the Gentile world was essentially motivated by strategic, imperial, political and even sincerely held moral considerations relating to the perceived injustices of Zionism and the extent that Gentile anti-Zionism was influenced by the fact that Zionism was a Jewish movement and Zionists were for the most part Jews. In other words, how much of Spears' refusal to work with the Fellowship was due to a prejudice against Jews?

Analysing anti-Zionism as a product of anti-Semitism has become a taboo issue. It has been attacked as Jewish oversensitivity[130] and a most unfair weapon in the debate over Palestine, and worse, an effort to tarnish those whose opposition to a Jewish state was motivated by a sincere concern for Jews rather than a profound hatred of them.[131]

Leading anti-Zionists of the post-war era, individuals closely connected to the CAA, such as Thomas Reid MP, Nevill Barbour, Robin Maugham and Maude Royden-Shaw, took great pains to stress that their opposition to political Zionism was not motivated by anti-Semitism.[132] Spears also echoed this position, telling one Jewish correspondent of 1948 who accused him of being 'an enemy of the Jews' that 'I am not an enemy of the Jews, I am an enemy of political Zionism which I consider an evil thing.'[133] And he concluded a letter to the Jewish commentator C.C. Aronsfeld in 1953 with the statement 'I am certainly not anti-Semitic and some of my best friends are Jewish.'[134]

Likewise the Arabs in their opposition to Zionism had always been concerned to show that their opposition was not a result of anti-Semitism, that Jews in the Arab world had not suffered from anti-Semitism and that it was only with the rise of political Zionism that these communities had begun to fear for their position and safety in Arab society. As an early Arab propaganda pamphlet setting out the Arab case in London stated, 'let it be understood that the Arabs of Palestine are not anti-Semitic'.[135]

On its formation the Arab Office reiterated this position and Musa Alami was keen that it should stress this aspect of the battle against Zionism. Indeed the importance that Alami attached to this can be seen by the fact that in a telegram in April 1945 to Oliver Stanley, the colonial secretary, the Palestine High Commissioner stressed that 'Alami assures us that offices [Arab Office] will provide a counter blast to Zionist publicity, they will not in any way become party to anti-Jewish propaganda.'[136] Early Arab Office pamphlets also stressed that 'anti-Zionism does not derive from anti-Semitism', and that 'the Arabs are irrevocably opposed to political Zionism but are in no way hostile to the Jews'.[137]

In 1947, in the wake of an FBI investigation into whether the Arab Office in Washington co-operated with anti-Semitic bodies, the Arab Office in London stressed that it 'has always ...

scrupulously avoided anything which might be regarded as racial or anti-Semitic propaganda'.[138] The following year the *Arab News Bulletin* was insistent in an editorial under the heading 'The Arab Cause and Anti-Semitism' in once again restating that 'the fundamental truth about the Arab struggle against Zionism in Palestine is that it does not derive from anti-Semitism ... the Arab Office in London has since its inception adhered with uncompromising rigour to these fundamental principles'.[139]

Within Jewry these claims were often met with scepticism and many of the attacks on anti-Zionists in these years were made in terms of their anti-Semitic motivations. There was for instance the *Jewish Chronicle*'s claim (subsequently retracted) that the reason that Spears, Storrs, Hope-Simpson and others opposed Zionism was because they were 'Jew-haters'.

However, the argument that anti-Semitism was at the heart of Gentile opposition to a Jewish state did not predominate in Zionist polemics in these years. For example, the veteran Zionist publicist Harry Sacher, writing in 1948, argued that the central motivation behind Gentile anti-Zionism was not anti-Semitism but a lack of 'a common interest in Jews and Judaism' or concern for the future of Jewry.[140] And it is possible to argue that it was this inability and a lack of inclination to view issues from a Jewish perspective rather than anti-Semitism that was primarily responsible for the Gentile inability to co-operate with Jewish anti-Zionists.

Spears exemplified this in his relationship with the Jewish Fellowship. And despite some negative private statements regarding Jewry and his offensive anti-Zionist rhetoric (especially his glib comparisons of Zionism to Nazism and his claim that Jewish Palestine was driven in its support for the Allies in the Second World War by the profit motive) it is much harder to argue that he was motivated in his anti-Zionism out of anti-Semitism than some other of his anti-Zionist contemporaries such as Freya Stark whose correspondence is full of derogatory remarks about Jewish history and Jews in general.[141]

But Spears' anti-Zionism had an added dimension and was made all the more fascinating by the fact that throughout his life he was dogged by accusations that he himself was Jewish. His biographer Max Egremont has chronicled Spears' obsession with not appearing Jewish (in 1918 he changed his name from Spiers to Spears for this reason). He also records how Spears could never escape this perception, noting how Patrick Coghill, who served under Spears in the security mission in Beirut during the war, recalled that 'my reaction was that he was a Jew – and I am not Jew conscious'.[142]

This apparent Jewishness which Spears always denied, and which it is impossible either to prove or disprove, followed him and was used against him at every stage of his career. For example, the Nazi propaganda machine in attempting to limit his popularity among Arabs in the Levant during the war claimed that he was of Jewish origin.[143] Later, his Gaullist enemies, attempting to minimise his role in de Gaulle's escape to London, argued that he was not assisting the French leader but running from the Germans because he was a Jew.[144] And one French reviewer of his book, *Prelude to Victory*, referred to Spears and Dreyfuss as two Jews who were enemies of France.[145]

But even at the height of his battle against a Jewish state Spears could not escape this label. Richard Crossman, for example, saw in Spears' anti-Zionist evidence before the AACIP proof that a Jew could be pro-Arab.[146] Indeed, the *Jewish Chronicle* in the wake of its particularly savage denunciation of Spears as a 'Jew-hater' in the May of 1946, retracted this claim the following week on the basis that Spears could not possibly be a Jew-hater because he 'is believed extensively by popular rumour to be of Jewish descent'.[147]

In his determined post-war opposition to Zionism one sees Spears make a final attempt, after a whole life of denial, to end such accusations once and for all. As such his refusal to work with the Fellowship must partly be seen as an extension of his effort to distance himself from the accusation that he himself was a Jew.

In 1948, in a last desperate attempt to find a way to halt Zionism, Spears drew up a memorandum on the feasibility of creating what he called a 'publicity fund' that could finance his plan to 'mobilise and organise [a] large body of pro-Arab and anti-Zionist opinion in Britain' and to form a 'Justice for Palestine' group to state the Arab case.[148] This was a move away from the quiet and elitist propaganda tactics favoured by the CAA throughout its existence. Spears now wanted to advertise for members and when enough people joined in a certain area a paid organiser would be sent to co-ordinate anti-Zionist activities.

He also set out his hope for a nation-wide publicity campaign, through posters, pamphlets and the press. But even in planning these extreme measures, as a drastic response to a crisis situation, Spears found no role for Jewish anti-Zionists. He had a place for the

Arab Office. It would take charge of the nation-wide publicity campaign. He also speculated on the possibility of arranging 'direct co-operation' with Kermit Roosevelt's parallel campaign in the United States. But there was no place and no role for the Jewish Fellowship.[149]

This ambitious plan came to nothing as it was too late to halt a Jewish state, but in ignoring the role of Jewish anti-Zionists one last time Spears was highlighting and reiterating what had been his fundamental inability and refusal to co-operate with the Jewish Fellowship in the battle against Zionism.

Unlike many other of his anti-Zionist contemporaries who accepted a Jewish state as a *fait-accompli*, Spears continued his anti-Zionist agitation in the years after Israeli statehood. Indeed, if anything the ferocity of his anti-Zionism only increased with the founding of Israel. In 1953 for example, he was publicly condemning Israel as a 'cancer in the heart of the Arab Middle East … an inoperable cancer I fear'.[150]

He continued to argue about the Jewish state in this manner until his death in the 1970s. It is one of the ironies of this story that the same factors that resulted in Spears' dominance and leadership of the Gentile anti-Zionist effort: a fearless determination in the face of criticism, a narrow-minded vision of right and wrong, an unalterable confidence in his own abilities and an inherent identity crisis relating to a possible Jewish ancestry were also the same characteristics that made it impossible for him to view the Palestine problem from a Jewish perspective or even understand the position of Jewish anti-Zionists. For these characteristics resulted both in Spears' total conviction that Zionism was evil and his inability and refusal to differentiate between Zionism and Judaism, which in turn made it impossible for him to view co-operation with Jewish anti-Zionists as a viable option.

Such dedication to the anti-Zionist cause over such a long period encourages the view that Spears' anti-Zionism, while brutal and unyielding, was motivated by a sincere belief in the danger a Jewish state caused to British interests and the Arabs of Palestine. This is given more credence by the fact that Spears, the lifelong francophile who had been sent to the Levant precisely because of his close and intimate past with the French, had been prepared to sacrifice Britain's relationship with France for Arab friendship during the crucial war years.

Yet Spears' refusal to co-operate with Jewish anti-Zionists

during the Mandate era, coupled with the uncommonly personal and intense nature of his anti-Zionism, also leads one to conclude that even if he was not motivated in his anti-Zionism by traditional anti-Semitism, he was influenced by the fact that Zionism was a Jewish movement and Israel a Jewish state. Given his determined attempt to end accusations that he was himself a Jew, how could he not have been? As the next chapter will show, his relationship with the Arab anti-Zionists of the Arab Office was free from the complications of his relationship with the Jewish Fellowship.

NOTES

1. See Hyamson and Newcombe, *Suggested Basis for Discussion on Reaching an Agreement on Palestine* (London: September 1937). For the contemporary correspondence on the Hyamson–Newcombe proposals see file 2, Box LXV, JEMP and material held in the PRO/CO 733/ 340/12. Also see Neil Caplan, in his second volume of *Futile Diplomacy: Arab–Zionist Negotiations and the End of the Mandate* (London: Frank Cass, 1986), pp. 78–84.
2. Ben-Gurion to Magnes, 24 February 1938, cited in Ben-Gurion's *My Talks With Arab Leaders* (New York: The Third Press, Joseph Okpaku, 1973), pp. 147–67.
3. Barbour, 'Some Less Familiar Aspects of the Palestine Problem', lecture to RCAS, 28 September 1938, reprinted in *JRCAS*, XXV: 4 (October 1938), pp. 544–70, p. 554.
4. Storrs, in his foreword to A.M. Hyamson's *Palestine: A Policy* (London: Methuen, 1942), p. v.
5. Newcombe, 'The Arab Countries', transcript of general meeting, RIIA, 17 September 1942, 8/860.
6. Elizabeth Monroe (Mrs Humphrey Neame) was director of the Middle East Division, Ministry of Information, 1940; Diplomatic correspondent of the *Observer*, 1944; member of the *Economist* staff, 1945–58 and Fellow of St Antony's College, Oxford, 1963–73. Her most famous work on the Middle East was *Britain's Moment in the Middle East, 1914–1956* (London: Chatto & Windus, 1963).
7. Caroline Moorehead, *Freya Stark* (London: Viking, 1985), p. 85.
8. For the above correspondence see Stark to Monroe, 10 December 1943; 20 December 1943; 17 April 1944, MONPA.
9. Shimoni, G., 'The Non-Zionists in Anglo-Jewry, 1937–1948, *Jewish Journal of Sociology*, XXVII: 2 (December 1986), pp. 89–115, p. 106.
10. See Thomas Kolsky, *Jews Against Zionism: The American Council for Judaism, 1942–1948* (Philadelphia: Temple University Press, 1990), p. 176.
11. See the Foreign Office report, *Jews for the Palestine Administration*, London, March 1920, PRO/FO 371/5113.
12. See Nachmani, *Great Power Discord in Palestine: The Anglo-American Committee of Inquiry into the Problems of European Jewry and Palestine, 1945–1946* (London: Frank Cass, 1986), p. 132.
13. Private Diary of R.H.S. Crossman, January 1946, file 2, CROSS.
14. Crossman, *Palestine Mission*, p. 68.
15. *Jewish Outlook*, 2: 2 (July 1947), p. 7.
16. See Newcombe and Beaumont, *A Constitution for Palestine* (London: 1945). Although only Newcombe and Beaumont were credited with authorship Nevill Barbour was also an author of this document. Newcombe stated this in a letter to Spears, 3 April 1945, Box 5/3, SPSP. Barbour's preference for anonymity was obviously part of his erratic but general desire not to be identified with public positions on Palestine because of his work at the BBC. Indeed, in referring to the document in his 1946 book he stated that Newcombe and Beaumont were the sole authors, *Nisi Dominus: A Survey of Palestine* (London: Harrap, 1946), p. 231.

188   *Divided Against Zion*

17. Newcombe to Barbour, 6 January 1940, Box 2/3, BARB.
18. Newcombe, Beaumont (and Barbour), *A Constitution for Palestine*, p. 2.
19. Newcombe to Spears, 3 April 1945, Box 5/3, SPSP; Newcombe to Storrs, 19 June 1945, Box 6/15, STOP.
20. Nevill Barbour, n.d., Box 2/3, BARB.
21. *New Judea*, February–March 1945, p. 72.
22. Brunel Cohen, *Address to Fellowship Council*, p. 2.
23. Spears to Henriques, 13 March 1945, Box 4/6, SPSP.
24. See *New Judea*, February–March 1945, p. 72.
25. 'Misrepresenting the Jewish Case', *Zionist Review*, 9 March 1945, p. 1.
26. Rosen to Spears, 15 March 1945, Box 4/6, SPSP.
27. See Spears–Hammersley correspondence of March 1945 on this affair, Box 4/6, SPSP.
28. Spears to Hammersley, 21 March 1945, Box 4/6, SPSP.
29. Gluckstein to Spears, 6 March 1945, Box 4/6, SPSP.
30. Keeling to Spears, 13 February 1945, Box 6/4, SPSP.
31. Spears to Brodetsky, 7 June 1945, Box 4/6, SPSP.
32. Evidence of Spears before the AACIP, p. 43.
33. Wigoder, *Zionist Review*, 22 February 1946, p. 9 and *Jewish Chronicle*, 22 February 1946, p. 17.
34. Hamabit (pseud.), *New Judea*, January–February 1946, pp. 64–5.
35. *New Judea*, March–April 1946, p. 94.
36. F.M. Landau, *Jewish Chronicle*, 15 March 1946, p. 15.
37. 'Sermon of the Week', *Jewish Chronicle*, 2 August 1946, p. 14.
38. Franklyn, *Jewish Chronicle*, 30 August 1946, p. 15.
39. Salomon to Greenberg, 1 March 1943, MS150 AJ 110/15, GREEN.
40. H. Newman, *Jewish Chronicle*, 28 December 1945, p. 12.
41. Spears to Hope-Simpson, 12 September 1945, Box 6/4, SPSP.
42. Hope-Simpson to Spears, 24 September 1945, Box 6/4, SPSP.
43. See the Aufheuser–Storrs correspondence and Rosenwald's 'Reply to Zionism', *Life*, 28 June 1943, Box 6/15, STOP. Aufheuser, a Munich Jew who had been a banker before the rise of Hitler, had travelled to Palestine in 1925 to investigate the possibility of settling there. He made contact with Storrs in 1933 and Storrs was very fond of him. In a letter to Humphrey Bowman, Storrs referred to Aufheuser as a 'charming and distinguished personage', Storrs to Bowman, 13 November 1933, Box 1/2, BOW.
44. MS Diary of Storrs, 4 August 1949, Box 6/8, STOP.
45. Hyamson to Storrs, 4 October 1954, Box 6/10, STOP.
46. Storrs to Spears, 9 September 1945, Box 7/2, SPSP.
47. MS Diary of Storrs, 29 May 1947, Box 6/8, STOP.
48. Ibid.
49. For Mattuck's writings collected by Storrs see Box 6/15, STOP.
50. Max Beloff has disagreed with the presentation of Montagu as a Jewish anti-Zionist on the basis that unlike other Jewish anti-Zionists of his era, such as Lucien Wolf or C.G. Montefiore, Montagu was in no way involved in or concerned with events within the Jewish community. However, in as much as Montagu used the fact that he was a Jew to give credence to his own anti-Zionism, it is fair to class him as a Jewish anti-Zionist. For Beloff's comments on Montagu see his review of Daniel Gulwein's *The Divided Elite: Economics, Politics and Anglo-Jewry, 1882–1917* (Leiden: E.J. Brill, 1992), in the *Jewish Journal of Sociology*, XXXIV: 2 (December 1982), pp. 152–5, p. 154.
51. MS Diary of Storrs, 2 November 1944, Box 6/5, STOP.
52. Waley Cohen, *The Times*, 7 November 1947.
53. For a recounting of this episode see J. Mendel's letter in the *Jewish Chronicle*, 22 February 1946, p. 16.
54. See Bustani to Waley Cohen, 14 July 1945, Box 5/4, SPSP. The fact that this letter can be found in Spears' papers does suggest that the 'us' Bustani referred to could well have included Spears.
55. Storrs to editor of *The Times*, 7 November 1947, Box 6/10, STOP.

56. On Newcombe and Storrs' discussion with Hyamson about Palestine, see Newcombe to Spears, 27 November 1945, Box 5/3, SPSP and MS Diary of Storrs, 12 May 1949, Box 6/8, STOP.
57. See Newcombe to Singleton, 23 January 1946, Box 5/3, SPSP.
58. Newcombe to Spears, 15 January 1946, Box 5/3, SPSP.
59. Newcombe to Spears, 3 July 1946, Box 5/3, SPSP.
60. Newcombe to Spears, 29 June 1946, Box 5/3, SPSP (emphasis in the original).
61. Newcombe, 'The Arab Countries', p. 5.
62. Newcombe to Singleton, 23 January 1946, Box 5/3, SPSP.
63. Newcombe to Spears, 25 January 1947, Box 5/3, SPSP.
64. Cassell, 'The Errors of the Jewish Fellowship', *Synagogue Review*, XIX: 12 (August 1945), pp. 90–1. See Brunel Cohen's claims in *Some Information for You*, p. 7 and in the Fellowship's evidence before the AACIP, p. 41.
65. Drummond Shiels to Spears, 11 September 1945, Box 4/7, SPSP.
66. See Barnett Litvinoff's 'Great Britain and the Arab States', *Zionist Review*, 22 October 1948, p. 14.
67. M.V. Seton Williams, *Britain and the Arab States: A Survey of Anglo-Arab Relations, 1920–1948* (London: Luzac, 1948), p. 7. The articles in question were published in the *Daily Telegraph*, 3, 6, 7 January 1947.
68. E.W. Elsworth to Spears, 14 February 1945, Box 4/6, SPSP.
69. Skinner to Spears, 13 March 1945, Box 4/7, SPSP. The article that Skinner sent to Spears to comment on had been written by the Revd Charles Fisher and was being circulated around the Victoria Institute.
70. Spears to Skinner, 27 March 1945, Box 4/7, SPSP.
71. Spears to Hammersley, 21 March 1945, Box 4/6, SPSP.
72. MS Diary of Storrs, 20 June 1944, Box 6/5, STOP. Liverman was the treasurer of the Board of Deputies for 13 years between 1933–46. He was opposed to the political Zionist control of the Board and was a founding member of the 'New Group' that was formed in 1947 to provide a caucus for members of the Board opposed to Zionist dominance of Board procedures.
73. Spears to Franklyn, 1 October 1945, Box 4/6, SPSP.
74. Ibid.
75. Spears to Henriques, 13 March 1945, Box 4/6, SPSP.
76. Storrs, foreword to A.M. Hyamson's *Palestine: A Policy*, p. v. Also see Maugham, *Approach to Palestine* (London: Falcon Press, 1947), p. 96 and Ionides, *Divide and Lose: The Arab Revolt of 1955–1958* (London: Geoffrey Bles, 1960), p. 40.
77. Storrs, *Memoirs*, p. 391.
78. Hyamson to Storrs, 24 November 1941, Box 6/10, STOP.
79. Hyamson to Storrs, 1 December 1941, Box 6/10, STOP.
80. Storrs to editor of *The Times*, 7 November 1947, Box 6/10, STOP.
81. Storrs, review of Weizmann's *Trial and Error*, in the *JRCAS*, XXXVI: 1 (January 1949), pp. 309–13, p. 312.
82. Newcombe to Spears, 24 January 1948, Box 5/3, SPSP.
83. Beloff later became Gladstone Professor of Government and was made a life peer in 1981. See his memoirs *An Historian in the Twentieth Century* (New Haven, CT, London: Yale University Press, 1992), especially chapter 6 'The Jewish Experience', pp. 91–103.
84. Hamabit (pseud.), *New Judea*, January–February 1948, pp. 69–70.
85. Spears to Newcombe, 27 January 1948, Box 5/3, SPSP.
86. Newcombe to Spears, 19 June 1948, Box 5/3, SPSP.
87. Newcombe to Spears, 15 December 1948, Box 5/3, SPSP.
88. On Isaacs see 'A Great Australian: Sir Isaac Isaacs', *Jewish Monthly*, 1: 12 (March 1948), pp. 32–7.
89. Bentwich, *My Seventy-Seven Years: An Account of My Life and Times, 1883–1960* (London: Routledge & Kegan Paul, 1962), p. 149.
90. Rose Henriques, TBJSBH, 3/38, 1948, MS132 AJ 195, HENP.
91. Hyamson to Spears, 6 February 1947, Box 4/6, SPSP.
92. Spears to Hyamson, n.d., February 1947, Box 4/6, SPSP.
93. Spears, 'The Middle East and our Policy There', p. 157.

94. Spears to Leimdoerfer, 7 November 1945, Box 4/7, SPSP.
95. Spears to Skinner, 27 March 1945, Box 4/7, SPSP.
96. Royden-Shaw to Spears, 1 November 1945; Spears to Royden-Shaw, 7 November 1945, Box 7/2, SPSP.
97. For the lists of members of the MEPC and the CAA see Box 6/3, SPSP.
98. Spears to Gluckstein, 31 May 1945, Box 4/6, SPSP.
99. Spears to Henriques, 27 September 1946, Box 4/6, SPSP.
100. Franklyn to Spears, 4 October 1946, Box 4/6, SPSP.
101. See minutes of meeting between Brodetsky, Mattuck and Gluckstein, 22 October 1945, ACC3121/C14/28, ABD.
102. Mattuck, sermon at the Liberal Jewish Synagogue, London, 30 June 1945. Also see Mattuck's earlier work *What are the Jews? Their Significance and Position in the Modern World* (London: Hodder & Stoughton, 1939) and Basil Henriques' *What is Judaism?* (London: St George's Settlement Synagogue, 1945).
103. Evidence of the Fellowship before the AACIP, p. 59.
104. 'A Time for Decision', *Jewish Outlook*, 2: 7 (February 1948), pp. 2, 8. Also see Basil Henriques' similar argument in the *Star*, 13 January 1947, and Franklyn's in 'Israel: State or Religion?', *Contemporary Review*, CLXXII: 979 (July 1947), p. 38.
105. Anon., 'The Repercussions of Zionism in Britain', *World Affairs*, I: 2 (April 1947), pp. 121–30, p. 124.
106. Brunel Cohen, address to Fellowship's second annual meeting, 10 December 1946, reprinted in abridged version in *Jewish Outlook*, 1: 9 (January 1947), pp. 4–5.
107. 'The Jews and Some Jews: Mr Pickthorn Knows the Difference', *Jewish Outlook*, 1: 4 (August 1946), p. 13.
108. Spears to Brodetsky, 15 May 1945, Box 4/6, SPSP (emphasis added).
109. Spears, 'The Middle East and our Policy There', lecture to RCAS, 7 February 1945, p. 157 (emphasis added).
110. See Spears to Stokes, 4 August 1945; Stokes to Maurice, 13 August 1945; Stokes to Maurice, 18 August 1945, Box 4/6, SPSP. There were a record 28 Jewish MPs returned to the House after the 1945 election. However, only D.L. Lipson, an Independent Conservative, and Phil Piratin, a communist, were outside the Labour Party. For an extensive study of Jewish involvement in national politics see Geoffrey Alderman, *The Jewish Community in British Politics* (Oxford: Clarendon Press, 1983).
111. Hyamson, *Palestine under the Mandate: 1920–1948* (London: Methuen, 1950), p. v. Newcombe was also well aware of the importance of this issue. In a review of Hyamson's book he welcomed the fact that throughout the work Hyamson had 'defined and maintained the difference between a Jew ... and a Zionist', *JRCAS*, XXXVIII: 1 (January 1951), p. 85. Also see the Revd Harold Reinhart's private letters to the editor of *The Times*, 24 August 1949 and 26 May 1950, asking that the word Jewish be not used out of context when reporting on Israel, MS171 AJ 246 122, REIN.
112. Hyamson to Spears, 23 September 1947, Box 4/6, SPSP.
113. Spears to Hyamson, 27 September 1947, Box 4/6, SPSP.
114. Spears to I. Shawa, 9 October 1948, Box 4/6, SPSP.
115. Evidence of Reid before the AACIP, p. 17.
116. Newcombe to Spears, 17 June 1948, Box 5/3, SPSP.
117. Spears to Newcombe, 21 June 1948, Box 5/3, SPSP.
118. See Simon to Magnes, cited in Arthur Goren (ed.), *Dissenter in Zion: From the Writings of Judah L. Magnes* (Cambridge, Mass, and London: Harvard University Press, 1984), p. 467.
119. For Roosevelt's anti-Zionist position see his pamphlet *The Arabs Live There Too*, published in 1945 in New York and his book *Arabs, Oil and History: The Story of the Middle East* (London: Victor Gollancz, 1949). Also see Alfred Lilienthal's account of the Zionist attacks on Roosevelt for his opposition to Zionism in *What Price Israel?*, pp. 131–3.
120. Stark to Monroe, 24 November 1943, MONPA.
121. See, for example, Roosevelt, 'The Partition of Palestine', *Middle East Journal*, 2: 1 (January 1948), pp. 1–16, p. 4. In this article Roosevelt referred to the position of

Judah Magnes, the American Jewish Committee and the American Council for Judaism as examples of Jewish opposition to Zionism to give credence to his own argument. Similarly, see his *Arabs, Oil and History*, pp. 173–96.
122. See for example, 'Roosevelt Hits Palestine Plan in Houston Talk', *Council News* (November 1947), p. 4. Ironically (given the lack of a relationship between the Fellowship and English Gentile anti-Zionists such as Spears), the Fellowship did give coverage to Roosevelt's anti-Zionist efforts in the United States, on one occasion summarising an article of Roosevelt's that had been published in *Harpers* magazine, *Jewish Outlook*, 1: 11 (April 1947), p. 14.
123. Kolsky, *Jews Against Zionism*, p. 173.
124. Ibid., pp. 187–8.
125. For example, copies of the Fellowship pamphlet *What the Jewish Fellowship Stands For* can be found in Storrs' papers with the words 'please peruse' written on top, Box 6/15 STOP and in the Spears papers, Box 4/6, SPSP. The Fellowship also sent copies of Fellowship resolutions and corresponded with Dr Cyril Garbett, the Archbishop of York, see Garbett to Henriques, 5 July 1946, 2/6, MS132 AJ 322, HENP.
126. Franklyn to Spears, 2 October 1945, Box 4/6, SPSP.
127. Hyamson to Spears, 6 February 1947, Box 4/6, SPSP.
128. Leftwich to Greenberg, 20 March 1944, MS150 AJ 110/7, GREEN.
129. See Beeley's report of these meetings in letter to J.M. Martin of the Colonial Office, 3 December 1946, PRO/FO 371/52646.
130. For example, an editorial 'The Palestine Problem' in the *National Review* in 1946 was of the opinion that it was the 'undue sensitiveness' and the 'hypersensitiveness' of Jewry that provided a 'clue to one of the difficulties in arriving at a settlement in Palestine', 1767 (December 1946), pp. 44–5. While Sir Arthur Rucker, speaking during a discussion 'Policy in Palestine' at the RIIA in the same year, echoed the general view that 'God forgive that anyone should deride the Jews', 29 November, 1946, 8/1345, p. 9.
131. See, for example, Christopher Mayhew and Michael Adams, *Publish it Not: The Middle East Cover-Up* (Harlow: Longman, 1975), p. 18.
132. Both Nevill Barbour and Thomas Reid emphasised this *inter alia*, in speeches at the RCAS. See Barbour's 'Some Less Familiar Aspects of the Palestine Problem', p. 565 and Reid's 'Should a Jewish State be Established in Palestine?', *JRCAS*, XXXIII: 2 (April 1946), p. 27. Robin Maugham also succinctly summed up this position when he asked 'is it wrong to assume that if a man is fond of the Arabs he must be against the Jews?', *Approach to Palestine*, p. 11.
133. See A. Jacobs to Spears, 22 October 1948 and Spears to Jacobs, 28 October 1948, Box 15/1, SPSP.
134. Spears to Aronsfeld, n.d., December 1953, WEINP.
135. See the 1921 pamphlet *The Holy Land: The Moslem–Christian Case against Zionist Aggression*, p. 10. Also see a later but similar claim (1936) in *The Arab Case*, p. 11.
136. Lord Gort to Oliver Stanley, 10 April, 1945, PRO/FO 371/45328.
137. See Edward Atiyah's *Arab Rights and the British Left* (London: AO, 1945), p. 6 and The Arab Office's *The Problem of Palestine: Summary of the Arab Point of View* (London: AO, 1945), p. 5.
138. *Arab News Bulletin*, 34, 4 April 1947, p. 1.
139. Ibid., 54, 16 January, 1948, p. 8.
140. Harry Sacher, 'Reflections', *New Judea*, March–April 1948, p. 87.
141. On Stark's disturbing attitude towards Jews and Judaism throughout her life see the six volumes of her collected letters edited by C. and L. Moorehead and her correspondence with Elizabeth Monroe held in Monroe's papers at the Middle East Centre, St Antony's College, Oxford.
142. See Egremont's *Under Two Flags: The Life of Major-General Sir Edward Spears* (London: Weidenfeld & Nicolson, 1997), pp. 1, 239. While examining this aspect of Spears' life, Egremont pays scant attention to the issues of Zionism and Palestine, neither of which even gain a reference in the index. Instead the author concentrates his study on Spears' life-long relationship with France.
143. On the Nazi presentation of Spears as a Jew see the letter from C.C. Aronsfeld to Spears, 17 December 1953, WEINP.

144. Egremont, *Under Two Flags*, p. 190.
145. Ibid., p. 285.
146. Private Diary of R.H.S. Crossman, January 1946, file 2, CROSS.
147. *Jewish Chronicle*, 24 May 1946, p. 10; 31 May 1946, p. 12. Also see 'Spears Denies he is Jewish', 8 November 1946, p. 16.
148. Spears, 'Memorandum on a Publicity Fund for Palestine', n.d. 1948, Box 15/3, SPSP.
149. Ibid.
150. Spears, *Arab World*, XVII (October 1953).

7 An Example of Anti-Zionist Co-operation: The CAA and the Arab Office

From its inception the Arab Office looked to have close ties with the foreign policy establishment in both the Colonial and Foreign Offices. As colonial official John Bennet informed his superiors in Whitehall in March 1945, 'the authors of this project and Atiyah himself have been almost embarrassingly forthcoming in their desire for advice and hints as to what to do and what not to do'.[1]

On arriving in London Atiyah wasted no time in asking the Foreign Office if he was eligible for diplomatic status (a request that was refused) and about receiving petrol rations and office accommodation, preferably near Fleet Street. The Foreign Office was aware that Atiyah wanted 'a government department or official body to take him under its wing and to vouch for him generally'. It was prepared to 'try to help him along and to keep him on straight lines' and requested that Mrs N.F. Oliver at the Ministry of Information be seconded to the Arab Office to liaise with Atiyah and provide him with assistance in establishing the London Office.[2]

Though this governmental involvement with the Arab Office was not as much as Zionists (or even some members of the United States Congress)[3] feared, there is no doubting the close ties and intimate support for the Arab Office in both the Foreign and Colonial Offices. For example, the Colonial Office argued in favour of issuing visas to members of the Arab Office on the ground that it was in 'the national interest'.[4] Even in Washington British Embassy staff met with Arab Office members to discuss their efforts and advise them on the best ways to carry on their tasks.[5]

The Arab Office also actively looked to work with anti-Zionist members of the British pro-Arab elite in these years. A confidential Arab League memorandum of December 1944 stated that one of the primary reasons that the Arab Office was founded was because 'our English and American friends consider it time for a serious effort to be made as quickly as possible and on a large scale to enlighten public opinion'.[6] This document also pointed out that the establishment of an office in London would be easier than in the United States, because there already existed more of a base and a network of friends in London.[7]

Nevill Barbour was to be appointed as the adviser to the Washington Arab Office, while the advisory committee for the Arab Office in London was to be made up of the Arab ministers in London (who in the company of Spears would found the CAA) and supportive Englishmen and women. Most interestingly, this group included Freya Stark, H.A.R. Gibb, Arnold Toynbee, Lord Winterton (who was head of the Arab Parliamentary Committee), newspaperman Philip Dunn (of the *News of the World*), whom Spears would attempt to recruit to the CAA, and future CAA members Hope-Simpson, Newcombe, Royden-Shaw, Richard Stokes MP and Kenneth Pickthorn MP.[8]

Spears was absent from this list due to the fact that at the time it was drawn up he was still minister plenipotentiary in the Levant. However, on his return to London he immediately involved himself in the efforts of the Arab Office.

Spears promoted the efforts of the Arab Office, which he believed was 'responsible for good propaganda activities',[9] and directed correspondents towards it as he promoted the Jewish Fellowship in correspondence. But more than welcoming the existence of the Arab Office and praising its propaganda efforts (which is how far his relationship with the Jewish Fellowship developed), he based many of his plans for the CAA's presentation of the Arab case in England on co-operation with the Arab Office.

Spears envisaged a situation where the resources of the Arab Office and the CAA would be combined in the battle against Zionism. On 9 August 1945, just one day after the CAA was founded at a meeting of the Arab Club, Spears stated his hope that 'it [the CAA] will keep in close touch with the Arab Office ... as the Arab Office develops, its information service will be at the disposal of members'.[10] In a letter to Kenneth Williams in April 1946, concerning the feasibility of setting up a newspaper on the Middle East, Spears informed his fellow committee member that if such a paper ever got under way he could rely on the Arab Office for much of the source information the paper would need.[11]

Spears' hopes for a newspaper presenting the pro-Arab position on the Middle East did not come to fruition, but from the time that the CAA was founded in August 1945, two months after the Arab Office officially opened, until both wound up in the wake of the creation of a Jewish state, there was very close co-operation between the two bodies – something that was in stark contrast to the relationship between the Fellowship and the CAA during the same years.

Indeed, when Ahmed Shukairi, member of the Arab Office (Washington) and future first leader of the PLO, told the 1946 AACIP that 'our case has won the hearts of noble friends on both shores of the Atlantic, noble friends who have supported us in no expectation of profit',[12] it is fair to presume that he was referring as much to the efforts of Spears, Storrs and their fellow members of the CAA as to any other group.

From its founding the Arab Office presented itself as a body with the objective of informing as wide a public as possible of the Arab position over Palestine. Musa Alami informed the High Commissioner of Palestine that the goal of the new body was to give 'accurate information and correct views about the Arab world' to the American and British public, and he maintained this claim in the following years.[13]

However, the reality was different and the Arab Office, like the CAA, concentrated on appealing to an elite audience rather than to the general public. This can be seen in a lecture by Edward Atiyah before the Middle East Discussion group at the RIIA in June 1945, the month that the Arab Office was officially launched. In the course of his talk, Atiyah set out the propaganda aspirations of the Arab Office in front of an audience that included future CAA members Nevill Barbour, Brigadier S.H. Longrigg and Colonel Elphinston, as well as Mrs N.F. Oliver of the Ministry of Information, who was acting as liasion officer between the Foreign Office and the Arab Office.

During his talk it became clear that the Arab Office was not really interested in appealing to the public in general, and Atiyah admitted that his body 'did not intend to address the rest of the British public at large, but merely people who were interested and in a position of influence such as Professors, MPs etc.'.[14] Atiyah added that because of this, materials such as pamphlets, lectures and the like would be presented to a 'somewhat restricted public'.[15] In this Atiyah was setting out a policy in contradiction to Alami's continual claims that the Arab Office's main objective was to educate the public, but one that would be adopted by the CAA when it formed two months later.

The London Arab Office was also similar to the CAA in its relationship with the Jewish Fellowship. Its constitution clearly stated that the body should work to influence and encourage the constituency of non-Zionist Jews.[16] However, in reality the Arab Office in London did not make the slightest effort to support or work with the Jewish anti-Zionists of the Fellowship. Apart from the publication of a pamphlet on the Balfour Declaration that emphasised the Jewish opposition to the document in 1917, the only other direct reference to Anglo-Jewish opposition to Zionism in the course of the Arab Office literature was Atiyah's reference in a 1945 pamphlet to Edwin Montagu's anti-Zionist efforts as proof of the fact that many Jews opposed Zionism.[17]

In fact the nearest that the *Arab News Bulletin* came to defending the efforts of the Fellowship was to take issue with a claim by Harold Laski that Daniel Lipson in a speech in the Commons had acted like 'a revolting animal' by commenting that it was the 'Zionist agitators' who deserved to be described as revolting animals.[18]

In contrast, the Fellowship reported on the position of the Arab Office on Palestine. The *Jewish Outlook* referred to an article by Atiyah in the *Spectator* in May 1946 to emphasise the Arab hostility to the recently published Anglo-American Committee report.[19] While in 1948 the same paper went even further than just reporting the position of the Arab Office, by actually reprinting two official Arab Office statements (that had originally appeared in the *Arab News Bulletin*) denying that it was an anti-Semitic body.[20]

This added credence to the continual Zionist claims that the Fellowship was simply a pawn of the Arab enemies of Zionism. It was claimed by the Zionist press that the Fellowship was but reiterating the position of the Arabs, most notably the Mufti and the Arab Office, in its opposition to Zionism. Robert Henriques' letter in *The Times* opposing the creation of a Jewish Brigade was attacked for setting out the Arab argument on this issue.[21] While the *Zionist Review*, under the heading 'Disgusting', attacked a Lipson letter in *The Times* as a piece of anti-Zionist propaganda that could 'easily have been signed without any hesitation by the Mufti's representative in London'.[22] The same paper condemned the

Fellowship's 1947 'Memorandum on the Jewish Problem', sent to the Foreign Secretary and foreign ambassadors in London, as a repetition of the same arguments found in 'any publication of the Arab Office'.[23]

The failure of the Arab Office to reciprocate in support of the Fellowship, or to refer to it or to its efforts, could be more easily understood if the Arab Office had not been aware of events within Jewry, or if it had not regularly noted the efforts of Jewish anti-Zionists outside England. For example, the *Arab News Bulletin* noted obscure meetings of Jewish anti-Zionist bodies, such as a 1946 meeting of the Jewish Socialist Party in Brussels (the source of the meeting given was a Yiddish paper, *Unser Steim*, which was published in France!).

Less obscure, but no nearer to home, the paper, under the heading 'Non-Zionist Jews' Meeting', reported on a gathering in Haifa (which was also reported in the *Jewish Outlook*) of 12 non-Zionist Jewish bodies and printed in full the resolutions condemning Zionism that were passed at the meeting. And in another issue, under the heading 'The Fate of an Anti-Zionist Jew', the decision of a well-known Jewish orientalist, Julian Kablivatsky, to begin a hunger strike in Palestine as a protest at Zionist fanaticism was welcomed. Coverage was also given to the efforts of anti-Zionist Jews in the Arab world, especially in Egypt and Iraq.[24]

It is not surprising that the Arab Office reported on the opposition to Zionism among oriental Jews, considering that it argued against Zionism in terms of its negative effect on these very same Jewish communities. Nor would one expect an official paper of the Arab League in London to preoccupy itself with affairs within Anglo-Jewry. However, it is interesting that the Arab Office did not devote even the most cursory of coverage to the efforts of the Fellowship, especially since men such as Atiyah and Hourani were well aware of the Jewish aspect of the Palestine debate. Indeed, Albert Hourani wrote a pamphlet on this very issue for the Arab Office entitled *Is Zionism the Solution to the Jewish Problem?*.[25]

On one occasion, Dr Robert Eisler, a regular correspondent of the Arabist Harry Philby in these years and a Jew who favoured a solution to the Jewish problem outside Palestine – two of his more eccentric proposals were the settlement of left-wing Zionists in a Jewish socialist state in East Europe and the settlement of non-socialist Zionists in what he called the Free City of Frankfurt – wrote to the Arab Office suggesting a public meeting between

Arabs, Jews and leading Englishmen in London that would be organised by the Arab Office and where the issue of Palestine could be addressed.[26] Albert Hourani replied to Eisler that although he personally thought that it was a good idea, it was impossible for the Arab Office to organise such an event because it could not deviate from its programme as laid out by the Arab League.[27]

This would be an acceptable answer except for the fact that the Washington Arab Office had a much closer relationship with the Jewish anti-Zionist constituency, and this relationship was not prevented or hindered because of the lack of provisions for such efforts in the guidelines laid down by the Arab League. For example, Cecil Hourani stated in his autobiography that Jewish anti-Zionists provided both financial and moral support for the Washington Office, even funding Arab Office advertisements.[28]

An example of the much closer relationship between Jewish anti-Zionists and the Washington Arab Office can be seen in Washington Arab Office member Najla Izzedin's book *The Arab World: Past, Present and Future*. In this work Izzedin was of the view that in opposing Zionism 'it is best to hear the objections from responsible Jews themselves', and went on to refer to the ACJ's 1944 publication *Zionism Versus Judaism*, which was a collection of editorials from the body's newspaper.[29] The equivalent would have been a member of the London Arab Office using a collection of editorials from the *Jewish Outlook* to argue against Zionism. This is unthinkable in view of the lack of a relationship between the two bodies.

As such, the differing relationship was due to different circumstances and attitudes that existed in London and Washington, rather than Arab League regulations. Given the larger network of Gentile support that was available to the Arab Office in London and the decision to concentrate on an elitist form of propaganda, the members of this office did not feel the need to look outside the constituency of leading Gentile anti-Zionist Englishmen and certainly not towards the Jewish anti-Zionists whom their mentor Spears ignored.

When the London Arab Office did reprint a speech by a leading Jewish anti-Zionist it chose Rabbi Morris Lazaron, a leading member of the ACJ. In an introductory note to the Rabbi's speech the *Arab News Bulletin* stated that

> Every now and then the courageous and honest voice of an American Jew makes itself heard, against the savage clamour

of Zionists, in words which sooner or later will prove their truth to the world. Amongst such utterances was the speech made at the meeting of the ACJ by Rabbi Morris Lazaron.[30]

From this statement one would think that there was no 'courageous and honest voice' within Anglo-Jewry which the Arab Office could listen to and take note of. The choice of a speech by Lazaron rather than Lipson, Henriques or Gluckstein highlights just how the London Arab Office ignored the anti-Zionist efforts of the Fellowship and underlines that, contrary to the Zionist claims, the Jewish anti-Zionists were not in league with Arabs any more than they were in league with Spears and the English anti-Zionist community.

However, the same cannot be said with regard to the Arab Office and the CAA. On the most superficial level their relationship can be seen primarily in the continual and fluid sharing of information and material that was believed to be of value in the fight against Zionist aspirations. Spears, through his secretary Nancy Maurice, was constantly sending information to members of the Arab Office, particularly Albert Hourani, on various issues relating to Palestine. The Arab Office did the same, with Mary Crook, an Arab Office administrator, sending material to Spears with covering notes such as 'Mr Hourani thought you might care to have a copy of this leaflet on partition'.[31]

While the relationship primarily concentrated on the Palestine problem, members of the Arab Office also asked Spears and the CAA to use their influence to help individual Arabs living in London. For example, on one occasion Hourani wrote to Spears asking him to help a young Tunisian with a visa problem by lobbying the Home Office on the young man's behalf.[32]

A system also developed where Miss Maurice would send any Arabic material that Spears needed translated into English to the Arab Office, where staff would go through the material, deem what, if any, was of value and then return the relevant translated pieces to Spears' office.[33]

Nor was Spears alone among members of the CAA in developing a close personal relationship with the Arab Office. Sir Ronald Storrs had discussed the Arab League's plan to open the Arab Office in London with Musa Alami during a stop-over in Baghdad in April 1945, as part of his tour of the Middle East and North Africa.[34] Once back in London, Storrs, like Spears, not only welcomed the Arab Office, but corresponded with its members on aspects of the Palestine issue about which he needed information.[35] Yet from the start of this close co-operation between leading members of both bodies there was an attempt to conceal the nature of the relationship.

Even in 1945 the actual relationship between the English anti-Zionists (who would form the core of the CAA) and the Arab Office did not go unnoticed in Jewish circles. The *Jewish Chronicle* was the first to draw attention to the intimate if blurred role of English anti-Zionists in the workings of the new Arab Office.

In July 1945 this paper quoted an extract from a letter in the *New Statesman* by the Arab Office as a 'grotesque historical misstatement and exaggeration' and concluded that the reason for this unimpressive presentation of the Arab case was because 'the chief pro-Arab propagandist General Spears was alternatively engaged'.[36] The following month an editorial on the Arab Office set out categorically the view that the 'principal workers' and 'the real brains behind the whole scheme' were not Arabs but men 'from the upper strata of British society'.[37]

By September 1945 a correspondence had begun in the letters page of the *Jewish Chronicle* on the issue of English involvement in the propaganda efforts of the Arab Office. One letter stated that it was the 'old colonial civil servants' who were the 'real power behind the Arab Office' and gave the example of a letter in *The Times* by Sir Nigel Davidson as a classic example of the English involvement in the work of the Arab Office.[38] Davidson was a former colonial civil servant in Iraq and the Sudan and vice-chairman of the Jerusalem and East Mission in England at the time. He was also a future member of the CAA.

Another letter in the same issue by one H. Fergusson Craig, who described himself as a Gentile who had become 'intrigued by the massive yet subtle development of Arab political activity in this country under the able direction of General Spears', warned readers about this English control of the Arab Office.[39] This warning was not wasted, and in two articles in two consecutive weeks in February 1946 the *Jewish Chronicle* stated first that Spears was 'connected with the Arab Office' and then that he was 'political director' of the same body.[40]

Not surprisingly both Spears and Atiyah, who was the true director of the Arab Office in London, wrote to the editor of the paper correcting this mistake. Spears did not deny his 'admiration' for the work of the Arab Office but pointed out that he was not an official of that body.[41] Atiyah, writing the following week, was adamant that any suggestion that Spears had a role within the Arab office was 'entirely baseless', and he went even further, saying 'Sir Edward Spears has no connection whatever with the Arab Office, save like every other person in this country who is interested in Arab affairs, as a friend.'[42]

Despite the *Jewish Chronicle*'s editorial apology for the 'exaggerated links ... between Spears and the Arab Office', Atiyah, in his letter to the *Jewish Chronicle*, as shall be seen later in more detail, was at best being economical with the truth in an effort to distance Spears from the Arab Office.

Throughout 1946 speculation continued in this paper's editorial columns and letters page, as to the true relationship between English anti-Zionists and the Arab Office. In March an editorial accused Thomas Reid MP of representing the Arab Office in parliament.[43] While in May, in the wake of the publication of the Anglo-American Committee report, the paper interpreted a visit to London by Musa Alami as part of a mission to meet 'with Storrs, Spears and other friends of the Arab cause' to organise the fight against the Anglo-American Committee recommendations.[44]

Likewise, the *Zionist Review* in October 1945 attacked the efforts of five anti-Zionist MPs, of whom three – Pickthorn, Stokes and Ernest Thurtle – were members of the recently formed CAA (and two, Pickthorn and Stokes, were also on the Arab Office advisory committee) for circulating an anti-Zionist memorandum to fellow MPs and accused this group of anti-Zionists of using 'material that is being supplied by the Arab Office'.[45]

This Zionist tendency to view the efforts of the Arab and English propagandists in London in conspiratorial terms was so prevalent that Storrs raised the issue at a meeting of the CAA and wrote to Spears in April 1946 to urge him to take measures to ensure that the two bodies were not perceived to be colluding.[46] But Storrs was voicing his concerns too late, and by May 1946 there was no doubt in the Zionist mind that men such as Storrs and Spears were intimately connected to, and working with, the Arab Office in its opposition to Zionist aspirations.

The letter in *The Times* of 23 May by the CAA opposing the Anglo-American Committee report was condemned precisely because it was an effort by Storrs and 'other friends of the Arab Office' to hurt Zionism.[47] Not surprisingly, Storrs, given his desire to be seen as a neutral figure in the Palestine debate, continued to correspond on this issue, warning Spears in June 1946 that not only was 'our committee ... said to emanate from the Arab Office' but that 'I consider that there is some substance in the remark'.[48]

One of the reasons for this belief, one that symbolised the much deeper links between the two bodies, was the fact that Spears' office (from which he organised all the efforts of the CAA) and the Arab Office headquarters in London shared the same building. This closeness in addresses was not a coincidence. Izzat Tannous recalled in his memoirs that the difficult problem of finding accommodation for the Arab Office in London was 'solved by the kindness and generosity' of Spears who gave the body two rooms in his own suite of offices.[49]

Storrs saw great danger in 'the tendency to confuse persons, to confound our stance' that resulted in Spears and the Arab Office using similar addresses (161 and 164 St Stephen's House respectively) in their public opposition to Zionism.[50] Spears ultimately agreed with Storrs as to the damage that the closeness in addresses was doing to the image and credibility of English Arabists, but replied to Storrs that 'I am afraid to say that the damage may have already been done, any ill-wisher can comfortably gloss over the small distinction between number 161 and 164, which certainly suggests a "just across the passage" propensity.'[51] This whole incident once more re-emphasises what was argued in chapter 3, that the credibility issue was a central concern in the propaganda battle over Zionism; and it was all the more damning given the existing perception in the minds of Zionists as to the close relationship that existed between Spears and the Arabs. In 1945, for example, the claim by the Lebanese minister in London that 'Sir Edward's home in London had become a centre for Arabs living in Britain and their British sympathisers' was reported on extensively in the Jewish press in both England and Palestine.[52]

Indeed, the Arab Office, in an effort to end any speculation regarding the nature of the relationship between itself and Spears, moved premises to 92 Eaton Place, London SW1, in June 1946. This decision to relocate must be placed in the context of Atiyah's assurance in the *Jewish Chronicle* just four months earlier that Spears 'has no connection with the Arab Office'.

Regardless of the denials and the constant effort to keep the closeness of the relationship a secret, the belief that Spears was close to the Arab Office persisted at every level and in every forum through these years. For example, Bartley Crum, in commenting on Spears' evidence before the Anglo-American Committee, was of the view that he had been 'associated' with the Arab Office.[53]

None of this speculation is surprising, in fact it was inevitable, given the reality of the relationship that did exist. For Spears acted as linkman between the English anti-Zionist community and the Arab Office (just as he acted as the linkman between English anti-Zionists and the Arab legations in London). On one occasion, for example, Spears received a letter asking for advice and suggestions on how best to help the Arab cause in Palestine (forwarded to Spears by the Iraqi legation). He replied promptly, informing the correspondent that the best thing that he could do in his home town of Cambridge was to set up a pro-Arab group, and promising that if he did this he would supply pro-Arab literature and speakers from the Arab Office to address the body.[54]

In his role as linkman Spears was behind a far more curious relationship between the Arab Office and a pro-Arab member of the public, H.T. Norris. Norris had written to Colonel Sayid Shakir al-Wadi of the Iraqi legation asking to be put in touch with any pro-Arab organisations in London.[55] As was usual for enquiries made by non-Arabs, Wadi forwarded the letter to Spears, who replied to Norris sending him 20 copies of a pamphlet, *The British, the Arabs and the Jews* that Henry Longhurst had written for the CAA.[56]

Thus began a correspondence between Spears and a soldier in the British army who was dedicated to the Arab cause. Norris was stationed in India at the time and he sent Spears information and material on the Palestine problem, cuttings from the Indian press and other sources at his disposal. Spears in turn forwarded this material to Albert Hourani at the Arab Office. By July 1946 Norris was writing to Spears to report that Hourani himself had made contact with him.[57]

This chain of events provides an insight into the relationship between Spears and the Arab Office, and highlights the pivotal position of Spears as a conduit between English and Arab anti-Zionists in London. For Norris would rise from his humble origins as an unwitting supplier of the Arab Office with press cuttings, to a contributor of articles to the *Arab News Bulletin* during 1948. Norris had three articles published in the Arab Office newspaper, the first of which, 'Views on UNO Trusteeship of Jerusalem', was prefaced by a note stating that

The author of this article was until recently an officer [Norris had reached the rank of Captain by 1948] in the British forces in Palestine. We publish his article as giving a neutral English view which is not necessarily identical with the views of this office.[58]

Given the fact that Norris had come into contact with the Arab Office through Spears, who himself had come to communicate with him after receiving his letter from the Iraqi legation offering to assist the Arabs in any way in opposing Zionism, it was disingenuous, to say the least, that the *Arab News Bulletin* went out of its way to emphasise that Norris provided a 'neutral English view'.

Norris hardly fitted within the parameters of any generally accepted definition of impartiality in the context of the debate over Palestine (as the content of his article, in which he strongly attacked Zionism, shows). This is especially so when one considers that the letter of introduction provided by Spears' secretary for Norris to the Arab Office stated that 'he is a real enthusiast, and has been keeping the General posted with news concerning the Arab case wherever he has been'.[59] Indeed, in a letter written the day before this introduction, Spears suggested to W.G. Baillie, the honorary secretary of the Anglo-Arab Association, that Norris should become the organisation's representative in Palestine, where he was stationed.[60]

Within CAA circles Spears and the Arab Office were perceived as almost interchangeable. Maude Royden-Shaw showed this tendency to view Spears and Atiyah as filling the same role when in November 1945 she wrote to Spears to apologise for not inviting him as a guest to the University Women's Club, explaining that because of rationing it was only possible to invite one guest a month 'and I had already asked Atiyah'.[61] Royden-Shaw continued to hold this view of Spears. After one F.S. Cragg wrote to her volunteering to help the Arab cause, she suggested he made contact with either Spears or Atiyah or both.[62]

Even Spears seemed to view himself and Atiyah as interchangeable. For example, Dr Georg Schwarzenberger, editor of the *London Quarterly of World Affairs*, wrote to Spears in May 1945 asking him to contribute an article on the Middle East for the journal. Spears was unable to undertake this because of the forthcoming election, but wrote back suggesting that Atiyah could do it instead.[63]

Similarly, CAA members such as Newcombe, M. Philips Price MP and Pierre Loftus all used Spears as an intermediary for dealings with the Arab Office in these years, and Philips Price on one occasion asked Spears to get the Arab Office to publish one of his articles as a pamphlet.[64]

Spears was also responsible for the Arab Office's publication of an article by the Revd Guillaume in pamphlet form attacking the Zionist right to Palestine on biblical grounds.[65] Thus began a relationship between the Arab Office and this convinced anti-Zionist theologian. And by the summer of 1946 Guillaume was writing to Spears informing him that he was speaking publicly on behalf of the Arab Office on the biblical aspect of Zionist claims to Palestine.[66]

Likewise Michael Ionides, whom Spears had brought into the CAA primarily to provide a public attack on Lowdermilk's claims on the economic absorptive potential of Palestine, and who subsequently became deeply involved in the committee's fight against Zionism, was another CAA member who through Spears established a close working relationship with the Arab Office. He not only provided the Arab Office with reports on specialised technical aspects of the debate on the economic absorptive capacity of Palestine, but like Guillaume represented it in public debates against leading Zionists. On one occasion Ionides represented the Arab Office against Aubrey Eban of the Jewish Agency in a debate organised by the Oxford University Jewish and Arab societies.[67]

The close connection between the two bodies, the CAA and the Arab Office, can be seen in any study of the *Arab News Bulletin* in these years. The paper reprinted a letter by Stephen Longrigg (that had originally appeared in the *Spectator* in 1947) and declared that this letter 'spoke for all Arabs and Arab sympathisers'.[68] It also published several articles on the Arab world by Robin Maugham.[69] And one could perhaps interpret the decision of the paper's editors to devote its precious space to a review of *Journey Down a Blind Alley*, a book by Mary Borden, as being as much due to the fact that its author was the wife of Sir Edward Spears, as for its literary or historical qualities.

When Kenneth Mills resigned his CAA membership on taking up a government post overseas, he wrote to Spears informing him of his resignation and enquiring whether he could continue to receive the *Arab News Bulletin*, which Spears duly organised.[70] The fact that a member of the CAA, who was leaving the country, saw it as part of Spears' duty as chairman of the CAA to help him to arrange subscriptions to the weekly paper of the Arab Office shows just how close Spears was perceived to be to the Arab Office.

But then this is perhaps not so surprising when one considers that on paying their subscription to the Anglo-Arab Association all members received the *Arab News Bulletin* on a weekly basis. Which in turn even resulted in one member of the above body writing to Spears to complain about the content of the Arab Office's paper.[71]

The closeness between the Arab Office and the CAA, as well as the governmental involvement in the Arab propaganda effort at this time, is evident in the case of Albert Hourani. The young Hourani, a leading member of the Arab Office, played a central role in the presentation of the Arab case over Palestine during these years. But had it not been for the permission and co-operation of the Foreign Office it is doubtful that Hourani would have ever joined the Arab Office in the first place. For Hourani, who had worked as a Middle East researcher for the Foreign Office and Chatham House in the early war years,[72] had been recruited into the Arab Office from the office of the minister resident in the Middle East where he had been working since 1943.

In 1945 Musa Alami requested that Hourani's superior in Cairo, Brigadier Iltyd Clayton, allow him to join the Arab Office, informing him that he was 'very anxious' that Hourani be permitted to do so.[73] Clayton had no objections and the Foreign Office was in favour of the move, as the unanimous feeling in Whitehall was that a man of Hourani's 'calibre' would be a great help to the Arab propaganda effort.

Hourani was based at the Arab Office in Jerusalem until the middle of 1946. This was partly because, as a British subject, he was still eligible to be called up to the army if he was not in government service. As such it was tacitly agreed between the Foreign Office and the Treasury that if Hourani worked for the Arab Office outside of England then his position would be overlooked and he would not have to go through all the documentation necessary for deferment as he would if he returned to England.[74]

This complicated and time-consuming effort to overcome bureaucratic niceties received endorsement from the highest levels of government, with the Foreign Office, in its correspondence with the Ministry of Labour and National Service, stating 'Mr Bevin [Foreign Secretary, Ernest Bevin] recommends this application and requests that it may be given early consideration'.[75]

In Jerusalem Hourani liaised with important British visitors to Palestine. One was M. Philips Price MP, a member of the CAA, who on a trip to Palestine in 1946 hosted by Hourani was taken to luncheon with Musa Alami.[76]

Hourani also played a central role in the presentation of the Arab Office case before the Anglo-American Committee, and in doing so established himself as a leading advocate of the Arab cause. On meeting Hourani during the Jerusalem hearings, committee member Richard Crossman noted in his diary that Hourani was a man of 'superior intellect';[77] While twice in the course of his oral testimony, committee member Judge Joseph C. Hutchinson complimented Hourani on his ability, at one stage telling him that 'if your character is up to your brains you are a pretty good man'.[78] The impression that Hourani made with his evidence before the AACIP drew comment both from the Zionist press and those journals sympathetic to the Arab position,[79] and Cecil Hourani was of the opinion that his brother's evidence was the best by any Arab at the hearings.[80]

Hourani, with reputation riding high, moved to the Arab Office in London after the conclusion of the Anglo-American hearings in Jerusalem. Much of the material that he had prepared for the Arab Office case in Jerusalem was drafted into the definitive Arab arguments published by the London Office. For example, *The Future of Palestine*, the largest pamphlet issued by the London Arab Office, although attributed only as the work of the Arab Office in London was in fact largely derived from the material that Hourani had prepared while at the Jerusalem office.[81]

Thus, although Hourani did not arrive in London until the summer of 1946 he was central to the Arab effort and was viewed as such by the English anti-Zionist community. He acted as something of a linkman with Spears between the Arab Office and the CAA. Robin Maugham, a member of the CAA who, as we have seen, contributed a series of articles to the *Arab News Bulletin* in 1948, dedicated his 1947 book on Palestine to Hourani and acknowledged in its prelude that much of the book was taken verbatim from no less a source than Hourani's unpublished work.[82]

However, if in this instance it was Hourani who was providing help to a member of the CAA, it must be stated that during these years it was Hourani through the support of the CAA who benefited most from the mutual relationship. For Hourani, at that time undoubtedly the golden boy of the Arab cause in London, counted amongst his admirers many of those who like Maugham were members of the CAA.

For example, Brigadier Stephen Longrigg, in a speech at the RIIA in 1946, stated his opinion that Hourani's book *Syria and Lebanon* 'is an excellent book and I recommend it to everyone'.[83] The historian Elie Kedourie included Longrigg in what could be called the Chatham House School – meaning that he belonged to that group of Arabists attached to the RIIA. Others included H.A.R. Gibb, Arnold Toynbee and W.G. Elphinston, Middle East secretary of the RIIA and member of the CAA.[84]

In this context it is not surprising that Longrigg was full of praise for Hourani's work, because it had been H.A.R. Gibb, the doyen of Chatham House Arabists and a member of the English advisory committee to the Arab Office, who had recruited Hourani into his section of the RIIA during the war.[85]

Richard Crossman rightly recognised the value to the Arab cause of Hourani's close links to leading English Arabists and noted that Hourani proved that 'effective propaganda is contacts in the right places'.[86] And it is fair to say that Gibb's patronage of Hourani was continued after the war by Spears and the group of Arabists connected to the CAA. Spears himself had such a high opinion of Hourani's value in the propaganda battle against Zionism that he was moved to write to him more than once simply to congratulate him on what he saw to be a valued exposition of the Arab case or an equally valued attack on Zionist claims.

On one such occasion Spears, on reading a scathing review of Crossman's *Palestine Mission* in the *Arab News Bulletin*, took the liberty of assuming (wrongly) that Hourani had written the review and wrote to congratulate him on the piece.[87] The review in question attacked the Crossman book in great detail under subheadings such as 'Anti-Arab Bias' and 'Irrelevant Arguments'.[88] It is perhaps excusable that Spears assumed that Hourani had written the review because he had publicly attacked Crossman in various forums.[89] However, on this occasion the author had been Edward Atiyah, who wrote to Spears correcting his misapprehension and belatedly accepting his praise.[90]

Although a minor incident, this affair exemplifies the different relationships that Hourani and Atiyah had with their English supporters. Hourani was very much seen as the shining light in the Arab effort and Atiyah his reliable, if somewhat unspectacular, associate.

But it was Sir Ronald Storrs whose championing of Hourani shows how the close links between leading members of the CAA and the Arab Office yielded practical and concrete results, which greatly benefited Hourani. Storrs wrote to Spears in June 1946 informing him that he had received a copy of Hourani's *Great Britain and the Arab World* from the publishers, 'of which it is impossible that too many copies should be circulated, particularly to the Labour party ... can anything be done about this?'[91]

Spears contacted fellow CAA member Richard Stokes MP, informed him of Hourani's 'very good little book' and asked him to circulate it in parliament, a request that Stokes was only too happy to fulfil.[92] As well as a further example of the co-operation between the Arab Office and the CAA, this is indicative of the effective promotion of the Arab case within the House by the CAA, which refutes the claims made at the time that the Arab cause had no access to the corridors of power.

But the CAA's relationship with Hourani did not stop with promoting him as suitable reading for ignorant MPs. Indeed, it was again Storrs who brought to the attention of a meeting of the CAA that Hourani's other book *Syria and Lebanon* was out of print and that only one thousand copies had been printed, and he called on Spears in his capacity as chairman of the CAA to find, on behalf of the committee, a publisher for Hourani's work.[93]

Storrs' advocacy of Hourani is all the more interesting given that he was one of the few leading Arabists of the time who was not totally adoring or uncritical of him. Storrs was aware of his contemporaries' general attitude to Hourani, noting at one stage that certain Arabists were 'devoted to Hourani'.[94] However, Storrs felt Hourani to have an 'unattractive' personality and to be 'unforthcoming' in conversation (which for a man like Storrs was perhaps the greater sin).[95] But Storrs also believed that as a writer and publicist he was 'engrossingly excellent'[96] and it was this that made him a patron of the young scholar.

At Storrs' behest Spears undertook to find a new publisher for Hourani, and did so in the form of the Rt Hon. Lord Astor, at the RIIA. What is of interest is that Spears in appealing to Lord Astor did so in his official capacity as chairman of the CAA, explaining that the CAA felt that a prompt reprint of Hourani's *Syria and Lebanon* was necessary as it was 'an extremely valuable contribution to British understanding of the Arab point of view'.[97]

Shortly after this request Hourani's book was being advertised on the 'new and forthcoming' list in the Chatham House review, the *World Today*.⁹⁸ Hourani was very appreciative of Spears' and the CAA's efforts.⁹⁹ He was right to be thankful, for his next book, *Minorities in the Arab World* (Oxford University Press, 1947), was also issued under the auspices of the RIIA. Thus, in the case of Hourani and the effort of the CAA to get his work published, one sees a relationship closer in quality and kind between the Arab Office and the CAA than that which existed between the Jewish Fellowship and the CAA.

Edward Atiyah also had a close, if more formal, relationship with the CAA during these years. He was the Arab representative on the council of the Anglo-Arab Association (a body the CAA had founded in 1946).¹⁰⁰ But it was his practical co-operation with Storrs in the battle against Zionism that highlights just how closely leading members of the CAA and the Arab Office worked during these years.

Storrs' diary is replete with references to his contacts with Atiyah, with entries such as 'visited Atiyah and his harem of pretty assistants', and 'looked into Atiyah's' and 'telephone conversation with Atiyah'.¹⁰¹ In a letter to Spears in the summer of 1946 Storrs informed his chairman that he was chairing a talk by Atiyah at the University of London and asked Spears if he would pass on this message to other members of the CAA, so that any member able to do so could attend and lend support.¹⁰²

This is but one more example of Storrs' lack of objectivity, feigning the role of neutral expert on Palestine, while at the same time attempting to organise the attendance of those sympathetic to Atiyah's position. Atiyah took even more practical measures to ensure that Storrs in his efforts to promote the Arab case was seen to have support, when on one occasion he sent ten Arab students to a lecture that Storrs was giving on Palestine. As it turned out, Storrs did not need to call on this group of Arab students for, as he notes, 'as hardly any Zionists [were] there they had no need to be vocal'.¹⁰³ However, this gesture does indicate just how organised much of the relationship between English and Arab anti-Zionists was.

One area where this close relationship was especially apparent was in the crucial area of drafting letters to the press on matters related to Palestine and Zionism. Throughout these years Atiyah, on behalf of the Arab Office, requested Storrs (whose penmanship, as we have already seen, was held in high regard by Spears) to write to the press opposing Zionist aspirations, and Storrs' diary contains several references to this, such as 'Atiyah and the other Arabs would like me to write to *The Times*'.[104]

But the best example of this co-operation between Storrs and Atiyah in drafting anti-Zionist letters (and one that truly highlights just how closely Arabs and English anti-Zionists co-operated in their everyday efforts, in comparison with the lack of co-operation with the Jewish Fellowship) occurred in November 1947.

As has been mentioned in chapter 6, Storrs was moved to write to *The Times* in defence of Daniel Lipson MP over a letter by Sir Robert Waley Cohen attacking Lipson for his unflinching anti-Zionism. What is interesting in the context of the lack of English anti-Zionist co-operation with the Jewish Fellowship, and the parallel close relationship with the Arab Office, is that Storrs, on finishing his letter defending Lipson, phoned Atiyah at the Arab Office and read him the finished version, discussed it and then noted Atiyah's suggestions for alterations to the letter (which, incidentally, Storrs did not agree with).[105]

It was not unusual for Storrs to read his letters on Zionism to Atiyah over the phone. This happened on a number of occasions.[106] However, the chain of events in regard to this particular letter is very illuminating. For Storrs, a leading member of the CAA, was moved to defend a leading member of the Jewish Fellowship from the public attacks of a highly placed member of the Jewish community, and in doing so consulted not a member of the Jewish Fellowship, nor a Jewish friend or acquaintance (and Storrs had many of these), nor even Lipson himself (although Storrs did send the MP a copy of his letter)[107] but rather turned to Edward Atiyah, secretary of the Arab Office, for his opinion and comments on the letter.

Thus we see in Storrs' decision to turn to Atiyah rather than to a Jewish anti-Zionist for consultation, an example of the fact that Storrs, like Spears and the membership of the CAA in general, felt more comfortable in dealing with the Arab Office in the fight against Zionism than with Jewish anti-Zionists, even when the issue in hand directly related to Jewish anti-Zionism and concerned a member of the Jewish Fellowship.

NOTES

1. See Bennet to Hankey, 29 March, 1945, PRO/FO 371/45238. For a similar view see Walter Smart, Cairo to FO, 17 April 1945, PRO/FO 371/45239.
2. See T. Wikeley to Mrs N.F. Oliver, 25 May 1945, PRO/FO 371/45238 and R.M.

Hankey, FO, to General Pollock, Ministry of Information, 19 April 1945, PRO/FO 371/45238.
3. See report on claims by Congressman Adolph J. Sabath of Arab Office and British collaboration in correspondence from British Embassy, Washington to FO, PRO/FO 371/52555.
4. W.W. Clark, CO, to Home Office Aliens Department, n.d., 1945, PRO/FO 371/45238.
5. See A.H. Tandy's 'Arab League Information Office in Washington', 22 November 1945, PRO/FO 371/45241.
6. See 'Memorandum on the Arab Office' (Cairo: Arab League, 1944), PRO/FO 371/45236.
7. Ibid.
8. Ibid.
9. Spears to Tawfik bey Said Toucan, 31 October 1945, Box 15/3, SPSP.
10. Spears' statement to prospective members, 9 August 1945, Box 6/3, SPSP.
11. Spears to Williams, 2 April 1946, Box 5/3, SPSP.
12. Evidence of Arab Office before the AACIP, p. 97.
13. See telegram from Lord Gort to the FO on discussions with Alami regarding Arab Office, 10 April 1945, PRO/FO 371/45328. Also see Alami's statement on the UN partition vote, 30 November 1947, reprinted in the *Arab News Bulletin*, 52 (12 December 1947), pp. 1–2.
14. Atiyah, 'Public Opinion and the Arab', lecture to Middle East discussion group, RIIA, 1 June 1945, 8/1176, p. 8.
15. Ibid., p. 8.
16. See the Arab Office constitution reprinted in full in the *Manchester Guardian*, 20 August 1945.
17. Atiyah, *Arab Rights and the British Left*, p. 3.
18. *Arab News Bulletin* (19 November 1948), p. 6.
19. 'Anglo-American Digest of Opinion', *Jewish Outlook*, 1: 3 (June–July 1946), p. 14.
20. See *Jewish Outlook*, 'Arabs not Anti-Semites', 2: 8 (March 1948), p. 8; 2: 9 (April 1948), p. 7.
21. *New Judea*, September 1944, p. 188.
22. *Zionist Review*, 'Disgusting', 7 November 1947, p. 7.
23. *Zionist Review*, 6 February 1948, p. 1.
24. See *Arab News Bulletin*, 'Jewish Socialist Party and Zionism', 24 (1 November 1946), p. 3; 'The Fate of an Anti-Zionist Jew', 41 (11 July 1947), p. 3; 'League for Combating Zionism in Iraq', 33 (27 March 1947), pp. 7–8; 'The Egyptian Jew and Zionism', 49 (31 October 1947), p. 2.
25. See Hourani's *Is Zionism the Solution to the Jewish Problem?* (London: AO, 1946).
26. See Eisler–Philby correspondence, Box 10/4, PHIL. For an example of his arguments see his article 'The Palestine Problem: A Reasonable Solution', *Oxford Mail*, 12 August 1946.
27. Hourani to Eisler, 15 June 1946, Box 10/4, PHIL.
28. Cecil Hourani, *An Unfinished Odyssey: Lebanon and Beyond* (London: Weidenfeld & Nicolson, 1984), pp. 61–3.
29. Najla Izzedin, *The Arab World: Past, Present and Future* (Chicago: Henry Regnery, 1953), pp. 252–3.
30. 'The Voice of Truth', *Arab News Bulletin*, 64 (4 June 1948), p. 4.
31. See Maurice to Hourani, 1 August 1946; Crook to Spears, 11 September 1946, Box 5/3, SPSP. Also see Atiyah to Spears, 26 January 1948; Spears to Atiyah, 28 January 1948; Atiyah to Spears 12 February 1948, Box 11/4, SPSP.
32. Hourani to Spears, 2 December 1946, Box 5/3, SPSP. On another occasion a resolution to help Arab students in London to find work and accommodation was passed at a CAA meeting. See minutes of the CAA meeting, 18 July 1946, Box 6/2, SPSP.
33. Atiyah to Maurice, 21 October 1946, Box 5/3, SPSP. Also see Maurice to R. Husseini, 28 November 1946; Crook to Maurice, 2 December 1946, Box 5/3, SPSP.
34. MS Diary of Storrs, 30 April 1945, Box 6/6, STOP.
35. Storrs to Hourani, 10 August 1946, Box 6/10, STOP.
36. *Jewish Chronicle*, 13 July 1945, p. 7. At the time Spears was in the process of

37. unsuccessfully fighting for his parliamentary seat in Carlisle.
37. *Jewish Chronicle*, 17 August 1945, p. 10.
38. 'Mabeet', *Jewish Chronicle*, 14 September 1945, p. 14.
39. H. Fergusson Craig, *Jewish Chronicle*, 14 February 1945, p. 15.
40. See the *Jewish Chronicle*, 1 February 1946, p. 14 and 8 February 1946, p. 10.
41. Spears, *Jewish Chronicle*, 15 February 1946, p. 14.
42. Atiyah, *Jewish Chronicle*, 22 February 1946, p. 17.
43. *Jewish Chronicle*, 1 March 1946, p. 10.
44. *Jewish Chronicle*, 10 May 1946, p. 1.
45. 'Superficial Approach', *Zionist Review*, 5 October 1945, p. 1. The other two were Thomas Reid and Harry McGhee.
46. Storrs to Spears, 10 June 1946, Box 5/3, SPSP.
47. 'Thank You Sir Ronald', *Zionist Review*, 31 May 1946, p. 6.
48. Storrs to Spears, 24 June 1946, Box 5/3, SPSP.
49. Tannous, *The Palestinians: A Detailed, Documented, Eye-witness History of Palestine under the Mandate* (New York: IGT, 1988), p. 371.
50. Storrs to Spears, 15 May 1946, Box 7/2, SPSP.
51. Spears to Storrs, n.d., May 1946, Box 5/3, SPSP.
52. See for example, 'Spears' Home an Arab Centre', *Palestine Post*, 7 May 1945.
53. Crum, *Behind the Silken Curtain* (New York: Simon & Schuster, 1947), pp. 60–1.
54. Spears to McGarvie, 29 May 1946, Box 4/6, SPSP.
55. Norris to Shakir al-Wadi, 30 September 1945, Box 7/1, SPSP.
56. Spears to Norris, 11 October 1946, Box 7/1, SPSP.
57. Norris to Spears, 24 July 1946, Box 7/1, SPSP.
58. Norris, 'Views of UNO Trusteeship of Jerusalem', *Arab News Bulletin*, 60 (9 April 1948), p. 7. He also contributed two further articles to the paper. See 'Tunisia Today', 70 (27 August 1948), p. 4 and 'The Tripolitanian Arab and his Future', 71 (10 September 1948), p. 3.
59. Maurice to Atiyah, 12 September 1946, Box 4/3, SPSP; Spears to Norris, 12 September 1946, Box 7/1, SPSP.
60. Spears to Baillie, 11 September 1946, Box 11/1, SPSP.
61. Royden-Shaw to Spears, 15 November 1945, Box 7/2, SPSP.
62. Cragg to Spears, 14 May 1946, Box 6/3, SPSP.
63. See Schwarzenberger to Spears, 26 May 1945; Spears to Schwarzenberger, 30 May 1945, Box 5/2, SPSP.
64. Philips Price to Spears, 3 March 1946; Spears to Philips Price, 7 March 1946, Box 7/1, SPSP. On this occasion Spears decided that the CAA would republish it instead. See also Loftus to Spears, 26 September 1946, Box 6/4, SPSP and Newcombe to Maurice, n.d., 1945, Box 5/3, SPSP.
65. See Guillaume, *Zionism and the Bible: A Criticism of the Establishment of an Independent Jewish State in Palestine as Prophesied in the Holy Scriptures* (London: AO, 1946).
66. Guillaume to Spears, 19 June 1946, Box 6/4, SPSP.
67. See Ionides to Spears, 6 April 1946, Box 6/4, SPSP. Also see report in the *Jewish Chronicle*, 22 November 1946, p. 14.
68. *Arab News Bulletin*, 35 (18 April 1947), p. 1. Longrigg's letter which made the point that the government treated Arabs more harshly than Jews, had appeared in the *Spectator*, 11 April 1947.
69. Examples of Maugham's articles in the *Arab News Bulletin* on Algeria, Tunisia and the Arab problem in North Africa respectively were published in 53 (2 January 1948), pp. 3–4; 54 (16 January 1948), pp. 4–5; 55 (30 January 1948), pp. 5–7.
70. Mills to Spears, 17 July 1946; Spears to Mills, 31 July 1946, Box 5/3, SPSP.
71. Ruth Foley to Spears, 18 September 1946, Box 11/1, SPSP.
72. On Hourani's work for the Foreign Office research department see R.M. Hankey to E.B. Boyd, 11 August 1943, PRO/FO 371/34958.
73. Alami to Clayton, 25 July 1945, PRO/FO 371/45239; Alami to Clayton, 8 November 1945, PRO/FO 371/45241. Also see Clayton to C.W. Baxter, FO, 28 November 1945, PRO/FO 371/45241.
74. See V.V.C. Saunders to C.W. Baxter, 21 September 1945, PRO/FO 371/45239.
75. C.W. Baxter, FO, to secretary, minister for Labour and National Service, 21 December 1945, PRO/FO 371/45241.

76. Diary of M. Philips Price, 8 January 1946, Diary of Travels in Palestine, Box 1/3, PPP.
77. Private diary of R.H.S. Crossman, March 1946, file 2, CROSS.
78. Evidence of Arab Office before AACIP, p. 129.
79. See, for example, *New Judea*, March–April 1946, p. 160; *Great Britain and the East*, LXII: 1759 (April 1946), p. 41.
80. Cecil Hourani, *An Unfinished Odyssey*, pp. 67–8.
81. See *The Future of Palestine* (London: AO, 1946). Hourani also published material under his own name for the Arab Office. See *Is Zionism the Solution to the Jewish Problem?*.
82. Maugham, *Approach to Palestine* (London, Falcon Press, 1947), p. 10.
83. Longrigg, 'Syria and Lebanon', lecture to RIIA, 3 May 1946, 8/1330, p. 7.
84. See Kedourie's *The Chatham House Version and Other Middle Eastern Studies* (Hanover, London, New Hampshire: University of New England, 1984), pp. 386–94.
85. See Cecil Hourani, *An Unfinished Odyssey*, p. 27.
86. Crossman, *Palestine Mission: A Personal Record* (London: Hamish Hamilton, 1947), pp. 124–5.
87. Spears to Hourani, 23 July 1947, Box 4/3.
88. See supplement to the *Arab News Bulletin*, 40 (27 June 1947), p. 4.
89. See for example Hourani's letter in the *New Statesman*, 25 May 1946.
90. Atiyah to Spears, 25 July 1947, Box 11/3, SPSP.
91. Storrs to Spears, 24 June 1946, Box 5/3, SPSP.
92. Spears to Stokes, 26 June 1946; Stokes to Spears, 2 July 1946, Box 7/2, SPSP.
93. See minutes of the CAA meeting, 18 July 1946, Box 6/2, SPSP.
94. MS Diary of Storrs, 13 November 1948, Box 6/7, STOP.
95. MS Diary of Storrs, 10 July 1946, Box 6/7; 24 October 1947, Box 6/7, STOP.
96. MS Diary of Storrs, 15 May 1946, Box 6/7, STOP.
97. Spears to Astor, 19 July 1946, Box 6/3, SPSP.
98. *World Today*, III: 1 (January 1947).
99. See Hourani to Maurice, 6 August 1946, Box 4/3, SPSP.
100. Atiyah to Spears, 9 September 1946, Box 11/2, SPSP.
101. See MS Diary of Storrs: 3 September 1947, Box 6/7; 3 May 1947, Box 6/7; 2 December 1948, Box 6/8; 30 January 1948, Box 6/8, STOP.
102. Storrs to Spears, 24 June 1946, Box 5/3, SPSP. Philips Price and Lord Altrincham did attend Atiyah's talk, MS Diary of Storrs, 26 June 1946, Box 6/7, STOP.
103. MS Diary of Storrs, 26 February 1948, Box 6/8, STOP.
104. MS Diary of Storrs, 4 March 1948, Box 6/8, STOP.
105. MS Diary of Storrs, 7 November 1947, Box 6/7, STOP.
106. See, for example, MS Diary of Storrs, 4 May 1948, Box 6/8, STOP.
107. Lipson thanked Storrs for his 'effective reply' to Waley Cohen. See Lipson to Storrs, 12 November 1947, Box 6/10, STOP.

8 Fundamental Issues, Fundamental Divisions

As we saw in the previous chapter it was not solely Spears but other CAA members who co-operated with the Arab Office much more than with the Jewish Fellowship. Indeed it was Storrs, not Spears, who in March 1944 had 'come to the conclusion that you can't make a Jew, even an anti-Zionist Jew understand the Arab point of view'.[1]

The isolation of the Jewish anti-Zionists of the Fellowship from non-Jewish anti-Zionists on issues central to the whole debate on Palestine – the White Paper of 1939 and Jewish immigration into Palestine – explains how Storrs, a man so interested in Jewish affairs, could make the above observation. But the isolation of the Fellowship from the Zionists on the same issues also underlines the prophetic nature of Stark's 1943 claim that the Jewish opponents of political Zionism were stranded between Scylla and Charybdis.

THE WHITE PAPER

Until the introduction of the Palestine White Paper in May 1939 Jewish immigration into Palestine was based on the principle of economic absorptivity.[2] This meant that the extent of Jewish immigration into the country was based on economic rather than political criteria and dependent on the number of extra immigrants that it was believed the economy of Palestine could adequately support. This principle was first laid down in the (Churchill) White Paper of 1922, which officially stated that 'immigration cannot be so great in volume as to exceed whatever may be the economic capacity of the country at the time to absorb new arrivals'.[3] This was most publicly reiterated in a letter from Prime Minister Ramsay MacDonald to Chaim Weizmann in February 1931.[4]

Even though the principle of economic absorptivity was

problematic, and adherence to it depended on the existing political circumstances (for example, after the 1936 Arab revolt the Palestine administration took political as well as economic considerations into account when deciding levels of Jewish immigration), it was still primarily perceived as a non-political approach to a controversial issue and as such it was a policy welcomed by Zionists as relatively fair.

But the 1939 White Paper officially changed Jewish immigration from an economic to a political issue. The immigration clauses of the White Paper set out the principle that the Arabs of Palestine had the final say on Jewish immigration levels into that country. It was this that particularly angered Jewry, for if adhered to, the document ruled out the possibility of a Jewish majority in Palestine.[5]

The Zionist attitude to the White Paper as an illegal and immoral document was encapsulated in a letter by Chief Rabbi Herzog of Palestine who wrote to *The Times* in May 1939 that the document was 'a sin against the spirit of God and the soul of Man'.[6] Attacks on the White Paper also became a central part of the post-war Zionist propaganda effort with pamphlets such as the Zionist Federation's *The Jewish Case Against the White Paper* and the Jewish Agency's *The MacDonald White Paper of 1939*, both published in 1945.[7]

It is true that in 1939 the Arabs, still hopeful of a complete victory on the Palestine issue, were not overly enthused by the White Paper and were wary of it, with the Arab Higher Committee stating at the time that the White Paper policy 'does not satisfy Arab demands'.[8]

However, in the more precarious days after 1945 there was a general Arab acceptance that the document was the main impediment to Zionist national aspirations and as such had to be upheld. An early Arab Office pamphlet clearly set out the Arab position. The White Paper had put 'a final limit on immigration' and the abrogation of that document would result in unlimited immigration, which in turn would result in the 'conversion of the country into a Jewish national state'.[9] Thus the Arabs viewed all post-war initiatives on Palestine, including Bevin's November 1945 statement on Palestine and the report of the Anglo-American Committee, in terms of how they affected the White Paper's position on limiting Jewish immigration.[10]

English anti-Zionists agreed with their Arab contemporaries that the White Paper meant only one thing in the post-war context: no expansion of the Jewish National Home by immigration unless the

Arabs acquiesced. For example, Robin Maugham in a lecture at the RIIA in 1946, informed his audience that 'the White Paper now means only one more thing to the Arabs, no more immigration'.[11]

Nevill Barbour was of the view that 30 March 1944 was the 'all-important date' in regard to Palestine because, under the terms of the White Paper, this marked the end of Jewish immigration that had been permitted between 1939 and 1944.[12] Brigadier Stephen Longrigg was of the view that the 'only possible course is to stick to the White Paper'.[13] While Storrs, who had publicly supported the White Paper policy as the solution fairest to all sides from its introduction, was of the view that any change by the government from the White Paper policy would be 'appeasement' of the Zionists.[14]

However, it is of interest that while all English anti-Zionists believed that the White Paper of 1939 had given legal authority to the moral right that had always existed in regard to the Arab veto on Jewish immigration, not all agreed that the best policy was to deny all Jewish immigration.

At the beginning of 1945, Newcombe told Spears that he believed the best policy for the Arabs was 'to come forward boldly under the White Paper and offer modest immigration to make the Zionists look bad'.[15] Michael Ionides informed Spears that although it was undoubtedly the Arab right to refuse Jews entry into Palestine, it did not mean that to do so was not 'wrong, stupid or intransigent'.[16]

Similarly, Thomas Reid during his evidence before the AACIP stressed that the White Paper gave the Arabs the right to control Jewish immigration, but also added his view that the Arab decision not to allow 6,000 Jews a month to enter Palestine while the committee sat was 'misguided and foolish'.[17] And Freya Stark, ever the strategist, told Harold Nicolson at the end of 1945 that the Arabs should admit up to 100,000 Jews as a way of emphasising to the world that it was they and not the British and certainly not the Zionists who controlled immigration into Palestine.[18]

Yet while these and other individuals at certain stages believed that the Arabs would be wise to allow Jews to enter Palestine in specified numbers for strategic, tactical, compassionate or political reasons, all opposed unlimited free Jewish immigration into Palestine and all agreed with Spears' statement that the Arabs 'take their stand on the White Paper of 1939, which restricts Jewish immigration ... they make it clear that there can be no question of their accepting unlimited Jewish immigration'.[19]

Thus it is hardly surprising that Albert Hourani, during a speech at the RIIA after the publication of the Anglo-American Committee report (which he claimed had 'no intellectual merits, no depth of understanding … no logical cogency'), decried the recommendations as an abrogation of the White Paper, precisely because it reneged on the most important paragraph of the 1939 document 'regarding immigration in the future'.[20]

The position of the Jewish Fellowship on the issue of the White Paper was somewhat different. When, during their presentation before the MEPC, Basil Henriques and Sir Jack Brunel Cohen were challenged by S.S. Hammersley as to the Fellowship's position on the White Paper, Henriques stated that the body did not have a policy on the document because it was a political issue, and the Fellowship as a religious body did not take a stance on political issues.

This answer did not satisfy either Hammersley or the anti-Zionist majority on the MEPC. Indeed, Spears, in his position as chairman, abruptly told Henriques that the Fellowship should make up its mind as to its stance on the White Paper, and that when it had done so it should submit its position on the issue to his committee.[21]

But the Fellowship never did make up its mind. In the wake of the leaking of this meeting to the Jewish press, Brunel Cohen, in a confidential memorandum to Fellowship members, once again denied that either he or Henriques had supported the White Paper at their talk before the MEPC, and explained that neither the executive nor the council of the Jewish Fellowship had adopted an official attitude to the White Paper.[22]

This explanation of the Fellowship's position on the White Paper formed the largest part of the statement issued to the press giving its account of what exactly had taken place at the meeting in front of the MEPC. This was reiterated by both Basil Henriques and Julian Franklyn in letters to the Jewish press that underlined the body's position of neutrality on such an emotive issue. As Franklyn informed the readers of the *Jewish Chronicle*, 'the Fellowship is not a political movement and therefore neither the executive nor council have adopted an official attitude to the White Paper'.[23]

During their evidence before the AACIP both Brunel Cohen and Basil Henriques restated this position. But Henriques went further and stated that 99 per cent of the Fellowship's members wanted the White Paper scrapped because it constituted anti-Jewish discrimination.[24] Indeed, throughout these years the official Fellowship position on the White Paper can be seen in an editorial in the *Jewish Outlook*, in September 1946, which stated that 'there are few Jews throughout the world who did not deplore both its substance and its terms, and who did not regret that expediency had once more prevailed over principle'.[25]

Given the importance that Gentile anti-Zionists attached to the White Paper, it is hardly surprising that Spears measured a person's anti-Zionist credentials on the basis of his or her support for the document. In a letter to Richard Stokes, Spears was of the opinion that Jews opposed to the White Paper were Zionists, 'as opposed to Lipson who is anti-Zionist'.[26]

Here Spears is providing an insight into his and the Gentile anti-Zionist mind that helps one understand the Gentile and Jewish anti-Zionist relationship. And it is in this context of the importance that Spears attached to the White Paper that one must view the refusal of Henriques and Brunel Cohen categorically to support the White Paper before the MEPC, which in turn gave Spears the impression that these Jewish anti-Zionists were perhaps not as much anti-Zionist as Jewish.

While Spears viewed Daniel Lipson as an anti-Zionist because he supported the White Paper, in reality Lipson had not voted for the document in parliament. He had voted for the Land Transfer Regulations that were enacted in February 1940 and, because they restricted the purchase of land by Jews in Palestine, were viewed by Zionists as an enactment of ghetto laws in Palestine.[27] Nevertheless, Colonel Gluckstein, who had been an MP at the time, did vote in favour of the White Paper. Nor was he alone among leading Fellowship members in advocating, or at least being perceived by Gentile anti-Zionists as accepting, the White Paper.

As has been seen, Albert Hyamson, Rabbi Mattuck and Emile Marmorstein, all members of the Fellowship council, participated with three Arabs and three English anti-Zionists in drawing up *A Constitution for Palestine*. This document omitted direct reference to, or support for, the more contentious (from a Jewish point of view) clauses of the White Paper, specifically clause 10(6) which called for an independent Palestinian state and clause 10(7) which gave the Arabs control over immigration.

This was despite the fact that the non-Jews on this committee supported the White Paper in full. Newcombe, one of the three English Gentile members of the committee (all of whom would become CAA members) set out his support for the White Paper repeatedly from the time the document was introduced in 1939. For example, his letter in *The Times* of 30 May 1939 endorsed the White Paper as a means of Jewish and Arab co-operation.[28] And in a letter written shortly after the publication of the *Constitution*, he told Storrs that the White Paper 'sums up the situation ... we must stick to paragraphs 10(6) and 10(7) ... let the White Paper be the final word'.[29] Newcombe even wrote to the colonial secretary in 1946, demanding that the government adhere to the White Paper.[30]

All this would seem to imply that the more controversial parts of the White Paper were excluded from the *Constitution* so that the Jews on the committee could endorse the document, which in turn implies that these three Jews, three leading Jewish anti-Zionists, were opposed to the White Paper.

Yet this was not the case. Newcombe in a letter to Spears in April 1945 stated that the exclusion of the contentious clauses of the White Paper from the final draft of the *Constitution* was not due to opposition from the Jews on the committee, because they had agreed on all the White Paper points. Rather, the proposal avoided mention of these clauses, in an attempt to appeal to a larger constituency within Jewry. As Newcombe explained, 'points ... were omitted which all the committee accepted, but which might raise controversy elsewhere'.[31]

This was for certain Newcombe's view of Hyamson's position, for in a speech at the RIIA in 1942 he stated that Hyamson in his book *Palestine: A Policy* 'accepts the White Paper'.[32] A fair statement, given the fact that Hyamson devotes the final chapter of this book to the issue of the White Paper and he presents the document as a means of finding a fair and long-term solution to the Palestine problem.[33]

Yet regardless of the personal views of influential Fellowship members such as Hyamson, Mattuck, Gluckstein and Marmorstein, the reality is that the Fellowship's official position was against the White Paper and that none of these individuals opposed this stance publicly during the Fellowship's existence. For example, Gluckstein, who as an MP had voted for the document, did not contradict Henriques' statement at the AACIP that 99 per cent of the Fellowship was opposed to the document. Thus, even while accepting that some individual members of the Fellowship accepted the White Paper, the Fellowship, by refusing to endorse the document, did not meet Spears' definition of an anti-Zionist body.

However, by refusing to condemn the document the Fellowship also failed to reduce its isolation within Jewry. From the date of its issuance the White Paper was condemned within all circles of Anglo-Jewry. Sir Robert Waley Cohen spoke for all the community when at the time of its introduction he called the document 'a complete surrender to the Arabs'.[34]

The Central Jewish Lecture Committee (which contained members of all sections of Anglo-Jewry, Zionist, non-Zionist and anti-Zionist), in a private and confidential 1940 memorandum drawn up to guide Jewish speakers in what they said in front of non-Jewish audiences, urged that speakers 'avoid expressing sectional views in matters which are controversial within the community', and concluded that 'it might be mentioned that Jews do not accept the policy of the White Paper'.[35] The implication was that whatever differences did exist within Jewry, division over the White Paper was not one of them.

As such the orthodox Zionist position on the White Paper was to claim that all Jews, regardless of their attitude to a Jewish state, opposed it, with Chaim Weizmann informing readers of *The Times* in 1944 that 'in reality every Jew, Zionist or non-Zionist opposed the White Paper'.[36]

However, when it came to the Fellowship the Zionists were unflinching in their efforts to paint the body as an advocate of the White Paper. Hammersley, who had led the attack on the Fellowship before the MEPC and who, it appears, was responsible for leaking the news of its appearance to the Jewish press, presented the Fellowship's stance at the parliamentary meeting as a vindication of the White Paper.

After the meeting took place, Hammersley felt it necessary to write to Spears to inform him that as a Jew it was his opinion that 'the Fellowship could offer little guidance and indeed might be misleading' in regard to its position on the White Paper and that it should not be mistaken for the general Jewish position on the issue. Hammersley also told Spears that 'a summary of what the [Jewish Fellowship] said was "we support the White Paper"' and he concluded with the claim that 'Jewish opinion is united as to at least ninety-five percent in opposition to the White Paper'.[37]

Hammersley's interpretation of the Fellowship leadership's position on the White Paper, which was leaked to the press, only intensified Jewish attitudes to the Fellowship on this issue. It is illuminating to note that the *Jewish Chronicle* condemned the appearance of Brunel Cohen and Henriques before the MEPC in an editorial entitled 'Friends of the White Paper'.[38] Yet the *Jewish Chronicle*'s negative attitude towards the Fellowship on this issue was not born purely out of the newspaper's understanding of the body's position as set out at the MEPC meeting.

Rather, the fact that Gluckstein and Lipson had given support in parliament to the White Paper and the Land Transfer Regulations respectively was seen as proof – not that any was needed – of both men's betrayal of, and isolation from, the rest of Jewry. Gluckstein's parliamentary support for the White Paper was used against him at every point in the battle between Zionists and anti-Zionists within the Jewish community. During their heated correspondence of 1942, Lavy Bakstansky ended his final letter with the words, more a promise than a statement of fact, that 'Jews will never forget that you voted for the MacDonald White Paper'.[39]

In the post-war years Zionist members of the Board of Deputies did their best to remind the community of this fact. They tended to dismiss all Gluckstein's views on Palestine because of his advocacy of the White Paper in the past. Schneir Levenberg, a leader of the socialist Zionist movement in Britain, speaking at a debate on Palestine at the Board, dismissed Gluckstein's vote against a pro-Zionist resolution with a reminder to deputies present that this man had voted in favour of the White Paper. Levenberg's statement contained the implication that one could not trust the views of any man who had indeed voted for such a policy.[40]

At another session of the Board, Councillor Abraham Moss was even more explicit in his instruction to Board deputies that they should not bother to heed the opinions of Gluckstein because as an MP he had voted for the White Paper.[41]

The Zionist press dismissed the Fellowship in the same terms. The *Zionist Review* in an editorial condemnation of Henriques' and Brunel Cohen's appearance before the MEPC concluded, as if to underline the scurrilous pedigree of these men, 'it will be recalled that Colonel Gluckstein, MP, and one of the leaders of the Fellowship, voted for the White Paper in the House of Commons'.[42]

New Judea, in an article on the Fellowship's evidence before the AACIP, denounced the body primarily in terms of Gluckstein's and Lipson's parliamentary records, and commented tellingly that 'the meaning of fellowship, Jewish honour, Jewish dignity, was strikingly illustrated by Colonel Gluckstein and D.L. Lipson who voted in the House of Commons for anti-Jewish discrimination in Palestine'.[43]

Thus there existed a tendency to judge the Fellowship's position on the White Paper on the past parliamentary records of its members rather than on the group's official position in the post-war era. That this was so can be seen in the course of *New Judea*'s extended coverage of the Fellowship's evidence before the AACIP. For while condemning the Fellowship for its members' past support of the White Paper, this journal was not only aware that Henriques had informed the AACIP that the White Paper was anti-Jewish and that 99 per cent of the Fellowship was against it, but commended him for doing so.[44]

This Zionist strategy of reiterating the White Paper past of some of the Fellowship leaders rather than its position as a body on the issue of the White Paper, was partly a way of attacking the Fellowship and emphasising the isolation of the body within Jewry. But there also existed a sincere belief that the Fellowship, by its very existence, was vindicating the White Paper policy.

Fellowship leaders did nothing to discourage this. Gluckstein refused to acknowledge that he had been wrong to vote for the White Paper. Indeed he defended his vote in favour of the White Paper because it was in 'the best interests of the country, British Empire, Jews and not least Zionists'.[45] After the war, Fellowship leaders continued to appear tacitly in favour of the document, never openly supporting it and yet (more importantly) never categorically refuting it.

For example, in 1947 in an article in the *Jewish Chronicle*, Rabbi Mattuck conceded that the White Paper was 'a mistake' but immediately added that 'it did not prevent any considerable number of Jews from getting into Palestine who could have got there'.[46] Not only was this a distortion of what actually happened but it could easily have been construed by willing Zionists as an intentional effort by this Fellowship leader to dilute his original criticism of the document.

'THE 100,000': RESPONSES TO THE ANGLO-AMERICAN REPORT

The idea of allowing 100,000 Jews into Palestine as a humanitarian gesture – a central recommendation of the Anglo-American Committee report – was not an original one devised by the committee in the course of its deliberations. Rather, it could be argued that the Anglo-American Committee was born out of

President Truman's 1945 suggestion that 100,000 Jewish refugees be allowed into Palestine as a humanitarian gesture.

Foreign Secretary Bevin's response to Truman was that such an act would only add to the bitterness that already existed, warning that although he was in favour of allowing in 100,000 refugees on humanitarian terms, the Zionists would view this as 'only the beginning'. Thus he called for the creation of an Anglo-American Committee to investigate the issue further.[47]

The Jewish Fellowship welcomed the Anglo-American Committee report that was published at the beginning of May 1946. An editorial in the May 1946 issue of the *Jewish Outlook* stated that the 'supreme task of Jewry' was to unite in supporting the committee's recommendations.[48] The Fellowship specifically welcomed the committee's recommendation in favour of opening Palestine to 100,000 Jewish refugees as an interim humanitarian measure to ease the position of Jewish refugees in Europe. Julian Franklyn, the secretary of the Fellowship, during the course of an interview he gave to a correspondent from the *Jewish Outlook* (something of an oddity, considering that Franklyn was coeditor of the paper), was asked whether he supported the 'notion of getting 100,000 DPs into Palestine', and he answered 'emphatically'.[49]

On the other hand, Gentile anti-Zionists were sceptical of the proposal for 100,000 long before the recommendations of the AACIP were made public. In 1945 Spears had argued that the White Paper had finally settled the political question of Palestine, and that to let in more than 75,000 Jews, as laid out in the document, would be a breach of the White Paper,[50] a view shared by the Arab Office at that time.[51]

Thus both the CAA and the Arab Office were extremely disappointed by the recommendations of the Anglo-American Committee report – and specifically by the recommendation to allow 100,000 Jewish refugees into Palestine as an interim measure – and all the more so because members of both the CAA and the Arab Office had been optimistic that the AACIP would legitimise the Arab position and confirm the White Paper policy (although Storrs was more circumspect and, on hearing Bevin's announcement of the plan for the AACIP, was of the view that the government was now 'playing with fire').[52]

Atiyah, for example, was optimistic, throughout his official reports on the London hearings sent to the Arab Office's Jerusalem headquarters, that the AACIP would find in favour of the Arab position. In one report sent after Selig Brodetsky's testimony to the committee on behalf of the Board of Deputies, Atiyah was of the opinion that the committee was 'thinking definitely, not in the direction of a Jewish state in Palestine, but of a general solution to the Jewish question'.[53]

Likewise, Albert Hourani informed a meeting of the RIIA, held after the publication of the committee's recommendations, that the general Arab impression once the hearings had concluded in Jerusalem in March 1946 was that the AACIP would decide against any more Jewish immigration, adding that the report's content was 'a great shock to Arab opinion'.[54]

This great sense of disappointment with the report was shared by English anti-Zionists. Storrs, writing in his diary the day the report was published, was of the view that it was 'a bombshell to the Arabs ... it's a triumph of Zion, abolishing the White Paper, pumping in 100,000 and giving no sort of limitation on numbers, time or space'.[55] While another CAA member, Sir Nigel Davidson, was equally disturbed, and in a letter to Spears stated that the recommendations will have a 'disastrous effect (1) on the good name of Britain through the Arab countries and in the Muslim world and (2) on the political and strategic interests of the British'.[56]

Thus the CAA met on 9 May 1946, to discuss the implications of the newly published report. At this meeting, and in one that followed on 30 May, it was agreed that the CAA should concentrate its opposition to the report on the recommendation concerning the opening of Palestine to 100,000 Jewish refugees as an interim, humanitarian measure.

The CAA argued that it was not the duty of the Arabs but of the 'United Nations to find a home for refugee Jews'. The body also decided to issue a public statement that included a clause urging His Majesty's Government to 'give [a] practical lead by offering to take a substantial quota of the 100,000 who did not wish to return [to] or remain in their countries of origin'.[57] The CAA took a stand on this issue precisely because this was the recommendation that most threatened the principle enshrined in the White Paper that the Arabs of Palestine had the right to decide on Jewish immigration into Palestine.

The decision by the CAA to set out in public its declaration of support for the opening of England to Jewish refugees, as an alternative to opening Palestine, does appear to demonstrate that the committee was interested in the plight of the Jewish refugees.

However, once put into its proper context the whole issue of the CAA's attitude to Jewish refugees coming into England shows the real distance between these Gentile anti-Zionists and the Jewish Fellowship.

While there was unanimity within the CAA for calling on the United Nations to help find refuge for homeless Jews, there was open dissent within the committee over the call for the government to allow more Jews into England. The Revd Dr Guillaume wanted the word 'substantial' deleted from the clause calling for the opening of England to Jews, on the basis that England had already accepted a very large number of Jews, and because

> Everywhere one hears complaints about their behaviour, their control of industry and finance and their very increasing weight in the Universities. I am not anti-Jewish myself, but I confess that I do not want to see this country dominated by Jews.[58]

Henry Longhurst also wrote to Spears echoing Guillaume's position on this issue, and adding that he did not want Jews taking jobs from Englishmen, warning Spears that there 'is a serious chance of our national stock being affected'.[59]

This distaste for Jewish Holocaust survivors coming to England was not unusual at the time, nor was it an attitude confined to members of the CAA. What is of interest are Spears' replies to both these men. In these letters Spears presented the decision to support the increased entry of refugees into England as necessary, not because the CAA members cared about finding a home for Jewish refugees, but because it was vital in the context of the opposition to the Anglo-American Committee's recommendation that 100,000 DPs be allowed to enter Palestine. As Spears informed Guillaume,

> Although nobody liked increasing the number of Jews in England ... we must give a lead in finding homes for ... refugees as otherwise we are not on nearly such strong ground in recommending that they should not go to Palestine.[60]

He was even more specific in his reply to Longhurst, informing him that there was 'a very strong feeling' among committee members that unless they supported this clause, 'we could not mobilise opinion against sending them to Palestine'.[61]

One should thus view the CAA's call for the opening of England to Jewish refugees in its proper context. The distinguished social scientist Albert O. Hirschman, in a study aptly titled *The Rhetoric of Reaction*, has referred to a situation where 'discourse is shaped, not so much by fundamental personality traits, but simply by imperatives of argument, almost regardless of the desires, character, or convictions of the participants'.[62]

From the time of the CAA's founding, leading members believed that it was vital that any arguments against Zionism must appear to be constructive. Both Hope-Simpson and Royden-Shaw wrote to Spears urging that the CAA be constructive in its opposition to Zionism. Royden-Shaw was particularly preoccupied with this issue, and in an earlier letter to Storrs had explained that 'I do not want people to feel that I am simply waving aside the promise of a national home ... people at once say "well what do you propose?", and I want to give them some kind of answer.'[63]

Thus, rather than proof of the CAA's compassion for the predicament of Jewish refugees, whom Spears on one occasion referred to as a 'motley collection of Europeans',[64] the body's call for the opening of England to Jews was (to borrow Hirschman's phrase) 'shaped ... by the imperatives of argument'. Michael Ionides, one of the two-man committee responsible for drafting the CAA's public response to the Anglo-American report, argued the case for allowing Jews into England primarily in political terms. He encouraged Spears to take a lead on this issue, as 'the political effect in the Mid East would be very great ... it would disarm the Zionists who cannot publicly do otherwise than urge the humanitarian aim'.[65]

That this support for opening England to Jewish refugees was motivated by political considerations rather than humanitarian concerns can be seen in Spears' lack of effort in following up this pledge. In June 1946, the same month as he was corresponding with Guillaume and Longhurst about the political necessity of calling for the entry of Jewish refugees into England, Newcombe wrote to Spears to inform him that he had been corresponding with Dr Isaac Steinberg, leader of the anti-Zionist Jewish Freeland League.

The League was a body that opposed the creation of a Jewish state in Palestine, and which laboured under the leadership of Steinberg to find a suitable territory outside Palestine, acceptable to both Jews and the indigenous population, where Jews could live in peace.[66] The Zionist attitude to this naïve if noble effort can be seen in the title of an article by Joseph Heller on the League in the *Zionist Review* in 1948. The article was entitled simply 'The Story of Failure'.[67]

Newcombe's proposal that Steinberg address the CAA once again illustrates how Gentile anti-Zionists, such as Newcombe, communicated on the Palestine issue with non-Zionist Jews; but it also emphasises the fundamental antipathy of Spears and his committee to opening England to Jews, or to helping in any scheme that provided relief for Jews outside Palestine. For Newcombe informed Spears that Steinberg supported the CAA's decision to call on the government to allow 30,000 more Jews into England, and that he had himself been lobbying both in England and in Australia to achieve this same goal. Newcombe then asked Spears if it would be possible for Steinberg to address the CAA.[68]

Spears ruled out the possibility of the CAA inviting Steinberg to speak because there was no real support for the idea of allowing 30,000 more Jews into England, and ended his letter, 'so I think we had better leave Steinberg alone'.[69]

The fact that Spears vetoed an appearance by Steinberg before the CAA on the ground that he supported the entry of a substantial number of Jews into England is curious, considering that this had been the same proposal as Spears' own committee had endorsed as an alternative to allowing more Jews into Palestine only one month earlier. Even the Foreign Office was more open to Steinberg's efforts than Spears. On arriving in England in 1946 Steinberg had approached the Foreign Office with a letter of introduction from Sir Norman Angell (journalist and former Labour MP) and Harold Beeley was of the opinion that Steinberg was 'not a negligible fellow and sincerely anxious to help us'.[70]

It is no surprise that it was Newcombe who had called on Spears to invite Steinberg, for he was the only significant member of the CAA who favoured opening England to refugees on purely humanitarian, as opposed to political, grounds. In his written submission to the AACIP he attacked the policy of the United States and Britain forbidding the increase of Jewish immigration above 3.5 per cent and 1.5 per cent of the population respectively.[71] Similarly, he informed Spears that 'It will not hurt us to take another 30,000 ... however unpopular it may sound ... if we want to be humane, do it ourselves and encourage others to co-operate we must take our share of Jewish refugees here.'[72]

During another correspondence with Spears he enclosed a

memorandum he had prepared which argued that far from hurting the English economy or threatening English jobs, new immigrants would bring new ideas and other advantages to the country.[73] But if Newcombe's position was an exception to the rule, it was Sir John Hope-Simpson whose position on the issue best sums up the CAA's indifference to the plight of the Jewish refugees.

As has been shown in chapter 3, the Zionists saw Hope-Simpson primarily as the man whose 'lamentable document'[74] of 1930–31 on immigration and land settlement had irretrievably damaged Jewish immigration prospects into Palestine during the previous decade. However, Hope-Simpson, a career civil servant who had moved from his post as vice-president of the Greek Refugee Board Settlement Commission to report on Palestine, had been an outspoken advocate of opening England to Jewish refugees in the years before the war, using his public position to lobby for the increased entry of Jews into England.

In one speech, in front of an audience at the RIIA, he presented an argument in favour of allowing Jewish refugees into England that was almost identical to the one Newcombe would espouse to both Spears and the AACIP after the war. Hope-Simpson told his audience that 'never has Britain suffered through the influx of refugees. On the contrary we have gained all the time.'[75]

So public was Hope-Simpson on this issue that the Jewish writer Louis Golding even referred to him in his own arguments for opening up England to more Jews.[76] Indeed, it has been surmised that his criticism of the Foreign Office's refugee policy during the interwar period cost him the prestigious appointment as high commissioner for refugees (as a replacement for Sir Neil Malcolm).[77]

Yet during the post-war discussion within the CAA on this same issue he was surprisingly quiet. Although he never openly opposed the CAA's decision to call upon the government to take Jewish refugees, he stated in his memorandum to the AACIP that a further influx of refugees would increase anti-Semitism in England and place a great burden on charitable obligations.[78]

This change on Hope-Simpson's part, from a position of advocacy to one of reluctance, symbolised a general decline in sympathy for and interest in the Jewish refugee issue, compared to those which existed before the war. Sir Ronald Storrs, not surprisingly, considering his interest in Jewish affairs, had been very concerned in the pre-war years over the position of Jews in the Nazi orbit and under direct Nazi rule.

In 1939 he approached the Board of Deputies, through the intermediary services of Norman Bentwich, to request information on the position of Jews,[79] and his private papers contain a large collection of material on the issue of the fate of Jewry under Nazism before the war. Even Spears showed an interest in the position of Jews in the Nazi orbit during the pre-war era, asking a parliamentary question on the subject in 1938 as to the efforts taken to protect British Jews caught in Germany.[80]

Yet after 1945 there was a tendency for these same men to minimise the Jewish refugee problem. There was a belief that Jews were receiving a disproportionate share of concern at the expense of other groups of refugees. This view was most publicly aired by Foreign Secretary Bevin. In a press conference following his Palestine statement of November 1945 he criticised the Jewish tendency to 'jump to the head of the queue' in demanding help for their refugees.[81] There was also a belief that the Jewish refugee problem was not as great as was generally claimed, with Spears, for example, arguing that refugee Christians provided a greater problem than Jews.[82]

In August 1945 Storrs went as far as to deem continued immigration into Palestine 'superfluous and unnecessary'. He justified this assessment on the basis that the extermination of so many Jews meant that less of a Jewish problem existed at this time than before the war.[83] The Arab Office also shared a similar view of the Jewish post-war situation and argued against any need for an increase in Jewish immigration into Palestine because the 'proportions of the Jewish refugee problem in Europe [in 1939] were more formidable than they are today'.[84]

Although this peculiar reasoning was proved wrong in the face of sheer numbers and social and economic conditions, it seemed to provide Storrs with an antidote for any troubled conscience that he might have had. For instance, during a lecture tour of Germany on behalf of the Admiralty, later in the same year, he never once visited a DP camp or mentioned the position of Jewish DPs in his diary, which, in the context of the other places he visited and the other issues that he dwelled upon in his diary during his visit, do stand out by their absence.[85]

Thus at the end of the war and in the wake of the Holocaust, within the CAA there was a tendency to view the Jewish position as less desperate than it had been before the war, and this was accompanied by less concern for the Jewish situation on the continent. This is interesting because the treatment of the Jews during the war and their subsequent refugee status have so often been presented as the prelude to, and in many cases did result in, an increase in emotional support for a suffering Jewry and even for the Zionist cause.

But not amongst this group of Englishmen. The CAA in advocating the opening of England to Jewish refugees was concerned not to help the Jewish refugees but rather to provide a 'constructive' alternative to recommendation 2 of the Anglo-American Committee report, while all the time aware that there was no possibility of a 'substantial' number of refugees being allowed into England.

Thus, ironically and even paradoxically, by advocating a policy that Spears admitted his committee did not favour, the CAA was not promoting a position favoured by Zionists, anti-Zionist Jews or by the English authorities, but one held purely by Arabs. As such the CAA's support for opening up England to Jewish refugees was an effort to move closer to the Arab position on Palestine.

The Arabs, as represented by the Arab Office, constantly attacked Britain (as well as other countries) for its refusal to take a share of Jewish refugees. Albert Hourani in his testimony before the AACIP referred to the 'guilt and shame' of the British (and American) refugee policy and he reiterated this in his speech to the RIIA in May 1946.[86]

Viewing the issue of Jewish refugees and immigration into Palestine from an Arab rather than a humanitarian perspective, English and Arab anti-Zionists refused to accept that this problem had anything to do with the issue of Palestine or that Palestine provided an opportunity to take the refugees.[87]

Secondly, these anti-Zionists refused to believe that the Zionist desire for homes for the refugees had anything to do with humanitarian concerns. Rather, this was a strategy adopted purely as a way of getting more Jews into the country with the objective of achieving a Jewish majority there. Robin Maugham exemplified this view when in 1947 he argued that the Zionists 'decided to concentrate on one demand – immigration – they realised that this was the humanitarian method to gain their political end in dominating the country'.[88]

Maugham's view was echoed by the Arab Office, which stated that the Zionists were not concerned with the humanitarian aspect of the problem but rather were 'determined to sabotage attempts to solve the Jewish refugee problem in a genuinely humanitarian manner and to refuse every alternative to Palestine, because their real object is political not humanitarian'.[89] Spears also argued that the Zionists saw Jewish refugees as political pawns rather than tragic victims of the war and was of the opinion that 'the Zionist's first care is not the infirm Jews of Europe'.[90]

Another charge made by the anti-Zionists was that the refugees did not particularly care about going to Palestine, and that any impression that they did was due to a lack of choice and Zionist propaganda. Professor Driver, in a letter to Spears in the wake of Foreign Secretary Bevin's 1945 Palestine statement – a letter that shows the frustration and disgust at perceived Zionist methods, stated that 'there is much harsh lying as you know only too well', and asked Spears in almost rhetorical manner: 'how many Jews "deem Zion their chief joy" as the Chief Rabbi so absurdly states?'[91]

Just how cynical was the Gentile anti-Zionist view of the Zionist effort to use Jewish refugees to gain their state can be seen in a comment by Storrs on this subject in his diary, that 'the only point upon which two Jews will agree: – how much money a third should pay to send a fourth to Palestine'.[92]

There was a belief that the Zionist strategy of using Jewish refugees for political purposes was achieved by denying them opportunities to rebuild their lives in Europe, or as Spears presented it, by offering European Jewry only 'a choice between penury and Palestine'.[93] Similarly, it was the anti-Zionist view that the Zionists, through constant propaganda, had brainwashed Jews into believing that Palestine was their only hope.

Spears on more than one occasion publicly called what he saw as the Zionist propaganda effort to manipulate refugees into believing that Palestine was their best hope 'the cruellest deception'.[94] Likewise, Sir John Hope-Simpson, the acknowledged expert on refugee issues, argued that any sincere desire on the part of Jews to go to Palestine was caused by the intense Zionist propaganda that had been carried on for many years, and that had instilled an artificial belief in Palestine as a haven for Jews.[95]

There is no doubt that the Zionist movement did use all the propaganda techniques at its disposal to try to convince Jewish refugees in Europe that the only solution to the Jewish problem was to go to Palestine.[96] What must be questioned is the anti-Zionist claim that it was *only* the existence of Zionist propaganda that made Jews go to Palestine. This is patently false and one should view the desire of Jews to go to Palestine as a result of their wartime experiences and the position facing them in Europe, rather than the result of insidious and repetitive Zionist propaganda techniques.

Richard Crossman, who visited the DP camps in 1946 with the specific intention of finding out whether the desire for Palestine of the Jews housed there was because of Zionist propaganda or their own wishes, came to the conclusion that although there was much Zionist propaganda in the camps, even if there had been none the great majority of DPs would have looked to Palestine, aware that it was 'their only hope of early release'.[97]

The Jewish Fellowship agreed wholeheartedly with the non-Jewish anti-Zionist argument that much of the desire for Palestine amongst Jewish refugees in Europe was a result of Zionist propaganda and the lack of other options. Ewen Montagu, speaking on behalf of the Fellowship at the AACIP, responded to a question, from committee member Wilfred Crick, as to whether Jewish refugees had been given an objective choice as to where they should live, with the view that they had been offered 'no alternative at all' to Palestine.[98] A 1947 editorial in the *Jewish Outlook* set out the Fellowship's view that Zionists tried to manipulate Jewish refugees into looking towards Palestine, informing readers that 'it would seem that Zionist agitators ... are working hard to instil Zionist ideas into people who show a preference for migration to the opposite point of the compass'.[99]

Yet regardless of the belief that the refugees looked to Palestine because of Zionist propaganda and a lack of other options, the Jewish Fellowship openly and categorically stated its support for free immigration for all those Jews who wanted to go to Palestine. This is understandable, given that it was a Jewish group that felt a need to support some option that gave hope to those Jewish refugees who did not want to be rehabilitated, without supporting a Jewish state. In his presidential address to the second annual Fellowship meeting in December 1946, Brunel Cohen informed his audience that 'the Jewish Fellowship fully realised that at the present moment Palestine alone offers a home on a large scale for the stateless Jews of Europe ... as many as want to go should be allowed'.[100]

The Fellowship was not alone in opposing a Jewish state but supporting free immigration. Other non-Zionist and anti-Zionist Jewish groups argued in similar terms.[101] But the differences between Jewish and non-Jewish anti-Zionists on the immigration issue were based on more than differing levels of sensitivity and concern over post-war Jewish homelessness.

Historically, Jewish anti-Zionists in England had favoured the right of free Jewish immigration into Palestine. Even Edwin Montagu, whose virulent anti-Zionism in the years of the Balfour Declaration may have been equalled by later anti-Zionists – but was certainly never surpassed – favoured this, at one point calling for Jews to be allowed 'complete liberty of settlement and life on an equality with the inhabitants [of Palestine]'.[102] And Basil Henriques, speaking during the debate on the Board of Deputies' November 1944 Palestine statement, opposed all references to a Jewish state or commonwealth in Palestine, but said that he wanted as many Jews as wished to go to Palestine to be allowed to do so. This was also the position advocated during the Fellowship's AACIP evidence.[103]

The Fellowship refused to see anything political deriving from this humanitarian position. One of its earliest pamphlets *A Challenge to All Jews* stated that the Fellowship's position in supporting and helping Jews find refuge in Palestine was 'fundamentally different from political nationalism'.[104]

However, the Arab and English Gentile anti-Zionists were not prepared to make the distinction between immigration and political Zionism. When speaking publicly at two prestigious engagements in February 1945 Spears told his audiences in no uncertain terms that immigration was at the heart of the whole Palestine problem and that 'the problem of Zionism is in fact to the Arabs one of unlimited immigration'.[105] This position was underlined by Edward Atiyah in his autobiography, written in the following year, where he stated that for the Arabs the immigration issue was 'a matter of life and death and their concern and their struggle largely centred on it'.[106]

The importance attached to immigration was due to the belief that it held the key to whether Zionists would succeed or fail in gaining a state. Newcombe exemplified this attitude, telling Spears that 'when the Zionists realise that immigration will shortly cease they may learn to co-operate with others', and in a subsequent letter he went even further, saying 'remove the question of immigration and Palestine will settle itself'.[107]

The Jewish anti-Zionist position, as embodied by the Fellowship, was exactly the opposite to this and was based on the belief that if the programme of political Zionism halted, then there would be no opposition to increased and free immigration into Palestine. For example, Daniel Lipson in a speech to a joint meeting of the Fellowship's council and executive in February 1946 called for the abandonment of the Jewish state idea as a way of enabling co-operation with the Arabs. He reiterated this view in parliament when he informed the House that 'I would like to see the large number of Jews who want to go to Palestine allowed to go there ... [the] chief obstacle ... is largely the policy of the Jewish nationalists'.[108]

Colonel Robert Henriques, in a speech to the Manchester Jewish Forum in April of the same year, stated that if an attempt was made to get Jews into Palestine on purely humanitarian grounds instead of making it a political issue the Arabs would have no reason for opposition.[109] Thus members of the CAA and the Arab Office saw stopping immigration into Palestine as the way to halt political Zionism, while the Jewish anti-Zionists of the Fellowship saw halting political Zionism as the way to increase Jewish immigration into Palestine.

At the heart of this contradictory position was a totally different view as to the moral right of Jews to be in Palestine in the first place. In the pre-war era Gentile anti-Zionists had not been unanimously opposed to Zionism on the ground that the Jews had no moral right to be in Palestine. Sir Ronald Storrs, in an article in the *Evening Standard* in 1939, echoed the position of the report of the 1937 Royal Commission on Palestine that the problem of Palestine was 'fundamentally a conflict of right and right' with the view that 'the issues of this unique and tremendous experiment are not a matter of right against wrong, but of right against right'.[110]

And in these years the Jewish and Gentile co-operative attempt to find a non-Zionist solution to the Palestine problem (from the pamphlets of Nevill Barbour in the 1930s through to *A Constitution for Palestine* in 1945) was based on an acceptance that there existed a certain moral equivalency on both sides of the Palestine dispute.[111] However, when it became apparent that a final decision over Palestine's future was fast approaching, and when the battle over Palestine revolved around Jewish statehood or Arab domination of the country, there was little support for a settlement in Palestine on the basis of moral equivalency.

Hope-Simpson, in an article in *International Affairs*, directly challenged the notion of moral equivalency.[112] Other CAA members such as Royden-Shaw and Stephen Longrigg also used their public platforms to do the same. During her radio debate with Wyndham

Deedes on Palestine Royden-Shaw stated, 'I cannot see that there are two rights'.[113] And Longrigg argued that the 'alleged rights' that the Zionists claimed in Palestine were 'unknown to law or reason'.[114]

Thus, in the final years of the Mandate, the constituency of English Gentile anti-Zionists believed that Palestine was no longer a matter of right and right, but right and wrong. In doing so they agreed with Musa Alami's view that the Arabs and not the Zionists had 'unanswerable right' on their side,[115] and with the editorial view of the *Arab News Bulletin* that 'this conflict is not, despite all the sophistry exercised to prove it [as] such, one between right and right, but a clear right on the one hand and an insidious attempt to defeat and suppress it on the other'.[116]

The unanimous agreement within Jewry that there should be free immigration into Palestine gave some comfort to the Zionist movement. Chaim Weizmann, speaking at the 1944 annual conference of the English Zionist Federation, saw the fact that no Jewish group opposed immigration as indicating 'a certain amount of progress'.[117] Yet the Zionists, like non-Jewish anti-Zionists, could not separate the issue of immigration from their political programme, for the simple reason that to a large extent immigration *was* their political programme.

Unlike the Fellowship, the Zionists could not comprehend, let alone advocate, a situation where the Jewish state policy should be put aside so that immigration could thrive. As has been seen, a central strand of Zionist attacks on the Fellowship was that the anti-Zionist body seemed to epitomise the profound lack of self-respect found in a certain sector of Jewry.

As a corollary to this it was the Zionist view that the Fellowship was motivated in its support for free Jewish immigration into Palestine because it despised Jewish refugees and did not want them in England. The Zionist columnist Zakan (pseud.) summed up this attitude when he stated that 'you get those Jews who ... dislike intensely seeing other Jews who look like Jews and who resent every overt manifestation of characteristics which are particularly Jewish'.[118]

Undoubtedly a gulf did exist between the 'anglicised Jew' that belonged to the Jewish elite that made up a large section of the Fellowship and the 'new Englishmen', those more recent arrivals in England. Robert Henriques, writing in 1966, referred to this group of 'new Englishmen' in some detail and it is worth quoting to show just why Zionists may have been forgiven for thinking that men like Henriques and his contemporaries in the Fellowship were opposed to more Jewish immigrants in England. In Henriques' view these 'new Englishmen'

> were not yet Englishmen ... even those who had been born and educated in England ... their taste in food, the way they dressed, walked, moved their hands, eyes and mouths, no less the way their minds worked ... they were still far away from understanding British usages, ethical standards, democratic practice.[119]

But the Zionist movement also viewed the Fellowship's support for immigration and its parallel refusal to accept that this support for immigration had political implications and could even lead to a Jewish state, as irresponsible, naïve, hypocritical and symbolic of both the body's isolation within Jewry and its disregard for the fate of Jewish refugees. For what was a Jewish state if not the surest way to achieve a situation where free immigration was a guaranteed inalienable right for the Jews that the Fellowship expressed so much concern for?

Dr Paul Riebenfeld, a member of the Board of Deputies and a leading member of the revisionist New Zionist Organisation (he was chairman of the British section of the NZO in 1945), most cogently stated the fundamental weakness of Jewish support for immigration and opposition to a Jewish state. Though never likely to be viewed as a neutral observer in the debate over Palestine (the Fellowship paper disparagingly referred to him as the 'authoritative spokesman of the Irgun'),[120] Riebenfeld first developed his argument in a letter to the *Jewish Chronicle* in September 1946 where he argued that the immigration issue as it related to Palestine was primarily an issue of 'power, politics and strategy'.[121]

One month later Riebenfeld expanded on this theme in an article in the Zionist organ, the *Jewish Forum*. He challenged those who refused to see that any call for immigration was a political act, and argued that once there were enough new immigrants (Riebenfeld gave the number as 600,000–700,000) then a Jewish state would follow naturally. In Riebenfeld's opinion,

> They [Jewish opponents of a Jewish state] still look at Jewish development in Palestine as a glorified undertaking on a mass

scale, and refuse as a matter of principle to discuss it in anything but these terms. In reality they no more than the Zionists can evade the political character of the Palestine problem.[122]

He also argued that regardless of the fact that the call for immigration was presented as a humanitarian necessity, it did not alter the simple truth that 'every humanitarian issue that concerns a great number of people is necessarily also a political one'.[123] This view was endorsed the following week in a *Jewish Chronicle* editorial which denounced those Jews who criticised Zionism merely because it was a political movement, calling this 'a conscious hypocrisy or else a degradation of the whole concept of politics'.[124]

On this issue, Riebenfeld, whose revisionist attitudes often found him in conflict with the orthodox Zionist movement, was speaking for all types of Zionism. For example, Moshe Shertok, in an earlier speech at the RIIA in 1945, set out the same argument as Riebenfeld, saying that one could not settle a large number of Jews (his figures of 600,000–700,000 were the same as Riebenfeld used later) in Palestine without achieving a Jewish majority, which in turn had a political implication.[125]

Indeed, there should have been no illusion on the part of the Jewish anti-Zionists that their position, unacceptable to Zionists, was any more appealing to non-Jewish anti-Zionists. As early as the summer of 1945, the Arab Office warned those who were opposed to the basic aim of Zionism – a Jewish state – not to be fooled or convinced by the Zionist plea for immigration into Palestine on humanitarian grounds.[126]

Such an appeal could have been directed specifically at the Fellowship's position. Even more importantly, the Arab Office in its public statements reiterated, in no uncertain terms, the Zionist argument, so clearly set out by Riebenfeld, that it was impossible to divorce the issue of immigration from the issue of a Jewish state.

In an article in the *Contemporary Review* in 1948, Edward Atiyah once again claimed that the real conflict in Palestine was over immigration, for 'Jewish immigration into Palestine involves acute political issues and cannot be regarded in a purely humanitarian light', and he went on, 'The continued arrival, against Arab wishes, of foreign immigrants who have a political design on the country is an act of aggression, and does not cease to be so merely because the immigrants in another sense are refugees.'[127] Atiyah in the above article was expressing a fundamental Arab (and English Gentile anti-Zionist) position that struck at the core of the Fellowship's philosophy. In another article during the summer of 1948, the Arab Office once again reiterated that there could be no co-operation between Jews and Arabs, but went even further and attacked those who called for immigration while at the same time supporting conciliation as 'merely indulging in futile wishful thinking', concluding that such a position was not really an attempt at compromise but a complete surrender to Zionist aspirations.[128]

This total isolation of the Fellowship on these vital issues is perhaps best seen by a four-sided correspondence in *The Times* in April 1948. Spears began the correspondence when he ruled out any Arab compromise on the issue of immigration and argued that immigration into Palestine should be decided, as it was in every other sovereign state, by the majority of the indigenous population.[129] In response to this letter Rabbi Dr Israel Mattuck called for the 'assured prospect for Jewish immigration into the country' and attacked Spears' position on immigration as a 'cause of profound regret ... [that] encourages intransigence'.[130]

This was followed by a letter from Bernard Lieberman, acting chairman of the Palestine committee of the Board of Deputies, which categorically rejected Mattuck's position, even with its attack on Spears. For Lieberman, 'Dr Mattuck seems to draw an artificial distinction between what he calls political Zionism and the need to secure a place of refuge for suffering Jews. No such distinction exists.'[131] Lieberman's letter was published the same day as a letter from Edward Atiyah, in which he defended Spears while deriding Mattuck's position, of claiming to support Arab rights in Palestine at the same time as calling for immigration, as 'contradictory, meaningless and dishonest'.[132]

This disagreement in April 1948 between Rabbi Mattuck on the one hand, and Spears, Atiyah and the leading Zionist Lieberman, on the other, on such a crucial issue as Jewish immigration into Palestine, at a time when the creation of a Jewish state was only one month away, symbolises just how isolated the anti-Zionists of the Jewish Fellowship were.

One month later the State of Israel came into being. Given the centrality of the goal of preventing a Jewish state in all or part of Palestine to Jewish and non-Jewish anti-Zionists throughout the Mandate years, it is hardly surprising that the Arab Office, the Committee for Arab Affairs and the Jewish Fellowship found themselves to be somewhat irrelevant in the post-Mandatory era.

The Jewish Fellowship wound up in November 1948, exactly four years to the day after it had held a press conference to announce its existence. The Zionist success in neutralising the Fellowship within Jewry can be seen in the fact that the body's leadership argued in favour of its closure because 'Zionist propaganda' had succeeded in giving the impression that the Fellowship was a political rather than a religious organisation, and thus had tarnished its reputation beyond repair inside Anglo-Jewry.[133]

Likewise the CAA, which lost its motivation for continuing once Israel was a reality, was slowly subsumed by the much larger Anglo-Arab Association that it had formed in July 1946, and it too wound up in the months after May 1948.

The Arab Office was the last of the three bodies to close its doors, arguing that it was needed more than ever in the wake of the massive Palestinian exodus following the 1948 war. However, in reality it was only the hope that the body would contribute to the prevention of a Jewish state that had enabled the Arab Office to survive as long as it did in the face of much bitter opposition to its existence from certain sections of the Arab League. And in April 1949, in the wake of the Arab defeat in the war in Palestine, the Arab Office finally shut its doors.

The anti-Zionists of the defunct CAA and the Arab Office would continue, in varying degrees, to oppose Zionism as constituted in the sovereign State of Israel (or as Spears saw it, the 'ugly little Spartan state dominated by a fierce little orthodox fascist movement').[134] And former CAA members such as Spears, Barbour, Ionides, as well as former Arab Office member Albert Hourani, all served on the Council for the Advancement of Arab British Understanding (CAABU), the Arab lobby group, during the 1970s.

Conversely, once Israel came into existence, Jewish anti-Zionist opposition was mostly intellectual and academic rather than public and polemical in nature. This relative silence in defeat must be viewed as an acceptance, albeit a begrudging one, that Israel was a *fait accompli*. That being the case it was the duty of Jews (just as it had been the duty of Jews to oppose a state before its creation) to wish it the best, hope it followed a true Jewish path or reserve criticism to scholarly works.[135]

Indeed, as time passed there seemed to be an increasing awareness of the incongruity of the position that the Fellowship had promoted during its existence. By 1966 Colonel Robert

Henriques, who had been one of the staunchest supporters of the Fellowship's opposition to a Jewish state, was conceding that 'today it seems very improbable that a national home could have been provided in Palestine without establishing there a Jewish state'.[136] This is the ultimate acknowledgement of the weakness of the Fellowship philosophy and an effective acceptance of the arguments of Zionists such as Bernard Lieberman and Paul Riebenfeld, and non-Jewish anti-Zionists such as Spears and Atiyah.

In a speech to the Jewish Fellowship Youth Conference in February 1948, in what was to be one of the last of the Fellowship's official gatherings, Sir Jack Brunel Cohen restated the Fellowship's position of supporting free immigration into Palestine on humanitarian, charitable and religious grounds but 'not more than that'.[137]

Brunel Cohen saw no contradiction in such a position, which incorporated virulent opposition to a Jewish state within a framework of accepting the need for and the right to free Jewish immigration into Palestine. But for Zionists and non-Jewish anti-Zionists alike this was an unacceptable position. For non-Jewish anti-Zionists 'not more than that' was too much, while for Zionists 'not more than that' was nowhere near enough.

NOTES

1. MS Diary of Storrs, 10 March 1944, Box 6/5, STOP.
2. Cmd. 6019, *Palestine, A Statement of Policy* (May 1939).
3. Cmd. 1700, *Correspondence with the Palestine Arab Delegation and the Zionist Organisation. And a Statement of British Policy on Palestine* (June 1922).
4. MacDonald to Weizmann, 13 February 1931. A copy of this letter can be found in Appendix 3 in Rose's *Lewis Namier and Zionism* (Oxford: Clarendon Press, 1980), pp. 171–6.
5. *Palestine, A Statement of Policy* (May 1939), part 2: Immigration, pp. 1–11.
6. Chief Rabbi Isaac Herzog, *The Times*, 16 May 1939.
7. *The Jewish Case Against the White Paper* (London: ZF, 1945); *The MacDonald White Paper of 1939* (London: JA, 1945). Also see Daphne Trevor, *Under the White Paper* (Jerusalem: Jerusalem Press, 1948).
8. See *The Reply of the Arab Higher Committee for Palestine to the White Paper* (Jerusalem: Arab Higher Committee, 1939), p. 13, BLYTH.
9. *Statement of the Arab Attitude Over Palestine* (London: AO, 1945), p. 1.
10. See, for example, the statement issued by the Arab Office in response to Bevin's Palestine statement, 13 November 1945. Also see the editorial in the first issue of the *Arab News Bulletin*, 1 (28 November 1945), p. 1 and Arab Office member Burhan Dajani's 'National Movements for Freedom in India and Palestine', *India Quarterly*, III: 1 (January–March 1947), pp. 135–43.
11. Robin Maugham, 'Impressions Gathered on a Very Rapid Tour of Egypt, Palestine and the Levant States', transcript of meeting of the Middle East group, RIIA, 5 March 1946, 8/1325, p. 5.

242   *Divided Against Zion*

12. Nevill Barbour, *Nisi Dominus: A Survey of Palestine* (London: Harrap, 1946), p. 225.
13. Brigadier Stephen Longrigg, 'Peril in Palestine', *Spectator*, 31 August 1945, pp. 191–2.
14. MS Diary of Storrs, 19 October 1945, Box 6/6, STOP. Also see Storrs' 'The British Plan for Palestine: Sir Ronald Storrs Says Nobody has Suggested Better', *Yorkshire Post*, 20 July 1939.
15. MS Diary of Storrs, 17 January 1945, Box 6/6, STOP.
16. Ionides to Spears, 15 May 1946, Box 6/4, SPSP.
17. Evidence of Thomas Reid before the AACIP, p.8.
18. Stark to Nicolson, 9 November 1945, cited in Lucy Moorehead (ed.), *Freya Stark: Letters, New Worlds For Old, 1943–1946* (London: Compton Russell, 1986), Vol. V, p. 239.
19. Spears, 'The Path to Arab Unity', *Great Britain and the East*, LXI: 1746 (April 1945), pp. 72–6.
20. Albert Hourani, 'Palestine after the Report', transcript of meeting of the Middle East group, RIIA, 17 May 1946, 8/1332, p. 2.
21. See Hammersley to Spears, 13 March 1945, Box 4/6, SPSP and the Jewish Telegraphic Agency's *Daily News Bulletin*, 12: 56 (8 March 1945), p. 2.
22. See *Some Information for You*, p. 2.
23. Franklyn, *Jewish Chronicle*, 18 May 1945, p. 15. Also see Basil Henriques' letter, 23 March 1945, p. 3.
24. Evidence of the Jewish Fellowship before the AACIP, p. 54, ACC3121/C14/30/5, ABD.
25. *Jewish Outlook*, 1: 5 (September 1946), p. 3.
26. Spears to Stokes, 14 August 1945, Box 4/6, STOP.
27. Regarding the Land Transfer Regulations see *Palestine, A Statement of Policy* (May 1939), part 3: Land, pp. 12–14. For an example of the Zionist view of these land regulations see the comments of Nathan Laski JP, president of the Council of Manchester and Salford Jews (the largest Jewish community outside London) at the council's first meeting after the Land Transfer Regulations had come into effect, reported in the *Jewish Chronicle*, 22 March 1940, p. 2.
28. Newcombe, *The Times*, 30 May 1939.
29. Newcombe to Storrs, 14 June 1944, Box 6/15, STOP.
30. Newcombe to Hall, 7 February 1946, Box 5/3, SPSP.
31. Newcombe to Spears, 3 April 1945, Box 5/3, SPSP.
32. Newcombe, 'The Arab Countries', p. 5.
33. See *Palestine: A Policy*, pp. 189–209. Also see Hyamson's similar argument in 'The Problem of Palestine', *Contemporary Review*, CLXXIV: 952 (April 1945), pp. 221–6, p. 223.
34. Robert Henriques, *Sir Robert Waley Cohen, 1877–1952* (London: Secker & Warburg, 1966) , p. 359.
35. See *Suggestions for Possible Guidance of Jewish Speakers Addressing Non-Jewish Audiences During War Time* (London: Central Jewish Lecture Committee, 1940), MS171 AJ 246 24, REIN.
36. Weizmann, *The Times*, 18 February 1944.
37. Hammersley to Spears, 13 March 1945, Box 4/6, SPSP.
38. 'Friends of the White Paper', *Jewish Chronicle*, 16 March 1945, p. 8.
39. Bakstansky to Gluckstein, 26 June 1942, MS150 AJ 110/8, GREEN.
40. Levenberg made his claim at the Board's debate on Palestine, 7 October 1945, see report in *Zionist Review*, 12 October 1945, p. 7.
41. Moss made his claim at a Board's debate on Palestine, 14 July 1946, see report in *Zionist Review*, 19 July 1946, p. 1.
42. *Zionist Review*, 16 March 1945, p. 3.
43. *New Judea*, January–February 1946, pp. 64–5.
44. Ibid., pp. 64–5.
45. Gluckstein to Bakstansky, 30 June 1942, MS150 AJ 110/8, GREEN.
46. Mattuck, 'American Jewry', *Jewish Chronicle*, 7 February 1947, p. 11.
47. See Bevin's comments, 25 February 1946, Parliamentary Debates, Vol. 433, 1946–47, p. 1909. On the issue of the 100,000 and its relation to the founding of the Anglo-American Committee see Ovendale's, *Britain, the United States, and the End of the*

48. *Palestine Mandate* (Woodbridge: RHS/Boydell Press, 1989), pp. 77–108.
48. *Jewish Outlook*, 1: 2 (May 1946), pp. 4–5.
49. 'The Jewish Fellowship: An Internal Interview', *Jewish Outlook*, 1: 6 (October 1946), p. 16.
50. See Spears, 'A Reply to Dr Parkes', in *Palestine Controversy: A Symposium*, Introduction by H.N. Brailsford, Fabian Colonial Bureau (London: Fabian Publications & Victor Gollancz, 1945), pp. 18–25, p. 23.
51. The Arab Office argued similarly at the same time in its *Statement of the Present Arab Attitude Over the Palestine Question*, p. 3.
52. MS Diary of Storrs, 17 November 1945, Box 6/6, STOP.
53. Atiyah, *Report on the Anglo-American Hearings*, London, No. 1 (26 January 1946), Box 4/3, SPSP.
54. Hourani, 'Palestine after the Report', p. 4.
55. MS Diary of Storrs, 1 May 1946, Box 6/7, STOP.
56. Davidson to Spears, 22 May 1946, Box 6/3, SPSP.
57. The CAA meeting of 9 May was entitled 'To Consider Action on the Report of the Anglo-American Committee of Enquiry on Palestine', see minutes, Box 6/2, SPSP and minutes of CAA meeting, 30 May 1946, Box 6/2, SPSP.
58. Guillaume to Spears, 3 June 1946, Box 6/4, SPSP.
59. Longhurst to Spears, 3 June 1946, Box 6/4, SPSP.
60. Spears to Guillaume, 7 June 1946, Box 6/4, SPSP.
61. Spears to Longhurst, 4 June 1946, Box 6/4, SPSP.
62. Hirschman, *The Rhetoric of Reaction: Perversity, Futility, Jeopardy* (Cambridge, MA, London: Belknap Press, 1991), p. x.
63. Royden-Shaw to Storrs, 3 April 1944, Box 6/15, STOP.
64. Spears, 'Draft Suggestions for Evidence before the AACIP', Box 4/3, SPSP.
65. Ionides to Spears, 15 May 1946, Box 6/4, SPSP.
66. See Steinberg's *Australia: The Unpromised Land* (London: Gollancz, 1948). Also see Michael Blakeney's 'Proposals for a Jewish Colony in Australia, 1938–1948', *Jewish Social Studies*, XLVI: 3–4 (summer–fall 1983), pp. 277–92 and Leon Gettler's *An Unpromised Land* (Fremantle: Fremantle Arts Centre Press, 1993).
67. Joseph Heller, 'The Story of Failure', *Zionist Review*, 31 December 1948, p. 10.
68. Newcombe to Spears, 29 June 1946, Box 5/3, SPSP.
69. Spears to Newcombe, 1 July 1946, Box 5/3, SPSP.
70. See minutes of discussion on the visit of I.N. Steinberg to England, 23 May 1946, PRO/FO 371/52569.
71. See Newcombe's memorandum to the AACIP, 23 January 1946, Box 5/3, SPSP.
72. Newcombe to Spears, 8 June 1946, Box 7/1, SPSP.
73. Newcombe, 'Memorandum on the Jewish Problem', n.d., Box 7/1, SPSP.
74. *New Judea*, December 1944, pp. 34–5.
75. Hope-Simpson, 'The Refugee Problem', transcript of general meeting, RIIA, 23 June 1938, 8/547, p. 19. Also see Hope-Simpson's *The Refugee Problem* (London: Oxford University Press, 1939).
76. Golding, *The Jewish Problem* (London: Penguin, 1938), p. 173.
77. See A.J. Sherman, *Island Refuge: Britain and the Refugees from the Third Reich, 1933–1939* (London: Paul Elek, 1973), p. 127.
78. Hope-Simpson to Spears, 18 January 1946, Box 6/4, SPSP.
79. Bentwich to A.G. Brotman (secretary of the Board of Deputies), 30 November 1939, Box 6/15, STOP.
80. *The Times*, 13 December 1938.
81. *The Times*, 14 November 1945. On the Foreign Office attitude to the Jewish refugee problem, see H. Henderson's 'Memorandum on Jewish Refugees', 19 October 1946, PRO/FO 371/52646. Box 4/3, SPSP. Also see Arieh J. Kochavi's 'The Displaced Persons Problem and the Formulation of British Policy in Palestine', *Studies in Zionism*, 10: 1 (spring 1989), pp. 31–48. Also see Bernard Wasserstein's *Britain and the Jews of Europe, 1939–1945* (London, Oxford: Institute for Jewish Affairs, Clarendon Press, 1979).
82. See Spears, 'Draft Suggestions for Evidence before the AACIP', Box 4/3, SPSP.
83. MS Diary of Storrs, 27 August 1945, Box 6/6, STOP.

84. *Statement of the Present Arab Attitude over the Palestine Question* (London: AO, 1945), p. 3.
85. MS Diary of Storrs, Admiralty visit to Germany, 23 October–18 November 1945, Box 11/6, STOP.
86. See evidence of the Arab Office before the AACIP, p. 107. Also see Hourani's speech 'Palestine after the Report', p. 7. Also see *Arab News Bulletin* editorial, 14 (13 June 1946), pp. 1–2 and Walter Stace's *The Zionist Illusion* (Washington: AO, 1947), p. 13.
87. For example, see Spears' articles 'Palestine's Future', *Sunday Express*, 18 November 1945; 'Crux of the Palestine Problem', *Daily Telegraph*, 8 October 1945. Also see Royden-Shaw's evidence before the AACIP, p. 59.
88. Maugham, *Approach to Palestine* (London: Falcon Press, 1947), p. 39.
89. *Palestine: The Solution*, p. 4. Also see Atiyah's 'Palestine', *Contemporary Review*, CLXXIV: 991 (July 1948), pp. 4–8 and Jamal Husseini's statement before the UN reprinted in a supplement to the *Arab News Bulletin*, 48 (17 October 1946), pp. 3, 6.
90. Spears, 'Draft Suggestions for Evidence before the AACIP', Box 4/3, SPSP.
91. Driver to Spears, n.d., November 1945, Box 4/6, SPSP.
92. MS Diary of Storrs, 28 November 1945, Box 6/6, STOP.
93. Spears, *Manchester Guardian*, 25 March 1946.
94. Spears, 'Crux of the Palestine Problem', *Daily Telegraph*, 8 October 1945; 'Reply to Dr Parkes', p. 24.
95. Hope-Simpson, 'The Palestine Statement', p. 24.
96. For a first-hand account of the Zionist efforts to use propaganda in the DP camps, see the autobiography of Lieutenant-General Sir Frederick Morgan, who was chief of the United Nations Relief and Rehabilitation Agency (UNRRA) operations in Germany, 1945–46. Morgan was the victim of harsh Zionist denunciations for what were interpreted as his anti-Jewish views while working with the DPs. Yet his descriptions of the Zionist propaganda efforts in the camps and of the organisation behind the Zionist movement of refugees to Palestine are made not without a sense of admiration. See *Peace and War: A Soldier's Life* (London: Hodder & Stoughton, 1961), pp. 234–62.
97. Crossman, *Palestine Mission: A Personal Record* (London: Hamish Hamilton, 1947), p. 88.
98. Evidence of Jewish Fellowship before the AACIP, p. 64.
99. 'Zion or USA?', *Jewish Outlook*, 1: 9 (January 1947), p. 12.
100. Brunel Cohen, presidential address to the second Fellowship annual meeting, 10 December 1946, reprinted in *Jewish Outlook*, 1: 9 (January 1947), pp. 4–5.
101. For example, see evidence of both Leonard Montefiore, chairman of the Jewish Colonial Association (ICA), and the AJA, before the AACIP, London, 26 January 1946, ACC3121/C14/30/5, ABD.
102. Edwin Montagu, 'Memorandum on the Anti-Semitism of the Present British Government', submitted to the British cabinet, 17 August 1917, PRO/CAB 24/24.
103. Basil Henriques' statement at the Board of Deputies debate on the Palestine statement, 5 November 1944, was reprinted in the *Zionist Review*, 10 November 1944, pp. 4–5.
104. *A Challenge to All Jews* (London: JF, 1944), p. 1.
105. See Spears' 'The Middle East and our Policy There', *Journal of Royal Central Asian Society*, XXXII: II (April 1945), pp. 156–65, p. 158, and his 'British Policy in the Middle East', transcript of general meeting, RIIA, 15 February 1945, 8/1155, p. 8.
106. Atiyah, *An Arab Tells his Story: A Study in Loyalties* (London: John Murray, 1946), pp. 203–4.
107. Newcombe to Spears, 8 June 1946 and 23 June 1946, Box 5/3, SPSP.
108. See Lipson's speech to the council and executive of the Fellowship, 15 February 1946, TBJSBH, 3/35, 1945–47, MS132 AJ 195, HENP, and his speech in the Palestine debate, 21 February 1946, Parliamentary Debates, Vol. 419, 11 February–1 March 1946–47, p. 1376.
109. See report on Henriques' speech, *Jewish Chronicle*, 19 April 1946, p. 10.
110. Storrs, 'Stand Firm in Palestine', *Evening Standard*, 20 July 1939. See Cmd. 5479, *The Report of the Palestine Royal Commission* (July 1937), p. 2.
111. See, for example, Nevill Barbour, *The Future of Palestine: How to Implement the White*

Paper (London: 1939), p. 3, Box 2/3, BARB.
112. Hope-Simpson, 'The Jewish World Since 1939: A Comment on Dr James Parkes' Paper', p. 101.
113. Royden-Shaw, 'The Future of Palestine', *The Listener*, p. 480.
114. Brigadier Stephen Longrigg, 'Peril in Palestine', *Spectator*, 31 August 1945, pp. 191–2, p. 191.
115. Geoffrey Furlonge, *Palestine is my Country* (London: John Murray, 1969), p. 115.
116. *Arab News Bulletin*, 30 (24 January 1947), p. 3. Also see Atiyah's *What was Promised in Palestine?* (London: AO, 1945), p. 1.
117. See Weizmann's speech, 30 January 1944, during the 43rd Annual Conference of the English Zionist Federation, 29–31 January 1944.
118. Zakan (pseud.), 'We Cannot Acquiesce', *Zionist Review*, 6 September 1945, p. 10.
119. Robert Henriques, *Sir Robert Waley Cohen*, p. 265. For an overview of the reactions to Jewish immigration into England see Geoffrey Alderman's *Modern British Jewry* (Oxford: Clarendon Press, 1992), chapter 3, 'Immigration and Social Control', pp. 102–51. For more detailed studies see Stuart Cohen's 'How Shall we Sing of Zion in a Strange Land?: East European Immigrants and the Challenge of Zionism in Britain, 1897–1918', *Jewish Social Studies*, 1 (new series): 2 (winter 1995), pp. 101–22. Also see David Englander (ed.), *A Documentary History of Jewish Immigration in Britain, 1840–1920* (Leicester, London, New York: Leicester University Press, 1994).
120. *Jewish Outlook*, 1: 4 (August 1946), p. 8.
121. Riebenfeld, *Jewish Chronicle*, 13 September 1946, p. 14.
122. Riebenfeld, 'The Politics of the Unpolitical Zionists', p. 38.
123. Ibid., p. 35.
124. *Jewish Chronicle*, 20 September 1946, p. 12.
125. Shertok, 'The Twin Problems of Palestine and the Jewish People', lecture to the RIIA, 27 November 1945, 8/1155, p. 11.
126. *Statement of the Present Arab Attitude Over the Palestine Question* (London: Arab Office, 1945), p. 3.
127. Atiyah, 'Palestine', *Contemporary Review*, CLXXIV: 991 (July 1948), p. 7.
128. 'The Arab Point of View', Arab Office, *Great Britain and the East*, LXV: 1785 (June 1948), pp. 37–8.
129. Spears, *The Times*, 15 April 1948.
130. Mattuck, *The Times*, 19 April 1948.
131. Lieberman, *The Times*, 21 April 1948.
132. Atiyah, *The Times*, 21 April 1948.
133. See 'Private and Confidential Memorandum' (London: JF, 1948), p. 2.
134. Spears, *Observer*, 24 May 1948.
135. For example, Sir Jack Brunel Cohen, the former MP and president of the Fellowship, does not even refer to his involvement in the group in his autobiography, *Count Your Blessingss* (London: Heinemann, 1956). Emile Marmorstein, who had been a member of the Fellowship council, wrote on the intellectual and religious roots of Jewish anti-Zionism rather than on the practical efforts of Jews like himself to oppose Zionism. See, for example, his articles in *International Affairs*, 'Religious Opposition to Nationalism in the Middle East', XXVIII: 3 (July 1952), pp. 334–59 and 'The Impact of Anti-Semitism on the State of Israel', XXIX:2 (April 1953), pp. 193–203. See also his article 'European Jews in Muslim Palestine', *Middle Eastern Studies*, 11: 1 (January 1975), pp. 74–87 and his book *Heaven at Bay: The Jewish Kulturkampf in the Holy Land* (London: Oxford University Press, 1969). This situation differed somewhat in the United States where leading Jewish anti-Zionists continued to chart their practical efforts to oppose a Jewish state long after the creation of Israel in 1948. See, for example, Elmer Berger's *Who Knows Better Must Say So* (New York: Bookmail, 1955) and *Memoirs of an Anti-Zionist Jew* (Beirut: Institute for Palestine Studies, 1978). See also Alfred Lillienthal's *What Price Israel?* (New York: Henry Regnery, 1954).
136. Henriques, *Sir Robert Waley Cohen*, p. 271.
137. Brunel Cohen's speech before the Fellowship Youth Conference was reprinted in *Jewish Outlook*, 2: 7 (February 1948), p. 2.

Conclusion

Lewis Namier, writing as an historian rather than as a Zionist, has stated that the goal of the historical approach should be to achieve an understanding of how things do not work. By examining the relationship between the leading Jewish and Gentile anti-Zionist bodies at a crucial time, 1945–48, in a crucial place, London, the capital city of the Mandate government, this book has attempted to abide by Namier's maxim and show how this relationship did not work.

In the Introduction, Freya Stark's use of the Scylla and Charybdis metaphor to describe the position of Jewish opponents of Zionism was adopted as the hypothesis at the heart of this study. As such, the preceding chapters have shown just how, and why, Stark was correct in her observation, in so far as it applied to the post-war relationship between Sir Edward Spears and the CAA, the Arab Office and the Jewish Fellowship.

As the early chapters showed, the CAA not only included the leading Gentile English anti-Zionists of the era, but the Zionist movement concentrated its polemical attacks on those same men and women who made up the CAA. Indeed, under the leadership of Spears, the CAA provided a conscious, albeit inconspicuous and sometimes stilted, attempt to organise opposition to Zionism among the political elite.

The fact that the Zionist publicists and the Anglo-Jewish media failed even once to refer directly to the existence of the CAA, while constantly condemning the anti-Zionist sentiments and efforts of its key members, does not so much reduce the importance of the CAA as a symbol of Gentile opposition to Zionism. Rather, it highlights the lack of Zionist awareness of the depths of the Gentile anti-Zionist effort. In fact the existence and activities of the CAA challenge, and in so doing disprove, one of the central misconceptions of the Mandate era, that the Arabs in the western world were struggling hopelessly without influential friends or committed supporters in their opposition to a Jewish state in Palestine.

There is no better testament to this than the close co-operation between the CAA and the Arab Office, particularly the intimate relationship that existed among leading members such as Spears, Ionides, Maugham and Storrs, and Arab Office luminaries such as Hourani and Atiyah. The close links between these two bodies also makes obvious the lack of an actual parallel relationship between the Committee for Arab Affairs and the Jewish Fellowship.

Indeed, where the Zionists were mistaken was not in their presentation of the widespread opposition that they faced, but in their claim that the Jewish anti-Zionists of the Fellowship shared a similar relationship of co-operation with English anti-Zionists as did the Arabs. This misrepresentation was undoubtedly due to the need for Zionist propaganda to present its Jewish opponents as enemies of Jewry and co-conspirators with Gentile enemies of Zion. But it was also very much due to the appearance of co-operation resulting from the common arguments, and the infrequent but much-publicised meetings of Jewish and non-Jewish anti-Zionists.

Yet regardless of this, the relationship (or lack of one), between the CAA and the Fellowship highlights the fact that, to borrow from Kipling, the real 'strangers within the gate' were the anti-Zionist Jews of the Jewish Fellowship.

That this was so was due to two reasons. The first derived from the fact that the leading anti-Zionist of the era, Sir Edward Spears, refused to co-operate with the Fellowship. That he entered the battle over Palestine only late in his career, with his appointment to the Levant in 1942, meant that unlike other post-war anti-Zionists he lacked both a past history of working with Jews in the Palestine administration and any past relationships with Jewish anti-Zionists. This goes some way to explain his lack of interest in the Jewish fight against Zionism.

Even more relevant was Spears' lifelong struggle to refute the haunting allegation that he himself was a Jew. Regardless of whether or not this was motivated by anti-Jewish prejudice, it is undeniable that his personal struggle with his possible Jewish identity greatly influenced his reluctance to be seen working with Jews, even those with the strongest anti-Zionist credentials. Given his total domination of anti-Zionist efforts in these years, this was a central and defining element in the Jewish and Gentile anti-Zionist relationship. For it not only prevented any possibility of co-operation between the Fellowship and the CAA, but also stifled the Arab and Jewish anti-Zionist relationship.

The creation of the Arab Offices in 1945 was the ultimate acknowledgement by the Arabs of their belief that their opposition to Zionism in the post-war era depended on a close relationship with those sympathetic to their cause in the western world. This was especially true in regard to London, where there already existed a network of willing and able men and women prepared to work for the Arab cause. The CAA epitomised this and the fact that on its formation the Arab Office in London (unlike its counterpart in Washington) had this constituency to draw upon meant that it believed that it could afford to ignore the efforts of the Jewish anti-Zionists of the Jewish Fellowship.

Thus, while Gentile opponents of Zionism, including Spears, never doubted the importance of the existence of Jewish anti-Zionists, and Jewish arguments were adopted in the public debate against Zionism, neither the CAA under the leadership of Spears nor the Arab Office turned these beliefs into close co-operation.

The second reason for the lack of a close relationship was that, despite publicly sharing similar arguments against Zionism, there existed fundamental differences between Jewish and non-Jewish anti-Zionists on key issues in the debate over Palestine. The Jewish Fellowship had a totally different understanding and perspective of, and attitude to, the Palestine White Paper of 1939 and the right of free Jewish immigration into Palestine than did English or Arab anti-Zionists.

Certain leading members of the Fellowship, most notably Gluckstein and Hyamson, may have sincerely seen the White Paper as a fair solution to the Palestine problem. Others such as Mattuck and Lipson might have viewed it as an imperfect but necessary way of dealing with the Palestine issue. However, the Fellowship, while refraining from any official attitude to the document, did not hesitate to admit that the majority of its members viewed the White Paper as a piece of anti-Jewish discrimination. Given the importance that Gentile anti-Zionists placed on adherence to the White Paper, close co-operation or even close identification with the Jewish Fellowship was not possible.

On the issue of the right of Jews to enter and settle freely in Palestine the division was much more clear-cut. For humanitarian reasons, and because of a refusal to view the opening of Palestine to refugees as a political act, the Fellowship never wavered in its support for free Jewish immigration; at the same time it virulently opposed a Jewish state.

This position was unacceptable to all members of the Gentile anti-Zionist constituency, who were fully aware of the political implications of free Jewish immigration into Palestine and who, unlike the Fellowship, were less concerned with the problem of Jewish refugees outside the context of how it would affect the final decision on the status of Palestine.

But on these issues the Fellowship was also very much isolated from Zionists and within Jewry. The fact that the Fellowship refused to endorse the White Paper policy, or that it supported free Jewish immigration into Palestine, gained it little credit within Jewry. Rather for Zionists all this emphasised was the *naïveté* and irresponsibility inherent in the Jewish anti-Zionist position.

There is no doubt that the Fellowship did hold a rather unrealistic attitude to Zionism and Palestine which lost it potential support within Anglo-Jewry. Gluckstein, for example, on one occasion concluded a speech to the Jewish Literary Society in 1945 by declaring that the solution to the Jewish problem could be found in the extension of toleration in the world. Nobody would have disagreed with Gluckstein's sentiments, but neither his words, dismissed as 'an amiable nothing'[1] in the *Jewish Chronicle*, nor the claim in the *Jewish Outlook*, that 'what the Jews really need is not a national state, but the right kind of world',[2] was a constructive argument against Zionism.

More than this, the Zionist movement was successful in presenting the Fellowship as a Liberal assimilationist body, motivated by the 'politics of fear',[3] and determined to deal a body-blow to the future of Jewry by opposing a Jewish state in the non-Jewish world.

In reality it was not an aversion towards its Jewish heritage, but a definite unmoveable faith in its own distinct conception of Judaism that motivated the Fellowship in its staunch opposition to Zionism. Its members perceived themselves to be a group of individuals forced by circumstance to defend all of Jewry from the false and dangerous claims of political Zionism.

Inherent in this attitude was the belief that Fellowship Jews were the only ones who had not been manipulated, deceived or brainwashed by Zionist propaganda. And it was in these terms that Fellowship leaders, such as Julian Franklyn, would claim that it was the duty of those Jews who found themselves 'blessed with the ability to distinguish between their religion and their nationality' to take a stand against Zionism.[4] This view was echoed in the *Jewish Outlook* which argued editorially that it was only those Jews who had 'not been blinded by blatant propaganda', and who could 'still distinguish' between charity and politics, religion and nationality, who understood the true value of the Fellowship.[5]

Yet however sincere the Fellowship position was, its perception of Jewish duty was at variance with that of the majority of Jews who, at least by 1945, equated support, or at least tolerance, of Zionism with Jewish self-respect and duty, and who could, for example, not fathom what denouncing Zionism as Nazism had to do with promoting the true Jewish view.

Thus, despite its convictions and its membership's claims to the contary, the Fellowship failed to gain credible support either at the Board of Deputies or in the wider community of Jewry by way of a large membership. It failed to counter Zionist propaganda and prevent itself from being perceived as a Liberal anti-Zionist conspiracy against the Jewish community. It failed to appeal to other Jewish bodies, even those like the AJA or Agudat Yisra'el that were not in support of a Jewish state in Palestine.

The Fellowship's mind-set also left this group of influential, and very able, Jews isolated from the position of Gentile anti-Zionists. Of course this was partly due to the instinctive and widespread anti-Semitism that was common in the relevant social and political circles of the time. And apart from the curious, if not downright peculiar, relationship between Spears and Jewry, this work has documented, though not exhaustively, occasions where many of the era's leading anti-Zionists (a list that includes, but is in no way limited to, Storrs, Stark, Guillaume, Longhurst and Toynbee) displayed an attitude that was derogatory to both Judaism and Jewry.

But more generally, the failure of Gentiles to work with the Jewish Fellowship was due to a lack of comprehension and a parallel suspicion, which could be most accurately described as prejudice against Jews as anti-Zionists, rather than prejudice against Jews as Jews. Fundamental to this situation was the contradiction that existed at the heart of the Jewish anti-Zionist position: its opposition to Zionism in the non-Jewish world out of a sense of Jewish duty and a desire to save Judaism.

One should remember Storrs' 1944 claim that not even an anti-

Zionist Jew could understand the Arab position. And it is perhaps the final irony that though the Fellowship never strayed from a virulent opposition to the creation of a Jewish state, and though it fought a ferocious battle with the Zionists inside the community of Jewry, its position on key issues such as the White Paper and free Jewish immigration into Palestine, proved Storrs correct.

Yet, in another sense Storrs' supposition explains only half the story. For if Jews, 'even anti-Zionist Jews', could never understand the Arab position, then equally, the relationship between the Fellowship, the CAA and the Arab Office shows that in the post-war era Gentile anti-Zionists could not fathom the fundamental Jewish anti-Zionist position: between Scylla and Charybdis indeed.

NOTES

1. See 'Is This the anti-Zionist case?', *Jewish Chronicle*, 8 June 1945, p. 10.
2. *Jewish Outlook*, 1: 7 (November 1946), p. 3.
3. This is the term used by Richard Bolchover to describe the assimilationist opposition to Zionism within Jewry in *British Jewry and the Holocaust* (Cambridge: Cambridge, University Press, 1993), p. 103.
4. Franklyn, 'Jewish Defence and the Jewish Fellowship', *Synagogue Review*, XIX: 9 (May 1945), p. 67.
5. *Jewish Outlook*, 1: 12 (May 1947), p. 2. Also see *Calling All Jews* (London, 1948) which asserted that it was the 'clear-sighted' members of Jewry who supported the Jewish Fellowship.

Bibliography

PRIMARY SOURCES

1. Archival Material

Archives of the Board of Deputies of British Jews:
Files ACC3121/C10–ACC3121/C20
Annual Reports of the Board of Deputies of British Jews, 1943–49
Statement on Post-war Policy on Palestine (November 1944)

BBC written archives, Reading:
Palestine Miscellaneous Correspondence A–Z 1939–48

Institute of Contemporary Jewry, Oral History Department, The Hebrew University of Jerusalem:
Project 2, 'Management of the Jewish Agency in London, 1938–1948'
Project 185, 'Zionism in England, 1917–1948'

Private Papers Collection, Middle East Centre, St Antony's College, Oxford:
Nevill Barbour papers
Estelle Blyth papers
Humphrey Bowman papers
Richard Crossman papers
Jerusalem and the East Mission papers
Miscellaneous file
Elizabeth Monroe papers
Edward Spears papers
Harry Philby papers
M. Philips Price papers
Hubert Young papers

Parkes Library, Special Collections Division, Hartley Library, University of Southampton:
Anglo-Jewish Association papers
Selig Brodetsky papers

Ivan Greenberg papers
Basil Henriques papers
Harold Reinhart papers

Pembroke College, Cambridge, Archives:
Ronald Storrs papers

Public Records Office, Kew:
Cabinet Papers: CAB 24
Foreign Office Papers: FO 371

Rhodes House Library, Oxford, Archives:
Fabian Colonial Bureau (FCBA) Papers, MSS Brit Emp.s. (365), Box 176, Palestine, 1935–48, files 1–7

Royal Institute of International Affairs, Chatham House, London, Archives:
Transcripts of General Meetings
Transcripts of Meetings of the Middle East Discussion Group

2. Official Documents

Cmd. 1700, *Correspondence with the Palestine Arab Delegation and the Zionist Organisation. And a Statement on British Policy on Palestine* (June: 1922)
Cmd. 3686, *The Hope-Simpson Report on Immigration, Land Settlement and Development* (October 1930)
Cmd. 5479, *Report of the Palestine Royal Commission* (July 1937)
Cmd. 5854, *The Palestine Partition Report* (October 1938)
Cmd. 6019, *Palestine: A Statement of Policy* (May 1939)
The Water Resources of Transjordan and their Development, Ionides, M.G., and Blake, G.S. (Amman: Government of Transjordan, Crown Agents for Colonies, 1939)
Survey Prepared in December 1945 and January 1946 for the Information of the Anglo-American Committee of Inquiry Regarding the Problems of European Jewry and Palestine (Jerusalem, 1946)
Report of the Anglo-American Committee of Inquiry Regarding the Problem of European Jewry and Palestine (May 1946)
Public Hearings of the Anglo-American Committee of Inquiry on Palestine and the Jewish Problem in Jerusalem, March 1946 (Jerusalem, 1946)

Official Reports 5th series, Parliamentary Debates, House of Commons:
1942–43, vols 385–93
1943–44, vols 396–406
1944–45, vols 407–12
1945–46, vols 413–29

1946–47, vols 430–42
1947–48, vols 443–56
1948–49, vols 457–71

3. Memoirs

Atiyah, E., *An Arab Tells his Story: A Study in Loyalties* (London: John Murray, 1946)
Bentwich, N., *My Seventy-Seven Years: An Account of My Life and Times, 1883–1960* (London: Routledge & Kegan Paul, 1962)
Berger, E., *Memoirs of an Anti-Zionist Jew* (Beirut: Institute for Palestine Studies, 1978)
Brodetsky, S., *From Ghetto to Israel: Memoirs of Selig Brodetsky* (London: Weidenfeld & Nicolson, 1960)
Brunel Cohen, J., *Count Your Blessings* (London: Heinemann, 1956)
Cohen, I., *A Jewish Pilgrimage: The Autobiography of Israel Cohen* (London: Vallentine Mitchell, 1956)
Crossman, R., *Palestine Mission: A Personal Record* (London: Hamish Hamilton, 1947)
Crum, B.C., *Behind the Silken Curtain* (New York: Simon & Schuster, 1947)
Henriques, B.L.Q., *The Indiscretions of a Warden* (London: Methuen, 1937)
Hourani, C., *An Unfinished Odyssey: Lebanon and Beyond* (London: Weidenfeld & Nicolson, 1984)
Loewe, L.L., *Basil Henriques: A Portrait* (London: Routledge & Kegan Paul, 1976)
McDonald, J.G., *My Mission in Israel, 1948–1951* (London: Victor Gollancz, 1951)
Meinertzhagen, R., *Middle East Diary, 1917–1956* (London: The Cresset Press, 1959)
Newton, F., *Fifty Years in Palestine* (Wrotham: Cold Harbour Press, 1948)
Spears, E.L., *Fulfilment of a Mission: The Spears Mission to Syria and Lebanon, 1941–1944* (London: Cooper, 1977)
Storrs, R., *Orientations* (3rd edn; London: Ivor Nicolson & Watson, 1937)
Tannous, I., *The Palestinians: A Detailed, Documented, Eye-witness History of Palestine under the Mandate* (New York: IGT, 1988)
Weizmann, C., *Trial and Error* (London: Hamish Hamilton, 1949)

4. Propaganda Pamphlets, Memoranda and Publications

Arab Office:
Arab News Bulletin
Atiyah, E., *Arab Rights and the British Left* (London, 1945)
——, *What was Promised in Palestine?* (London, 1945)
Guillaume, A., *Zionism and the Bible: A Criticism of the Establishment of an*

Independent Jewish State in Palestine as Prophesied in the Holy Scriptures (London, 1946)
Hourani, A., *Is Zionism the Solution to the Jewish Problem?* (London, June 1946)
Stace, W., *The Zionist Illusion* (Washington, 1947)
The Arab World and the Arab League (London, 1945)
The Problem of Palestine: Summary of the Arab Point of View (London, 1945)
Statement of the Present Arab Attitude Over Palestine (London, 30 July 1945)
The Secret History of the Balfour Declaration and the Mandate (London, 1945)
Partition (London, 1946)
The Future of Palestine (London, 1946)
Palestine: The Solution (London, 1947)

Committee for Arab Affairs:
Driver, G.R., *Palestine: The Historical Background* (London, 1945)
——, *Considerations on Palestine* (London, 1946)
Lipson, D., *Is Jewry a Nation?* (London, 1945)
Longhurst, H., *Britain, the Arabs and the Jews* (London, 1945)

English anti-Zionist:
Anglo-Arab Friendship Society, *The Truth about the Mufti* (London, 1946)
Barbour, N., *A Plan for a Lasting Peace in Palestine*, (London: PIC, 1938)
——, *Zionism, Palestine and the Jewish Problem* (Jerusalem, 1939)
——, *The Future of Palestine: How to Implement the White Paper* (London, 1939)
Beaumont, R. and Newcombe, S.F., *A Constitution for Palestine* (London, 1945)
Newcombe, S.F., *The Future of Palestine* (London, PIC, 1938)
Palestine Information Centre, *The Task of the Royal Commission: Has there Been a Breach of Faith?* (London, 1937)

Jewish anti-Zionist:
Hyamson, A.M., and Newcombe, S.F., *Suggested Basis for Discussion on Reaching an Agreement on Palestine* (London, 1937)
League of British Jews, *The Need for the League* (London, 1917)
Magnus, L., *Old Lamps for New: An Apologia for the League of British Jews* (London: League of British Jews, 1918)

Jewish Fellowship:
Brunel Cohen, J., *Address to the Jewish Fellowship Council* (London, 1945)
Henriques, B., *Statement to Fellowship Members* (London, 1946)
Henriques, B., and Marmorstein, A., *What is Judaism?* (London, 1945)
What the Fellowship Stands For (London, 1944)
A Challenge to All Jews (London, 1944)
The Constitution of the Jewish Fellowship (London, 1945)

Some Information for You: Confidential Memorandum (London, 1945)
Memorandum to the United Nations Commission on Palestine, as adopted at a JF Council Meeting (London, July 1947)
Memorandum on the Jewish Problem (London, 1947)
Calling All Jews (London, 1948)
Private and Confidential Memorandum (London, 1948)

Zionist:
Dugdale, B., *The Balfour Declaration: Origins and Background* (London: JA, 1942)
Feuer, L., *Why a Jewish State?* (London: APC Book Service, 1944)
Frankenstein, E., *An Open Letter to Rt Hon. Ernest Bevin, MP* (New York: American Zionist Emergency Council, 1945)
Goodman, P. (ed.), *The Jewish National Home: The Second November, 1917–1942* (London: ZF, 1943)
——, (ed.), *A Jubilee Record of the English Zionist Federation, 1899–1949* (London: ZF, 1949)
Goodman, P. and Lewis, A. (eds), *Zionism: Problems and Views* (London: ZO, 1916)
Heller, J., *The Zionist Idea* (London: ZF, 1945)
Hyamson, A.M., Sacher, H. and Simon, L. (eds), *Zionism and the Jewish Future* (London: ZO, 1916)
Jewish Agency, *Palestine, Land Settlement, Urban Development and Immigration: Memorandum Submitted to Sir John Hope-Simpson* (London, 1930)
——, *The MacDonald White Paper of 1939* (London, 1945)
——, *Political Report of the London Office of the Executive of the Jewish Agency, submitted to the 22nd Zionist Congress, Basle, 1946*
——, *Memorandum on the Position of the Jewish Communities in the Oriental Countries* (Jerusalem, 1947)
Jewish Dominion League, *Palestine and the British Commonwealth of Nations* (London, 1945)
Landman, S., *Zionism: Its Organisation and Institutions* (London: ZO, 1916)
Lewis, A., *Cosmopolitanism and Zionism* (London: ZF, 1919)
Parkes, J., *Palestine: Yesterday and Tomorrow* (London: British Association of the Jewish National Home, 1945)
Sacher, H., *Jewish Emancipation: The Contract Myth* (London: ZF, 1917)
Sidebotham. H., *British Policy and the Palestine Mandate: Our Proud Privilege: A Memorandum* (London, 1929)
Simon, L., *The Case Against the Anti-Zionists* (London: ZO, 1917)
Zionist Federation, *Arab v. Arab: The Inner Arab Terror in Palestine* (London, 1939)

——, *A Jewish State* (London, 1944)
——, *The Jewish Case against the White Paper* (London, 1945)
——, *Keep Faith with the Martyrs of Israel* (London, 1945)
Zionist Organisation, *Great Britain, Palestine and the Jews: A Survey of Christian Opinion* (London, 1918)

Anglo-Jewish journals and press:
Concord
Gates of Zion
Information Bulletin (WJC)
Jewish Chronicle
Jewish Forum
Jewish Monthly
Jewish Outlook
Jewish Telegraphic Agency, London: Daily News Bulletins
New Judea
Palcor News Agency
Palestine Information Bulletin (Jewish Agency)
Synagogue Review
TAC Bulletin (Trade Advisory Council)
Zionist Review

Newspapers and news agencies:
Arab News Agency, London
Daily Express
Daily Telegraph
Evening Standard
Manchester Guardian
News Review
New Statesman and Nation
Observer
Spectator
Sunday Express
Sunday Times
The Times
Wiener Library press cuttings collection
Yorkshire Post

SECONDARY MATERIAL

1. Books

Abcarius, M.F., *Palestine: Through the Fog of Propaganda* (London: Hutchinson, 1946)
Alderman, G., *The Jewish Community in British Politics* (Oxford: Clarendon Press, 1983)

——, *Modern British Jewry* (Oxford: Clarendon Press, 1992)
Antonius, G., *The Arab Awakening: The Story of the Arab National Movement* (London: Hamish Hamilton, 1938)
Atiyah, E., *The Arabs: The Origins, Present Conditions and Prospects of the Arab World* (London: Penguin, 1955)
Barbour, N., *Nisi Dominus: A Survey of Palestine* (London: Harrap, 1946)
Bermant, C., *The Cousinhood* (London: Eyre & Spottiswoode, 1971)
Black, E., *The Social Politics of Anglo-Jewry, 1880–1920* (Oxford: Basil Blackwell, 1988)
Bolchover, R., *British Jewry and the Holocaust* (Cambridge: Cambridge University Press, 1993)
Brailsford H.N. (ed.), *Palestine Controversy: A Symposium* (London: Fabian Publications and Victor Gollancz, 1945)
Bullock, A., *Ernest Bevin: Foreign Secretary 1945–1951* (London: Heinemann, 1983)
Caplan, N., *Futile Diplomacy, Vol. II: Arab–Zionist Negotiations and the End of the Palestine Mandate* (London: Frank Cass, 1986)
Cesarani, D., *The Jewish Chronicle and Anglo-Jewry* (Cambridge: Cambridge University Press, 1994)
Cohen, I., *The Progress of Zionism* (7th rev. edn; London: ZO, 1944)
Cohen, M., *Palestine and the Great Powers, 1945–1948* (Princeton, NJ: Princeton University Press, 1982)
——, (ed.), *The Rise of Israel, Vol. 35, The Anglo-American Committee on Palestine, 1945–1946* (New York, London: Garland, 1987)
Cohen, S., *English Zionists and British Jews: The Communal Politics of Anglo-Jewry, 1895–1920* (Princeton, NJ: Princeton University Press, 1982)
Egremont, M., *Under Two Flags: The Life of Major-General Sir Edward Spears* (London: Weidenfeld & Nicolson, 1997)
Englander, D. (ed.), *A Documentary History of Jewish Immigration in Britain, 1840–1920* (Leicester, London, New York: Leicester University Press, 1994)
Evensen, B., *Truman, Palestine and the Press: Shaping Conventional Wisdom at the Beginning of the Cold War* (New York: Greenwood Press, 1992)
Feldman, D., *Englishmen and Jews, Social Relations and Political Culture, 1840–1914* (New Haven and London: Yale University Press, 1994)
Furlonge, G., *Palestine is my Country: The Story of Musa Alami* (London: John Murray, 1969)
Gilman, S.L., *Jewish Self-Hatred: Anti-Semitism and the Hidden Language of the Jews* (Baltimore, London: Johns Hopkins University Press, 1986)
Golding, L., *The Jewish Problem* (London: Penguin, 1938)
Goren, A. (ed.), *Dissenter in Zion: From the Writings of Judah L. Magnes* (Cambridge, MA, and London: Harvard University Press, 1984)
Halpern, B., *The Idea of the Jewish State* (Cambridge, MA: Harvard University Press, 1961)

Hanna, P., *British Policy in Palestine* (Washington: American Council for Public Affairs, 1942)

Henriques, R., *Sir Robert Waley Cohen, 1877–1952* (London: Secker & Warburg, 1966)

Holmes, C., *Anti-Semitism in British Society, 1870–1939* (New York: Holmes & Meier, 1979)

Hope-Simpson, J., *The Refugee Problem: Report of a Survey* (London, New York, Toronto: Oxford University Press, 1939)

Hourani, A., *Great Britain and the Arab World* (London: John Murray, 1946)

——, *Syria and Lebanon: A Political Essay* (London: Oxford University Press, under the auspices of the RIIA, 1946)

Hurewitz, J.C., *The Struggle for Palestine* (New York: Norton, 1950)

Hyamson, A.M., *Palestine: A Policy* (London: Methuen, 1942)

——, *Palestine under the Mandate* (London: Methuen, 1950)

Ionides, M.G., *Divide and Lose: The Arab Revolt of 1955–1958* (London: Geoffrey Bles, 1960)

Izzard, M., *Freya Stark: A Biography* (London: Hodder & Stoughton, 1993)

Izzedin, N., *The Arab World: Past, Present and Future* (Chicago: Henry Regnery, 1953)

Jeffries, J.M.N., *The Palestine Deception: A Daily Mail Enquiry on the Spot* (London: Daily Mail, 1923)

——, *Palestine, the Reality* (London: Longmans Green, 1939)

Jones, M., *Failure in Palestine: British and United States Policy after the Second World War* (London: Mansell, 1985)

Kaplan, R.D., *The Arabists: The Romance of an Arab Elite* (New York: Free Press, 1993)

Katz, J., *Emancipation and Assimilation* (Westmead, Hants: Gregg International, 1972)

Kedourie, E., *In the Anglo-Arab Labyrinth: The McMahon–Husayn Correspondence and Interpretation, 1914–1939* (Cambridge: Cambridge University Press, 1976)

——, *The Chatham House Version and Other Middle Eastern Studies*, (London, Hanover, New Hampshire: University of New England, 1984)

Kershen, A.J. and Romain, J.A., *Tradition and Change: A History of Reform Judaism in Britain* (London: Vallentine Mitchell, 1995)

Kirk, G., *The Middle East in the War, 1939–1946* (London: Oxford University Press, under the auspices of the RIIA, Survey of International Affairs, 1950)

——, *The Middle East, 1945–1950* (London: Oxford University Press, under the auspices of the RIIA, Survey of International Affairs, 1954)

Kolsky, T., *Jews Against Zionism: The American Council for Judaism, 1942–1948* (Philadelphia: Temple University Press, 1990)

Kushner, T. (ed.), *Jewish Heritage in British History: Englishness and Jewishness* (London: Frank Cass, 1992)

Levenberg, S., *The Jews and Palestine: A Study in Labour Zionism* (London: Poale Zion, 1945)
Lilienthal, A., *What Price Israel?* (Chicago: Henry Regnery, 1954)
Lipman, V.D., *Social History of the Jews in England, 1850–1950* (London: Watts, 1954)
Louis, W.R. and Stooky, R. (eds), *The End of the Palestine Mandate* (London: Tauris, 1985)
Maugham, R., *Approach to Palestine* (London: Falcon Press, 1947)
Mayhew, C. and Adams, M., *Publish it Not: The Middle East Cover-up* (Harlow: Longman, 1975)
Montefiore, C.C., *Race, Nation, Religion and the Jew* (Keighley: Rydal Press, 1918)
Moorehead, C., *Freya Stark* (London: Viking, 1985)
Moorehead, L. (ed.), *Freya Stark, Letters: New Worlds for Old, 1943–1946* (London: Compton Russell, 1986)
Nachmani, A., *Great Power Discord in Palestine: The Anglo-American Committee of Inquiry into the Problems of European Jewry and Palestine, 1945–1946* (London: Frank Cass, 1986)
Namier, L., *Facing East* (London: Hamish Hamilton, 1947)
Ovendale, R., *Britain, the United States and the End of the Palestine Mandate* (Woodbridge: RHS/Boydell Press, 1989)
Parkes, J., *Emergence of the Jewish Problem, 1889–1939* (London: Oxford University Press, under the auspices of the RIIA, 1946)
Podet, A.H., *The Success and Failure of the Anglo-American Committee of Inquiry, 1945–46: The Last Chance in Palestine* (Lewiston and Queenston: Edwin Mellon Press, 1986)
Rose, N. (ed.), *Baffy: The Diaries of Blanche Dugdale, 1936–1947* (London: Frank Cass, 1973)
——, *The Gentile Zionists: A Study in Anglo-Zionist Diplomacy, 1929–1939* (London: Frank Cass, 1973)
——, *Lewis Namier and Zionism* (Oxford: Clarendon Press, 1980)
Sacher, H., *Zionist Portraits and Other Essays* (London: Anthony Blond, 1959)
Sherman, A.J., *Island Refuge: Britain and the Refugees from the Third Reich, 1933–1939* (London: Elek, 1973)
Shimoni, G., *The Zionist Ideology* (Hanover, London: Brandeis University Press, 1995)
Sidebotham, H., *Great Britain and Palestine* (London: Macmillan, 1937)
Sokolow, N., *History of Zionism, 1600–1919*, 2 vols (New York: Longmans, 1919)
Spears, E.L., *Two Men Who Saved France* (London: Eyre & Spottiswoode, 1966)
——, *Assignment to Catastrophe*, 2 vols (London: Heinemann, 1954)
Stark, F., *East is West* (London: John Murray, 1945)
Stein, L., *The Balfour Declaration* (London: Vallentine Mitchell, 1961)

Sykes, C., *Crossroads to Israel* (London: Collins, 1965)
Toynbee, A., *A Study of History,* Vol. VIII (London, New York, Toronto: Oxford University Press, under the auspices of the RIIA, 1954)
Tuchman, B., *Bible and Sword: How the British Came to Palestine* (London: Papermac, 1988)
Vital, D., *Origins of Zionism* (Oxford: Clarendon Press, 1975)
——, *Zionism, Vol. 2, The Formative Years* (Oxford: Clarendon Press, 1982)
——, *Zionism, Vol. 3, The Crucial Phase* (Oxford: Clarendon Press, 1987)
Wasserstein, B., *The British in Palestine: The Mandatory Government and the Arab–Jewish Conflict, 1917–1929* (Oxford: Basil Blackwell, 1990)
Ziff, W., *The Rape of Palestine* (New York, Toronto: Longmans Green, 1938)
Zurayk, C., *The Meaning of the Disaster* (Beirut: Khayyat, 1956, trans. R. Bailly Winder)
Zweig, R., *Britain and Palestine during the Second World War* (London: Royal Historical Society, 1986)

2. Monographs

Henriques, B., *What Is Judaism?* (London: St George's Settlement Synagogue, 1945)
Henriques, B. and Marmorstein, A., *The Religion of the Jew* (Leicester: Newry Welsey, n.d.)
Hope-Simpson, J., *Refugees: A Review of the Situation Since September 1938* (London: Oxford University Press, under the auspices of the RIIA, 1939)
Mattuck, I., *What are the Jews? Their Significance and Position in the Modern World* (London: Hodder & Stoughton, 1939)
Storrs, R., *Palestine and Zionism* (London: Penguin, 1940)
Wasserstein, B., *Wyndham Deedes in Palestine* (London: Anglo-Israel Association, 1973)

3. Articles

Alami, M., 'The Lessons of Palestine', *Middle East Journal*, 3: 4 (October 1949), pp. 373–405
Anon. (Nevill Barbour), 'Palestine: The Commission's Task', *Round Table*, XXVII: 105 (December 1936), pp. 79–94
Anon., 'The Repercussions of Zionism in Britain', *World Affairs*, I: 2 (April 1947), pp. 121–30
Atiyah, E., 'The Arab League', *World Affairs*, I: 1 (January 1947), pp. 34–7
——, 'Palestine', *Contemporary Review*, CLXXIV: 991 (July 1948), pp. 4–8
Barbour, N., 'Some Less Familiar Aspects of the Palestine Problem', *Journal of Royal Central Asian Society*, XXV: 4 (October 1938), pp. 554–70
——, 'England and the Arabs', *Journal of Royal Central Asian Society*, LII: 2 (April 1965), pp. 102–15

Bayme, S., 'Claude Montefiore, Lily Montagu and the Origins of the Jewish Religious Union', *Jewish Historial Studies, Transactions of the Jewish Historical Society of England*, XXVII (1978–80), pp. 61–71

Beeley, H., 'The Middle East in 1939 and 1944', *Journal of Royal Central Asian Society*, XXXII: 1 (January 1945), pp. 7–23

Black, E., 'Edwin Montagu', *Jewish Historical Studies, Transactions of the Jewish Historical Society of England*, XXX (1987–88), pp. 199–218

Cesarani, D., 'Anti-Zionist Politics and Political Antisemitism in Britain, 1920–1924', *Patterns of Prejudice*, 23: 1 (1989), pp. 28–45

Cohen, E., 'The Errors of the Jewish Fellowship', *Synagogue Review*, XIX: 11 (July 1945), pp. 82–4

Cohen, I., 'The Palestine Problem', *Contemporary Review*, CLXIX: 961 (January 1946), pp. 14–19

Cohen, M., 'The Genesis of the Anglo-American Committee on Palestine, November 1945: A Case-Study on the Assertion of American Hegemony', *Historical Journal*, 22: 1 (January 1979), pp. 186–207

Cohen, S., 'The Conquest of the Community? The Zionists and the Board of Deputies in 1917', *Jewish Journal of Sociology*, XIX: 2 (December 1977), pp. 157–84

——, 'Sources in Israel for the Study of Anglo-Jewish History: an Interim Report', *Transactions of the Jewish Historical Society of England*, XXVII (1978–80), Miscellaneous, Part XII, pp. 129–47

——, 'Selig Brodetsky and the Ascendancy of Zionism in Anglo-Jewry: Another View of his Role and Achievements', *Jewish Journal of Sociology*, XXIV: 1 (June 1982), pp. 25–38

——, 'Ideological Components in Anglo-Jewish Opposition to Zionism Before and During the First World War: A Restatement', *Jewish Historical Studies, Transactions of the Jewish Historical Society of England*, XXX (1987–88), pp. 149–62

——, 'How Shall we Sing of Zion in a Strange Land? East European Immigrants and the Challenge of Zionism in Britain, 1897–1918', *Jewish Social Studies*, 1 (new series): 2 (winter 1995), pp. 101–22

Dajani, B., 'National Movements for Freedom in India and Palestine', *India Quarterly*, III: 1 (January–March 1947), pp. 135–43

Deedes, W., Royden-Shaw, M. and Storrs, R., 'The Future of Palestine', *The Listener*, XXXIV: 877 (1 November, 1945), pp. 479–95

Deighton, H.S., 'The Arab Middle East and the Modern World', *International Affairs*, XXII: 4 (October 1946), pp. 511–20

Finestein, I., 'Changes in Authority in Anglo-Jewry since the 1930s: A Critical View', *Jewish Quarterly*, 32: 2 (118) (1985), pp. 33–7

Franklyn, J., 'Jewish Defence and the Jewish Fellowship', *Synagogue Review*, XIX: 9 (May 1945), pp. 66–7

——, 'Israel: State or Religion?', *Contemporary Review*, CLXXII: 979 (July 1947), pp. 35–9

Gibb, H.A.R., 'Towards Arab Unity', *Foreign Affairs*, 24: 1 (October 1945), pp. 119–29
Glubb, J.B., 'Britain and the Arabs', *Journal of Royal Central Asian Society*, XLVI: 3 (July 1959), pp. 232–41
Henriques, R., 'Unity and Expedience', *Jewish Monthly*, 1: 2 (May 1947), pp. 9–15
Himmelfarb, M., 'Anti-Zionism as Ideology', *Commentary*, 17: 2 (November 1954), pp. 194–6
Hocking, W., 'Arab Nationalism and Political Zionism', *Moslem World*, XXXV: 3 (July 1945), pp. 216–23
Hope-Simpson, J., 'The Palestine Mandate', *Fortnightly*, CLVI (December 1944), pp. 341–9
——, 'The Palestine Statement', *Fortnightly*, CLIX (January 1946), pp. 21–7
——, 'The Jewish World since 1939: A Comment on Dr. James Parkes' Paper', *International Affairs*, XXI: 1 (January 1945), pp. 100–5
Hurewitz, J.C., 'Recent Books on Palestine', *Middle East Journal*, 3: 1 (January 1949), pp. 86–91
Hyamson, A.M., 'The Problem of Palestine', *Contemporary Review*, CLXXIV: 952 (April 1945), pp. 221–6
Ionides, M.G., 'Water Development in Palestine and Transjordan', *Journal of Royal Central Asian Society*, XXXIII: 3 (July 1946), pp. 271–80
——, 'Irrigation in Palestine; A Key to Economic Absorptive Capacity', *World Today*, III: 2 (April 1947), pp. 188–98
Issawi, C., 'The Arab World's Heavy Legacy', *Foreign Affairs*, 43: 3 (April 1965), pp. 501–12
Kochavi, A.J., 'The Displaced Persons Problem and the Formulation of British Policy in Palestine', *Studies in Zionism*, 10: 1 (spring 1989), pp. 31–48
Laqueur, W., 'Zionism and its Liberal Critics, 1896–1948', *Journal of Contemporary History*, 6 (1971), pp. 161–82
Leftwich, J., 'Are we a Philistine Community?', *Jewish Monthly*, 1: 9 (December 1947), pp. 11–23
Levene, M., 'Lucien Wolf: Crypto-Zionist, Anti-Zionist or Opportunist *Par Excellence*?', *Studies in Zionism*, 12: 2 (autumn 1991), pp. 133–48
Levy, S., 'Zionism and Liberal Judaism', *Jewish Forum*, 1: 1 (October 1946), pp. 88–96
Lewin-Papanek, M., 'Psychological Aspects of Minority Group Membership: The Concepts of Kurt Lewin', *Jewish Social Studies*, XXXVI: 1 (January 1974), pp. 72–9
Marmorstein, E., 'Religious Opposition to Nationalism in the Middle East', *International Affairs*, XXVIII: 3 (July 1952), pp. 334–59
——, 'European Jews in Muslim Palestine', *Middle Eastern Studies*, 11: 1 (January 1975), pp. 74–87
Mattuck, I., 'The Jews' Problem', *Liberal Jewish Monthly*, 15: 7 (July 1944)

Montefiore, L., 'B.L.Q.H.', *Jewish Monthly*, 1: 8 (November 1947), pp. 9–11
Morris, C.J., 'The Labour Government's Policy and Publicity over Palestine, 1945–1947', in *Contemporary British History, 1931–1961: Politics and the Limits of Policy*, eds Gort, A. and Lucas, W. (London: Institute for Contemporary History, 1992)
Morrison, S.A., 'Arab Nationalism', *Middle East Journal*, 2: 2 (April 1948), pp. 147–59
Ovendale, R., 'The Palestine Policy of the British Labour Government in 1947: The Decision to Withdraw', *International Affairs*, LVI: 1 (January 1980), pp. 73–93
Parkes, J., 'The Jewish World since 1939', *International Affairs*, XXI: 1 (January 1945), pp. 87–100
Perret, M., 'The Arab League and World', *Contemporary Review*, CLXXX: 1020 (August 1951), pp. 84–6
Philby, H. St J.B., 'The Arabs and the Future of Palestine', *Foreign Affairs*, 16: 1 (October 1937), pp. 156–66
Reid, T., 'Should a Jewish State be Established in Palestine?', *Journal of Royal Central Asian Society*, XXXIII: 2 (April 1946), pp. 27–42
Riebenfeld, P., 'The Politics of the Unpolitical Zionists', *Jewish Forum*, 1: 1 (October 1946), pp. 34–46
Roosevelt, K., 'The Partition of Palestine', *Middle East Journal*, 2: 1 (January 1948), pp. 1–16
Roth, C., 'The Collapse of Anglo-Jewry', *Jewish Monthly*, 1: 4 (July 1947), pp. 11–17
Royden-Shaw, M., 'Arab Palestine', *Newsletter*, 7: 8 (August 1944), pp. 233–6
Sharot, S., 'Reform and Liberal Judaism in London, 1840–1940', *Jewish Social Studies*, XLI: 3–4 (summer–fall 1979), pp. 211–28
Shimoni, G., 'Selig Brodetsky and the Ascendancy of Zionism in Anglo-Jewry, 1939–1945', *Jewish Journal of Sociology*, XXII: 2 (December 1980), pp. 125–62
——, 'From Anti-Zionism to Non-Zionism in Anglo-Jewry, 1917–1937', *Jewish Journal of Sociology*, XXVIII: 1 (June 1986), pp. 19–47
——, 'The Non-Zionists in Anglo-Jewry, 1937–1948', *Jewish Journal of Sociology*, XXVIII: 2 (December 1986), pp. 89–115
Soref, H., 'They were Ringing the Bells', *Jewish Monthly*, 1: 11 (February 1948), pp. 8–18
Spears, E.L., 'The Middle East and our Policy There', *Journal of Royal Central Asian Society*, XXXII: 2 (April 1945), pp. 156–65
——, 'The Path to Arab Unity', *Great Britain and the East*, LXI: 1746 (April 1945), pp. 72–6
Stansky, P., 'Anglo-Jew or English/British? Some Dilemmas of Anglo-Jewish History', *Jewish Social Studies*, 2: 1 (Fall 1995), pp. 159–79
Toynbee, A., 'Jewish Rights in Palestine', *Jewish Quarterly Review*, LII: 1 (July 1961), pp. 1–11

——, 'Britain and the Arabs: The Need for a New Start', *International Affairs*, XL: 4 (October 1964), pp. 638–46
Wasserstein, B., 'Clipping the Claws of the Colonisers: Arab Officials in the Government of Palestine, 1917–1948', *Middle Eastern Studies*, 13: 2 (May 1977), pp. 171–94
Weber, G., 'The Present Position of Anglo-Jewry', *Jewish Forum*, 1: 1 (October 1946), pp. 75–85
Williams, K., 'The Arab League', *Fortnightly*, CLXIV (November 1948), pp. 302–6
——, 'Are the British and Arabs in Step?', *Great Britain and the East*, LXI: 1744 (February 1945), pp. 35–7
Wistrich, R.S., 'Zionism and its Jewish "Assimilationist" Critics (1897–1948)', *Jewish Social Studies*, new series, 4 : 2 (winter 1998), pp. 59–112
Wolf, L., 'The Zionist Peril', *Jewish Quarterly Review*, XVII: 3 (October 1904), pp. 1–25
——, 'The Jewish National Movement', *Edinburgh Review*, 225: 460 (April 1917), pp. 1–17
Woolbert, R.G., 'Pan Arabism and the Palestine Problem', *Foreign Affairs*, 16: 2 (January 1938), pp. 309–22
Zollschan, I., 'The Arabian Race of Palestine: The Facts', *Jewish Forum*, 1: 1 (October 1946), pp. 46–51

4. Unpublished PhD theses

Leifer, M., 'Zionism and Palestine in British Opinion and Policy, 1945–1949' (University of London, 1959)
Stellman, H., 'The Ideology of anti-Zionism 1881 to the Present Day' (University of London, 1982)

Index

Abcarius, M.F., 31, 48, 58, 67, 126, 127
Abrahams, Sir Lionel, 98
Abrahams, Robert, 114
Afnan, Bedia, 15
Agudath Yisra'el, 6–7, 19 n6, 94, 114, 250
al-Ahram, 25, 31
al-Alami, Musa, 15, 183; and the Arab Office, 195–6, 199, 201, 206–7, 236
Alexandria, 15
Altounyan, Lieutenant-Colonel, E.H.R., 149
Altrincham, Lord, *see also* Sir Edward Grigg, 27, 42, 46, 127, 146
American Council for Judaism (ACJ), 158–60, 180–1, 198
American Geophysical Union, 34
American University of Beirut, 12
Angell, Sir Norman, 228
Anglo-American Committee on Palestine and the Jewish Problem (Anglo-American Committee, AACIP) (1946), 32, 35, 39, 40–3, 46, 48, 61, 65, 66–7, 75–6, 85, 92–3, 96, 100, 107, 109–10, 112, 126, 128, 136, 143, 148, 160, 163, 168–9, 196, 201, 203, 207, 216, 218, 220, 222–3; Report of, 223–31
Anglo-Arab Association, 18, 29–30, 31, 170, 204, 206, 210, 240
Anglo-Arab Friendship Society, 18
Anglo-Jewish Association (AJA), 6–7, 92, 106, 114, 121, 137, 149, 250; non-Zionism of, 9
Anglo-Jewry, 25, 77, 83, 104, 108, 112, 136–7, 143, 173, 197, 199, 221, 239
Anti-Semitism, 82, 183–5, 229, 250
Antonius, George, 27, 69
Arabs, 24
Arab Centre, 10, 12–13, 16, 18, 156
Arab Centre Bulletin, 13–14
Arab Charter for Palestine, 13–14
Arab Club, 25–6, 43
Arab Higher Committee, 12, 20 n22, 129, 216
Arab Labour Union of Jaffa, 12
Arab League, 2, 15, 26, 30, 60, 76, 98, 193–4, 197–8, 240
Arab Listener, 32
Arab News Bulletin, 11, 122, 132, 184, 196, 198, 203–6, 208, 236
Arab Office, 1–2, 5, 36, 64, 77, 127, 139, 156, 184, 193, 195–6, 216, 230–1, 238, 240, 247; and Committee for Arab Affairs, 4, 125, 199–211, 215, 235, 239–40, 246–7, 251; antecedents of, 10; as propaganda body, 11, 32; and Anglo-American Committee, 41; on Balfour Declaration, 98; claim Jews a religious community not state, 122–3; and dual loyalty charge, 132–3; and Albert Hourani, 134, 197–9; comparison of Zionism to Nazism, 147–8; and anti-Semitism, 183–4; in Washington, 183, 195, 198; and Sir Edward Spears, 194–6, 199–211, 246; and Jewish Fellowship, 196, 199, 239, 246, 251; and Jewish anti-Zionists, 196–200; and White Paper, 224–5; and Report of Anglo-American Committee, 224–5, 231; and Jewish immigration into Palestine, 238–9
Arab Revolt, 13, 20 n22, 58, 216
Aron, Major Wellesly, 65
Archbishop of York *see also* Cyril Garbett, 55, 181
Aronsfeld, C.C., 141, 183
Ashbee, C.R., 13
Association of Synagogues of Great Britain, 89
Astor, Lord, 210
Atiyah, Edward, 15, 32, 69, 77, 247; and Arab Office, 193, 195–7, 200–2, 204, 208, 210; and Sir Ronald Storrs, 210–11; and the Anglo-American Committee, 224–5; and Jewish

immigration into Palestine, 234, 238–9, 241
Aufheuser, Siegfried, 166, 188 n43
Australia, 174
Azzam Bey, Abd al-Rahman, *see also* Azzam Pasha, 30, 47

Baillie, Major G.W.G., 29, 30, 140, 204
Bakstansky, Lavy, 97, 104, 108–10, 222
Balfour Declaration (2 November 1917), 1, 8, 61, 67, 74, 84, 97–8, 121, 125–6, 130, 196, 234
Balfour, Lord, 55
Barbour, Nevill, 13, 17, 28, 30, 31, 55, 57–8, 61, 70, 122–3, 156–7, 160–1, 175, 183, 187 n3, 194–5, 217, 235, 240
Bazzaz, Abdur-Rahman, 12
Bearsted, Viscount, 6, 158
Beaumont, Ralph, 17, 25, 28, 76, 160, 175
Bee, John, 30
Beeley, Harold, 25, 182, 228
Beirut, 17
Beloff, Max, 173, 188 n50
Belsen, 136, 142
Ben-Gurion, David, 4 n1, 156
Bennett, Sir Ernest, 11, 58
Bennet, John, 16, 193
Bentwich, Norman, 77, 174, 230
Berger, Rabbi Elmer, 181
Bernard Baron Settlement, 90
Bevin, Ernest (Foreign Secretary 1945–51), 41, 46, 111, 138, 206, 216, 224, 230, 232
Biltmore Declaration (May 1942), 1, 4 n1, 6, 9, 130–1
Blyth, Estelle, 11
Board of Deputies of British Jews, 61, 84, 92, 97–8, 111–12, 121, 225, 230, 239; the Jewish Fellowship at, 103–11, 113, 130, 134, 144, 164–5, 222, 234, 250
Borden, Mary, 205
Bowman, Humphrey, 69
Bradford and Sinai Synagogue, 88
Britain, 23, 24, 40, 55, 129, 135, 168, 222, 228, 231
British Broadcasting Corporation (BBC), 73; Nevill Barbour and, 31–2
British Embassy, Warsaw, 138
British Embassy, Washington, 193
Brodetsky, Professor Selig, 61, 89, 104, 106, 108, 111, 113, 116 n28, 126, 135, 162–3, 170–1, 176–7, 225
Broido, Ephraim, 35

Brotmacher, David, 110
Burrows, Bernard, 87
Bustani, Emile, 167
Buxton, Frank, 66

Cairo, 26, 82, 146, 206; Minister of State's Office in, 15
Callan, Norman, 63
Canada, 157–8
Carvahlo, Robert, 106
Cassell, Rabbi Curtis, 88–9, 169
Cecil, Lord Robert, 103
Central British Fund, 136
Central Intelligence Agency (CIA), 180
Central Jewish Lecture Committee, 221
Central Synagogue Council of the Zionist Federation, 91
Chief Rabbi of Poland, 138
Chief Rabbi's Religious Emergency Council, 137
Chatham House *see also* Royal Institute of International Affairs, 23, 36, 61, 206, 208, 210
Cherrick, Revd Bernard, 77
Churchill, Winston, 16, 23
Clayton, Brigadier Iltyd, 26, 206
Coghill, Patrick, 184
Cohen, Dr Ernst, 85
Cohen, Israel, 62, 67
Cohen, Sir Jack Brunel, 5–6, 89, 92, 159, 169, 241; as Fellowship publicist, 95–7, 100, 101, 112, 124; at the Middle East Parliamentary Committee, 161–3, 165, 171, 177, 218–19, 222; and White Paper, 218; and Zionist propaganda, 233
Cohen, Sir Leonard Lionel, 89, 159; first Jewish Lord Justice, 5
Cohen, Maurice, 87
Cohen, Percy, 106
Colonial Office, 44, 139, 193
Committee for Arab Affairs (CAA), 1, 5, 16, 25, 26, 29, 38, 63, 73, 76, 125, 131, 165, 168–9, 175, 195, 240; as forum for anti-Zionist propaganda, 3, 27–8, 33–4, 55, 185; and Jewish Fellowship, 4, 171, 182, 210, 239, 247–8, 251; and Arab Office, 4, 171, 182, 199–211, 215, 235, 239–40, 246–7, 251; Sir Edward Spears and, 31, 194, 246; antecedents of, 10; and Nevill Barbour, 13, 32; as pro-Arab body, 27; influence on Parliament, 34; and Anglo-American Committee, 41–3; and debate

on dual loyalty, 132–3; and rehabilitation of Jews in Europe, 139–41; and Report of the Anglo-American Committee, 225–9; and Jewish Refugees in England, 230–3
Committee for Justice and Peace in the Holy Land, 179–81
Conjoint Committee of the Board of Deputies *see also* Joint Foreign Committee, 97, 117 n76
Contemporary Review, 145–6
Cornwallis, Sir Kinahan, 28
Council for the Advancement of Arab British Understanding (CAABU), 10, 240
Council News, 180
Cragg, F.S., 204
Cromer, Earl of, 42
Crook, Mary, 199
Crossman, Richard, 46, 65, 75, 160, 185, 207–8, 233
Crum, Bartley, 65, 203

Daily Mail, 13, 38, 121, 141
Daily Telegraph, 24, 29, 60, 169
Dajani, Burhan, 15
Dallyi, Abdul Ghani, 12
Damascus, 17
Daoudi, Awni, 12
Dartle, Isaac, 99
Davidson, Sir Nigel, 200, 225
Deedes, Sir Wyndham, 69, 73–4, 235–6
Diaspora, 82, 122
Driver, Professor G.R., 36, 41–2, 44–5, 46, 48, 55, 59, 128, 232
Drower, Lady, 29,
Drummond Shiels, T., 169,
Dual Loyalty, 3, 129–36
Dugdale, Mrs Edgar (Blanche), 55, 60–1, 63, 66, 135, 148–9
Dunn, Philip, 194

Easterman, Alexander, 104, 109
Eban, Aubrey (Abba), 58, 205
Edinburgh Review, 95
Egremont, Max, 184
Egypt, 16, 197
Eisler, Dr Robert, 197–8
Elphinston, W.G., 29, 208
Elsworth, E.W., 170
England, 23, 84, 158, 166, 206, 226–9, 231; Arab cause in, 29, 159–60, 166, 234
Erskine, Mrs Steuart, 11, 13

Evening Standard, 68

Fabian Colonial Bureau, 64–5, 169
Faisal, Emir, 13
Federation of Synagogues, 162
Ferguson Craig, H., 200
First World War, 16, 17, 98
Foreign Office, 44, 138, 159, 193, 206, 228
France, 16, 24, 186
Franklyn, Julian, 87, 112, 144–6, 149–50, 164–5, 171, 174, 176, 181, 218, 224, 249
Freeden, Herbert, 61
Freud, Sigmund, 135
Friedman, Benjamin, 129, 173

Garbett, Dr Cyril, *see also* Archbishop of York, 55
Gates of Zion, 90, 92, 135
Gaulle, Charles de, 17, 23, 185
Gentile anti-Zionism, 10, 18, 66
Gentile Zionists, 37
Germany, 17, 88, 137, 142, 230
Ghoury, Emile, 11, 12
Gibb, Professor H.A.R., 25, 49 n27, 194, 208
Gildersleeve, Virginia, 179
Glasgow Jewish Institute, 96
Gledhill, Henry, 91
Glubb, Lieutenant-General Sir John, 25, 61
Gluckstein, Colonel Louis, 6, 89–90, 97, 106, 112, 113, 159, 182; at the Board of Deputies, 108–11, 130, 143–5, 160, 163–4, 168; and the Middle East Parliamentary Committee, 175–6; and the White Paper, 219, 222–3, 248–9
Golding, Louis, 229
Goldmann, Nahum, 51 n69
Goldstein, William, 19
Gollancz, Victor, 37
Goodman, Paul, 89, 91, 102
Graf, Rabbi Gerhard, 88–9
Great Britain, 29
Greek Refugee Board Settlement Commission, 229
Greenberg, Ivan, 33, 58–9, 74, 99–101, 142, 149–50
Grigg, Sir Edward see also Lord Altrincham, 27, 146
Grunis, H., 91
Guillaume, Revd Dr Alfred, 17, 28, 41, 55, 127, 205, 226–7, 250

Haganah, 149
Haifa, 197
Haining, General Sir Robert, 45
Hale, William, 158
Hall, George, 105
Halpern, Ben, 8
Hamabit (pseud.), 59, 164, 173
Hammersley, S.S., 62, 162–3, 170, 218, 221
Hardman, Revd Leslie, 142
Heller, Joseph, 134, 228
Henriques, Basil, 5, 88–9, 92–3, 101, 107, 113, 143, 167; as warden of Bernard Baron St George's Jewish Settlement, 5, 90; as magistrate in Juvenile cases, 5; as Fellowship publicist, 91; on Liberal Judaism and Zionism, 93–4; at the Board of Deputies, 108–9, 234; at the Middle East Parliamentary Committee, 112, 161–3, 165, 171, 218–19, 222; and the charge of dual loyalty, 130; and Sir Edward Spears, 171, 176; and Arab Office, 199; and White Paper, 218, 223
Henriques, Colonel Robert, 89–90, 95, 100, 106, 108, 112, 124, 196, 240–1; and Jewish immigration into Palestine, 235–7
Henriques, Rose, 110, 136, 174
Herzog, Chief Rabbi Isaac, 216
Hewitt, Professor R., 64
Hinden, Rita, 65
Hirschman, Albert O., 227
Histadrut, 70
Hitler, Adolf, 83, 123–4
Hocking, William, 122
Hodson, H.V., 57
Holocaust, 7, 40, 83–4, 135, 137, 141–3, 226, 230
Hope-Simpson, Sir John, 31, 33–4, 38, 41–2, 44, 55, 56–7, 61, 70, 76–7, 123–4, 128, 131, 140, 194, 227, 232, 235; and Jewish anti-Zionists, 165–6, 168
Hourani, Albert, 15, 69, 240, 247; and Arab Office, 134, 197–9, 203, 206–10, 218; and Report of the Anglo-American Committee, 225–6, 231
Hourani, Cecil, 15, 129; and Arab Office, 198, 207
House of Commons, 17, 29, 45, 131
House of Lords, 29
House of Representatives, Foreign Affairs Committee of, 35
al-Husseini, Al-Hajj Muhammad Amin, see Mufti of Jerusalem, 10
al-Husseini, Jamal, 57, 129
al-Husseini, Musa, 12
Hutchinson, Judge Joseph C., 207
Hyamson, Albert, 69, 107, 144, 156–7, 159, 161, 166, 168, 174; and Sir Ronald Storrs, 172–3; and Sir Edward Spears, 178–9, 182; and the White Paper, 219–20, 248

Ichud, 182
International Affairs, 123–4
Ionides, Michael, 29, 39–40, 42, 44, 63, 227, 240, 247; and Arab Office, 205; and White Paper, 217
Iraq, 197, 200
Isaacs, Sir Isaac, 174
Israel, State of, 1, 10, 113, 123, 128, 132, 166, 239–40
Issawi, Charles, 15
Izzedin, Najla, 15, 198

Jackson, J. Hampden, 59
Jacobson, Lionel, 19
Janner, Barnett, 86, 96, 109
Jeffreys, Major-General Sir George, 28
Jeffries, J.M.N., 11; as correspondent of *Daily Mail*, 13, 28, 121
Jerusalem, 34, 40, 207; Arab Office in, 15, 206, 224; Bishop of the Church of England in, 126; Anglo-American Committee in, 225
Jerusalem and East Mission, 200
Jews' College, 91
Jewish Agency, 9, 58, 60, 62, 64, 70, 92, 105–6, 107, 131, 216
Jewish Brigade, 95, 100–1, 124, 196
Jewish Chronicle, 25, 33, 58–9, 60, 66, 67, 74, 76, 90, 92, 93, 96, 218, 221, 223, 237–8; and the Jewish Fellowship, 99–102, 107, 125, 137, 142, 149, 163–4, 173, 184, 200, 249
Jewish Committee for Relief Abroad, 136–7
Jewish Dominion League, 62, 74
Jewish Fellowship (Fellowship or JF), 1, 5, 77, 82, 95, 156, 164, 239, 241; giving credibility to Gentile anti-Zionists 3; relationship with Arab Office and Committee for Arab Affairs, 4, 16, 170, 182, 196, 210, 215, 239, 247–8, 251; in Anglo-Jewry, 6, 111–14; product of Jewish emancipation, 7–8; as successor

to League of British Jews, 9; at the Anglo-American Committee, 41, 233–4; and anti-Zionist propaganda, 85–7; and Liberal Judaism, 87–94; and *Jewish Chronicle*, 99–102; and the Board of Deputies, 103–11; argument that Jewry a religion not a nation, 123–5; and charge of dual loyalty, 129–32; and rehabilitation of Jews in Europe, 136–42; claim that Zionism was successor to Nazism, 142–50; and the American Council for Judaism, 158–60; at the Middle East Parliamentary Committee, 161–3, 171; relationship with Sir Edward Spears, 164–5, 176, 179–81, 183, 185–7, 194, 246; annual meetings of, 177; and White Paper, 218–23, 248; and Report of the Anglo-American Committee, 224–5; and Zionist propaganda, 233–5; and Jewish immigration into Palestine, 235–7, 240–1, 248

Jewish Forum, 135
Jewish Freeland League, 227
Jewish Guardian, 8
Jewish Labour Committee, 141
Jewish Literary Society, 249
Jewish Monthly, 92, 137
Jewish National Home, 25, 59, 159, 216
Jewish Opinion, 8
Jewish Outlook, 89, 92, 95, 102, 105, 113, 123, 127, 129, 130, 138, 141, 145, 160, 177, 180, 196, 198, 219, 224, 233, 249–50
Jewish refugees, 24
Jewish Telegraphic Agency, 60, 65
Joint Foreign Committee, *see also* Conjoint Committee of the Board of Deputies, 106, 117 n76
Joint Palestine Appeal (JPA), 85,

Kablivatsky, Julian, 197
Kedourie, Elie, 4 n2, 208
Keeling, E.H., 17, 45, 163
Keen, Dr B.A., 39
Keith Roach, Edward, 68
Keren Hayesod *see also* Palestine Foundation Fund, 35
Khairi, Khulusi, 15
Khalidi, H.F., 39
Khalidi, Walid, 15
Khazars, 128–9, 134
al-Khouri, Faris, 129

Killearn, Lord (Sir Miles Lampson), 16
King Sinusi of Libya, 12
Kirk, George, 27, 36
Kirsch, Dr L., 19
Koestler, Arthur, 151 n39
Kolsky, Thomas, 158

Labovitch, Mark, 19
Labour Party, 45–6, 177
Landau, F.M., 164
Landman, Samuel, 58, 84
Land Transfer Regulations (of 1939 Palestine White Paper), 14, 219, 222
Laqueur, Walter, 9
Laski, Harold, 196
Laski, Nathan, 242 n27
Laski, Neville, 106
Lawrence, T.E., 166
Lazaron, Rabbi Morris, 180–1, 198–9
League for Peace with Justice in Palestine, 129
League of British Jews, 8–10, 20 n13
Lebanon, 17, 23, 134
Leftwich, Joseph, 83, 95, 101, 182
Leimdoerfer, Dr Emile, 138, 175
Levant, 169, 247
Levenberg, Schneir, 222
Lewin, Kurt, 86
Liberal Judaism, 7, 88–9, 93, 115 n26; and the Jewish Fellowship, 87–94; and anti-Zionism, 114
Liberal Synagogue, 88–90, 92–3, 108, 176
Lieberman, Bernard, 239, 241
Lipson, Daniel, 5–6; as leading anti-Zionist, 102–3, 124, 131, 141, 148, 158–9, 163, 166–7, 173; and the Middle East Parliamentary Committee, 175; and Arab Office, 196, 199, 211; and the White Paper, 219, 222, 248; and Jewish immigration into Palestine, 235
Litvinoff, Barnet, 86
Liverman, Gordon, 171
Lloyd, Lord, 127
Loewe, Raphael, 91
Loftus, Pierre, 28; and Arab Office, 205
London, 40, 121, 166; Arab delegation in, 10; Arab Office in, 15, 183–4, 194, 197–9, 202, 207, 248; as capital city of Mandate Government, 15; Arab legations in, 26, 41, 43, 203; Arab representatives in, 25, 172; importance of, 27; Jewish Agency in, 70, 156
Longhurst, Henry, 17, 26, 28, 45, 48, 59,

73, 203, 226-7, 250
Longrigg, Brigadier Stephen, 73, 133, 205, 208, 217, 235–6
Lowdermilk, Walter Clay, 34–40, 46, 48, 55, 205

Mack, Dr John, 109
MacDonald, Ramsay, 215
MacMichael, Sir Harold, 43, 71
Magnes, Judah, 156, 179, 182
Malcolm, Sir Neil, 229
Manchester Guardian, 15, 43, 46, 138
Mansour, George, 12
Marmorstein, Dr Alfred, 91
Marmorstein, Emile, 140, 161; and the White Paper, 219–20
Martin, J.M., 139
Mattuck, Rabbi Dr Israel, 6, 86, 88–9, 93, 94, 113–14, 130, 159, 161, 166; and the White Paper, 219–20, 223, 248; and Jewish immigration into Palestine, 239
Maugham, Robin, 29, 33, 146–7, 183, 205, 207–8, 217, 231, 247
Maurice, Mrs Nancy, 26, 39, 199
Mayhew, Christopher, 10
McDonald, James, 112, 160, 176–7
McGhee, Harry, 47
Meinertzhagen, Richard, 70
Mendel, J., 91–2
Melbourne, 174
Mesquita, Revd Bueno de, 92
Michaelis, Herbert, 19
Middle East, 14, 24, 25, 36, 46, 131, 199, 204, 206; British Minister Resident in, 27, 82, 195
Middle East Parliamentary Committee (MEPC), 17, 25, 27, 43, 112, 161–3, 165, 170–1, 174–5, 181–2, 218, 221–2
Mills, Kenneth, 205
Milner, Lord Robert, 103
Ministry of Information, 159, 193, 195; Freya Stark as propagandist for, 3, 14
Mocatta, A. Alan, 92, 107
Monroe, Elizabeth, 149, 157–8, 187 n6
Montagu, Edwin, 98, 102, 111, 121, 130, 166, 196, 234
Montagu, Hon. Ewen, 91, 233
Montagu, Lilly H., 93
Montefiore, Claude G., 8, 10, 19 n12, 124, 130, 133
Moorehead, Caroline, 157
Morris, Harold, 94
Morris, Lieutenant-Colonel Harry, 102

Moss, Councillor Abraham, 99, 222
Moss, Ben, 89, 93, 108
Moyne, Lord, 27, 114 n1; assassination of, 82, 96
Mufti of Jerusalem *see also* Al-Hajj Muhammad Amin al-Husseini, 10, 11, 12, 196; co-operation with Nazis, 18, 20 n22, 156

Nabarro, Joseph, 92
Nachley, Esa, 12
Nachmani, Amikam, 160
Namier, Professor Lewis, 92, 139, 246
Nasir, Jamal, 15
Nathan, Louis, 19
Nazis, 65, 122, 141; the Mufti's co-operation with, 18, 20 n22, 156
Nazism: comparison of Zionism to, 3, 142–50, 165, 172, 230, 250
New Judea, 25, 35, 56, 57, 58, 61, 62, 65, 72, 73, 86, 104, 112, 161, 164, 182, 222
New Statesman and Nation, 69, 165, 200
New York, 166
New Zionist Organisation, 237
News of the World, 68, 194
Newcombe, Colonel Stewart, 11, 13, 17, 33, 36, 38, 41, 44, 55, 121, 125, 131, 156–7, 159, 160–1, 168–9, 194; relationship with anti-Zionist Jews, 173–5, 179, 227–8; and Kermit Roosevelt, 179; and Arab Office, 205; and White Paper, 217, 219, 229; and Jewish immigration into Palestine, 234
Newman, H., 165
Newton, Frances, 11–13, 18, 58, 126
Nicolson, Harold, 217
Nordau, Max, 83–4
Norris, H.T., 203–4

Observer, 59, 69
Oliver, N.F., 193, 195
Orthodox Judaism, 88
Orwell, George, 56

Palcor News Agency, 60
Palestine, 2, 156, 169, 186, 203, 207, 210, 224, 227, 230–2, 235–6, 247; Arabs of, 56, 183, 197, 216, 232–3; Arab Revolt in, 20 n22, 216; autonomous Jewish state in, 3, 6, 9, 17, 24, 25, 84–5, 140, 143, 158, 195, 225, 250–1; British Mandate for, 1, 13; diplomatic battle over, 5; partition of, 13; Jewish

immigration into, 13, 34, 40, 56, 74, 216–17, 229, 234–41; unitary state in, 13, 26; limits on Jewish immigration into, 14, 35–6, 215–17, 225, 249, 251; Arab propaganda over, 27; Jewish settlement in, 35, 40; as Land of Promise, 35; Biblical argument over, 125–9, 205; Jewish historical claims to, 125–8; White Paper, 215–25, 248
Palestine Arab Reform Party, 39
Palestine Foundation Fund *see also* Keren Hayesod, 35
Palestine Information Centre (PIC), 10–13, 16, 18, 58, 121, 131
Palestine Liberation Office (PLO), 15, 195
Palestine Post, 71
Pan Arab Conference (Alexandria, October 1944), 15
Paris, 159
Parkes, Revd Dr James, 123, 148
Partition, 13; debated at United Nations, 15; Sir Ronald Storrs opposition to, 74
Pasha, Azzam, *see also* Abd al-Rahman Azzam Bey, 30, 76
Passfield White Paper (1930), 56
Philby, Harry St John, 18, 68, 197
Philips Price, M., 17, 45–6, 139, 146–7; and Arab Office, 205, 207
Pickthorn, Kenneth, 17, 45–8, 132, 139, 177, 194, 201
Pinner, Walter, 86
Poalei Zion (Labour Zionist Movement), 70
Poland, 136–7, 141–2
Poliak, Abraham, 134
Popular Front (in France), 1
Pro-Arab League, 10
Pro-Arab Parliamentary Committee, 44
Propaganda: Arab, 10, 206; Gentile anti-Zionist, 11, 121; of the Arab Office, 11, 32; of the Arab Centre, 13; of Arabs in London, 14; Zionist, 27, 90, 159, 230–3, 249; of the Committee for Arab Affairs, 28, 31, 33–4; of the Jewish Fellowship, 84–7

Raikes, Victor, 47
Rank, Otto, 135
Rees, Leon, 89, 108
Reform Judaism, 88
Reid, J.C.S., 41
Reid, Thomas, 33, 41, 45, 47, 55, 112, 121, 179, 183; and Arab Office, 201;

and White Paper, 217
Reinhart, Revd Dr Harold, 88, 93, 110, 144, 149
Reiss, A., 141
Reynaud, Paul, 17
Richmond, Ernest, 13
Riebenfeld, Dr Paul, 67, 237–8, 241
Roosevelt, Kermit, 179–81, 186
Rosen, Rabbi Kopul, 162
Rosenwald, Lessing, 159–60, 166
Rosette, Moshe, 58–9, 98–9, 102, 140
Roth, Cecil, 83
Rowson, Shabtai, 19
Royal Central Asian Society (RCAS), 31, 33, 40, 131, 156–7, 175
Royal Commission on Palestine (1937), 9, 11, 31, 61, 235
Royal Institute of International Affairs (RIIA), *see also* Chatham House, 23, 131, 134, 146, 148, 157, 169, 195, 208, 210, 217–18, 220, 225, 229, 231, 238
Royden-Shaw, Dr Agnes Maude, 17, 33, 41, 45–6, 48, 55, 58–9, 61, 69, 73–4, 77, 126, 133, 175, 183, 194, 204, 227, 235–6
Russell, Sir John E., 37

Sacher, Harry, 86, 90, 130, 136, 159, 184
Salmon, Samuel Isidore, 107
Salomon, Sidney, 105, 165
Samuel, Frank, 91
Samuel, Sir Herbert, 20 n22, 159
Sandelson, D.I., 109
Schonfeld, Rabbi Dr Solomon, 137
Schwarzenberger, Dr Georg, 204
Second World War, 16, 27, 184
Sergeant, Dr R.B., 64
Seton Williams, M.V., 169
Shaftesley, John, 100–1
Shavit, Yaacov, 142
Shaw, C.V., 139
Shertok, Moshe, 148, 238
Shimoni, Gideon, 7–8, 158
Shukairi, Ahmed, 15, 195
Silver, Rabbi Abba Hillel, 93
Simon, Sir Leon, 95, 159, 179
Singleton, Sir John, 65
Skilbeck, Wing-Commander, 37–8, 46
Skinner, T.C., 170, 175
Sloan Coffin, Henry, 179
Snowman, Councillor Emanuel, 85
Sokolow, Nahum, 125
Solel Boneh, 71

Soref, Harold, 92
Spears, Sir Edward, 19, 23, 30, 41, 44, 58, 70, 75–6, 85, 121, 125, 131, 161, 169, 194, 226–9, 231, 247, 250; and the Anglo-Arab Association, 29; and the Committee for Arab Affairs 16–17, 170, 194, 215, 240, 246; as British Minister Plenipotentiary in the Levant, 17, 23; as leading anti-Zionists, 17, 55; and the Middle East Parliamentary Committee, 25, 161–3, 171; long-time francophile, 23; before the Anglo-American Committee, 24, 42–3; on Walter Lowdermilk, 37–9; and Parliament, 43–8; and the Zionist movement, 60–8; and the Jewish Fellowship 89, 179, 183, 185–7, 194, 246; and the biblical argument against Zionism, 126–8; and charge of dual loyalty, 132–4; and the rehabilitation of Jews in Europe, 138–41; his comparison of Zionism to Nazism, 147–8; and Jewish anti-Zionists, 165, 169–76, 181, 247–8; correspondence with R.R. Stokes, 177–9; and Albert Hyamson, 178–9, 182; and Kermit Roosevelt, 179–81; and anti-Semitism, 183–7; and Arab Office, 186–7, 194–6, 199–211, 246; and Albert Hourani, 208–10; and the White Paper, 217; and Jewish immigration into Palestine 234, 239, 240–1
Spectator, 36, 102, 124, 125, 131, 163, 196
St. George's Settlement Synagogue, 89, 108
Stanley, Oliver, 183
Star, 143
Stark, Freya, 3, 87, 175, 184, 215, 246, 250; and Pro-Arab League, 10; in the United States, 14, 55, 157–9, 180; and *East is West*, 69; and Arab Office, 194; and White Paper, 217
Stein, Hannah, 141
Stein, Leonard, 6, 19 n4, 107, 149
Steinberg, Dr Isaac, 227
Steward, J. Henderson, 47
Stewart, Rt Revd W.H., 126-7
Stokes, R.R., 17, 43–4, 48, 55, 139, 194, 201, 209, 219; correspondence with Sir Edward Spears, 177–8
Storrs, Sir Ronald, 17, 32, 33, 41–2, 44, 45, 48, 57, 59, 63, 85, 126, 147, 151 n22, 157–9, 161, 170, 229–30, 232, 247, 250; and *Orientations*, 27, 69; and CAA, 28, 30; and the Zionist movement, 67–78; relationship with Jewish anti-Zionists, 98, 166–8, 171, 175, 251; and charge of dual loyalty, 133; and Albert Hyamson, 172–3; and Arab Office, 199–202, 215; and Albert Hourani, 209–10; and Edward Atiyah, 210–11; and White Paper, 217; and Report of the Anglo-American Committee, 225; and Jewish immigration into Palestine, 235
Strabolgi, Lord, 62, 74
Streatham News, 150
Stretton, Hallburton, 69
Sudan, 200
Sunday Express, 66
Sunday Times, 69, 71–2
Swaythling, Lord, 6, 107, 158
Sykes, Christopher, 70
Sykes, Sir Frederick, 42
Synagogue Review, 89, 93, 96, 169
Syria, 17, 23, 134

Tal, Wasfi, 15
Tannous, Dr Izzat, 10–13, 31; as head of Arab Centre, 14; as member of Arab Office, 14, 127, 156, 202
The Times, 33, 39, 42, 59, 76, 95, 96, 97, 101, 124, 132, 144, 167, 173, 196, 200, 211, 216, 220–1, 239
Thurtle, Ernest, 47, 201
Toynbee, Professor Arnold, 146, 194, 208, 250
Transjordan, 39, 63
Truman, President Harry S. (1945–53), 224

Union Theological Seminary, 179
United Jewish Relief Organisation, 137
United Nations, 1, 129, 226; debate on partition at, 15; Zionist argument at, 148
United Nations Special Committee on Palestine (UNSCOP), 111, 129
United States, 166, 179, 186, 194, 228; and Palestine, 2; Freya Stark in, 14, 157–9
United States Soil Conversation Service, 34
United Synagogue, 91–2, 159, 167
Unterman, Rabbi I.J., 19

Vienna, 135
Vital, David, 97

al-Wadi, Col. Sayid Shakir, 41, 203

Waley Cohen, Sir Robert, 5; as member of the Jewish Fellowship, 91, 159, 167, 211; and the White Paper, 221
Washington, 40; Arab Office in, 15, 129, 183, 195, 198, 248; British Embassy in, 193
Waters, Donovan, 37–8
Webb, Maurice, 66
Weiler, Rabbi M.C., 93
Weizmann, Chaim, 4 n1, 35, 55, 70, 97, 133, 166, 173, 215, 221, 236
West London Liberal Synagogue, 88–9
White Paper on Palestine (1939), 14, 21 n42, 84, 157, 215–25, 248–9, 251
Wigoder, Dr Philip, 19, 163
Williams, Kenneth, 17, 25, 29, 31, 42, 55, 59, 70, 194
Wingate, Sir Reginald, 42, 44, 125
Winterton, Earl, 44, 194
Wise, Rabbi Stephen, 51 n69, 93
Wittgenstein, Ludwig, 135
Wolf, Lucien, 8, 10, 95, 98
Women's Mizrachi Society of London, 35
Woodhead Commission (1938), 31, 33
World Congress of Progressive Judaism, 93
World Jewish Congress, 35, 104–5

World Zionist Organisation, 25, 105

Yishuv, 6, 56, 100, 121, 131
Yorkshire Post, 170

Zakan (pseud.), 236
Zangwill, Israel, 83
Ziadeh, Nicola, 12
Ziff, William, 72
Zionism, 8, 35, 121, 183, 238, 246, 250; active opposition to, 5, 176, 210–11, 227, 248; in England, 17; British support for, 24; Arab case against, 32; Sir Ronald Storrs and, 67–78; Sir Edward Spears and, 60–8, 179; Jewish Fellowship's antipathy to, 82–3, 176, 196; and dual loyalty, 129–36; as successor to Nazism, 142–50, 184, 250
Zionist Congress, 8, 83, 135
Zionist Federation of Great Britain and Ireland, 35, 85, 87, 104, 216, 236
Zionist Review, 35, 37, 55, 56, 57, 58, 63, 66, 72, 74, 76, 85, 90, 97, 98, 104, 111, 112, 141, 159, 163, 196, 201, 222, 228
Zionist press, 92, 222
Zollschan, Ignaz, 134